£3

D1631576

THE GLORY OF SCOTLAND

GALLOWAY AND THE SOUTHERN HIGHLANDS OF SCOTLAND
Norman Wilkinson

Fr. *Courtesy L.M.S. Rly.*

The GLORY *of* SCOTLAND

By

J. J. BELL

WITH A FOREWORD BY
COMPTON MACKENZIE

Coleridge hailed us with a shout of triumph, . . .
exulting in the glory of Scotland.
DOROTHY WORDSWORTH, *Journal*, 1803

FOURTH IMPRESSION REVISED

LONDON
GEORGE G. HARRAP & CO. LTD.
BOMBAY & SYDNEY

First published June 1932
by GEORGE G. HARRAP & CO. LTD.
39–41 *Parker Street, Kingsway, London, W.C.*2

Reprinted : June 1932
June 1932
August 1932

Printed in Great Britain by Neill & Co. Ltd., Edinburgh

FOREWORD

MR BELL's book is likely to become a standard work. I have read almost every topographical work about the Highlands, and I have read many about the Lowlands, and I cannot recall any which offers as much information in the same space. I understand that Mr Bell's original manuscript exceeded 2200 pages and that what remains is hardly more than a quarter of what he originally wrote. In these circumstances it is remarkable that he has managed to preserve his proportions as well as he has.

No country in Europe can offer so much variety as Scotland in so small a space, as no doubt Mr Bell found to his cost when he began to compress his bulky manu-script, and the trouble is how to achieve the ubiquity one desires. I know that if I were not fettered to my desk by literary work I should spend the whole of my life tearing about all over the country. And wherever I was at any given moment I should be seized with a sudden desire to be somewhere else. In the fullness of time I shall have to decide where I propose to die, and it is going to be a very difficult matter, if I am granted the necessary length of life, to settle what prospect in Scotland shall receive the last blink of my rheumy eyes, what *duthaich* the last tread of my doddering footsteps.

He who reads *The Glory of Scotland* from cover to cover will appreciate the perplexity that threatens my old age, but he who after reading *The Glory of Scotland* from cover to cover sets out to obtain personal knowledge of every place and district Mr Bell mentions will wonder how it is possible for any man to hope to find a solution of the problem that besets me. The Emperor Tiberius never discovered exactly where on the island of Capri he wanted to build his palace. So in the end he built twelve palaces, and even with such prodigal building he left out one view which one of these palaces should have overlooked. Not being an emperor, I might manage to be scenically content with twelve cottages instead of twelve palaces, live in a different one each month, and in a manner of speaking not mind in which one of them I died.

Mr Bell, who has in this book set up so many signposts to every part of our beloved country, needs no signpost from me. He holds a secure place in the affections of his fellow-Scots, and I am grateful to him for according me the privilege of associating my name with his in a book which so excellently achieves what its author set out to achieve. Good weather to those who take Mr Bell for a guide!

COMPTON MACKENZIE

EILEAN AIGAS
BEAULY
INVERNESS-SHIRE

PREFACE

THIS book has been written primarily for readers who have never been in Scotland, yet I hope it may have some appeal to Scottish readers not too well acquainted with their own country. To the Scot who knows his Scotland by heart it will, of course, appear quite inadequate, and its errors of omission and commission be many.

It is a guide in the sense that it directs the reader's attention to the scenes, sights, and pleasures which I conceive to be the most inspiring, interesting, and inspiriting that Scotland can offer to a stranger; a guide also in the sense that it is intended to inform and assist a stranger in various ways; but it does not pretend to be a gazetteer, a road book, and an hotel-list bound into one. Essentially a holiday book, it has been written with the wish that it may suggest and promote light-hearted journeys, rather than solemn educational pilgrimages.

In designing the book I sought to consider alike the convenience of the traveller by rail and the traveller by road, and now I realize how much simpler, though not happier, my work would have been in the old days, when there was only one way of getting about the country. I realize, too, that there must be some pages in the book on which, having attempted to satisfy both travellers, I have satisfied neither; nevertheless, I feel that they will understand and appreciate the difficulty, and be lenient accordingly.

The divisions of the country in the book have not been made arbitrarily. Scotland, small as it is, is really a group of little Scotlands, each with its own particular characteristics, natural and human. For example, the Borders are quite different from Ayrshire and Galloway, while Fife is as different from either as it is from the Western Highlands. You can see the differences in passing from one to another; you can feel them by making a brief sojourn in each. With this idea in view, the divisions have, as far as was practicable, been made, and the sections arranged. I need hardly add that each little Scotland is worth a holiday devoted to itself.

While I have sought especially to serve the visitor who desires to explore each part of Scotland from a base, I trust that the chapters so planned may be serviceable also to the visitor who prefers to make a general tour of the country; and I have taken some thought for the visitor—the business visitor to Edinburgh or Glasgow, for instance—who finds he can spare just one day "to see Scotland."

As for my sins of omission, which will be so apparent to some of my compatriots (should they read the book), while many of them were unwilling, I must confess that not a few were deliberate. Regretfully I left out, or struck out, towns and castles and kirks and scenes and stories which deserved pages to themselves. On the other hand, I cheerfully ignored such things as sites which have nothing to show for their pasts, and birthplaces of, for example, poets whose names are locally cherished as faithfully as their works are neglected; and gladly I refrained from noticing a thousand or so buildings represented by "the imposing modern mansion on the left, the residence of Lord (or Sir or Mr) So-and-so."

No man loves his country as much as he loves a part of it. Perhaps because of the part he loves the whole. Here and there in this survey, or rather series of impressions, of my country it is possible that I have betrayed a preference; yet I trust I have been impartial enough generally, and at the same time descriptive enough, to enable a distant reader to choose for himself the part of Scotland he will visit—to begin with.

May 1932   J. J. B.

CONTENTS

ILLUSTRATIONS

9

10   THE GLORY OF SCOTLAND

The
GLORY OF SCOTLAND

INTRODUCTION

I

"Now we are a-going into Scotland, but with heavy
hearts. They tell us here at Berwick what terrible living
we shall have there."—The first words of the *Journal of
an English Surgeon with the Duke of Cumberland's Army
in* 1745.

"The entrance into Scotland has a very unpromising
look."—Pennant's *Tour*, 1769.

"We reckoned there would be some inconvenience and
hardships, and perhaps a little danger. . . . When I
[Boswell] was at Ferney, in 1764, I mentioned our design
to Voltaire. He looked at me as if I had talked of going
to the North Pole."—*A Journal of a Tour to the Hebrides
with Samuel Johnson, LL.D., in* 1773.

So, you see, it is not so very long since Scotland
was generally imagined as a bleak, inhospitable country,
scarce touched by the finger-tip of Civilization, the prospect of a visit evoking gloomy misgivings, if not the
blackest of forebodings; and it may be that even to-day,
not necessarily in the remoter parts of the world, there
persists the idea of a Caledonia whose sternness, wildness,
and shagginess are not confined, though so applied by Sir
Walter Scott, to its scenery alone. Indeed, it is not a
score of years since, as a sojourner in the South—in
Devon, to be precise—I became aware that my rustic
neighbours were peeping at me as at a prodigy—a Scotsman, yet a fellow human being, though one composed
mainly of oatmeal and whisky, native of a mountainous

country still in its glacial period, whose inhabitants, when at home, wore ruddy hair and tartan garments, and where the sound of the bagpipes was heard continuously.

It is true enough that, about the time of those visitors whom I have quoted, Scotland, with her internal troubles and comparative poverty, was still sadly lacking in many of the material boons and social niceties of the civilization possessed by her southern partner; yet she had learned something, as those visitors were to discover, from her old ally, France; and the roughness and rudeness were often a matter of economics. One may also read the tributes of travellers to the fine courtesies of Highland gentlemen—also to their claret, which seems to have been better stuff than English cellars generally provided. Moreover, Scotland was then beginning to realize certain benefits of her union with England, and to 'find herself' commercially and financially. Forty years earlier it was reckoned that the whole country, with its million inhabitants, contained little more than half a million, sterling, in coin. Yet less than fifty years after Dr Johnson's visit—in 1819, to be exact—we find it written that no country in Europe had made such rapid advances in the elegancies and comforts of life as had Scotland within those last eight decades. And in that year there appeared a volume entitled 'Pleasure' Tours in Scotland—I must ' quote ' the adjective in what was, I imagine, its earliest application to my country as a holiday resort.

That was only seven years after the Comet, first commercially successful steamship in Europe, had begun to flap the waters of the Clyde with her feeble floats; but already a fleet of little paddle-wheelers was plying on the Firth and its lochs, while there was a weekly service to Ireland; and one may regard Henry Bell's puny craft, 42 feet in length, spluttering along at four miles an hour, assisted by a sail, the breeze being favourable, on her tall, slim funnel, as pioneer in the first real tourist service given to Scotland. A good many years were to pass before the railways caught up with the steamboats for long-distance transport. In 1840 my grandfather, bound from Glasgow to London, travelled by sea to Liverpool, thence by train, the journey, which by rail to-day takes 8 hours, requiring three rounds of the clock.

Scotland is a small country—utmost length 280 miles, utmost breadth 146 miles—but its coast-line runs to thousands of miles, and in those early tourist days many 'places of interest' were accessible only from the sea. To-day some of them, though easily reached by highway and railroad, may fail to charm the approaching visitor as they charmed the visitor long since departed. The truth is that much of Scotland, in its noblest and loveliest aspects, is viewable only from the deck of a ship, and I cannot but regret the overwhelming advance in motor transport, since the visitor who confines himself to land travel is bound to sacrifice countless opportunities of inspiration to ease and speed—not that our pleasure steamers are either comfortless or slow. No man should say that he has seen a country with a coast-line when he has toured it only from within. But I must hasten to add that, thanks to motor transport, very many places of beauty, historic association, and recreation which not so many years ago were 'at the back of beyond' are now pleasantly within reach.

You have but to glance at the map to imagine Nature's prodigious agony when Britain "first arose from out the azure main," and there is little of Scotland that does not bear evidence of fiery upheavals, icy grindings and gougings, watery engulfments. Grim enough, despite intervals of smiling sands, are the cliffs and rocky shores facing the east; but on the north and west coasts, and in the Western Isles, there is scarce a mile without a memorial of ancient rendings and shatterings, of heights scoured by Atlantic gales and rains; while, from Loch Linnhe to the Moray Firth, Scotland has been all but split in twain—cleft so deeply that, with the Caledonian Canal linking three lovely lochs, there is a water-way from sea to sea.

Yet the very forces that wrought those upheavals and all that ruggedness gave Scotland a softer side, as it were, in her straths and glens, both north and south, where she can be mild and gentle, of tender beauty, and even a little enervating. She has her woods and gardens, her green pastures and rich fields, her quiet streams and sheltered lochs, her seaside and inland playgrounds. If you prefer the restful to the energetic holiday, she can give it you and in full measure. But I fancy you will want to move about and see things, or take your recreation in some form of sport, and here I would venture a word of warning. If you must have an Ostend, or a Deauville, or a Brighton, or a Blackpool—*don't* come to Scotland. The popular resorts provide music, pierrots, dancing, and other entertainments, but we have no gaieties on the Southern scale, and a pier is only a place of embarkation.

A few words on the beginnings of Scotland in its relation to man. A controversial subject, but from the evidence of prehistoric remains found in various parts, one may take it that there were people in Scotland—I am here using the name for convenience sake; it was not established as the general title of North Britain till the twelfth century—5000 years ago—*i.e.*, about 3000 years after the end of the last Ice Age. The first inhabitants were probably descendants of people of the Old Stone Age, and were called the 'Harpoon Folk,' because among their relics have been found harpoons made of deerhorn. Similar remains have been found in Denmark, and it is significant that Britain was then joined to the Continent. A thousand or two years later came New Stone Age people, long-headed and dark, a 'Mediterranean' type, who had crossed what we know to-day as the Straits of Dover, possibly dry-footed. Later arrived adventurers from the Eastern Mediterranean, also dark, but round-headed, seekers after metals, whose blood survives in the West and North. Then to the East Coast drifted people, some of whose distant forebears had emigrated from Central Asia, who made pottery and had bronze, or copper, axes. Next, about 1150 B.C., through England, came Gaelic-speaking Celts, with bronze leaf-shaped swords, and, a thousand years later, appeared the Brythons, or Britons, who knew about iron. In A.D. 80 Rome, represented in the person of Agricola, entered Scotland, and for three hundred years thereafter Roman legions were more or less in occupation, conquering, yet always having to conquer again. On Scotland Rome never impressed her civilization as she impressed it on England, and it is noteworthy that while we have the remains of a great wall—Antonine's—and numerous stations and camps, we have no city or town whose founding can be credited to the Romans, nor in all the country—save, possibly, in the Borders—are there place-names which may be declared with certainty to be of Roman origin. Perhaps the most far-reaching effect of the Roman invasion was to force the different native tribes into defensive alliances, thus opening the way to their one day becoming the nucleus of a nation.

The Romans were not, however, the last of the in-comers. Not long after their departure came the Scots —*Scoti* may mean either 'tattooed' or 'broken' men— from Ireland, and, a few centuries later, the Norsemen. Finally, at the time of the Norman Conquest, there was an English infusion, later a Norman one, and, with the awakening of commerce, a Flemish tincture. What a mixture we are!

It took many centuries to make of Scotland a

peaceable country and its inhabitants a united people. War between tribes or races, war with the Romans, Norsemen, and English, civil war, religious war, war between this clan and that—a reading of my country's history leaves me wondering whether Scotland holds a square mile of sod, flat enough for men to strive on, that has not, at one time or another, soaked in some human blood. Yet, amid all that brutal turmoil, fourteen hundred years ago, Christianity, the slow but sure civilizer, was stealing over from Ireland, by way of Iona and other isles, to the mainland, and through the western glens into the very heart of the country; and the seeds of learning were here and there falling and taking root in that unpromising, uncultivated soil, so that in due season the Scottish people, while yet poor in material things and lacking the amenities of life, were to have an education surpassing that of their more softly situated southern neighbours. Even before Columba's day St Ninian had come as a missionary to Galloway, while, no doubt, other early Christians had found a perilous way farther north.

To many men and women the Yesterday of a land and its people—though that land and people be their own—does not greatly matter; but I have ventured, only lightly, to touch on these few things of the past, in the hope that they may interest those of you who are coming to see and know my country, rather than to use it merely as a playground. Still, those of you who in your holiday visions can perceive little but a glorious golf-links or a splendid river may, when your dreams have come true, be mildly intrigued by the reflection that, once upon a time, some old Scottish king played where you are playing, with a funny-looking club and a ball stuffed with feathers; or that, long ago, in yonder ruined castle men whose names are writ in history feasted uncouthly upon a forty-pounder, such as you are about to hook in the pool at your feet. At any rate, this book is written in the hope of its being of some friendly service, whether you come with camera or clubs, with road-maps or rods, with antiquarian appetite or desire for adventure, sport, discovery, or simple peace and quiet.

II

Scotland, as already remarked, is a small country, but in no sense can it be called compact. Its configuration apart, nothing could be more erratic than the disposition of its inhabitable places, nothing more irregular than the distribution of the means whereby modern man seeks to make a living. Scotland's population is nearly five millions—less than a seventh of England's—and more than a third of it is contained in two cities, Glasgow and Edinburgh.

In both cities, though more so in Edinburgh, you will find things characteristic of Scotland; but you will find also things characteristic of London, and, indeed, of any great city. You will, in short, be in a strange place full of familiar things. The Scottish characteristics will not obtrude themselves; you will have to look for most of them. In this respect it is perhaps enough to say that you will see more tartan in one shop window than you will see in the whole length of street—unless it should chance that a company of soldiers or Boy Scouts passes along in swinging kilts. As for the language of these cities, you are not likely to hear much but English—as good English as the citizens can make it. You may, in a crowd, hear snatches of the vernacular, now a mixture of English, old 'Braid Scots,' and 'American.' There Gaelic (sometimes pronounced 'Gallic') is an alien tongue, though were you to walk along the pavement shouting an urgent question in it you would presently get an answer, and a kindly one, from some Highlander— possibly a police officer—whose business keeps his body in the crowded South, while his heart is, almost certainly,

B

in the open West or North.   There are still in Scotland about 7000 people who have no tongue but the Gaelic, but you would have to seek them in the remotest corners. You will hardly find out the real Scotland in her two chief centres, though in them, particularly in the capital, you will learn much of the story of her past.

I am assuming that you are coming—or have come— to Scotland for the first time.   If, as is quite likely, this little book fails in giving details which you think ought to have been given, I would crave not only your leniency, but your generosity in the form of a postcard indicating the fault.   And if you feel that you must punish me, don't put a stamp on the card.   That, if you believe all you have heard about Scotland, will be pretty severe punish-ment upon a Scotsman.

So far as Scotland in the open is concerned, I am hoping that you will read this book before you start on your journey, or, at any rate, read the necessary pages before beginning the day's excursion.   When I see visitors, books in hand, diligently checking off the names of the mountains, streams, islands, and so forth, I cannot help feeling that in acquiring information, which will prob-ably pass with the hour, they are missing inspiration which might remain for many a year.   I'd rather you kept the vision of one mountain than the memory of a score of names.   If you must, keep your map handy; but I believe you will get more out of it if you refrain from studying it till the end of the day.   Indeed, if you have not read my pages the night before, I suggest that you do not read them till the evening after your ex-cursion.   There is a good deal to be said for the child's method of looking at the pictures before reading the story.

There are two things which, obviously, so small a book as this cannot do.   It cannot describe a country in any-thing like detail; it cannot, like a newspaper, supply the very latest information about this, that, and the other place. But in nearly every town in Scotland you can get, either gratis, or for a few pence, a little guide-book, official or otherwise, to the place itself and its neighbourhood, in which you will find much which could not be put into these pages. For example, an ancient building may lately have been restored, a new bathing-pool may have been constructed, an archæological discovery of importance may have been made. Also, such guides usually give particulars of local motor services, useful knowledge to many people. If you are planning to make a stay it is worth while to write in advance to the Town Clerk for a copy of the local guide; and if your stay is to be in one of the large centres I should advise you to do so. Supposing, for instance, that you are going to spend only a few days in Edinburgh, the Corporation's *Guide Book* (9*d*., including postage) will certainly assist you to make a programme for each day, besides being helpful in questions of transport and other details. The railway companies' and motor transport companies' publications are also very useful in a general way.

Scotland has this advantage: there are no vast distances between hostelries. I cannot think of a road passable on a car that includes a stretch of twenty miles between one hotel, or inn, and another. But it should be remembered that many of these houses are not large, and that in some of them the entertainment is best described as 'homely'; also that, whether large and fully equipped, or small and plain, they may, in the summer season, be fully occupied. This is most likely in fishing districts, where accommodation is booked far in advance, often by anglers who return to the same hotel, or inn, year after year. It is therefore expedient to use the telephone, or telegraph (reply paid), as far as possible ahead of the proposed arrival. This applies not only to the outlying places, but to the cities and towns. There

Its remaining rough stretches need not deter any motorist from taking the most wonderful route in all Scotland. There are still bad roads—not main roads—and some of them, for reasons which will be apparent if you travel on them, are not likely ever to become good roads. Yet certain of them lead to places and things which you ought to see. Of the faults and difficulties of such roads your Road Book should warn you.

There is no place that invites visitors which has not its golf course, tennis courts, and bowling greens, and I shall not mention these things on every occasion. As to angling, Scotland has so many fishable rivers and lochs that it would be impossible even to name a hundredth of them, while the man bent on a fishing holiday will, almost certainly, choose a place of which he has heard good reports. All the same, I shall, here and there, tell what I happen to know about a river or loch.

And now a word about the weather—a subject which the patriotic writers of some Scottish guides seem inclined to shirk. Some eighteen hundred years ago, the Roman historian Tacitus, in his *Agricola*, wrote: "The climate is disagreeable from the constant rains and fogs; great cold is, however, unknown"; and, the other day, on our West Coast, an old Highlander, being asked his opinion on holiday prospects, replied: "Well, well, I am thinking it will be fery wet, or more rain." But, apart from the possibility of a big climatic change (for the better) in the course of all those centuries, it should not be forgotten that the Romans did not have much of a picnic in Scotland, and I cannot but suspect that the estimable Tacitus may have received his weather report from some disgruntled person, perhaps his father-in-law, Agricola. As for that more recent observation of a native, I would merely remind you that the Celtic temperament tends to foreboding.

To be frank, I advise you to come prepared for a rainy

and, perhaps, chilly day or two. You may not get them. Scotland can have her droughts, her long periods of sunshine, while elsewhere dullness prevails. Her districts with the rainiest reputations may provide the finest summer in Britain. You never can tell. Generally speaking, in the East fair weather is probable, but in the West the mountains stand in wait for the clouds from the Atlantic, and the risk of rain is greater. Yet Scotland's supreme beauty is in the West, and the weather, in its infinite variety, has had much to do with the making of that beauty. Take your chance, come prepared—and hopeful.

CHAPTER I

EDINBURGH

USUALLY the visitor to Scotland has the capital included, if not underlined, in his programme, while the chances are that his visit begins there. That in itself would be a logical and polite reason for giving Edinburgh prime place in this little book; but the simple, natural reason for doing so is that Edinburgh, with her wealth of historic, romantic, artistic, and modern interests, is indispensable to anyone who comes to Scotland with a desire to look into the tempestuous Past, as well as to observe the peaceful Present.

You may come to Edinburgh by rail, by road, by sea, and, of course, by air, and whatever the approach the prospect is worth while; but the finest effect is gained by arriving in the train. For the two stations are so situated that you come almost abruptly into the middle of things; not the dingy and drab things such as too often provide one's first impression—or depression—of a city, but things of beauty and splendour in a truly noble setting.

Emerging from either of the stations, you find yourself standing with To-day and Yesterday on the broad pavement of the Present, looking upward at a panorama of the Past. Here are the brightest and most modern things that Scotland has to show, in shops and hotels; yonder are many of her most ancient buildings, sombre heights of stone, memorials royal, homely, romantic, tragic.

You are in Princes Street, which is one of the world's most beautiful streets, and in the New Town of

24

Edinburgh, which, with its spacious ways and squares and gardens, came into being a century and a half ago, when the wise men of the Old Town over yonder, with its narrow 'gaits' and huddled houses, must surely have been inspired to think of it. To-day the grey Castle on its craggy mount frowns austerely across the Gardens, where once was a loch, at the traffic and business and gaiety and luxury of Princes Street; and Princes Street, debonair, serene, smiles back. Those bridges over the hollow are bridges across the centuries.

It is not my intention to pepper these pages with statistics. The balance-sheets of municipalities, the price-lists, so to speak, of public buildings, and so forth, are not for the light-hearted traveller; but you may care to know that Edinburgh, with its 300 miles of streets, has a population of about 425,000, or a little more than a third of that of commercial Glasgow, 40 miles away, over which Edinburgh, though far from uncommercial, is entitled to queen it, with her culture, her educational institutions, her art and letters, which have flourished through the centuries. The Church, the Law, and many learned societies have their headquarters in her centre, and, if it be not bathos, most of the Scottish banks their chief offices. Should our Nationalists have their way, she will one day have her ancient Scottish Parliament restored to her. As she is, she has a dignity, a character, all her own.

It was a young Englishman, visiting Edinburgh nearly a hundred years ago, who wrote:

I believe I shall never hear the name of the Capital of Scotland without a thrill of gratitude and pleasure. I shall love, while I have life, her hills and her houses—even the stones of her streets!

He was Charles Dickens. And the other day another Englishman, Wilfred Whitten (so widely known as 'John o' London'), wrote:

Incomparable city, by Nature mothered, by time made reverend, by man kept young, who shall praise her but in naming her for what she is—the monument and nursery of a great people !

Well, well! I can see that this chapter would be far better done by a generous English visitor, or even an 'intelligent foreigner,' than by a Scot who at the very outset realizes that the magnitude of the picture is hope-lessly beyond the size of his canvas.

Of the beginning of Edinburgh, set upon hills among hills, we know as much as we know of the beginning of Scotland—which is nothing that can be proved. There are theories and theories, and I respect them all, though they have been drawn forth from the fog of the far-off centuries, when people were too much occupied in keep-ing alive to give thought to the possibility of an inquisi-tive posterity. Traditions also I respect, for nothing comes out of nothing, and the grain of truth is blown hither and thither.

According to one tradition, and that not the least pic-turesque, Edinburgh was founded, a thousand years be-fore the Christian era, by a certain King Ebranke, who further distinguished himself not only by founding the City of York, but by being the father of twenty sons and thirty daughters. The flippant person may remark that he provided the citizens, as well as the cities; but until we hear of a better founder I do not see why we should not accept King Ebranke.

Edinburgh's early name was Dunedin—"Fort on the Hill Slope." This would suggest that it came into being on the slope of the Castle Rock, though it might equally well have begun on the eastern slope of Arthur's Seat— King Arthur has his traditions too—most dominating of the city's surrounding hills, as some of our archæo-logists opine that it did, though allowing that the Castle Rock may have provided a later site. No doubt from very early times both heights, like the Rocks of Dumbarton and Stirling, were used as places of refuge and defence. No actual traces of the Roman invaders have been found, though it is known that Roman roads ran below and past the Castle Rock. In those days lakes, or swamps, surrounded almost entirely the Rock and the ridge whereon Old Edinburgh was to be built, thereby adding to the attractions of the Rock as a place of safety and defence. We find, too, the fortress called 'Castle of the Maidens,' but the pretty word is under suspicion of being the corruption of a Welsh one, meaning 'stones.'

Edinburgh does not quite emerge from the prehistoric mists till two thousand years after the period allotted to the fatherly King Ebranke. We read that in 1004 King Malcolm II sojourned there, and that toward the end of the century, when Scotland's capital was Dunfermline, Malcolm III (Canmore) had a sort of hunting-lodge on the Rock, where his Queen Margaret (afterward Saint) caused a little chapel, which still stands, to be built. There, too, in 1093, she died—some say in the Chapel—soon after learning of the death of her husband and first-born in battle with the English. We shall meet Margaret again in these pages. She and Canmore—Canmore means 'Big Head'—meant much to Scotland, which in their time became, at last, something like a kingdom. David I took after his mother in religion and founded many religious houses, including Holyrood Abbey.

Then came the Normans, town-planners and castle-builders, or Scots and English who had learned of them, and the Old Edinburgh that was to reach from the Rock, down the ridge, to Holyrood began to take form. The stretch is now known as the Royal Mile, but I think a brother scribe has named it better as the Mile of Memories. Edinburgh's earliest—so far as has been discovered—city charter was granted by King Robert the Bruce, who held parliaments in the Banqueting Hall of the Castle,

which was not then a very imposing building. But, as
already indicated, centuries were to pass ere the Edinburgh in which you will eat and sleep beeame so much as
a thought. Not till after the last Jacobite Rising, in
1745, did the Old reach out to bridge the gulf and build
the New, to cover vacant land with those splendid streets
and squares which to-day are the admiration of strangers
—and ourselves. There was no Napoleon to order those
things. Blessed with a rare vision, free of dictatorship
and hampering regulations, the citizens of their skill and
good taste achieved them. By the end of the eighteenth
century the New Town was in being; in 1820 it was
beginning to expand; it is still expanding. No great
city is without its drab and dreary districts, reminding
man that he has still a lot to learn; but Edinburgh has no
square mile without park or garden, wide open space or
golf course, and the air is remarkably clean. The air can
also, when the wind's in the east, be remarkably keen,
and the sensitive visitor is warned accordingly, though
he may reproach me if the extra wrap should never be
needed.

As I want, if possible, to be of service to the visitor who
can spare but a day, as well as to the visitor who need not
count the hours, I must now try to promote for both a
bowing acquaintance with Edinburgh, which for the
sojourner may develop into a close and friendly one.

The New Town

I propose that we approach the Ancient by way of the
Modern, which happens to be the convenient method,
since you are almost certain to start the day in the New
Town, as I would still call it. So I suggest that we meet
at the west end of Princes Street, at the corner opposite
the L.M.S. Railway Station, and then walk eastward over
the mile of broad pavement, which knows the tread of all
nations, of all grades of society. I have known people,

EDINBURGH CASTLE FROM PRINCES STREET GARDENS
Photo Alexander B. Beattie   28

PRINCES STREET, LOOKING WEST

Photo Valentine and Sons, Ltd.

come to spend a day in 'seeing' Edinburgh, who have
never got out of Princes Street, what with the attraction of
the shops in the morning, the pleasures of a midday meal
at a window looking over the Gardens to the Castle and
the Old Town, and the delight of the afternoon promenade. Especially on a fine summer afternoon the street
has a charm, an atmosphere, indescribable. Eastward
the vista is broken only by the lofty, ornate monument
to Sir Walter Scott, and closed by the Calton Hill, with
its classic buildings. But the eye will ever be turning to
Old Edinburgh, spired and peaked and massed against
the sky. Blue skies or bleak, sun, rain, snow, or North
Sea haar, there she abides, beautiful, withal a formless
mountain of stone and lime thrown up by generations of
men who comprehended not the wonder they were working for the eyes of generations to come. Sombre she is,
as though brooding on "old, unhappy, far-off things and
battles long ago," and dire secrets that shall never be
told. Not the tomb of a dead past, but the prison of its
unquiet spirit lies yonder. Only one wholly ignorant of
Edinburgh's history, void of imagination, could linger
there without being aware, if only vaguely, of presences.

But now we are walking in the shine and safety of the
twentieth century, and the eye comes back to the Present.
To obtain an impression of the architecture of Princes
Street—its hotels, clubs, warehouses, cafés, picture
houses, and so forth, we must cross to the other side,
which we may do when opposite the Mound, an artificial
elevation lying between the West and East Gardens.
There stand two dignified buildings which might be
temples, as indeed they are, being dedicated to Art.
That facing Princes Street is the Royal Scottish Academy,
and in its rooms, no less dignified than its exterior, you
may learn something of Scotland's artistic activities, for
the Academy holds its annual exhibition from April to
the end of August. The second building is Scotland's

National Gallery, which, in addition to representative
works by Scottish painters of the past, harbours fine
examples of the foreign schools. Among its treasures
is a series illustrating the characteristics of early paintings and some Gothic sculptures; works by Tiepolo
and Bassano and wax models by Michelangelo of the
Medici Chapel statues; works by Rembrandt, Franz
Hals, Ruisdael, Vermeer, Van Dyck, Watteau, Boucher,
Greuze, Goya, Corot, Millet, Monticelli, Monet, etc. The
works of my countrymen are shown in a suite of octagonal rooms, and, if you are interested, the following names
will be sufficient to draw you in: George Jamesone, earliest
Scottish portrait painter, Allan Ramsay, son of the genius
who combined poesy with wigmaking, and Raeburn, who
is splendidly represented; in *genre*, Wilkie, Scott Lauder,
Dyce, and John Phillip; in figure, Noel Paton, Pettie,
and Orchardson; in landscape and seascape, that celebrated divine, John Thomson of Duddingston, Horatio
Macculloch, Wintour, Sam Bough, and McTaggart. On
the same side of the gallery are some notable English
works by Gainsborough, Hogarth, Crome, Cotman, Turner,
and Sargent.

I had better here mention the National Portrait
Gallery, though it is situated over in Queen Street, one
of the grand thoroughfares running parallel with Princes
Street—a building of red sandstone, described by Sir
J. L. Caw, our expert in all matters pertaining to Art,
as "a Gothic palace, half Venetian, half Flemish in style,
avowedly historical rather than artistic." There you
ought to go, even if your time be limited and your appetite for Art, as Art, not particularly keen, for there are
the likenesses, many of them contemporary and authentic,
of men and women who played leading parts in the drama
of Scottish History, whose names you have known from
your school days, or will learn presently, as you pass
through Old Edinburgh. To set down only a few, there

are portraits of the early Stuart kings, Queen Mary of Scots, her third husband, Bothwell, and her arch-antagonist, John Knox; of Montrose and Argyll, Claverhouse ('Bonnie Dundee'), and Lord Stair, with their memories brilliant, bitter, tragic; of, in their later periods, Bonnie Prince Charlie, Adam Smith, who wrote *The Wealth of Nations*, Boswell, Burns, and Scott. The collection is representative of Scotland's sons and daughters, distinguished in one sphere or another, from the fifteenth century almost to the present day.

Within the same building is housed the Scottish National Museum of Antiquities, which, like the Portrait Gallery, ought, if possible, to be visited before the Old Town, though sections of the exhibits belong to very much more distant ages. The antiquarian for a day or two will probably forget about regular meals, while the most modern-minded young person may possibly allow that many of the "funny old things" are quite intriguing: implements, homely, sporting, and warlike, of the Stone, Bronze, and Iron Ages; weapons, utensils, and ornaments recovered from Pictish underground dwellings; varied objects from Scottish lake-dwellings; gold and silver armlets, necklets, brooches; memorials of the Roman and Norse invasions; relics of Robert the Bruce; antique artillery and firearms; John Knox's pulpit; instruments of the prison and torture chamber; Lochaber axes—fearsome weapons; 'The Maiden,' the Scottish guillotine of the sixteenth century; personal belongings of Bonnie Prince Charlie; a pair of pistols carried by Robert Burns in his capacity of exciseman. . . .

But we are still in Princes Street, and close to the Scott Monument, a notable landmark, perhaps familiar to you from its representations in railway guides and on posters, not to mention advertisements of Scottish merchandise. The Monument was raised nearly a century ago, and its architect was George Kemp, a Peeblesshire man who, it is said, was inspired by Melrose Abbey. He saw Sir Walter on two occasions, but never met him. *Murray's Handbook*, a guide amazing in its detail, and unfortunately out of print, neatly describes the Monument as "a pile of arches, gradually decreasing in size till the whole terminates in a single pinnacle." Whether or no you admire the Monument, the statue of Sir Walter and his dog—by the sculptor Steell—in the shelter of the main arches, will appeal to you. For a small sum you may climb, by an inner stair, 200 feet and gain a wide and impressive view. Just beyond the Monument is a statue of David Livingstone, not the least of Scotland's most warmly remembered great men. It stands at the corner of Waverley Bridge, which affords one of the passages over the hollow to the Old Town.

Let us move on, however, passing the L.N.E. Railway's great hostelry and the General Post Office, crossing the end of the North Bridge, another route to the Old Town, thence to the end of Waterloo Place and the Calton Hill. The Hill in itself is not impressive, but from it the views of Edinburgh are truly, to use a much abused word, glorious. The buildings upon it were, doubtless, the inspiration of somebody's naming the City "the Modern Athens." Yonder 'temple,' the National Monument, commemorating the part of Scottish soldiers in the Peninsular War and at Waterloo, was begun in 1822, and left unfinished for lack of money. Each column cost £1000—a large sum a hundred years ago. We need not regret that the purse was not long enough. As a memorial the building would have gained nothing, as a feature the landscape would have lost something, by its being completed. The Nelson Column is not worthy of its hero and its position, but strikes a note of utility, bearing a staff, down which, every day (except during "summer time"), a big ball descends at the firing of the one o'clock gun over at the Castle. A juvenile visitor

witnessing the ball's descent was heard to observe that
the gunner must be a jolly good shot.
Near the summit of the mount is the City Observatory.
You will notice also a massive cenotaph, which bears the
name of Professor Playfair (1748–1819), and, to the south-
west, a memorial, reproduction of a monument in Athens,
to Professor Dugald Stewart (1753–1828). Looking downward, you find the classic idea still further developed
in the buildings of the Royal High School and the Burns
Monument. While I write this a building very different
in sentiment as well as architecture is being brought low
—the old Calton Jail, a much be-turreted pile, once one
of Edinburgh's landmarks to the just, no less than the
unjust. The question of filling its place seems likely to
produce considerable controversy.

Lastly, let me mention, set a little way aloof, the
Calton Cemeteries, Old and New, where one reads
Scottish names of note, and where the visitor from the
United States may pay respect to the memory of Presi-
dent Lincoln—a really fine statue.

Edinburgh possesses many fine monuments, yet sometimes, whether in Edinburgh or elsewhere, the eye may
admire a memorial while the imagination remains cold as
the material of which it is formed; and I will confess that
when I would have visions of famous people of the past I
must seek inspiration where they lived and moved, warm
and worldly, though it be only in the streets they trod.
So—hoping you can agree with me—we shall go back and
get among buildings that, more than a century ago, were
homes, as many of them are still to-day. Let us return
along Waterloo Place, but on the north side, crossing the
opening of Leith Street, and find ourselves again in
Princes Street, in front of the Old and New Register
Houses. Old Register House, which must have been one
of the first public buildings in New Edinburgh, was
designed by the brothers Adam, whose never-palling

c

architecture we shall discover in many other places, particularly the University and Charlotte Square. Among its treasures are letters of Mary Queen of Scots, and many precious State Papers and autographs. Behind it lies St James's Square, of note only because Robert Burns lodged there—No. 30, third floor—with his friend William Cruickshanks, the schoolmaster, during the winter of 1787—the winter in which he met 'Clarinda.'

Turning into St Andrew Street, we go down to St Andrew Square, where we shall not regard with any particular reverence the offices of the Scottish Union and National Insurance Company, unless we remember that in their place stood once the Douglas Hotel, under whose roof Sir Walter Scott, toward the end of his weary journey from Italy to Abbotsford, passed his last two nights in his beloved Edinburgh.

Let us walk along George Street—parallel with Princes Street—magnificent in its breadth, for at first it was intended to be *the* street of the New Town. It now harbours banks, insurance offices, the old Assembly Rooms, Masonic Hall, and St Andrew's Church, memorable as the birthplace of the Disruption in 1843, and here are several statues, which may speak for themselves. But not because of things visible need we tread softly. Many human beings whose names were assuredly not "writ in water" must have walked, if they did not live, in George Street. Shelley, de Quincey, Scott, Burns, Sidney Smith, Mrs Siddons, the great Free Churchman Dr Chalmers, Sir James Young Simpson, who introduced chloroform as an anæsthetic, Dr John Brown, author of *Rab and his Friends*, Raeburn the artist, Dickens and his *fiancée*, Carlyle, Robert Louis Stevenson—only a few names quickly chosen, yet surely enough to stir the fancy so that presently its eyes are open to behold visions.

For a little while after his marriage, in 1797, Scott had rooms at 108, but his town home for the following twenty-

eight years was at 39 North Castle Street, which runs up
to Princes Street. You cannot miss the house, though
it is now a place of offices; for, besides an inscription on
the front, Sir Walter's bust is to be espied behind the fan-
light over the door. Most of his literary work was done
in that house. The financial disaster of 1826 ended his
blithe days there, but it is good to picture him in the
years before—in his study, at the back, its walls book-
lined to the ceiling, with space only for a portrait of
Claverhouse and some broadswords and dirks over the
mantelpiece. There we may imagine him seated at the
stout table that bore his writing-desk—"a very handsome old box, richly carved and lined with crimson
velvet"—Maida, his favourite dog, at his feet; or, in the
dining-room next door, on a Sunday evening, entertaining his friends; and we may wonder how so prodigious
a worker could find time for frequent and lavish hospitality. I never pass the house without remembering
the story of Menzies, the young barrister, who lodged in
rooms the windows of which looked across to Scott's
study. Night after night, on the study window's blind,
Menzies used to see a shadowy hand and pen ceaselessly
travel to and fro, hour after hour, over page upon page.
The sight fascinated him; gave him an 'uncanny' sensation; and at last he forbade himself to look. It was that
busy hand, as Lockhart tells us, which, within the period
of three weeks, wrote Volumes II and III of *Waverley*.
What that means physically only a writing man who
uses the pen can appreciate. Very few fingers and wrists
could do it.

Eighteen years after Scott left the world Robert Louis
Stevenson came into it—at 8 Howard Place. To-day it
is his Memorial House, the property of the Stevenson
Club, where you may look upon many relics, literary,
personal, some pathetically intimate. If you have read
the play, written in collaboration with W. E. Henley,

The Double Life, you will give more than a glance to the tall, beautifully made cabinet, the handiwork of Deacon Brodie, prototype of the 'hero' of the play. At 17 Heriot Row, down the hill from George Street, looking out upon Queen Street's gardens, was the home of the delicate little boy's upbringing. Many of the flowers of his *Child's Garden of Verses* must have been seedlings there. Edinburgh is starred with his associations—even the Castle Rock, for he scaled it once, in full view of Princes Street. Without in any way suggesting comparison between his fame and that of Scott, the giant, one feels that his name would be uttered oftener to-day in those grey streets, had but the wind that so often scours them been tempered to his bodily weakness. In May 1887, gallantly withal, he turned his back to the unkindly airs, on Edinburgh and the " hills of home," for the last time, to cherish what life was left for him on a foreign sunny isle. A far cry from Edinburgh to Samoa, where he died in 1894; but the lock of hair cut by his loving and beloved nurse, 'Cummy,' from his child's head, and now treasured in the Memorial House, is at least a symbol of his abiding memory in the old place.

Princes Street Gardens

If you would pause awhile between the New and the Old, take a walk or a rest in the charmingly laid-out Gardens. Or if you are staying in a Princes Street hotel, and the morning is sunny, take a stroll there before breakfast, and you will acquire inspiration as well as appetite. At all events, you ought to enter them, if only to look at the American Memorial to Scottish Soldiers, which many people regard as one of the most beautiful War memorials in Europe. You will find it in the West Gardens, built into a grassy bank, facing the Castle Rock. In the stonework is set a bronze frieze, with a representation of soldiers of various regiments and corps on the

march; and in front is a bronze kilted figure, rifle in
hand, with so poignant a look of listening on the face
that it all but lives. This is the main part of the inscription:

THE CALL

1914

A TRIBUTE

FROM MEN AND WOMEN OF SCOTTISH BLOOD AND
SYMPATHIES IN THE UNITED STATES OF

AMERICA

TO

SCOTLAND

The Old Town

To the visitor with little time the Castle is the sight of
Old Edinburgh that demands first attention, and, even
if time be plentiful, it is usually taken at the beginning
of the pilgrimage—logically, as well as conveniently, so,
for it was the beginning of Old Edinburgh; was there,
indeed, before the town on the ridge came into being.

At this point it seems worth while to consider the word
'castle,' which is bound to make frequent appearances
on these pages. For some hundreds of years the word has
conveyed the idea of a large stone building, probably with
towers and turrets, possibly with obvious fortifications.
But that is a large development of the original idea.
Before the Norman Conquest there were no castles, as we
figure them, in Britain, and it is unlikely that there were
any in Scotland until well on in the thirteenth century.
A castle before then was not a building, but an elevation
of the ground, natural or artificial, with a ditch around
the base, a palisade about the summit, and within the
palisade a hut of timber. As time went on, the palisade
was replaced by a stone and turf wall; but not so quickly
did the timber building give place to a stone one, though

it expanded into a sort of house, which later became a
tower-like structure. Roughly, that was the beginning
of the castle, or 'castell,' as it was written in the old days.
The first stone wall of Stirling Castle was in course of
construction in 1288, but, almost certainly, wood, then
more plentiful in Scotland than it was to be later, continued to serve for the erections within. Even in
England, always in advance, the buildings of Durham
Castle were of wood till the year 1345, while in Scotland
at least one castle retained timber erections till the
middle of the fifteenth century. (This tardy use of stone
did not apply to religious buildings.) The primitive
stone building of refuge and defence was the Pictish, or
early Celtic, broch—a curious mortarless construction of
two concentric towers, the space between being roofed
over.

So, if we would picture, for example, Macbeth's castle,
we must not imagine—being influenced, maybe, by certain elaborate stagings of Shakespeare's play—a place
of mighty strength and lofty magnificence. At best it
was possibly a broch, but probably it was a wooden
affair, daubed with clay to keep out some of the draughts,
set on a fortified hillock, and internally very squalid and
insanitary. Shakespeare, however, wrote the play at a
time when the English castles had attained to great
outward splendour and considerable inward luxury.
You will see ruined castles in Scotland that *look* as though
they had been built in the year one, while your guide may
talk impressively of the tenth century—the other day a
lady assured me that the castle near her home was 3000
years old—and your best plan is to accept the statement
blandly. Moreover, the ruin you behold may be that
of the second or third castle to occupy the site.

We may picture Edinburgh Castle, when first mentioned as a Royal Residence, in 1004, or even at the time
of Margaret's death, ninety years later, as enclosing

sundry wattle erections—hall, domestic and sleeping
quarters, stables, and so forth; and the solitary stone
building—assuming that it did exist then, for its date is
undoubtedly not later than the twelfth century—would be
the little Norman Chapel. When, in 1312, Earl Moray,
with a few score men, scaled the Rock and drove out the
English garrison, he demolished the buildings, excepting
the chapel. For the next twenty years the place was
neglected, if not deserted; then we have accounts of new
buildings set up, all of wood, turf, or wattle and clay,
while, incidentally, four glass windows were provided for
the chapel. Hence it may well be that the Castle's first
secular building of stone was the tower raised in 1368, by
David II, and known by his name.

The shortest route from Princes Street to the Castle is
by way of the Mound, and then up the slope past University Hall. This brings us to the Esplanade in front of
the Castle gateway, which was reconstructed in 1888.
The monuments on the Esplanade tell their own tales.
Short of scaling precipices, this is the only approach to
the Castle—an easy, pleasant approach compared with
the rough road of the old days when, too, there was the
dry moat with its drawbridge. On either side of the gateway is a recently erected statue in a niche—on the right,
Sir William Wallace, by Alexander Carrick, R.S.A.; on
the left, King Robert the Bruce, by T. J. Clapperton.

Immediately within the gateway we come up against
the Half-moon Battery, constructed by order of the
Earl of Morton, then Regent—craftiest, greediest, most
shameless noble of an ignoble age—after the Castle was
taken, in 1573, from Kirkcaldy of the Grange, who had
been holding it for Queen Mary. Within the Battery
are the long-buried remains of the David Tower, once 60
feet high, but doubtless battered to bits during the siege.
They were laid bare as lately as 1913. The Argyll
Tower, originally the Constable's Tower, stands on guard,

and we pass under it, through an archway at one time barred by a portcullis and no less than three gates. It was well renamed the 'Argyll.' In one of its chambers lay the Marquis before his execution in 1661; from its fastness, in 1683, escaped his son, the ninth Earl, only to be brought back, two years later, to pay the extreme price of failure. There, too, Montrose, to many people the most gallant figure in Scotland's story, awaited his tryst with the executioners.

The modern building which we are now passing is the military hospital; the older one, which belongs to Queen Anne's day, is the Governor's House. Then up through Foogs Gate—who or what Foog, or Foogs, was, or were, I have been unable to learn—we come to the chapel known as Queen Margaret's, or Saint Margaret's, although she was not canonized until two hundred years after her association with the Rock. Whether she or her devoted son, David I, caused its building matters very little. It is the oldest building in Edinburgh and, perhaps, the oldest intact building in Scotland. It is very small, only $16\frac{1}{2}$ feet by $10\frac{1}{2}$ feet within the nave. It was restored in the last century, after having been used as, of all things, a powder magazine. We may guess that its ancient stones have echoed to more sorrowful prayers than glad thanksgivings, and there is, after all, no reason why we should not peer through the mists of sentiment, as well as of the ages, and behold in that bleak shelter Queen Margaret, worn out by her religion, receive the last priestly consolation, and then, on that November day, learn from her son, David, the news of her husband and first-born slain in battle. The Castle at this time was besieged by a rival faction, and those who had loved her, already regarding her as a saint, took advantage of the prevailing fog, and bore her body down yonder western precipice for conveyance across the Forth to the tomb in Dunfermline.

On the ramparts in front of the Chapel stands that famous old piece of artillery, Mons Meg, forged in 1486, but whether at Mons of Belgium, or at Castle Douglas, in our own Galloway, by blacksmith McKim and his three stout sons, is a question that has not been answered with decision. Built of iron bars hooped together, Meg had a long life for a big gun. She was two centuries old when, in honour of the Duke of York, she belched her last— and burst. In 1745 she was removed to the Tower of London, and to the influence of Sir Walter Scott we owe her restoration to her proper place.

May the day be clear when you stand on those ramparts. As well as of the New Town, with Princes Street in all its charm, you will have a refreshing view of the expanding Forth, its great Bridge and islands, beyond them the hills of Fife and the Ochil Range, and, westward, Ben Ledi in Perthshire, and Ben Lomond.

The summit of the Rock carries the Crown Square, formed by the Palace, the Great Hall—sometimes referred to as the Parliament or Banqueting Hall—the Barracks, and the Scottish National War Memorial. One might catalogue a thousand 'notables' who in those bygone centuries trod where we are treading now—and none of them would be more than a name. But in a small room of the Palace lingers a memory with a human interest for nearly all the world. In that room which you may know by the Royal initials " H " and " M " Queen Mary, three months after witnessing the horror of Riccio's murder in Holyroodhouse, gave birth to a son whose father was Lord Henry Darnley, degenerate and scoundrel—the son through whom the Crowns of Scotland and England were one day to be united. Lying there, in June 1566, she must have thought much of that, perhaps more fearfully than hopefully. Yet she could hardly have dreamed that her baby would grow up to fail her in her desperate need; to make no manly effort to save her from the block in Fotheringay Castle; to accept, without protest, the written statement of Elizabeth to the effect that she had cut off his mother's head "by accident."

Yet there is another story. Long afterward a hollow was suspected in the wall; which being opened, there was found, built into it, a small coffin containing the bones of an infant; and on the remnant of the little shroud was embroidered the initial 'I,' or something like it, which might have stood for 'Iames' or 'Iacobus.' Now it is known that Mary's was not the only baby to come into the Castle at that time. One of her ladies-in-waiting also bore a son. What if Mary's boy were still-born, or died soon after birth? What if there was a substitution? What if James Sixth of Scotland and First of England was not the Queen's son? What if he had no heart for Mary because he had never lain under her heart? Scotland has her mysteries.

In the same building you will find the Regalia of Scotland — Crown, Sceptre, Sword of State. The double golden circlet, the oldest part of the Crown, may have rested on the brow of Robert the Bruce; the Crown, as it is, with the additions made by James V, the father of Mary, last served its purpose at the Scottish coronation of Charles II. From first to last it must have touched some uneasy heads. The sceptre too belongs to James V, having been wrought in 1537; while the Sword, a thing of beauty in its way, was the gift of Pope Julius II to James IV in 1507. Beside the Regalia are some memorials of James VI, including insignia of the Order of the Garter presented to him by the lady who effected the death of his mother.

The Great Hall, which dates from 1424, was last used for State purposes in 1648, when Oliver Cromwell was chief guest at a banquet. For a long period thereafter it served as a military hospital, and the fabric was badly knocked about. Thanks to Mr William Nelson, one of

Edinburgh's notable publishers, it was fully restored at the end of last century, and now contains a fine display of arms and armour. Its old walls must have witnessed some strange dramas; and perhaps the strangest, and certainly the most sensational, was that of 'the Black Dinner,' enacted when the walls were almost new. In November 1440 Sir William Crichton, Governor of the Castle and Chancellor of Scotland, and Sir Alexander Livingstone, his colleague, jealous of the influence of the eighteen-year-old Earl of Douglas over the boy King, James II, invited the young man and his younger brother to a feast, the little King being present. While the feast was in progress the portcullis in the Castle gateway was lowered and all the doors were secured, thus excluding Douglas supporters. The feast had come to its end, but yet another course was brought to the table—the head of a black bull, sure sign of death in old Scotland. The Douglases, knowing the sign, strove to defend themselves, but were easily overpowered by Crichton's armed servants, and after being given a mock trial, at which the weeping small King was forced to preside, were taken forth and beheaded, along with their aged friend, Fleming of Cumbernauld.

From the horrid squalor of self-seeking, so evident in the early chapters of Scotland's history, let us turn for a little while. From the Hall across the quadrangle is not so many paces, but in taking them we are stepping over centuries, for we are approaching the Scottish National War Memorial, emblem, first and last, of self-sacrifice. Designed by Sir Robert Lorimer, noble in conception, it is built close to the wall of the eighteenth-century Barracks. The lovely Shrine is floored with polished granite, through which obtrudes the topmost pinnacle of the Rock, whereon is set a green altar-stone. Thus does the rock on which Abraham was prepared to sacrifice his son Isaac obtrude through the floor of the Mosque of Omar, on the site of Solomon's Temple, in Jerusalem. Above the green altar-stone is the Archangel Michael, sword at Satan's throat, and upon it rests the coffer containing the Rolls of Honour—names of a hundred thousand Scottish soldiers who died in the Great War. Records in bronze and stone are on the walls and in the stained-glass windows. And resting upon tables of stone, each under a carved inscription embodying the name of a regiment, lie great folio volumes bound in scarlet, their many pages, alas! closely printed—the Books of the Dead.

The Royal Mile

The Royal Mile extends between the gate of the Castle and the entrance to Holyroodhouse. It is made up by the Esplanade, Castle Hill, Lawnmarket, High Street, and Canongate, and is not far from being a straight line. Canongate, by the way, should be written 'Canongait'—'Street of the Canons' belonging to the Abbey. It is long since lords and ladies had their town dwellings in these quarters, but here and there you will come upon houses once the homes of those whose names are written in Scotland's History—maybe in the world's also. Drab and uninviting may such dwellings be to-day, yet this one may have a doorway for you to envy, and that a ceiling which you would surely covet. There are courts into which you may enter, to look up at windows whence bright eyes, long since dust, looked smilingly down for approaching lovers, or white, terrified faces peered furtively forth at the *tramp-tramp* and *clink-clank* of soldiery. You may peep into wynds where fugitives have paused for breath, into closes where assassins have awaited their victims. (A 'wynd' is a narrow thoroughfare; a 'close' a private passage, its entrance having, in the old days, a gate which could be shut at night.)

Impossible for me here to tell a tenth of the story; but if you have the time and will to make a leisurely progress, let me commend as guide Mr Robert T. Skinner's *The Royal Mile*, a little book which tells much and suggests more.

Coming from the Castle you will notice, on the right, a house, in the western gable of which, under the centre window, is stuck a cannon-ball. How the ball got there —whether it was a good or a bad shot from the Castle, or was put there for ornament—nobody knows. But the building is known as Cannon-ball House, and three hundred years ago it belonged to Alexander Mure, an honest furrier. (I have put in the 'honest,' because it has a nice old-fashioned flavour.) He and Mrs Mure, and possibly the little Mures, must have witnessed stirring and gruesome—especially gruesome—sights in their day, for the site of the Esplanade was often the scene of torturings and beheadings, stranglings and burnings; and, no doubt, they obtained good prices for the use of their windows on such occasions, for people then were just as hungry for entertainment as they are to-day.

East of the Castle the villa with the octagonal tower was built by Allan Ramsay, who, in the eighteenth century, sold wigs and books at "The Sign of the Mercury" in the High Street—and wrote poetry. However fleeting his fame as a wig-maker, his *Gentle Shepherd* was destined to become a classic. The villa must have a literary atmosphere, for later its roof sheltered Mrs Grant of Laggan, whose very charming *Letters from the Mountains* are cameos of Highland life toward the close of the eighteenth century, and John Galt, whose novels are big pictures of Lowland life in the beginning of the nineteenth.

On Castle Hill (north side; No. 541) is Sempill's Close, the mansion within bearing the date 1638. Even then the Sempills were an old Scottish family, originally of the West, though their estates are now in Aberdeenshire. A Sempill married one of Queen Mary's "four

Maries," and, about two hundred years later, the twelfth Baron commanded the left wing of the army that routed Bonnie Prince Charlie's Highlanders at Culloden. The mansion is now the kitchen of New College.

Over the way is Boswell's Court, where lived in the eighteenth century a man of physics and lancets, uncle of *the* Boswell. Imagine yourself standing there on a morning in 1773, watching two figures, one stout and elderly, in brown suit and bob-wig, the other young and slim, coming slowly up the street. It is the Biographer conducting the Sage to call upon his relative. They arrive at the door, Johnson's hand on his young friend's arm, and read the motto on the lintel—

O—LORD—IN—THE—IS—AL—MI—TRAIST

Hush! The Doctor is making an unkindly remark concerning our Scottish notions of orthography. But never mind! We are glad to know, later, that they spent a pleasant forenoon in the house of the physician; at all events, the great man was pleased to be pleased with his young friend's uncle's company. Regrettably, in the same place, he was to suffer being baited by Edinburgh's wits and wags of the day.

The Doctor and his companion were then lodging at the White Horse, which stood in the Canongate. This inn had stabling for 50 horses but only 13 bedrooms, which seems to indicate that a guest would not always get a room to himself. Boswell tells of a little 'scene' which took place there. The Doctor asked for more sugar, and the waiter took a lump in his "greasy fingers" and dropped it in. In high indignation the Doctor—can't you hear his snort?—shied the tumbler out of the window.

A little way down the street is the Assembly Hall of the Church of Scotland, built in the pointed Gothic style, its tower and spire 240 feet high. It is, however, in the Assembly Hall at the top of the Mound that the

Supreme Court of the Church, commonly called the General Assembly, gathers annually in May. The meetings are presided over by a Moderator (a minister chosen yearly), and the Sovereign is represented by a Lord High Commissioner, who resides for the period in the State Apartments of Holyroodhouse. He may be a noble or a commoner; in either case during the period of his Commissionership he takes precedence of the dukes of Scotland, and ranks next to the Lord Chancellor of Great Britain. For ten days or so Edinburgh, including Princes Street, is gay, black coats and all, for the afternoons and evenings are not, by any means, entirely devoted to solemn debates. For many country ministers and their wives it is the outing of the year.

The West Bow, now a flight of steps, was once a steep, tortuous lane, the main passage between the West Port, or gate, and the City. It leads down to the Grassmarket, a frequent setting for public executions between 1666 and 1784. Kings and queens and nobles with their retinues, martyrs and criminals with their mobs, have passed to their pleasures, or pains, through the West Bow.

In the inner court of Riddle's Close, toward the end of the sixteenth century, lived Bailie John MacMorran, who is remembered for his entertainment of James VI and his Queen in his mansion, now a University Students' Settlement, which you should see, especially the panelled hall, where the banquet took place. The Bailie, however, is still better remembered through the circumstances of his death. Boys of the High School, annoyed by a curtailment of their holidays, became refractory, and the Bailie stepped along to admonish them. The boys barred him out, and, when he sought to force an entrance, one of them shot him dead with a pistol.

When we were in the New Town, I mentioned, in connection with Robert Louis Stevenson, Deacon Brodie— and here we are at Brodie's Close, where the man lived

his two lives: an excellent cabinetmaker and Town
Councillor by day, a burglar by night.   In 1788 he made
his last haul—a few guineas from the Excise Office—and,
panic-stricken, fled to Amsterdam, only to be arrested
there and brought back to Edinburgh.   In those days
capital punishment had a wider application than now,
and he was hanged at the Tolbooth, a little way down the
street.   The story goes that he induced the hangman to
let him wear a steel collar, but the noose did its deadly
work, and though friends bore him away with all speed,
they failed to revive him.

There is little about the Lawnmarket—not Linen but
Land Market—to tell us that once upon a time it was an
avenue of fashion, where one could meet the illustrious
persons of the day.   Yet so it was.   In the seventeenth
century we read that Mylne, of Mylne's Court, on the
north side, removed two old houses to make room for
a fashionable square.   Gladstone's Land—a 'land' is a
tenement, as we call it in Scotland, of flats owned, or
tenanted, by different persons, or families—is over three
hundred years old.   While the Lawnmarket was the
'right place,' the 'best people' did not deem it beneath
their dignity to live in a land, and to climb the steepest of
stone stairs to a home, even on the topmost storey.   In
the Grassmarket there is still a land eleven storeys high.
It must have been a business getting up the fuel and
water, but servants had no 'rights' in those days, and
perhaps they used as little fuel as possible, while their
employers were not too reckless with the water.   Incidentally, there was no difficulty in the disposal of
dirty water and garbage.   The good folk simply threw it
out of their windows, with the perfunctory warning to
pedestrians of "Gardeyloo" (*Gare de l'eau*).   At the rear
of Gladstone's Land you will find walls with timber
facings.   Many of the more ancient houses were originally timber-faced, but in Queen Mary's time occurred a

fuel famine, and the facings were converted into heat. Lady Stair's House, in the close bearing her name, open to visitors, contains many interesting items. Almost opposite, Burns, on his visit in 1786, found lodgings with a friend in the house of Mrs Carfrae, who deserves to be remembered for the moderation of her charges—three shillings a week for both guests.

In *The Royal Mile* Mr Skinner indicates the variety of trades followed in this neighbourhood in the eighteenth century—money scrivener, mantua-maker, inspector of window lights, gumflower maker, clothes cleaner, setter of elegant rooms, extractor, harpsichord and spinet maker.

Talking of odd trades, did you ever hear of the firm of Burke and Hare which, for a brief space, flourished here, over a hundred years ago?   In all the annals of business that firm's trade was surely unique.   For a long time after its winding up, mere mention of the names of the partners produced shudders in any part of Britain; for Messrs Burke and Hare committed murder on at least sixteen occasions, and sold the bodies to an enthusiastic ana- tomist of the respectable name of Knox.   Their method was admirable in its simplicity: they enticed the pro- spective 'subjects' into Hare's abode, where, assisted by a woman, they drugged them with hospitality into helplessness, and then suffocated them.   The accidental discovery of one murder led to the discoveries of fifteen more; but probably others remained hidden.   Hare, viler, if anything, of the two, turned king's evidence, and eventually betook his vileness to America; Burke was duly hanged in the Lawnmarket.   You will find in the roadway three cross stones, which mark the situation of the gallows; and if you glance up at the building bearing the number 423, you may guess the window from which Sir Walter Scott and a friend witnessed the spectacle in 1829.

D

At George IV Bridge, almost in a line with the west pavement of Melbourne Place, was the close in which the Bank of Scotland had its beginning in 1695. Long before that James VI stayed there for a time, and there in 1581 the Earl of Morton, cornered at last, awaited the summons to his doom—at the blade of 'The Maiden,' it has been said, though a contemporary diarist records that he was sentenced, in the good old-fashioned, efficient way, to be "hanged, beheaded, quartered and demeaned as a traitor."

The Tolbooth, which loomed so largely in the life of Old Edinburgh, once harboured the Scots Parliament, but was the City Prison from 1640 till its removal in 1817. Paving-stones set in the form of a heart commemorate it, while other distinctive stones mark the site of its walls. There is no end to the tales of the Tolbooth, but for a little while let us escape from scenes and memories of cruelty and misery and turn to that which—outwardly, at least—stood for mercy, peace, and loving-kindness.

Where rises the High Kirk of St Giles to-day was a little chapel, 800 years ago, probably built by David I. Richard II, on his visit to Scotland in 1385, may have burned its successor, along with most of Edinburgh, such as it then was; but we know that two years later a church there was being enlarged, and during the next two centuries its expansion continued. Describing St Giles, as it is now, Murray says:

A cruciform building, with slightly projecting transepts, originally of great architectural beauty, but at various times so mutilated—both intentionally and unintentionally—it has at length been admirably restored (by the munificence of Mr William Chambers), so far as regards the interior. The exterior has been so lamentably spoilt by previous 'restorations' that nearly all traces of the original have disappeared, with the exception of the choir and square central tower.

Whatever the building's graces just before the Reformation, its 'purification' by the Reformers, or the mob that always accompanied them, was drastic, and to many an eye then the interior must have become a sad and vacant place. John Knox was minister from 1559 to 1572. I cannot see St Giles without seeing Knox in his prime, thundering his sermons through that denuded House at the crowded, quivering people; and, toward the end, the eager spirit struggling with the failing flesh, still forcing feebly, scarce audibly, his message upon them. A great man, he remains a great figure, in some ways the greatest, in Scotland's earlier story. One may hate or admire him; one cannot despise him, for he wrought not for himself. Picture him coming out of St Giles on a Sabbath afternoon, bearded, sombre, looking sterner, perhaps, than he felt. He has preached for the second time that day, and has attended, in the vestry, to the more or less spiritual problems of men and women—mostly women—for they do flock around him, the women, if they do not actually run after him! Leisurely—for he is getting old, has never been robust, and those nineteen months on the French galleys have taken it out of him— leisurely he walks toward his home, wherever it may have been, for nobody knows for certain. Arrived, he rests awhile, then welcomes to his supper-table some of his supporters and those whom he has supported in the Faith, including the highest in the land. And we need not assume that the talk, moistened from the cask of claret, will be a continual whine on religious matters. Knox himself tells us that they had their good stories— 'merrie bourdes,' he calls them—and we may believe that he relaxed in quite an ordinary human fashion. For he was neither inhumanly hard nor inhumanly wise. When, an old widower, he married a lass of sixteen, his enemies rejoiced over his folly, and when he died they wrote of him that he had been the servant of Satan all along. But

Morton, standing at the graveside, said: "Here lies one who neither flattered nor feared any flesh." In Parliament Square, close by, you may see the stone marking his resting-place. It bears the date and the initials 'I. K.'

By the way, in those days the only permanent seats in the church were stone benches along the walls, a circumstance which, I have been told, gave rise to the saying, "The weakest goes to the wall."

No finer ornament has Edinburgh than the open-arched crown steeple of St Giles. From up yonder men have witnessed strange and stirring and horrible spectacles; bells have sent forth merry peals, slow dirges, frantic summons, wild alarums. St Giles has told the time for centuries. Away back in 1585 we read of a clock—or 'knok,' as we funny Scots may still call it—being purchased from the Abbey of Lindores, in Fife, for £55. Another clock that came from London, in 1721, did its duty for nearly two hundred years, when it was replaced by a gift from Messrs Ritchie, of Princes Street. Two of the bells, which hang among beams recovered from a ship of the Spanish Armada wrecked on the Fife coast, are dated 1706 and 1728. A much more ancient vesper bell, used before the Reformation, rests, silent, in the Moray Aisle below. The author of *Robinson Crusoe*, visiting Edinburgh in 1727, admired the chimes, remarking that the ringer well earned his wage. He remarked, too, on the white stockings of the Edinburgh ladies, and the display thereof.

During the course of its existence the church, outrages of the Reformation apart, has suffered many indignities. At different periods it was partitioned into separate places of worship—well, not always of worship, for parts served as grammar school, court of justice, jail, and store for the hangman's paraphernalia. Along the outer walls merchants planted their booths and called their wares.

Now in its restored dignity it harbours many monuments and memorials.

In Parliament Square the modern building which is part of St Giles is the Chapel of the Order of the Thistle. The old Parliament House was burned in 1824; but the Great Hall, in which Scots Parliaments met from 1640 till the Union in 1707, survived, with its splendid timber roof, to be contained in the present building. Therein, too, is the College of Justice, now known as the Court of Session, where the majesty of Civil Law holds its dreary sway. The Criminal Court is at the east end of the House. Below Parliament House is the recently founded National Library of Scotland, incorporating the Advocates' Library, in existence for two and a half centuries. Among its supreme treasures are letters of Mary Queen of Scots and Prince Charlie, and the original manuscript of *Waverley*.

We are now in the High Street proper, "the goodliest street that ever mine eyes beheld," wrote Taylor, the Water Poet, early in the seventeenth century. Well, we must take his word for it, remembering, however, that his soubriquet had nothing to do with Temperance. Yet, no doubt, there were elegancies in the old place, as there were evidences of wealth. In a house that stood between Byres Close and Advocate's Close lived Sir William Dick, who must have been a plutocrat of his time, for not only did he lend money to James VI and finance the Covenanters, but he advanced £20,000 for the cause of Charles II, for which last little deal the Parliamentary Party fined him £65,000. Broken, he went to London, hoping to recover £160,000 which he had lent on Government security. Alas! there was 'nothing doing,' and the poor fellow, after suffering imprisonment for small debts, died in poverty. I am glad to have this opportunity of naming a Scotsman who could not possibly be described as 'canny.'

Peep into Old Post Office Close, and reflect that when George I was King one postman served all Edinburgh. Look at that corner house with the quaint projections and outside stair. It was built by Queen Mary's gold-smith; his initials and his wife's are upon it still, also a carving said to show "Moses receiving the Law on Mount Sinai," the Almighty being suggested by a gilded disc. It has been said also, rather flippantly, to represent Moses directing attention to the sun coming out of the clouds, possibly in order to encourage the tourist on a wet day. The building, the rooms of which are small, low-ceiled, and dark, is known as John Knox's House, and we have proof in the City's records that he spent his last days there. On November 9, 1572, he preached in St Giles, came home a 'done man,' lay down, and died a fortnight later.

In Knox's day, and for two centuries after, just below his house, the Netherbow Port extended across the street, dividing Edinburgh from the Canongate, then a suburb. It was removed about 1765. An old print shows it as a charmingly elegant building, with clock-tower and steeple. Some of its stones have been placed within the railings of the Moray-Knox church, which stands on the site of the old Balmerino mansion. The last of the Balmerinos died for Prince Charlie; arrested after the Culloden *débâcle*, he was taken to London and beheaded on Tower Hill.

What happened to the old Mercat Cross when it was removed, in 1756, nobody seems to know. In 1885, William Ewart Gladstone, M.P. for Midlothian, had the present Cross erected, and the shaft carrying the Unicorn is thought to have belonged to the old one. Here to-day, as of yore, Royal Proclamations are made by the Lyon King at Arms in his gorgeous dress, accompanied by trumpeters. Till 1666 the Mercat Cross stood farther down the street—its place is marked—and was the scene of many executions. There died Kirkcaldy of Grange, who had held the Castle for Mary, and whom a word from Elizabeth could have saved from the revengeful Morton; also Montrose and, later, his arch-enemy Argyll, along with the Rev. James Guthrie; and, later still, the son of that Argyll, the ninth Earl, of whom we spoke in the Castle. All died bravely in the face of the rabble.

In the neighbourhood lodged Lord Braxfield, the terrible judge, Lord Auchinleck, father of Boswell, and the Doomster, or hangman. Within the proverbial stone's throw of that sinister person's abode were the Assembly Rooms, which suggest visions of Edinburgh's beauty and quality, coifed and corseted, borne through the murk and mire in sedan chairs, link-boys in front with flaring, dripping torches. By 1787, the High Street having become unfashionable, Edinburgh's fourth Assembly Rooms were inaugurated in George Street, where to-night the ghosts of those who knew the graces of minuet and sarabande, as well as the intricacies of country dances, may smile pityingly at the 'floor walkers' of the twentieth century.

In Blackfriars Street Chepman and Myllar, in 1508, printed Scotland's first book; Mary passed through it in the darkness, returning to Holyrood from visiting her invalid husband at Kirk o' Field, where Murder was biding its time. At the far end, for a time, lived Cardinal Beaton, who was to come to a bad end in the Castle of St Andrews. The only existing house with a history is the Earl of Morton's. Four years earlier had died in gentler fashion Thomas Bassendyne, who, in Fountain Court, a little way down the High Street, printed the New Testament in the first version to be published in Scotland. After all, Scottish industry, even in the sixteenth century, was not confined to getting on in the world by foul means, and Bassendyne with his types makes a fine contrast to Morton and his like with their daggers and pistols.

The Canongate for a long time was Edinburgh's most aristocratic quarter. It was walled by fine houses, with long gardens behind, occupied by dukes, earls, barons, and lesser nobility. Its glory began to fade with the removal of the Jacobean Court to London.

The big projecting clock proclaims the presence of the Canongate Tolbooth, built in 1591, at first the Council Chambers, afterward, and till the middle of the nineteenth century, the prison—a quaint, old-world building, modelled on French and Scottish ideas of architecture. The Canongate Church was dedicated about the end of the seventeenth century and was built for the congregation ejected from Holyrood Abbey Church by James VII, who wanted the old place for his chapel royal, and cared not a groat for the offence given to his Presbyterian subjects. In the churchyard are stones bearing the names of many Scotsmen eminent in their native country, or of wider celebrity, such as Adam Smith, author of *The Wealth of Nations*, the argument of which, as the writer of *The Royal Mile* succinctly puts it, is that every man best promotes the interests of his fellows by attending to his own; the brothers Ballantyne, printers of Scott's novels; Horatius Bonar, "the beloved hymn-writer," as somebody called him; Burns's 'Clarinda,' who reached the age of eighty-two; and that worthy professor of physic, whose fame for generations has flourished on an ingenious, beneficent compound, abhorred of juveniles—and grown-ups, too—"Dr Gregory's Stomachic Mixture." Under a carved stone at the south-east corner of the church lies what was left by his murderers of David Riccio, exhumed from under the Chapel passage at Holyrood and brought hither.

Look into Brown's Court, Campbell's Close, and Whitehorse Close; also up at Golfer's Land (No. 81), which was built with a wager won at a golf match. In a tavern in Callender's Entry, John Gay, of *Beggar's Opera* fame,

used to hobnob with boon friends and admirers.   Poor
Gay was hard hit by the refusal of a licence for his opera
Polly; but the Duke and Duchess of Queensberry stood
his friends, and made him provision for the rest of his life.

On the south side are two mansions at which you will
pause.   The first is Moray House, dating from the reign
of Charles I, a dignified building, readily recognizable by
reason of the obelisk pillars at the entrance.   Its domed
ceilings and carved woodwork give it a beautiful interior.
It has many associations, but none so memorable as that
of May 18, 1650.   A day or two earlier, Lord Lorne, son
of the Marquis of Argyll, had been wed to the Lady Mary,
a daughter of the house, and the celebrations were still
going merrily on.   But now comes an interruption—a
tumult in the street.   A straggling procession approaches,
squalid and brutal.   The guests crowd to the windows
and balcony to see it pass—not with pitying eyes, for the
principal figure in the procession is their enemy, the
Marquis of Montrose—Montrose broken yet gallant still,
roped to a cart, on his way to Parliament House, there
to hear the sentence of doom.   Does he raise his eyes?
Certainly he does—and smiles!   Not Montrose, did he do
otherwise.   And do not the Argylls, through the flush of
triumph and wine, feel a faint, chill breath?   For it is
written that within five-and-thirty years they, father
and son, shall pass into the darkness now awaiting
Montrose—and pass just as gallantly.

Your eye will be caught by Huntly House, the sixteenth-century mansion with the timber-breasted gables.
It has lately been restored to serve as a city museum,
of which the interior itself will surely be the most intriguing and illuminating exhibit.   No thrilling tales
are attached to it, but the front bears sculptured tablets
with mottoes, and the date 1570.   Here is one of the
mottoes, an odd piece of philosophy:

To-day for me—to-morrow for you : why therefore worry ?

Holyrood

Holyrood — spelled by old-time writers Halirud, Halierude, Holyruid, etc.—means Holy Cross, a natural enough name to give to an abbey, though here the early monkish chroniclers invested its application with the supernatural. Not so long ago excavations in the choir of the ruined church revealed the foundations of a Celtic chapel, and we may imagine that King David I, while in residence at the Castle, where the holy men then lived, came down with them to worship there. David also went a-hunting in adjacent Drumselch (now Drumsheugh), which in the twelfth century was, as a chronicler quaintly tells, "ane gret forest full of hartis, hyndis, toddis [foxes], and siclike maner of beastis." David, like his Old Testament namesake, while a deeply religious man, could go astray. On a certain Holy Day, falling on September 14, he duly attended Mass; but thereafter, rejecting the admonition of his confessor, rode off with a bunch of young sparks belonging to his retinue, amid "sic noyis of rachis [hounds] and bugillis [horns] that all the beastis war raisit fra their dennys." Near the foot of Salisbury Crags—'Salis' is almost certainly derived from a word meaning 'willows'—David, separated from his friends and servants, was attacked by a monstrous hart, "with awful and braid tyndis [broad antlers]," and unhorsed. To save himself from being gored he grasped at the antlers, but, lo and behold, seized, instead, a mystic luminous Cross, whereupon his antagonist—the Evil One in disguise—fled away "with gret violence." In acknowledgment of his miraculous deliverance, David proceeded to found, build, and richly endow the Abbey of the Holy Rood. Such is the legend, more or less, and I should have liked to accept it as, at least, based on fact; for, after all, a miracle might befall an unsophisticated king, like David I, in 1128, which could hardly happen to, for instance, a stockbroker, in 1932. Unfortunately, a modern writer, whose judgments I must respect, coldly remarks that the tale was invented by some pious persons, a couple of hundred years or so after David's death, with the object of "shedding over the building the mystery of a divine origin."

Still, without a doubt, the Abbey owes its beginning to David I. The choir, with its apse and crossing, seems to have been completed at his death in 1153, but of it only a Norman doorway stands to-day. Building operations then lapsed for the space of half a century; during the next fifty years, however, the northern and southern aisles were raised and the nave completed. One of the square towers of the western front remains, and its most beautiful doorway has survived those seven centuries of Nature's aggression, and man's—especially man's. About the middle of the fourteenth century the Abbey was fired by English invaders. A hundred years later, in the reign of the mild and cultured James III, it was restored, while the buttresses and flying arches on the north and south fronts were added. But, in 1544, over the Border came Earl Hertford—otherwise the Lord Protector Somerset—and in his smashing up of Edinburgh the Abbey and Palace did not escape. One of his lieutenants, Sir Richard Lee, looted the brass font and lectern of the church, and the lectern may now be seen in the chancel of St Stephen's Church at St Albans. Hertford, however, though he had ruined the Palace, was not satisfied with what he had done to the Abbey; so, on his return, three years later, he 'went for it' with such enthusiasm that little was left standing except the nave.

After her appointment to the Regency, Marie of Lorraine, mother of Queen Mary, rebuilt the Palace in the French style and restored the nave; the destruction of choir and transepts had been so thorough as to render their restoration beyond her. The Reformers have been blamed for, and were guilty of, much vandalism, but in the instance of Holyrood comparatively little was left for their energies; still, they did what they could in the way of 'purification' by felling and shattering all Romish monuments and effigies. So it must have been a bare and dreary place on the morning of Mary's marriage to Bothwell—that May morning when she wept and wished she were dead. In 1688 the Abbey was again visited by the rabble, who, among other doughty deeds, rifled and desecrated the royal tombs. Eighty years later, the roof of the nave gave way, and for long the ruin was left to the ravages of the weather; but recently there has been extensive restoration.

If the Palace of Holyroodhouse—to give it its proper title—stands for anything, it stands for Tragedy. True, its walls have witnessed feasting, dancing, and masquerading, have hearkened to music, song, and laughter; but it is the weeping of a Queen, the shrieks of a courtier being done to death, the whisperings of plotters, the brief acclamation of a Prince, whose soaring star was only a rocket, that they seem to echo to-day. Memories of Mary Stuart alone would make it a sorrowful place; and there is no place I know of in Scotland, excepting St Andrews, where memories crowd so closely, where the sigh of the Past is so poignant, where one, in broad daylight, may conjure up the ghosts of those who were destined to survive as something more than mere names in a nation's history.

Till the beginning of the sixteenth century Royalty visiting Edinburgh lodged at the Abbey, which maintained Royal apartments and provided all the creature comforts and luxuries then available in Scotland. But a history of the Royal Stuarts is likewise a history of expanding ideas; and when James IV, during whose reign Scotland's economic value was trebled, decided to accept in marriage the thrice-offered hand of the English

Princess, daughter of Henry VII, he determined to build
a Royal residence on the site adjoining the Abbey.
James was responsible for at least the great north-
western tower, with its four turrets—that is, the tower
on the left, as one approaches from the Canongate.
James did fairly well by his people. His likeness, hanging with those of the other Jameses in the Scottish
National Portrait Gallery, is that of a thoughtful person,
though he was a keen warrior, as well as a ladies' man.
If you would see what his wife was like, you must go
to the National Portrait Gallery, London. According
to the artist, Margaret was more buxom than bonnie,
albeit oddly alluring—I feel sure that James, even
when thinking of somebody else, called her 'Maggie'—
though she was slight enough on her wedding-day, in
1503; but then, poor thing, she was barely fourteen. It
was through this marriage that the two Kingdoms became eventually united. Ten years later the chivalrous,
wise, yet headstrong and flirtatious James was slain at
Flodden—a disaster as well remembered by Scotsmen as
the victory of Bannockburn—but in those years of comparative peace we may fancy him getting some enjoyment
out of his new palace. His son, James V, extended the
building and had his private apartments in the southern
turret. He, too, had his pleasures and pains there. We
see him bringing home his first wife, Princess Madeleine,
whom we may assume he loved, since she was not the
lady he had journeyed to France to marry—and in two
months she was dead. We can imagine his second wife,
Marie of Lorraine, a clever woman, if ever there was one,
creating some liveliness in Holyroodhouse; yet trouble
was never far away from a Stuart, and two years later
the two little Princes died. In the following year the
Queen, removed to the Palace of Linlithgow, gave birth
to a daughter, and received the tidings that her husband,
broken-hearted by the farcical rout of his army at Solway

Moss, lay dying at Falkland. The baby girl was Mary, in a few days to be Queen of Scots.

Had Mary, as queen, never lived in it, Holyroodhouse would matter but little to us now. Compared with her and those about her, friends and foes, all who lived there before and after her are shadows—if we omit Prince Charles Edward, who during his brief triumph of 1745 entertained in the Palace, though he never slept under its roof. It is Mary, hopeless as a queen, far from admirable as a woman, but as herself fascinating to half the world, who, though for centuries dust, still draws us thither. She came to it, a girl of nineteen and a widow, in August 1561, when the sea-fog lay thick on Edinburgh; six years later—what years of stress!—she rode away from its door for the last time, a prisoner.

The greater part of Holyroodhouse, as we see it now, belongs to the reign of Charles II. Mary knew it as her father had left it, or, rather, as her mother had restored it after the destruction wrought by Hertford. You will pass through its spacious throne chamber, its state apartments, its royal suite, and in passing see many beautiful and curious things—ceilings, chandeliers, furniture, tapestries, portraits. You will perambulate the fifty yards of picture gallery, wherein Prince Charlie gave a ball, at which the more sagacious guests exchanged whispered doubts along with their snuff-boxes; on the walls you will observe a long series—over a hundred—of portraits of the early Kings of Scotland, all painted 'out of his own head' by a Flemish artist, who received £120 per annum for the 'job.' The series has been described in modern parlance, rudely but not unjustly, as 'a scream'; yet the Gallery has redeeming features in several portraits and panels by Hugo van der Goes.

All these rooms and their exhibits have, undeniably, their historic and antiquarian interests, but it is when you reach the apartments of the Queen of Scots that the

'museum feeling' is dispersed in an atmosphere inti-
mately human. In these apartments—audience chamber,
bedroom, boudoir—you will 'see' those sad, bad, mad
people of the past, not as puppets in a toy theatre, but
as warm, live beings on the stage of life. You can watch
Mary pitting her woman's wit, her obstinacy, her charm,
against the persuasions, trickery, threats of her self-
seeking advisers. You can glimpse her rapture as
bride of the handsome, dissolute Henry Darnley, and, a
little later, her utter disenchantment; her even briefer
matrimonial affair with that vainglorious 'bounder'
Bothwell. You can peep at her, exasperated into a fury
of hysterical weeping by the cold, stern, uncompromising
John Knox. You can behold her beside the overturned
supper-table, screaming for mercy upon her favourite,
David Riccio, while Darnley pins her arms that would
shield him, and George Douglas, reaching over her
shoulder, drives in the first of the dagger-thrusts which
my Lord Ruthven and the others are to raise to the
ghastly grand total of fifty-six. A year later, in the first
chill hour of a February morning, you can spy her in that
boudoir, receiving the news of the murder of her invalid
husband at Kirk o' Field, two miles away—found
strangled in the garden, and the house blown up. Only
a few hours ago she returned from paying him a visit, and
you may judge for yourself whether that pale fair face
is a mask of innocence, or otherwise. Finally, in a June
midnight, her mad moon of marriage with Bothwell
ended, her supporters defeated at Carberry Hill, her
ears still full of the foulness of the rabble in her own
capital, you can watch her drearily descend the stair
and, closely guarded, ride away to her prison in Loch
Leven Castle, there to sign her abdication and be a
Queen no more.

The bed in Mary's chamber is so short that you will be
glad to know, unless you bear her a grudge, that she

never lay in it. It is certainly not the couch beneath which, on the night of February 12, 1563, Châtelar, the lovelorn swain who had followed in her train from France, concealed himself; it belonged to a lady of a century later. Châtelar, on that occasion let off with an admonition, repeated the offence, two nights later, in the castle at Burntisland. The execution took place at St Andrews.

In Holyroodhouse, nigh to midnight on March 26, 1603, James VI was roused from sleep to be hailed King of England. The messenger, Sir Robert Carey, who brought the news of Elizabeth's death, had covered the 400 miles in 62 hours—not bad travelling, allowing for the state of the roads then, and a fall from his horse. James lost little time in betaking himself to London. Life was softer, money more plentiful in the South, and there was nothing really ineradicably Spartan about James and the Scottish gentlemen who accompanied him, and who were pleasantly astonished by London's luxurious ways. Naturally, James had to find posts for them, and did so largely at the expense of the English courtiers. It seems probable that Mr Punch's most celebrated Scottish jest, "Bang went saxpence!" had its origin in the year 1603, and that the first 'Aberdeen story' was invented by a disgruntled English nobleman about the same date.

Charles I was eight years King before, after several broken promises, he came, in 1633, to be crowned at Holyrood. Edinburgh received him with acclamations and loyal orations. In the paving of the Canongate is a circle of stones marking the spot where he knighted the Lord Provost, who had presented, on behalf of the City, a golden bowl containing a thousand double-angels— about £1000, sterling—which gift, doubtless, was as highly appreciated by Charles as it was to be grudged by the citizens. At the end of a month he departed, leaving a people with their enthusiasm evaporated, and suspicious of his attitude to the Reformed Religion. If he did not then put the fat in the fire, he left it in the pan, all ready to spill and blaze up, four years later, at the attempted reading of Laud's Liturgy in St Giles—the beginning of a conflagration that was to mutter or roar for fifty years, despite all the blood and tears poured upon it.

Cromwell, in 1658, quartered his troops at Holyrood. The Palace was badly damaged by fire, but repaired to his orders. Charles II, after his Restoration in 1660, had the idea of an entirely new building, but, happily, could not find the money. With his additions, it stands to-day pretty much as he left it, though the fine gateway of James IV was pulled down in 1753, and the Abbot's house, a lovely example of sixteenth-century architecture, was removed about 1830. "Queen Mary's" sundial in the gardens was really erected by Charles I.

In 1679 the Duke of York, afterward James VII, made a stay in the Palace. The Duchess, who was accommodated, more or less, by the bed now in Queen Mary's Room, gave all sorts of entertainments, at some of which tea was served, not unlikely for the first time in Scotland. Prince Charlie, as we know, made it his Court in 1745; the Duke of Cumberland lodged in it in the following year; Charles X of France found a haven there; and in 1822, through the influence of Sir Walter Scott, George IV paid a visit and held several levees. In 1850 Queen Victoria and the Prince Consort made a short stay. The great fountain in front was their gift, and many improvements in the surroundings were brought about by the Prince Consort. King Edward VII held a levee in 1903; and, more than once, King George V and the Queen have lived here—not in those Royal Apartments which, to the ordinary person, appear much too stately to be comfortable, but in rooms on the floor above.

E

From the Heights

Holyroodhouse stands on the edge of the King's Park, which slopes up into the heights of Salisbury Crags and Arthur's Seat (800 feet). One may associate the Seat with *the* King Arthur, of whom there is tradition of battles fought victoriously in the South and West of Scotland; but, more likely, the Arthur here was a three-headed giant of far more distant days, who was given the name, after the Arthurian tales had made it popular, in the fifteenth century.

On the way up you may pause at St Anthony's chapel, looking down on little St Margaret's Loch, and, farther up the Queen's Drive, at the pool of Dunsappie. Below, southward, lies Duddingston Loch, a bird sanctuary, and the pretty village of the same name, which is Saxon, and is recorded as far back as 1150. It comes into Scott's *Heart of Midlothian*.

A mile south of Duddingston, on a mound, are the still impressive ruins of Craigmillar Castle. It was an old place when Mary rode thither to rest and recover from the horror of the Riccio affair. The vaulted apartment adjoining the tower is known as her chamber. A little later came that unholy quartet, Bothwell, Huntly, Maitland, Argyll, to pledge themselves, in writing, to do away with Darnley. Apart from its own interest, its situation affords a remarkably fine view of Edinburgh; which having enjoyed, you may, if so disposed, go to Blackford Hill, or the Braids, for more fine views or a round of golf.

Inchcolm

Edinburgh's northern boundary is the Firth of Forth, on which stands Leith, Scotland's second largest port. "The Port of Leith" had its beginning in the reign of Robert the Bruce. What a procession of shipping since then—galleys with toiling rowers; carracks with lofty,

lantern-crowned poops, painted sails and far-streaming
pennons; bulky, square-rigged men-o'-war with black-
and-white hulls and tiers of muzzle-loaders; clippers
and wind-jammers; the earliest of steamboats, tall-
funnelled, spluttering little things; all the elegancies of
shipbuilding and the practical uncouthness of the
present day. These docks receive hulls salted by the
Atlantic, Mediterranean, Baltic; there you may embark
for Holland, Germany, Denmark, Russia, Norway,
Sweden, Finland; also London, Aberdeen, Orkney and
Shetland Isles, Faroes, Iceland. The chief islands of
the Forth are Inchcolm and, farther out, picturesque,
fortified Inchkeith.

To the archæologist in particular Inchcolm (Isle of
Columba) is vastly interesting. In 1123 Alexander I,
elder brother and predecessor of David I, was crossing
the Forth at a point just above where the great railway
bridge stands to-day when a gale sprang up, driving the
frail vessel down the Firth. In his extremity the King
made a vow to St Columba, which was apparently
accepted, he and his companions finding refuge on
Inchcolm. There a solitary hermit gave them shelter
and sustenance—you will still find a little cell in a
corner of the garden—and before he died, in the following
year, Alexander made good his vow by founding the
Augustine Priory, and his successor, David, carried on
the work. Tales most miraculous are told of the sacred
place. In 1355, for example, an English ship carried off
the images of the saints, but ran forthwith into such
foul weather that the skipper was fain to put back and
restore the loot, with apologies in the form of an offering;
after which the weather improved. Next year another
English ship, having plundered a church in Fife, belonging
to the Abbot of Inchcolm, sailed past the isle with
sounds of trumpets and merry-making. But, as she was
rounding the south point, all of a sudden down she went

with all hands. The Priory, which became an Abbey, flourished for centuries, from time to time receiving additions and undergoing alterations. In its prime it must have been a fair sight to sailors, and neither fire nor tempest, nor even religious passion has blighted all its ancient beauty. Above the chapter-house, octagonal in form, is the Scriptorium where the old monks bent diligently and, one may believe, cheerfully—for it was the only room with a fire—over manuscripts in the making.

Education

Edinburgh and Education have been said to be synonymous, and the truth of the saying is far from new. For amid all the tumult and turmoil of the sixteenth century Learning was beginning to raise its head; worthy citizens were doing their utmost to encourage it. The University, though youngest of the four Scottish universities, was founded in 1582. Two hundred years later the existing buildings were erected on the original site, in Chambers Street, to the design of the famous Robert Adam. The Medical Department, however, is now housed in the New University Buildings, reached through Lothian Street, and there also is the splendid University Hall. The students, men and women, number about 4000.

Edinburgh's three great boarding-schools are not ancient, but their names are known to the world— Fettes, Loretto, and Merchiston—the last, until lately, occupying Merchiston Castle, once the home of John Napier (1550–1617), who invented logarithms.

The oldest school is the Royal High School, founded in the twelfth century. We saw it from the Calton Hill. It provided the model for the system of High Schools in the United States and Canada. Of the schools known as 'Hospitals'—the scholars were boarders—I must say something about Heriot's, the oldest, which stands under the shadow of Greyfriars Church, within whose walls the National Covenant was signed, on a February eve, in 1638. Scott, in *The Fortunes of Nigel*, gives a rare presentment of 'Jingling Geordie' (George Heriot), gold-smith to James VI, who, in 1624, left over £23,000—a huge sum in those days—to found a hospital for the education and maintenance of poor and fatherless boys, sons of freemen of the City. The material result of this munificence has been called the handsomest old building in Edinburgh. Architecturally a combination of Palla-dian and Gothic, it stands four-square about a spacious quadrangle, with corner towers carrying turrets, and two hundred windows, all ornamented differently. It is now a day school, with a roll of some 1300 scholars.

For George Watson's College, near to the magnificent Royal Infirmary and to George Square, the place of Scott's home in his boyhood, Edinburgh and the nation are indebted to an accountant of the Bank of Scotland who died in 1723.[1] Close by are the Meadows, a public park, and Bruntsfield Links, where James IV reviewed his army before marching to fatal Flodden, and where Edinburgh Burgess Golfing Society, which claims to be the oldest existing club in Scotland, began operations in 1735. The *Golfers' Handbook* tells how, in the gay old days, two merry members lofted balls over the spire of St Giles, and how another won a gallon of whisky by driving a ball from Bruntsfield over Arthur's Seat in forty-five strokes.

Talking of golf, for news of the local courses I refer you to the Official Guide. As to the outlying courses, I shall mention some of them in their own places. A list would be too long, but I have just met an Edinburgh man who on thirty-seven consecutive days played over thirty-seven different courses, some famous, all good, and slept every night in his own bed.

[1] The College has been removed to new buildings in Colinton Road.

CHAPTER II

THE PENTLANDS—LINLITHGOW—EAST LOTHIAN

EDINBURGH is justifiably proud of her Little Highlands, the Pentland Hills, which rise almost at her door and extend south-west for 16 miles into Clydesdale. They have not the tremendous effect of the bens of the North and West; at no point do they reach 2000 feet in height; but they have their own particular charms of contour and colouring, of open and secret places, of stream, pool, and reservoir; and no hills in Scotland have looked down for a thousand years on more varied doings, brave or terrible, sad or strange, solemn or silly, of humanity. Scarce a furlong around them lacks a story; every little village is a place of history and tradition.

If you would know all about them and their surroundings, for it is little enough I can put into these pages, you should read Will Grant's *The Call of the Pentlands*, which, though written primarily for the tramper, is a delight for anyone, even in an easy chair. The quaint place-names alone are alive with suggestion—Hunter's Tryst, Fairmilehead, Lang Whang, Cauldstane Slap, Ninemileburn, Stonypath, Silverburn, Windy Gowl, and so forth. Druids, Romans, Saxons, Norsemen, have left memorials in material or nomenclature on hilltop and in hollow. The monks arrived early; some of Scotland's most ancient families had their homes there; Stuart kings hunted on the moors and woods; Covenanters held their conventicles in the clefts of the hills; their psalms rose fearlessly into the pure air; their blood ran bravely into the clean soil. On a wintry day in 1666, at Rullion Green, in the shadow of Carnethy Hill, nine hundred of them, with sixty muskets and eight pistols for firearms, stood up against three thousand trained soldiers under Sir Thomas Dalyell, of whom more presently, and showed how men could do or die. Nightfall saved the majority, but the fifty who fell were more fortunate than those taken prisoners. The tale of torture, administered under the auspices of an Archbishop, makes a very dirty page in the History of Scotland. Ten were eventually hanged on one gibbet in Edinburgh; thirty-five were sent home —to be hanged in front of their own doors. And yet, as one of our historians, Principal Rait, has put it:

> In other circumstances, they would, probably enough, have been guilty of the crimes for which we execrate the Restoration Government, and their opponents would have evinced a similar courage and devotion.

Yet despite 'alarums and excursions' those Pentland villages have had their centuries of quiet industry. Kings died, but the weavers went on with their weaving; nobles plotted, murdered, or were murdered, but the workers in wood and stone considered their designs and plied their tools; battles were won or lost, but the shepherd took his flock to the hills, the smith sweated at his forge, the poet in some secluded corner made his songs.

Leaving the City by Craiglockhart Hill, with its tower, we are presently in Colinton village, where the old and the new mingle. In 1650 Redhall Castle was surrendered to Oliver Cromwell, after its garrison had run out of ammunition. Oliver, while complimenting the commander on his valour in "holding out so stoutlie," allowed his men to plunder the very garments of the prisoners.

Colinton House, with its cedars and holly hedges planted nearly three centuries ago, is now part of Merchiston School; Dreghorn Castle, a mile away, is a preparatory school for boys. And, talking of education,

it is recorded that, in 1655, Mr John Craw, the village
schoolmaster, lost his job because he brewed and sold
ale in the schoolhouse, "near to ye kirk and hard by ye
minister's gate." For shame, Mr Craw! Still, the teach-
ing profession of his day had a pretty thin existence, and
I hope he had better luck as brewer than as dominie.
Anyway, his little memoir is a quaint sidelight on the
times, as interesting in its way as the ancient sculptured
stones of Hailes House, or the stone coffins recently found
in the neighbourhood, or the old stronghold, Colinton
Castle.   At the church in the Dell you will find an iron
'mort safe,' ghastly relic of the days of Burke and Hare;
it was fixed across the new grave, so that the poor
mortality might rest till useless to the 'resurrectionists.'

Through the woods to Juniper Green, where Thomas
Carlyle, as a young married man, resided; on to Currie,
with its aged bridge over the Leith Water, its antique
ale-house, its Knights Templar stones at the Kirk; and
then we come to ivy-clad Lennox Tower, where Mary
rested with Darnley on hunting expeditions, while yet
the glamour lasted.

Running up the Lang Whang ('Long Stretch') we
reach eventually the town of Carnwath, whose ancient
importance may be judged from the fact that 400 years
ago it boasted a jail.   Its Cross, now naturally the worse
for wear, was set up in 1516.   Yonder mausoleum, an
aisle of a church that was, has a fine Gothic window and
arched roof;   its outer walls carry coats of arms of
famous families and the effigy of a Crusader.   Dunsyre
village is rich alike in beauty, history, and legend.   Do
you happen to know what 'jougs' are?   There is an
unusually fine specimen on the wall of the church, and
you may picture a luckless sinner, man or woman, of the
old days, with his neck confined in the unkindly iron
collar, chained to the stone, for all to despise or pity.

By a woody winding road we come to Dolphinton—

odd name so far inland; but, 800 years ago, the land here came into possession of a Dunbar from the East Coast whose name was Dolphine, and whose arms included that small relative of the whale. There's a reason for everything. The men of Dolphinton were always in the fight. A local historian blandly says: "In early times but a small proportion of our parishioners died in their beds." Perhaps that is why the old Parish Church is one of the smallest in Scotland.

About four miles farther on is West Linton, a veritable bower. Its traditions go back to the sixth century. Its name, says Mr Grant, ought to be Linton Roderick—the Roderick, with whom it was then associated, being ruler of Strathclyde, and one of the earliest Kings to champion the Christian cause. Its most joyous memory concerns one James Giffard, a small landowner and keen amateur sculptor, who, in 1666, as a proud husband and father, presented to Linton, as a Mercat Cross, a pedestal bearing the effigies of Mrs Giffard on top, and the four little Giffards at the corners. Presumably it was admired by the sober Pentland folk; quite likely the sculptor himself surveyed it with pride as representing his masterpiece. But women in those days, if not so hard to please, were just as uncertain as now; and, lo and behold, Mrs Giffard presented him with a fifth jewel! Yet was the good man confounded? Not at all! A place ought to be found for an effigy of Quintus—or was it Quinta? —and a place *was* found. Having carved the new effigy, this most resourceful of sculptors stuck it on the maternal head. What a pity the whole thing could not have been preserved! Alas, one by one, victims of the weather— not, one hopes, of mischievous laddies—the childish figures dropped off. One, being salved, now reposes in Spitalhaugh House, but the others are no more. Happily Mrs Giffard survives to adorn the little clock-tower built over the old public well of West Linton.

Three miles up the road, Carlops ('Old Woman's Leap') was, in the fourteenth century, on the border of England's dominion—but only for a few years. Near by was " raised "—his father a shepherd—George Meikle Kemp, designer of the Scott Monument. Passing Ninemileburn, which has its stories too, a short stretch brings us to Glencorse, with its fine Kirk window and 'cup and ring' stone. From the road, presently, we have an outlook toward Fife and Haddington, which on a clear day is worth the miles we have covered. Then the road descends to Hillend, where we have a view of what man can do in adding to the landscape—great mounds of shale refuse from the workings of a company extinct. Not far from Hillend is Swanston, prettiest of villages, and the Cottage, so often Stevenson's abode between 1867 and 1880, whence he made his excursions among the "hills of home," as he thought of them during his exile in Samoa.

Roslin

Roslin, with its Castle and Chapel, is in the Pentlands district, not far from Glencorse, but you will probably want to give it a special visit; it is only seven miles by road and a little more by rail from Edinburgh. The Castle, a splendid ruin, on an almost isolated rock overhanging the wooded steeps of the Esk, is, oddly enough, more romantically than securely situated, for, at a second glance, you realize that it is, in its turn, overhung by a commanding height. Its oldest parts, the peel tower south-east of the entrance and the great south-western tower, are of the fourteenth century. Early in the next century it seems to have been a place, inwardly as well as outwardly, of considerable grandeur. We read that its owner, the third Earl of Orkney, kept up great style, having his meals served on platters of gold and silver, his chamberlain, cupbearer, and carver being all noble lords.

His lady enjoyed the attendance of seventy-five gentle-
women in silks, velvets, and gold chains, and had a body-
guard of 200 fine gentlemen for her outings to Edinburgh
and elsewhere. At the same time, she had her simple
tastes, was fond of dogs, and did not mind them having
pups in her bed-chamber. The Castle was badly damaged
by Hertford on his 1544 invasion; repaired and, in 1650,
battered and plundered by General Monk; restored again,
and ill-used by the mob in 1688. Captain Grose's drawing
of 1790 shows it in sorry state, but the least ancient part
of the building is still intact and inhabited, and preserves
a fireplace, ceiling, and carvings of the early seventeenth
century.

The Chapel, a furlong distant, is really the chancel and
Lady Chapel of what was intended to be the Collegiate
Church of Roslin, founded by the aforesaid Earl, who,
evidently, did not confine his attentions to high living.
The whole building, excepting the crypt, is a marvel of
ornamentation, the curtest description of which would
fill pages. It is of the richest interest to the student, but
only an expert could give any impression of the architectural features.

I believe that of the thousands who visit Roslin Chapel
annually, the majority is intrigued mainly by the quainter
carvings, the Prentice Pillar, and the burial place of the
St Clair Barons, ten of whom were laid to rest in their
armour. There was a belief that on the night before the
death of a Baron the Chapel would appear to be in flames
(see Sir Walter Scott's ballad *Rosabelle*), and Dr Hill
Burton once witnessed the phenomenon. As to the
carvings, to mention but a very few, the short pillars
dividing the centre aisle from the side aisles carry figures
of the Crucifixion, Samson killing the Lion, the Prodigal
Son, and angels playing musical instruments, including
the bagpipes; the arches bear designs of, for example,
Samson bringing down the house of the Philistines, the

Dance of Death, the Seven Deadly Sins, and a fox running off with a goose, pursued by a farmer. One feels sure that those old masons enjoyed themselves. The Prentice Pillar in the Lady Chapel, with its opulence of ornament, shows on its capital Abraham offering up Isaac, attended by a figure performing on the bagpipes. The Pillar has its name from a legend. While the Pillar was in the making, the master sculptor suffered from what would now be termed brain fag, and went off to Rome for inspiration. On his return, he found that his apprentice had completed the work, and done it better than he could have done himself. Perhaps he was a trade unionist, but, whether or no, instead of congratulating the young man, he raised his hammer and struck him dead. At the risk of your smiling at our Scottish frugality, I confess that we use the same legend for another ecclesiastical place in Scotland.

The Reformers seem to have dealt lightly with the building, though the church lost its lands and revenues, but the mob of 1688 was less tender, and for a time it was almost a ruin. In the middle of the eighteenth century, General St Clair did much toward its restoration; his good work was carried on by the Earls of Rosslyn; and since 1862 it has been a place of worship of the Scottish Episcopal Church.

Linlithgow

Seventeen miles west of Edinburgh lies Linlithgow in the midst of a wide agricultural and industrial district, not in itself, for all its long history, a show place. Its great attraction, the Palace, is hardly to be seen from the streets, and its own appearance is old-fashioned, rather than old-world.

In its main street a bronze tablet marks the place of the assassination of the Regent Moray in 1570. Behind a curtain in the window of the house of his uncle the Archbishop, Hamilton of Bothwellhaugh looked to his

THE PALACE OF HOLYROODHOUSE

Photo Valentine and Sons, Ltd.

[*Pp.* 58–65]

LINLITHGOW PALACE AND LOCH
Photo Valentine and Sons, Ltd.

priming and took aim. In a museum the hackbut, or arquebuse, of the sixteenth century may not appeal to the eye of the twentieth as a particularly capable instrument; yet that scoundrel's gun banged its big leaden ball clean through the victim and killed a horse into the bargain. We are told that the stricken man felt no pain; dismounting he walked back to the house he had recently left; but a few hours later he died. Sir Walter Scott, in a ballad, uses the crime as an act of revenge for personal injury; but it seems to have been purely, or, rather, foully, political. Had not Moray given Bothwellhaugh his life after the Battle of Langside? At all events, we may take it that the murderer did not shoot for himself alone, for, fourteen months later, his uncle, the Archbishop, was hanged at the Mercat Cross of Stirling, "as the bells struck six hours to even."

James I began the building of the Palace in the third decade of the fifteenth century; James IV added the Lyon Chamber, or Parliament Hall; and to his son's credit is the southern gateway, also the courtyard fountain, still, in its decay, a thing of charm. The fountain in front of Holyroodhouse is modelled upon it. The Jameses, when they chose, could do the thing handsomely. Marie of Lorraine deemed the Palace the most 'princely' in Scotland, and when you stand in the courtyard and look up at those majestic towers, and those walls with the many windows in their five storeys, you can imagine what a tremendously imposing and richly splendid place it must have appeared to the eyes of the common folk of her day.

The best days of Linlithgow were over when James VI deserted his native porridge and bannocks for the fleshpots of the South. In 1646 the Scottish Parliament met in the Lyon Chamber for the last time. One imagines it in a pretty shabby state when, a century later, Prince Charlie unexpectedly paid a visit; one would like to believe that the fountain was still in working order to run the wine of the legend attached to that September Sunday. Five months later General Hawley's dragoons, sore from the whipping given them at Falkirk by the Highlanders, then retreating northward, made the Palace their headquarters. Shortly after their departure it was found to be on fire—mere carelessness, one may allow—and we see it to-day, a roofless shell, very much as it must have appeared immediately after the disaster.

As you move among those aged walls, the Palace guide will tell you many things, and maybe you will imagine more. Maybe you will see Margaret Tudor, with her year-old son, at a window in the watch-tower, in the falling dusk looking—not, perhaps, over-anxiously—for tidings of her husband, James IV, then lying dead on Flodden field; or in the courtyard that son, grown to manhood, 'showing round' his bride, dwelling particularly, we may be sure, on his new gateway and fountain; or, once more, that same Marie, while yet mourning her two little boys, who had died at Holyroodhouse, gazing out upon the December-darkened waters of the Loch, wondering what the Fates were spinning for her baby girl, Mary, whose father lay dying in the Palace of Falkland, over yonder in Fife, heart-broken by the defeat and disgrace of Solway Moss—a young man, only thirty, a King who, whatever his failings, had won the regard of the common people.

Alongside the Palace stands the Kirk of St Michael, founded by the pious David, though the present building belongs to the days of James III and his son. As James IV knelt at the altar to pay his vows, before setting out with his army on his last adventure, a mysterious blue-gowned figure, yellow-haired, bearing a pike, appeared and, bending beside him, warned him not only against the adventure, but against the society of women and their counsels. James being rather given to gallantry,

as well as superstitious, it has been suggested that the
mysterious figure was simply a disguised emissary of the
Queen, who wanted to keep her man at home; it has
even been hinted that the figure was Margaret herself, in
which case she must have worn a wig, her own hair being
dark. While we may smile at such things to-day, it is
credibly recorded that, about the same time, another
mysterious figure appeared at the Mercat Cross, in
Edinburgh, prophesying woe to the adventurers.

The Church, one of Scotland's finest examples of the
Gothic, suffered at the Reformation, when enthusiasts
removed all the images, save St Michael's, which was
beyond their reach; and in the next century Cromwell's
dragoons used it as a stable. Nevertheless, it survived
the Palace, and in 1894 was completely restored as a
place of worship. To view the tree-sheltered Palace and
Kirk from across the Loch, with its swans, is alone worth
the run from Edinburgh. If the day chance to be in
early autumn, with a hint of sunny haze, I think you will
have the picture at its loveliest.

Linlithgow belongs to a green and pleasant countryside, though not far from great areas scarred and seared,
pitted and befouled by the works of man. Six miles
west, on the main road, is Falkirk, an important town,
famous for its iron-works. It has its historic associations
in memories of Sir William Wallace and the ubiquitous
Prince Charlie, and in remains of the Roman Wall of
Antoninus, once stretching across Scotland from the
Forth to the Clyde, a barrier, not always effectual,
against the 'barbarians' of the North.

Blackness and Forth Bridge

From Linlithgow I suggest a run back by the shores
of the Forth, where stands Blackness Castle, one of the
grimmest, most forbidding things of stone in the country.
Much of its past is not less horrid. With it is associated

the name of Sir Thomas Dalyell, or Dalziel, whose Tower
of Binns you may have spied in the distance—an evil man,
even for his day.   They called him the Muscovy Brute,
because he had lived for some years in Russia, and had
added its savagery to his own original brutality.   His
Tower witnessed his private orgies, his Castle and its
dungeons the miseries of captive Covenanters.   He
raised a troop of horse to ride them down; but one never
knows, and the troop was the origin of that very gallant
regiment, the Scots Greys.   His portrait exists—a great
bald dome of a head, with long hair hanging from the sides,
malevolent eyes, the lower part of the face mercifully
lost in a big beard.   The Castle must have been new
then, or just rebuilt, for I find in an old diary this curious
entry, which shows that the earlier building had its own
bad name:

> 3 Apryll 1652.   The castell of Blaknes, situat upone the
> sea syde neir to Burrowstouns [now Bo'ness], wes blawn
> up with a powder trayne.   It was reportit that the Devill
> was vesiblie sene upone the wallis at its upblowing.

The road running inland goes through the estate of
Hopetoun, which you, if an Englishman and in compli-
mentary mood, will admit to be quite English in its sylvan
serenity.   There is an ancient castle, Midhope, beyond
the woods on the left, and in the small flowery village of
Abercorn a restored Norman kirk.   Hopetoun House
stands magnificent amid avenues, lawns, and gardens.
There are deer in the park and among the trees.

We run back to the Forth at The Society, or Sea City,
odd name for a small group of houses, and then along the
shore to Port Edgar, named after the brother of Queen
Margaret, and South Queensferry.   The ferry was established by Margaret for the free passage of pilgrims to
Dunfermline and St Andrews.   Into the Forth, in, or
about, the year 1070, came the little ship bearing the

Saxon Princess and her relations, seeking a refuge from
the Normans.   King Malcolm Canmore heard the news in
Dunfermline and hastened to pay his respects.   'Tis said
she was none too willing, but never mind that.   Let your
fancy rest on the frail barque and the quaint courtesies,
and your eyes look up at that prodigious monument of
man's genius and labour raised more than eight centuries
later; for Malcolm and Margaret had something to do
with the making of the Scotland that made the Forth
Bridge, still one of the engineering marvels of the world.

The shortest road back to Edinburgh, a very pleasant
one, skirts the Earl of Rosebery's Dalmeny estate, on which
is ancient Dalmeny Church, lately restored, and passes
through Cramond Bridge, where James V, on one of his
incognito democratic expeditions, got into trouble with
gipsies, and was rescued by a more genuine democrat,
Jock Howieson, a miller, who provided water and towel
to remove the blood from the Royal countenance.   James
presented him with land, on the condition that he or his
successors should be ever ready with a hand-basin and
ewer when the King crossed the bridge, or came to
Holyroodhouse.   And so, when in 1822 George IV came
to the Palace, a descendant of the miller was there with
a silver basin and ewer.

East Lothian

To-day, when Scots people speak of East Lothian,
they mean only Haddingtonshire; but at one time they
meant all the country along the North Sea, right down
to the Tweed.   Let us, for our present purpose, take the
older meaning and include Berwickshire, or most of it,
in our round.   The route proposed is as follows: Out of
Edinburgh, by Newington, to Dalkeith; across to the
main road that runs over Soutra Hill, in the Lammermuirs, down to Lauder, thence eastward to Greenlaw
and, by Duns, to Berwick-on-Tweed; then up the coast,

F

with digressions, to Dunbar and North Berwick—and so, once more, to Edinburgh.

Dalkeith Palace looking down on the North Esk, a seat of the Dukes of Buccleuch, has a long history, but it was rebuilt in the eighteenth century to the plans of Sir John Vanbrugh, who, whatever his skill as a playwright, had certainly no light touch as an architect. It is an 'imposing' affair of reddish stone; yet if it be poor in art outside it is rich within—Holbein, Rembrandt, Van Dyck, Gainsborough, Reynolds, Wilkie, and other great artists being represented. In 1745 Prince Charlie, though he entertained at Holyroodhouse, preferred Dalkeith for his own quarters.

The Soutra Hill road is well worth while for its views alone. It allows one a full prospect of Haddingtonshire and vistas of shires beyond. The last time I passed over it was on a winter day, but it was very clear weather; and from the snowy summit, nearly 1200 feet up, I saw northward across Fife to the Sidlaws, southward to the Eildons; then from looking down on Traprain Law, Berwick Law—a 'law' is a small, isolated green hill—and the Bass Rock, I turned to see Edinburgh's Castle and Arthur's Seat. For varied beauties it is one of Scotland's notable highways, and it must be one of her oldest. The Romans, Saxons, and Normans came by Soutra Hill; the early pilgrims went by it to the holy places of the Borders. The name means literally 'Outlook-house.' It runs above a land rich for the farmer, the shepherd, and the golfer; a land with a modest rainfall and few streams, large or little, except the Tyne, where the angler may find trout and, maybe, salmon.

The Lammermuirs, which stretch across Haddingtonshire, are gentle hills, and the road goes easily down to Lauder, where, in 1482, as arranged at a meeting in the Kirk, of all places, the Scottish nobles, led by the celebrated 'Archibald Bell-the-Cat'—Earl of Angus—

seized the low-born Earl of Mar and other minions of James III, and hanged them over the bridge before, as one chronicler says, his Majesty's eyes, and with their own scarves. Neither Kirk nor bridge now exists—the present church is late seventeenth century—but Lauder Fort, a stout tower, with its foundations in the days of Edward I, remains as part of Thirlestane Castle, belonging to the Earl of Lauderdale.

From Lauder, through the little town of Greenlaw, on the Blackadder—'adder' means nothing more sinister than 'long water'—with its roomy market square, we come to Duns, Berwickshire's county town, which came into being about the close of the sixteenth century, an earlier Duns, perched on the Law, 700 feet high, having been wiped out by the English. A hundred years after that event, on the Law, beside a great boulder, since known as the 'Covenanters' Stone'—souvenir hunters have left very little of it—General Leslie stood with a big army, under banners bearing the legend " For Christ's Crown and Covenant," all ready to dispute the advance of the Royalist forces; while among the musketeers, pikemen, armed ploughmen, and Highlanders from Argyll went many black-coated ministers with prayers and admonitions. A brave sight it must have been on the Law, though in the end fighting was avoided by mutual arrangement.

Lots of British people, including Scots, still imagine that Berwick is in Scotland, though it was yielded "in perpetual surrender" to England away back in 1482. The actual boundary is at Lamberton Old Toll, where there is, or was, a pigsty that looks as if it were in Scotland, but is really in England. Both countries can enjoy the grunts. Approached from the south, red-roofed Berwick is surely the most picturesque of towns, and I will readily admit that I never so approach the bridge over the Tweed without forgetting that Berwick is not a bit of my own country. Before its final delivery to

killed and 10,000 prisoners; the English but 30 men.
Cromwell wrote home: "The Lord hath showed us exceeding mercy." Which was true, though he owed
something also to those black-coated servants of the
Lord who had misled the luckless Leslie. The good Scot
still frowns when he thinks of Dunbar. It is poor
comfort to reflect that, three centuries earlier, Edward II
came fleeing to the Castle from Bannockburn, and that,
a century later, General Johnny Cope came clattering
frantically into the town from the fiasco of Prestonpans.

Of Dunbar's Castle, once so massive and impregnable,
not much remains to illustrate its stories, the most
cheerful of them being that of 'Black' Agnes, Countess
of March, who, in 1339, during her man's absence, pluckily
held it against English besiegers. Mary came to it with
Darnley three days after the murder of Riccio; she
returned to it with Bothwell less than three months
after the murder of Darnley, and from it rode with him
to Carberry Hill, where they were destined to see the
last of each other.

Dunbar town, hugging the rocky shores and sandy
beaches, knows the tang of salt spray; it can be a keenly
cold place in winter, especially with a nor'easter blowing,
and it is a fine fresh place in summer, when, quite apart
from its grand golf course, its popularity is understand-
able. Its chief antique is the sixteenth-century town-
house, spired and gabled, which once served as a jail,
and an ancient Cross near the entrance.

North Berwick, next only to St Andrews and Carnoustie in golfing fame, is set on a broad, blunt promontory, and on the cliff's verge, dark against the blue,
stands Tantallon, castle of a hundred stories and a
thousand secrets, frowning across the water at the Bass
Rock, which grins back whitely in the sunshine. To-day
there are scaffoldings against the walls, and small figures
at work with steel and cement, stiffening them against

future assaults of the autumn and winter blasts that tear
across the promontory.

It has had many owners, beginning, they say, with
Macduff, Thane of Fife. In 1371 it passed to the Earl
of Monteith; in 1425 it was in the hands of the Douglases;
fifty years later in those of the Earl of Angus, whose son
became stepfather of James V, then a youngster. There
was no love in the relationship; Angus overdid the heavy
hand, and eventually James slipped away from Falkland
Palace, where he was virtually a prisoner, rode to
Stirling, collected sympathizers, borrowed a couple of
cannon from Dunbar Castle and, with other artillery of
queer names, set to work on Tantallon. The walls, 12
feet thick, withstood the granite cannon-balls, and
eventually James had to raise the siege. But he was a
boy of determination, and coming back with more men
and heavier cannon, bombarded and starved the place
into surrender. After the King's death Angus got back
his castle, which James had strengthened by blocking up
windows and repairing other weaknesses, and spent the
remaining years of his life in poverty, but at home. What
did those old warriors think of when they sat at their
windows, looking out on the North Sea?

It was from Tantallon's gateway that Sir Walter made
Marmion escape so narrowly that the falling portcullis
grazed the plume of his helmet.

Under the shadow of the Castle lies sandy Canty Bay,
once the embarking place for unhappy souls doomed to
imprisonment on the Bass Rock—or 'the Bass,' as one
calls it after a day or two's residence in North Berwick.
For its size, only a mile in circumference, it has known
much human misery. It rises from the sea, a lump of
pallid lava, moulded in a crater, the softer stone around
it having disintegrated, to a height of 313 feet, its north
side wellnigh sheer. There is some pasturage, and it is
the home of countless gannets, or solan geese, while it

serves mankind by supporting a lighthouse. Its earliest
and, I imagine, its only willing inhabitant was St
Baldred. The island is only a mile and a quarter from
the nearest point of land, and, given a calm sea, with no
wind from the east or south-east, you may land on it and
see the remains of fortifications and the places where they
kept political prisoners and those who suffered for conscience' sake. As far as I know, the only romantic thing
about the Bass is the exploit of the four young Jacobite
captives who, in 1691, tricked the garrison of fifty men,
who were busy landing coal, by barring them out of the
fort. The four were later joined by twelve others; food
was somehow got to them by the French Government;
and the sixteen 'held the fort' for almost three years, and
then made favourable terms for their capitulation. If
staying at North Berwick, you should read, or re-read,
Stevenson's *Catriona*.

The town is three miles from the Castle—breezy, but
milder of climate than Dunbar. There are two courses,
the West, the favourite, dating from 1895. But, for
all its charm and popularity, it has never become a
ground for championships, and if you take a walk over
the fine turf, with its sandy margin, you will understand
why. Championships mean spectators, and there are at
least two passages on the course where a crowd would
mean hopeless congestion. July and August are the
'family' months; in September North Berwick becomes
'fashionable.'

From afar the Law is North Berwick's landmark.
East Neuk of Fife folk—unless they be Largo folk, who
have a very good Law of their own, and a loftier one, too
—point it out to strangers. The town has few antiquities.
Of a Benedictine nunnery there are fragments; and the
old Kirk, down at the Harbour, which used to stand on
an islet bridged to the shore by arches, is represented by
a doorway and font. It was dedicated to St Andrew,

but that did not keep away the witches. At a trial in 1591 it was shown that ninety-four witches and six wizards had danced in the kirkyard to the music of a Jew's harp played by one Geilie Duncan, and that the Devil himself, as a black man, had popped up in the pulpit to receive their allegiance. All of which may appear funny in these days, but to the poor witches and wizards on trial it must have been very much the reverse. They had a delightfully simple method of deciding whether a woman was guilty. They tied her thumb to her big toe and tossed her into a pool. If she sank, she was innocent; if she floated, they took her out and burned her.

We must not miss Dirleton village, two miles farther on—its church, school, inn, and modern cottages, with their flowery plots, set about a triangular green. It has been called the loveliest village in the Lothians, and from the stir of North Berwick it must be a blessed occasional retreat to many people. Close by the village, amid fair gardens with yews for background, are the ruins of de Vaux Castle, with gateway, ivied walls, moat, and dungeon, to give Dirleton an old-time atmosphere, if it did not possess that already. They say that these same walls were standing at the end of the thirteenth century, as they were standing when Generals Monk and Lambert, in 1650, gave orders for dismantling.

Golf again!—two courses at Gullane (pronounced 'Gillen'), almost next door to Dirleton, and, a couple of miles on, another at Aberlady. Here, however, we must turn inland to see Haddington.

Its Abbey Church must have been a wonder of its day, for it was called the Lamp of Lothian. Edward III destroyed most of it in 1356. The old nave, preserved, is now the Parish Church. Two of the bridges over the Tyne are very old—the Abbey Bridge, a mile east of the town, and the Nungate Bridge within it. Some ancient houses remain; and by the river side, in the sunshine, the red roofs glow warmly above the slow, cool water. There are trim, old-fashioned streets, with excellent shops, and quietly dignified dwellings in old-fashioned gardens. If you like quietude and mellowness, you will like Haddington very much.

In the High Street is the house where Thomas Carlyle tutored and courted Jane Welsh. Haddington was her home then, and after forty years of wedlock she came back to lie in St Mary's Kirkyard, where lie others of by no means so fair memory. Was it not at the grating of the Earl of Lauderdale's tomb—Lauderdale the persecutor—that an old woman was found dancing and screaming in impotent fury, because she could not get in to "rax the banes o' him"?   What an elegy!

In my reading, the other day, I came upon this: "Haddington was the birthplace of the destroyer of all Scotland's monasteries—John Knox." Well, though Haddington has claimed him, there is no proof of his birth there, and the rest of the statement is surely an exaggeration.

Five miles upon a level road and we come to East Linton, and within hail of another Law—Traprain. From its top one can see thirteen counties; its interest for most people, however, is in its tale of buried treasure. Stray Pictish and Roman relics had occasionally been unearthed, but in the present century was discovered the plum of plums—a pirate's hoard of silver vessels, 600 ounces, over the origin of which learned men still have their differences. You will find the treasure in Edinburgh's Museum of Antiquities.

CHAPTER III

THE BORDERS

Tweeddale, Ettrick, and Yarrow

By 'the Borders' I mean more—much more—than a strip of country north of the line between Scotland and England; I include the shires of Peebles, Selkirk, Roxburgh, and parts of those of Berwick and Dumfries. This may seem like taking liberties with geography, yet I have the old Scots Acts of Parliament for precedent, and, what is more to the point, it simplifies the making of this chapter.

From Edinburgh the route, by rail or road, is through Peebles.

Peebles lies in the lap of mild-featured hills, grassy, woody, or heathery, at the confluence of the Eddleston Water and Tweed, and with its population of over 5000 is the chief town of Peeblesshire, or, to use the old name, Tweeddale. The New Town, as it is still called, though it began in the sixteenth century, is built partly on the slope, and a street name, Portgate, as well as some traces, tells us that it was once walled. The Old Town, most of it on the right bank of the Eddleston, has become touched with modernity and enlarged by many villas and gardens.

In the parish burying-ground there is a tower, which may have belonged to a church dedicated to St Andrew in 1195, but more likely to a chapel of nearly two hundred years later. Little remains of the Kirk of the Holy Rood, which was raised in honour of "a stately and venerable cross" unearthed at Peebles in 1261, close to a stone urn containing ashes and bones. Many miracles were wrought by this cross, for centuries held to have been formed from a portion of the True Cross and hidden away by some very early Christians during persecution, about the year 300.   James V saw and revered it in 1529, but after the Reformation it is not mentioned.

The Cross Keys Inn, or, thanks to Sir Walter and his 'Meg Dods,' 'the Cleikum,' began as a private dwelling in 1653.   Under an arch, from the Northgate, you enter a courtyard, at the end of which is the hostelry.   The Tontine Hotel, in the High Street, was built in 1808, and, if you do not happen to be familiar with the word 'Tontine,' I may explain that it was an investment, usually in stone and lime, made by a number of persons, who agreed that it should fall to the survivor.   The Chambers Institution, also in the High Street, was given to the town by Dr William Chambers, who, with his brother Robert, founded *Chambers's Journal* and the famous Edinburgh publishing house.   The Mercat Cross, one of the oldest crosses in the country, stands at the junction of High Street, Eastgate, and Northgate.   Peebles provides all outdoor sports, and is a centre for anglers.

Not far out of Peebles, westward, Neidpath Castle overlooks the Tweed, where it bends and runs deep. The massive, turreted keep, with walls ten feet thick in places —some, at least, of the stones were laid together in the fourteenth century—is partly roofed, and is inhabited, I believe, by a caretaker.   The best view of it is from the river.   Its early lords were of Norman ancestry, and, as Earls of March, possessed also Dunbar Castle.   Its most interesting owner was the Duke of Queensberry, the notorious 'Old Q.,' who flourished, like the green bay-tree, during the greater part of the eighteenth century, and for ten years after.   He loved not his entailed Scottish estates any more than he loved the person who should succeed him; wherefore, as far as possible, he did his utmost to spoil the one and spite the other by felling the timber—Wordsworth and Burns wrote uncompli-

NEIDPATH CASTLE, PEEBLES
Photo Robert McLeod

ABBOTSFORD, FROM THE TWEED

Photo Valentine and Sons, Ltd.

93

mentary lines about him—and lived most of his unloyal,
unlovely life in London. There, in his house, at No. 138
Piccadilly, he planned carefully, though not meanly, his
selfish pleasures until, at length, the only pleasure possible
for him, aged, toothless, half-blind, deaf, and diseased,
was to sit on the balcony there, in the sunshine, under a
parasol, peering down at the passing show, in which he
had once been so prominent. His is one of the ghosts,
not of Scotland's gloomy towers, but of London's gayest
thoroughfare. Neidpath has a tale of a fair daughter of
the Castle who loved a youth of insufficiently high degree;
but the end being tragic, or, as a matter-of-fact com-
patriot expressed it, 'unsatisfactory,' I do not propose to
set the poem before you. Even in sentimental Scotland
the tear for the medieval maiden who pined away is apt
to be sluggish nowadays.

The stream that hereabouts joins the Tweed is the
Manor Water. The cottage known as the 'Black
Dwarf's' has been much altered since Sir Walter saw it.
It no longer suggests the abode of 'Bowed Davie,' who
built it to 'fit' his poor little misshapen self. Manor's
now peaceful vale used to have half a score of 'peels,' or
round towers—not 'brochs'—and that of Barns has been
well preserved, with alterations. If you go inside you
will realize that, so far as creature comforts were concerned, the old Scots were indeed a hardy race. The
inmates must have been horribly huddled. There would
have been more towers left here, had not Sir Walter
Scott's father—of all people—pulled down several in
order to provide stone for road metal.

Up the stream from Lyne you will find the tower and
roofless walls of a palace, rather than a castle, which was
never completed. Its name is Drochil, and, in 1581,
Morton, the Regent, was looking forward to enjoying it,
when he was called to the scaffold. Turning south, we
come to wooded Stobo, its modern Normanesque castle

very prominent. Not long ago Stobo added to its antiquities with the discovery of a cell attributed to Mungo,
saint of Glasgow. In 1863, while restoration work was
proceeding on the quaint old kirk, they found in a tomb,
along with a skeleton, four German coins and a Scots
piece of James V—one of those queer finds that set one
wondering. The tomb itself is queer, every stone being
marked with a 'W,' though whether the 'W' was meant
to be an initial, ornament, or symbol I should not like to
say. On the other bank of the Tweed are the ruins of
Dawyck, Tinnies, and Drummelzier castles. Dawyck has
glorious woods—the first larches and chestnuts to grow in
Scotland were planted here (Dunkeld, in Perthshire, dis-
putes the honour of the larches) two hundred years ago;
and near Drummelzier is the grave of the wizard Merlin,
whose magic failed him at the last, so that he died uncouthly under the stones and clubs of barbarous folk,
falling from a steep bank upon a pointed stake.

Broughton, near by, was the home of John Murray, Prince
Charlie's secretary, whom fear made a traitor in the end.

The vista of the valley becomes wilder, but the road
has its traffic. Before the days of motors I walked here
with a friend, and it seemed then that it must be the
loneliest place in the world. The only people we met
were two anglers; the burns around are noted for their
yellow trout, and were less strictly preserved then. The
Crook Inn, busy hostelry in coaching days, has been
replaced by an hotel. The Tweed flows faster, and we
follow it to Tweedsmuir. The hills here are the highest
in the South of Scotland; among them lies Loch Talla,
whence Edinburgh draws much of its water supply.

From Tweedsmuir post-office you get a pretty picture
of Talla Glen, and I think you might step in among the
trees for a minute, where Tweedsmuir Kirk stands on a
mound at the river's brink, if only to glance at the grave
of one of the old Covenanters—

John Hunter, who was cruely murdered at Corehead by Col. James Douglas and his party for his adherance to the Word of God and Scotland's covenanted work of reformation—1685.

Doubtless Col. James Douglas was also doing his duty, as he saw it, whether he liked it or no; but it is surely the saddest of all chapters in Scotland's story, that of the hunting and slaying of men who had courage to worship according to their convictions. And if the Covenanters retaliated, it was because they were men, not saints. Here, gazing up at the hills, it is easy to imagine solitary figures in homespun, lying in the heather—sentries on the lookout for companies of dragoons—while from a hidden hollow in the glen rises the preacher's voice, or the slow, terribly fervent singing of a psalm.

Not far from the bridge at Tweedsmuir is a solitary standing-stone, called the Giant's, sole survivor of an ancient Circle. Where are its one-time neighbours? The rude forefathers of the hamlet had less regard for such things than for their pigsties. Some five miles farther on we pass Tweed Shaws—'shaw' meaning 'a wood'—and Tweed's Well; then, having surmounted the hill, arrive at the verge of a great gloomy gulf, known as the Devil's Beef Tub, with water at the bottom. Here a Jacobite prisoner broke from his guards and escaped by rolling down the precipitous slope.

We shall do better by rolling down to Moffat ('long, deep mountain hollow'), and into its spacious High Street, which, were it in France, would be called a *place*, and which looks as if it had just been swept and tidied in your honour—so much so that you may feel like saluting the bronze ram on the red-stone fountain. As a spa Moffat has been known since the middle of the seventeenth century. Its golf and tennis are excellent; its bowling greens, on which a great tournament is held annually in the late summer, are famous.

You may be relieved to learn that its oldest church dates only from 1880. The Court House is a hundred years older and has a bell dated 1620. Moffat House was built by Earl Hopetoun in 1751. Therein, a few years later, the once prominent Macpherson translated or 'invented' many poems of Ossian, the ancient Celtic bard. Samuel Johnson believed him to be a 'fraud,' but the dear Doctor was occasionally wrong, and I have met many good Highlanders who disagree with him. At all events, Macpherson was himself a real poet, and no one need grudge him his profits, which were considerable.

The Annan, just beginning to grow up, flows by Moffat; and while the scenery in the near neighbourhood is of the amiable sort, we are not far from scenery very different. Our course is now more or less uphill to the pass at Birkhill. Near the summit we turn aside, as everybody does, to see the Grey Mare's Tail, most apt of names for the cascade with a fall of three hundred feet on the stream that comes from Loch Skene, which lies sulking among precipices under the frown of White Coomb, second loftiest of the southern mountains. It can be grim, indeed, here in grey weather; and perhaps the most sinister feature of all is Dob's Linn ('pool'), near to Birkhill, above which Dob and a Covenanter friend, Davie, lived in a cottage and had great times with the Devil, who tormented them of nights. Eventually they got the better of him with a Bible and a staff cut from a rowan-tree (mountain ash). Do not smile! Were you spending a night up there you would want a Bible too. The rowan, by the way, is a sure protection against many evil things. Countless cottages in Scotland have a tree at the door.

The scenery here greatly impressed Sir Walter Scott when Hogg, the Ettrick Shepherd, was his guide; he refers to the Linn in *Old Mortality*. It cannot be called a happy countryside. All these inhospitable hollows have been the hiding-places of hunted men, some of them the deathbeds of brave men, shot down where they stood by dragoons. You would understand were you to read Hogg's *Brownie of Bodsbeck*.

St Mary's is *the* loch of the Borders for size, though that is only some seven miles round about, and for associations, which are innumerable. In coming to it we come to Tibbie Shiels.

"What is Tibbie Shiels?" says somebody, as somebody once, long ago, asked, "What are Keats?" Well, in its own way, the name Tibbie Shiels is just as illustrious as that of the poet. We are now in Ettrick, and away back in 1813 an Ettrick servant-girl married a mole-catcher from Westmorland, and they came to live at the head of Loch o' the Lowes. Ten years passed, and they removed to a cottage on the isthmus between it and St Mary's Loch. A year later her husband died, leaving her with six children. It looked like being a sore struggle for the widow, but one day Robert Chambers, the Edinburgh publisher, came seeking material for his book on Scotland and took a room in the cottage. He liked it so much that his book, when published, contained a kindly little 'advertisement' of Tibbie's cottage and capable self. That was the beginning. The cottage became an inn—a small, homely place, to be sure, but so hospitable and comfortable that its fame, coupled with the name of Tibbie Shiels, went far abroad. Scotland's learned and literary men came to it; the Visitors' Book holds also many great names not of Scotland. Tibbie must have been a rare hostess, as well as a prime cook of country fare, and things were more free and easy than they are to-day. There were jolly nights in the Inn, when Hogg, sweetest singer of the singing Borders, and the other poets and good fellows met together. Tibbie, who used her maiden name as hostess, lived to be ninety-five. There is a picture of her—an old

G

woman in knitted shawl and mutch, shrewd, kindly, humorous. To-day Scotland has her big luxury hotels, yet I think 'Tibbie Shiels'—the lowly, white-washed cottage—will outlast them all. There is now a modern house attached to the gable, but you may step into the old place and imagine that you have walked all the way from Peebles on a wintry day, as no doubt many of Tibbie's customers did, and without thinking much about it. Near by, at the Lochside, you will find, in effigy, the Shepherd-Poet, whose eyes she closed, and who lies in the same yard, over at Ettrick Kirk.

The Loch, a mirror of moods, is bounded by green hills. Scott, who loved it for its silence and solitude, no less than its beauty, might not love it so much to-day; nevertheless, for those of us who are come from the rush and racket of cities, the lovely road along the hillside may still seem quiet enough. But it is a road, like so many others in the Borders, that should be walked, and walked leisurely. Only so may one absorb the spirit of that strangely sad, yet comforting, countryside.

The Yarrow Water flows from the north end of the Loch, and accompanies us into a smiling valley and past the Gordon Arms, at the cross-roads, and Yarrow Kirk to Newark Castle among its birches. It was to the widowed Lady of Newark that Scott's "Last Minstrel" sang his "Lay." A great stronghold it must have been in its prime, and the grand tower still stands firm, while you can see that the walls, with their high, small windows, rise to four storeys.

If Yarrow means 'rough river,' as a scholar has suggested, it deserves the adjective here, and we pass through much wild beauty to rejoin our friend the Tweed. At one point on the road we are almost within signalling distance of Selkirk Town, but Selkirk is for another day, and we carry on toward Clovenfords, turn to the left, and are presently on the Peebles main road,

in the spacious meadow-land of the Tweed valley. We
may catch a glimpse on the hillside of ruined Elibank
Castle, built by Sir Gideon Murray about 1600.

At Innerleithen, a neat little town, as an eighteenth-
century English traveller in Scotland called every town
where he got plenty to drink—I shan't tell you what he
called the others—we may turn down, if you please, to
Traquair House. The original part of the House is very
old; the greater part of it belongs to the time of Charles
I. Plain and austere of aspect, it is one of our finest
examples of *châteaux*, and is still inhabited, or was when
I saw it a few years ago. Its romantic interest, however,
belongs to the gates, which have never been opened since
1796, when the seventh Earl, after the death of his lady,
decreed that they should remain closed till the coming of
another lady worthy to take her place. That is one of
the tales. Another, generally discredited, runs to the
effect that, in 1746, after Culloden, the Earl, a staunch
Jacobite, had them shut, never to be opened till the
Stuarts returned to their kingdom. Anyhow, the gates
are there for all to see, hung from two heavy square
pillars, with queer stone bears on their tops—closed upon
a grass-grown carriage-way; a pathetic sight when you
reflect that, whatever may happen, they will never be
opened to a Traquair, for the last of the house died in
1875, an old lady in her hundredth year.

Five Border Towns

Within a circle of some six miles' radius are four towns,
each with a story to fill a book, each a likely centre for
the explorer; and some five miles outside the circle, eastward, is a fifth town, of which the same may be said.
The five towns are Selkirk, Melrose, Kelso, Jedburgh,
and Hawick. Do not assume, pray, that they are here
named in order of importance. Every Borderer,
whether business man, antiquarian, or football 'fan,'

is warmly jealous for his own town, and some day I may want to revisit one, or all, of them.

I take Selkirk first, simply because it seems most convenient for our purpose, whether we are coming to it from Peebles, or from Edinburgh.   If from Peebles, by road, we shall come round by Clovenfords and Galashiels.   The history of Galashiels, as a writer has succinctly put it, is mainly the history of the Tweed Trade, yet it has its attractions, and we must certainly stop in the wide and airy Square, if only to look upon the impressive War Memorial, so characteristic of the Borders.   The shrine, sheltering the Angel of Peace, is within a recess in the base of a tower, a hundred feet high, the bronze plate therein bearing over six hundred names.   On a pedestal in front is a Border horseman in panoply of war.

Set on a steep hillside, mostly modern, Selkirk seems to smile on our approach, its workaday features, mills, being down in the hollow.   They tell me that the town can show nothing over two hundred years old, yet it had an Abbey in 1113, and its men went out to the great battles of the Middle Ages.   As Andrew Lang, Selkirk-born and one of Scotland's most distinguished men of letters, wrote: "Its air is full of ballad notes borne out of long ago."   There may be nothing ancient in the spacious Market Square, but to stand there in moonlight is to be aware of something not of the present.   Moreover, Selkirk is not seeking to forget the past.   Every June the townspeople keep the festival of the Common Riding—*i.e.*, the riding of the marches—as their forebears have done for hundreds of years.

It is a picturesque ceremony or, rather, series of ceremonies.   On the Thursday evening the burgh officer, in uniform, accompanied by drum and fife, parades the streets, and summons all interested to be ready on the morrow "at the sound of the second drum."   Then follows the "bussing of the colours."   The various trades corporations and associations have their standards, and each chooses a standard-bearer and a lady to kiss the flag. There are speeches, and were you to hear them you would appreciate my remark about every Borderer being jealous for his native town. Next morning, at five, the fifers and drummers parade the streets; at six they are followed by the town band which, rain or shine, opens its programme with *Hail, Smiling Morn!* At the Victoria Hall, beside the Flodden Memorial, the Burgh standard is duly 'bussed,' and the procession, led by perhaps 150 horsemen, moves off, following the standard-bearer through the town to the bank of the Ettrick. The horsemen ford the river, proceed to ride the marches, and recross the river, a mile farther down. Galloping up the hill, they rejoin the procession, and all make for the Market Square, where the final ceremony takes place— the "casting of the colours." 'Casting' means waving the flags in a peculiar fashion, which involves considerable practice, to the old tune of *Up wi' the Souters o' Selkirk*. After that there is a little period of solemnity; the band plays *The Flowers of the Forest*, most moving of Border airs. Then smiles again, and breakfast, and a holiday, and games.

The note of sadness in an otherwise joyous celebration is Selkirk's tribute to her sons who fell at Flodden, more than four hundred years ago. Her men in those days were mostly shoemakers—for centuries Selkirk was famous for a certain kind of brogue—and 'Souter' is Scots for shoemaker. So in August 1513 the Souters joined up with the host that James in his folly was leading into England and to the greatest disaster that ever befell Scottish arms. Just over the Border, on September 9, the armies met, the English under the Earl of Surrey. The fighting did not begin till late in the afternoon; it continued upon that rain-soaked, blood-sodden ground till men could no longer see one another, enemy or friend.   Not till the new day came did Surrey know that he had won.   As for the men of Selkirk, the story goes that of the seventy odd who crossed the Border only one came home.   But he brought with him an English pennon, which you may see in the Public Library, and his deed is immortalized in the bronze figure on the Flodden Memorial.

Sir Walter Scott, as plain 'Mister,' was sheriff of the Shire—a monument to his memory stands in front of the Court House—but his heart was over at Melrose, and we are going there now, a short run through lovely country. The name suggests a fragrance, though it probably means 'blunt' or 'bare promontory.'   Centuries before the noble Abbey was even a thought, there was a little monastery two miles east of the site.   Founded by St Aidan, it stood on a peninsula in the Tweed, and was called Melrose.   So fair is this situation that when the Wordsworths were there, in 1803, Dorothy wished the famous ruins might have been transported thither.   When in 1136 David I founded a new abbey at Little Fordell, he transferred to it the old name from the peninsular monastery, then extinct, and so Little Fordell became Melrose.   Yet the ruins we see to-day are not those of David's abbey, which, thanks to invaders from the South, was in fragments by 1300; they are those of a recon-structed abbey begun in 1326, under the practical en-couragement of King Robert the Bruce.   One must admire the spirit of the old monks, as well as that of the fighting men.   Like people living in an earthquake area, while yet they wept over the wreckage of their homes they were planning to raise new and finer ones in the same perilous places.   But earthquakes could hardly have done more damage than, for example, the Earl of Hertford in 1545.   Within a fortnight his armies in the Borders destroyed four abbeys, sixteen castles and towers, five market towns, and 243 villages.   It was then that

Melrose suffered for the last time. Generals Evers and Layton burned it. There is an ironic end to their story. The day after the burning, their army was badly beaten on Ancrum Moor, a few miles away, and both were slain. And, a little later, their bodies found Christian burial at the Abbey, under its still warm walls.

Constructed in the decorated and perpendicular styles of Gothic, the Abbey in its good days must have been a glorious spectacle. Even its remnant gives the impression not only of rich magnificence, but of delicate grace. We can still form pictures of its pristine splendour from an inspection of the nave, choir, transepts, cloisters, and chapter house; of its infinite beauty from the sculptured figures, canopies, and pinnacles of the buttresses, and the exquisite traceries of the windows. It is no wonder that every year thousands of people come to look at Melrose Abbey, the most precious jewel of the Borders; no wonder that Scott, who loved its every gleam and gloom, was inspired to tell the world about it. I have doubts as to whether 'poetical quotations' are welcome in a book like this, but so illuminating are these lines of Scott's that I am asking you to read them—slowly:

> Through slender shafts of shapely stone,
>   By foliaged tracery combined,
> Thou would'st have thought some fairy's hand,
> 'Twixt poplars straight the osier wand,
>   In many a freakish knot, had twined ;
> Then framed a spell, when work was done,
> And changed the willow-wreaths to stone.

That is the wonder of Melrose Abbey in a thought.

Though the body lies at Dunfermline, in Fife, it is appropriate that the heart of Bruce should be here, on the eastern side of the Abbey which he had helped to raise. A Scotsman, at any rate, knows from his school history how the dying King desired that his heart should be buried in the Holy Land, and how Lord James

Douglas undertook to bear it thither. But, passing
through Spain, in a fight with the Saracens Douglas was
slain, and the heart in its casket was brought back to
Scotland. The hint of human tenderness in the tale
comes sweetly into Scotland's long chronicle of blood-
shed and burnings.

Melrose Town is a trim little place, unafflicted by
industries, with an antique Cross in its principal street.
As well as hotels, it has a hydropathic, " The Waverley."
Its one apparent crime is that bygone generations allowed
buildings to be erected so close to the Abbey that one
of them is all but nudging it. If ' the good old days,'
with their vandalism and irreverence, had lasted a little
longer, this story of mine would have been a great deal
shorter.

From Melrose Abbotsford is only three miles, but we
have scarcely passed over one of them when we must stop
to see what to many people must be the most entertaining sight in the Borders. Ruins are all very well in
their way, but here is a tower complete, as it was four
hundred years ago, and occupied by descendants of the
man who built it. Better still, by paying a shilling, we
may enter and learn in a few minutes what no lecture,
however erudite, on empty walls could teach us. Dar-
nick Tower, built in 1425, burned by our friend Hertford
at the same time as Melrose, was rebuilt by Andrew
Heiton, under a new charter granted by Queen Mary, in
1569. A battlemented square, weather-worn and grim,
with a peaked roof, its old doorway has an outer 'yett'
(gate) and inner door, oaken and nail-studded, with
'tirling pin' still serving as knocker. Above the lintel
is the date, 1569, and the initials of Andrew Heiton and
his spouse, Kate Fisher; also the sacred monogram,
I.H.S., implying that the owner held the tower in fief
to the monastery of Melrose Abbey. You go along a
narrow passage to the dining-room, which contains some

family heirlooms. In the central hall, low-roofed and long, lighted by four windows, are three contemporary portraits of Mary Queen of Scots, one on copper; a six-legged seventeenth-century couch; a powder-horn bearing Prince Charlie's initials, also his dirk, with knife and fork; and a piece of tapestry believed to have been worked by Mary. Go up the narrow, twisting stair, and you will see two bedrooms, one with a bed of carved oak, in which Mary may have slept at Linlithgow Palace. There are other treasures and relics in the armoury. The old Heitons were warriors. One fell at Flodden, another in the fight that finished the struggle between the brothers Scott of Buccleuch and the Earl of Angus for the person of the boy King, James V. Two Heitons, brothers, went out with the Covenanters and fought in the Battle of Bothwell Bridge, in 1679—one being killed, the other taken prisoner. In 1820 John Heiton parted with the last of his land to Sir Walter Scott, who would fain have purchased the Tower also.

Of Abbotsford Ruskin wrote: "Perhaps the most incongruous pile that gentlemanly modernism ever designed." And if you are a good housewife you will exclaim: "Oh, Heaven, what a house to run!" Alas! there is no getting away from the impression that it is more extraordinary than beautiful. But let us remember what it meant to Scott, who, first of all, desired the place for its outlook and romantic surroundings, including Melrose. When he first saw the site, there was a sort of farm cottage, with a barn on one side, a cabbage-patch on the other, and a duck-pond in front. The place, Cartley Hole, commonly called "Clarty [dirty] Hole," was almost bare of trees. Its present sylvan beauty is of Scott's creation; tree-planting was one of his first cares. The House itself was fourteen years in the making—addition after addition, till the small villa that had replaced the cottage became the 'imposing,' castellated, turreted mansion we see to-day. And what a continual feast the gradual growth must have been to him; to read of its progress in his letters is a joyous experience; and all the time he was the most generous and genial host to relays of visitors. Domestic service was another story then, but it does occur to one that there may have been times when Lady Scott and her daughters found it a little difficult to keep smiling. A visitor, in 1823, found other visitors there and workmen engaged on "new buildings," but he records no particular impression of his hostess, only of his host, whom he describes as "the best-natured man I ever saw." That being so, and since the House gave him happiness, what matters the form of stone and lime? Besides, tastes differ, and, only the other day, I read this of Abbotsford:

> Notwithstanding many oddities, the general effect is pleasing and surprising. Abbotsford was reared on no set plan, but with the desire to reproduce some of those features of Scottish Architecture which Scott most venerated.

We enter by a turreted gateway in an embattled wall, the entrance porch copied from Linlithgow Palace. There is the grave and marble effigy of his favourite deerhound, Maida, and the fountain once at the Cross in Edinburgh's High Street. The walls are adorned with inscriptions of sayings from various sources. The rooms open to the public constitute a treasure-house of personal memorials and historic relics—an amazing collection for one busy man to have made. The study, they say, is as he left it: reference books and so forth in their old places. The library adjoining, the largest room in the house, has a ceiling of Jamaica cedar, its carvings modelled from Melrose and Roslin. It is a place where the antiquarian murmurs soft "Ah's!" Here, for instance, is a seal once used by Queen Mary—a fragment of one of her dresses;

a lock of Prince Charlie's hair and his *quaich* (drinking-cup); Rob Roy's purse and Helen Macgregor's brooch; Flora Macdonald's pocket-book; the blotting-book and pen-tray taken from Napoleon's coach after Waterloo.

The drawing-room is notable for its furniture and paintings, but the armoury overwhelms one—no private collection like it in the world. It is not confined to Scotland; the weapons and curios represent every country, and many carry historic associations. Quite vain to attempt to convey the smallest idea of it all; a descriptive guide is necessary to the earnest visitor, and I would recommend *Abbotsford*, by the Rev. W. S. Crockett, which tells the whole story of the house. The spacious entrance-hall, with which, when I last visited the place, the stranger's privilege terminated, is panelled and roofed with dark oak from Dunfermline Palace, and floored with black-and-white marble; the effect of these is not lessened by the subdued, wine-tinted light from the emblazoned windows. Around the cornice are escutcheons of many Border families; while down from the centre of the roof, with its pointed arches, run sixteen shields with the arms of Scott's own ancestors.

Like the armoury, the hall is filled with weapons and trophies, of which I can name but a few. Here is a suit of armour which belonged to Sir John Cheney, surely a giant, and his two-handed sword—he must have been a spectacular figure in action; a Jeddart axe, dreadful weapon; the keys of Edinburgh's Old Tolbooth; a clock once Marie Antionette's; and relics from Culloden and Waterloo. Had ever man so catholic a taste in curios? And—pathetic sight—here are the last garments he wore—dark green coat, striped waistcoat, drab trousers, beaver hat of fawn colour. . . .

The dining-room is private. Within it, on a lovely autumn afternoon in 1832, he escaped from the weakness and weariness of his latter days.

From Abbotsford it is natural that we should go back, through Melrose, to Dryburgh Abbey, where he and another brave man, with near a hundred years, but only a few yards of earth, between them, were laid, each mourned by the whole British nation. The Abbey is about the same age as Melrose, and its fate was the same.

Sir Walter Scott lies in St Mary's Aisle, under a great granite sarcophagus, and a few paces away lies Field-Marshal Earl Haig. Their one-time homes are but a few miles apart; though, when Abbotsford was in the building, there had been Haigs at Bemersyde for 700 years. If you are making a stay in Melrose, you should go there to see the quaintest of old houses, of which, in the thirteenth century, Thomas the Rhymer prophesied:

> Tyde, tyde, whate'er betyde,
> There shall be Haigs at Bemersyde.

With Sir Walter Scott Kelso and its neighbourhood have the most intimate associations. A delicate little boy, in 1773 he was sent, for his health's sake, to his grandfather's farm of Sandyknowe, six miles from the town. There was born his love of nature; there he began to absorb the lore of the Borders. From that ridge the young eyes enjoyed an unfailing feast—hills, moors, and valleys; plains, woods, and rivers. Near by was Smailholm Tower, which you have only to see to guess how the sight of it must have influenced the imaginative child. It has been called the most perfect remaining example of a feudal stronghold in the South of Scotland. Built for security about 1400, it rises to a height of 60 feet, and stands square and stern and stark on a moorland crag, overhanging a sullen pool—not a hint of decoration on its eight-foot thick walls, unless the blood-red sandstone forming the door-posts and lintels, set in that mass of grey whinstone, may be called ornaments. You enter a dusky arched vault, above which is the hall, with a great fireplace. The timber roof of this chamber has gone, likewise the roof of the chamber above, but the top storey is still covered by a massive roof of stone. A winding stair, amazingly preserved, leads up to the battlements, and the view is magnificent. Scott often came back to Smailholm. His last visit was in 1831, when he brought with him Turner, and the famous painter made a sketch for the new edition of the *Poems*.

> Then rise those crags, that mountain tower,
> Which charmed my fancy's wakening hour.

So wrote Scott, in his *Marmion*, of Smailholm. You must see it, though it lies a little way off the regular tourist track. It is one of the many surrounding sights that may tempt you to spend a night in comfortable Kelso, where Scott spent a little time at school, meeting there his future publishers, the brothers Ballantyne, and where, twenty years later, his *Minstrelsy of the Scottish Border* was printed; whereupon connoisseurs of printing exclaimed: "What a beautiful book! But where on earth is Kelso?" Of all the Border towns it would seem that Scott loved Kelso best.

It is charmingly set at the meeting-place of Teviot and Tweed, which you may view, as part of a splendid prospect, from Chalkheugh Terrace—the word Kelso has something to do with 'chalk'—a few minutes' walk from the Market Square. Once more the Eildons are the background of a picture, which contains St James's Fair Green, where once stood Roxburgh town; Marchmount, on the peninsula between the rivers, with its remnant of Roxburgh Castle, strongest and most famous in all the Borders, razed by the Scots in 1460 to prevent its passing again into the hands of the English; Floors Castle (it should be the French *Fleurs*), white in the sunshine above its terraced lawns, not ancient, but surely the stateliest of palaces, home of the Duke of Roxburghe; and afar, on a height, the Waterloo Monument. Kelso, like its neighbour towns, was particularly interested in Waterloo, for many French soldiers had been sent to the Borders as prisoners on parole.

Away back in 1547 Kelso was described by a traveller as a "pretty market town," and the description holds to-day. The pale stone used in most of its buildings gives it a cheerful air, and there is a hint of prosperity too in the fine spaciousness of its Market Square. Kelso has a long history, religious and warlike. Although the ruined Abbey has not the moving beauty of Melrose, the comparatively recent discovery of a description by a traveller early in the sixteenth century shows that it was the most sumptuously planned building in Scotland. Founded, like so many of our ecclesiastical buildings, by David I, it must have known vicissitudes as the centuries followed; but it would seem to have been at the peak of its grandeur not long before those fatal years between 1523 and 1545. The troops that came from England in 1545 had in their ranks almost every European nation, save Turkey and Russia, and destruction was their "chiefest joy." On that occasion, however, Kelso put up a good fight for its Abbey. It will probably strike you that the great square tower is worthy of a castle; and as such it was used by monks and townsmen after the walls of the main building had been breached by cannon; and there they held out till the bitter, bloody end. Of the once great church, which may have been modelled on Ely Cathedral, only enough remains to suggest its former dignity. It saw many pageants in its time; but the solitary coronation at its altar could hardly have been a gladsome affair—that of James III, immediately after his father had been killed by the bursting of a cannon, while besieging Roxburgh Castle.

Before you leave Kelso for Jedburgh, about 15 miles southward, take a last look at it from the south bank of the river, a little way below the bridge. Years after, if you remember Scotland at all, you will remember that scene.

It may be that you have come into Scotland by the road over Carter Bar, in the Cheviots; if so, given clear weather, you have had from the summit, 1400 feet up, the best possible view of the Border country. On the ten miles' run to Jedburgh you have passed through Old Jeddart, site of the first Jedburgh, and have glimpsed among the trees the towers of the restored Ferniehurst Castle. Considering its past, the wonder is that there was anything left to restore.

'Jedburgh' is the town's formal mode of address. The people call it 'Jeddart.' You may have heard the expression 'Jeddart justice,' which means "Hang him now, and try him later"—a libel on the place, for its men of the olden time were no worse than their neighbours on both sides of the Border, though they were great fighters with their terrible axes and staffs, the latter poles 7 feet long with a hook and hatchet at the end. Their slogan "Jethart's here!" could put heart into their friends and take it out of their foes. 'Jeddart justice' was only once, so far as we know, executed, and it was done by Lord Home on a band of raiders. You may notice, by the way, that I have given several spellings of the name, and I believe there are about seventy others. 'Jed,' meaning 'turning' or 'twisting,' describes the course of the impetuous stream, which has seven bridges within a mile.

"The charm of Jedburgh itself," says Dr Crockett in *The Scott Country*, a helpful book to anyone who has leisure to do the Borders justice,

consists in a kind of old-world character that clings to it, and in the half-Continental traces which it exhibits. It reminds one, too, in some respects, of an English cathedral town ; and there are not wanting certain resemblances to the capital of Scotland.

That gives a very true idea of the little town so snugly set by the river, and I would only add that, approached from the higher ground, it is to-day an epitome of peace, though no spot in all the Borders has had a less peaceful past. Strangely enough, out of all the hate and horror the Cathedral has emerged a less shattered object than any other cathedral of the Borders; sufficient has been spared of the great central tower, the nave, and the western bays of the choir, to afford an idea of its one-time extent and splendour. Part of the tower and the choir are early Norman; the whole Abbey through its architecture speaks of three, if not four, periods. Of its many fine features I may name the tiers of arches on either side of the nave, the western and southern doors, and the wheel window high up in the west gable; but, unless one is a student of architecture, or an archæologist, the way to take in the beauty of Jedburgh Cathedral is to regard it from the other side of the river, at an hour when the tower and walls overlooking the woody slope are mirrored in the quiet waters, and let your imagination have liberty.

High Street and Castlegate, both about half a mile in length, are the most important thoroughfares. In Queen Street, which runs parallel to High Street, you will find Queen Mary's House. Until 1928 the old building was in private hands; then it was acquired on behalf of the community. Sir James Barrie came to open a bazaar for the purpose of raising funds for its preservation and for making its garden a public pleasure-ground; and during his visit he received the Freedom of the Town.

In October 1566 Mary, on her way to preside at a Circuit Court in Jedburgh, learned that Bothwell, wounded in attempting the capture of a notorious free-

THE TWEED AND CHEVIOT HILLS, COLDSTREAM

Photo Valentine and Sons, Ltd.

JEDBURGH ABBEY, FROM THE RIVER
Photo Valentine and Sons, Ltd.

booter, "Little Jock Elliot," who did not long survive
the Earl's blow, had been carried to his Castle of Hermitage. According to the historian, George Buchanan,
who can never impute enough vileness to Mary—you
have only to see the man's portrait to think of him as a
mean little creature—she flew forthwith on the wings of
unholy love to Hermitage; but we should do better to
credit contemporary official documents, which state that
she did her business, lasting a week, in Jedburgh, ere she
set out. And, in either case, her stay at Hermitage
Castle must have been brief, since she did the double
journey—near fifty miles of rough riding—between dawn
and dusk. Next day she was unwell; during the following week desperately ill. There was an hour when they
thought her dead, but her French physician persevered
and drew her back. In days to come she was heard to
murmur: "Would God that I had died at Jedburgh!"

It is a tall, pretty, three-storeyed house, with three
crow-stepped gables and a stair-turret in the angle.
The roof, now red-tiled, was thatched in Mary's day. It
was in a room on the second floor that the Queen lay ill.
Convalescent, she would look down to a garden—perhaps
an orchard, for Jedburgh has ever been known for its
fruit-growing: "Jethart pears" used to be a cry in the
streets of London—and over to the Jed. Lift your eyes
to those second-floor windows, and maybe at one of them
you will see her.

To Jedburgh, in 1803, came Wordsworth and Dorothy,
to be welcomed and shown around by Scott. Sixteen
years before that, Burns was a visitor, receiving the
Freedom of the Town.

Ten miles to Hawick. Half-way we pass through
pretty, flowery Denholm village. In a thatched, white-
washed cottage was born, in 1775, John Leyden, son of
a shepherd, remarkable for the life he crammed into
thirty-six years. Poet, brilliant scholar and linguist,

H

preacher, though not a very successful one, doctor of
medicine, all at twenty-eight, he entered the service of
the East India Company at Madras, and within seven
years performed the duties of Professor, Commissioner,
and Assay-Master of the Calcutta Mint. Java was then
a French possession; in 1811 his services were required
in a military expedition ordered thither, and he died
suddenly at Batavia. His verse won him the friendship
of Scott. His monument stands on the village green.
Denholm, too, was the birthplace of Sir James Murray,
editor of the *New English Dictionary*, also of John Scott,
naturalist, whose works were highly praised by Darwin.

In this neighbourhood is Minto House, birthplace of
Jean Elliot, whose version of *The Flowers of the Forest* is
immortal. On Minto Crag stands a tower with the un-
prepossessing name of Fatlips—I have been unable to
discover the meaning. High above dark larch woods, it
is astonishingly perched on the round, flat summit of a
peak of blue-grey rock, so steep that you must use steps
to reach it. On the Teviot side there is a sheer drop of
four hundred feet. The Tower has been well cared for
by the Earl of Minto. At Cavers, beyond Denholm, the
mighty Douglases have had their home for six centuries.
Here were long kept the gauntlets taken from Hotspur at
Otterbourne in 1388, also a Douglas pennon—both now
in the National Museum of Antiquities, in Edinburgh.

Hawick has become big, modern, and commercial—
not that its commerce has been allowed to interfere with
its regard for its past. Its Common Riding Festival is
the most elaborate of all such ancient Border celebrations. I have briefly indicated the nature of the pro-
ceedings at Selkirk, and to do Hawick justice in detail is
not here possible. Hawick's Standard Bearer is called
Cornet, and Hawick has its own song, beginning:

Teribus ye Teri Odin,
Sons of heroes slain at Floddin.

Nobody knows what the first line means; it seems to have come down from Saxon worshippers of the old gods; and the wild tune suggests "battles long ago." The Hawick men are known as 'Teries' (pronounced 'Teeries'), just as the Selkirk men are known as 'Souters.' Hawick, too, has the replica of an English flag, captured in 1514 by a band of daring young men from a party of marauders, at Hornshole, on the outskirts. So much does Hawick enjoy its annual festival that every year, after it is over, you may overhear remarks like "Ah, weel, it's bye; but, thank the Lord, it's only fifty-twa weeks till the next time." Enthusiasm appears to be increasing with the years, and Border communities who have neglected their ceremonies for generations are now reviving them. June is the month.

Hawick town stands in a basin, in which the rapid Slitrig Water joins the Teviot. Busy with its manufacture of tweeds, woollens, leathers, and so on, it has retained few of its ancient landmarks. The notable building is the Tower Hotel, its western side being part of a Douglas stronghold. Mary, on that wild ride from Jedburgh to Hermitage, drew rein here, and no doubt her honoured host made haste to draw something for her refreshment. Hawick's outstanding feature is the Moat—a mound, as to the meaning of which learned men have wrangled. Its commanding situation suggests that Hawick's Moat, which is 30 feet high, 312 feet around the base, and 117 around the top, was, at all events, a place of public importance in the old days.

Border Landmarks

From Hawick there are—as I write—few first-class roads running south and west; and the Borders still to be explored are largely a land flowing with little waters. None the less, you will get a very good outing if you take the road through the green valley of the Teviot to Langholm

and Canonbie, returning through Liddesdale. Just out
of Hawick, you will notice, high up and lifting above the
trees, a square tower, which bears the pretty name of
Goldielands—an old 'peel' in wonderfully good condition. It used to serve as a look-out for Branxholme
Castle, a mile or so farther on. You may be disappointed
in Branxholme's appearance—a white-washed, inhabited
mansion, built against a tower; but it was a mighty inspiration to Scott, and there is additional interest in the
fact that it was a Sir Walter Scott who, in 1571, set about
rebuilding the tower after it had been four times burned
by the English. Above the arched doorway you will see,
in the quaint spelling of the time, his name and that of
his wife—"Schir Walter Scot of Branxholme, Knycht:
Margret Douglas." One likes to think of its Knights who,
in order to be 'aye ready,' kept on their steel gloves at
dinner, drank red wine through the bars of their helmets,
and went to bed in their armour.

Beyond the Allan Water—not the only Allan Water in
Scotland—and near Teviothead, we find, at Caerlanrig,
site of a Roman camp, a tablet which records, in no
tender terms, the treachery, if such it really was, of
James V to Johnny Armstrong, of Gilnockie, down in
Eskdale. The Armstrongs lived so close to the Border
line that they were sometimes English, sometimes
Scottish, and occasionally both. They helped themselves to cattle on either side, thus solving the oldest
human problem, how to 'have it both ways.' At that
time James was striving to put the Borders in order.
The evidence of 'treachery' is confined to the *Ballad of
Johnie Armstrang*—a splendid ballad too. It relates
how the King has written a loving letter, which brings
Johnny and forty of his friends to Caerlanrig; how on his
arrival the King, in spite of protestations of allegiance,
dubs him traitor, and, in the face of frantic offers of
"milk-white steids," men-at-arms, and rentals, continues

to dub him so; and finally, how Johnny, in his golden girdle and hat with nine tassels, each worth "three hundred pound," is "murdered," along with his "galant companie." The ballad says nothing about 'hanging,' but there is another story which pictures the "galant companie" suspended from trees, which afterward withered away. It is impossible for us to judge of the rights and wrongs, but Johnny has always been the popular hero. Another monument here is of a gentler memory—Henry Scott Riddell, whose fame rests secure on a solitary song —though he wrote others as fine—*Scotland Yet*.

The road rises till near Mosspaul Inn, and then descends easily to Ewes Church, whose bell may still hang from a tree, runs alongside the Ewes Water into Langholm, which consists of an Old and New Town, the latter begun in 1778, and originally designed in the form of a triangle. There is fine fishing in the district.

Along the beautiful banks of the Esk we go on to Canonbie, a little way beyond it, turn into the Liddesdale Road, and presently pass Hollows Tower, often confused with Johnny Armstrong's Gilnockie Castle, of which nothing now exists. When Scott first came to this wild country, in 1792, there were no roads; eight years later his was the first vehicle to be seen in the place. At Castleton Church a road strikes to the left, and five miles of it brings us to Hermitage Castle, with its great, brown, square twin-towers and enormous, darkly yawning, ominous gateway, standing starkly on the moor—a place of legends, mostly evil. Its earliest tales are of one Nicholas de Soulis, in the thirteenth century, whose sorceries and cruelty to his fellows at last so outraged the people that, having captured him, they took him to the Nine Stane Rig, a stone circle, a mile or so away, and there, if you please, boiled him in a great copper pot— boiled him not in decent water, but, according to John Leyden:

They rolled him up in a sheet of lead—
A sheet of lead for a funeral pall;
They plunged him in the cauldron red,
And melted him, lead and bones and all.

No wonder the rushes and grass on the spot would never grow again! But, of course, a learned man now comes along with the information that de Soulis really died in Dumbarton Castle, a prisoner accused of a commonplace crime like treason. Fortunately there are other horrid legends, though I cannot repeat them here. Enough to say that, because of the weight of crime upon it, the building has been declared to be slowly sinking into the ground.

It was to Hermitage, you may remember, that Mary came to visit the wounded Bothwell. Then—in the distance, at any rate—it would appear pretty much as it does to-day. The outside has worn better than the interior—at night, surely, a place of shudders. Not far away, on the bank of Hermitage Water, are the remains of a little chapel, as old as the Castle. After all, it is ill work condemning dead men; and even Bothwell, when his blood was cool, may have bowed in its shadows, with a contrite heart.

To cheer you, just a little story from Lockhart's *Life of Scott*. In those days the good Liddesdale folk thought nothing of buying smuggled liquor. Scott was spending the night with a farmer, a hospitable soul, but darkness had come without the production of a dram. It was time for family worship. All were kneeling when a slight sound was heard outside; whereupon the farmer jumped up, crying, "By ——, here's the keg at last!"

CHAPTER IV

FIFE

Soon or late all good golfers—and some pretty bad ones, too—go to Fife; yet Fife, long ago a Kingdom by itself, named, perhaps, after Fib, its founder, is far from being dependent for its distinctions and attractions on its golf courses. The promontory reaching between the Firths of Forth and Tay into the North Sea is a veritable treasure-ground of Scotland's past. It has been said that to know the story of Fife is to know the history of Scotland—a true enough saying, as far as most of Scotland's earlier days are concerned.

Fife, with its place-names that strike the newcomer as comical or pretty—*e.g.* Auchtermuchty, Collessie, Pittenweem, Leslie, Elie, Largo, Blebo, Ceres—contains Scotland's most ancient cities, St Andrews, with her oldest University, and Dunfermline, the Capital long before Edinburgh. When much of Scotland was still poor and in some respects barbarous, Fife was prosperous and, in comparison, civilized. To-day it is a land so well furnished, though not crowded, with towns and villages, each having a history of its own, that if you are one of the surviving few who seek remote solitudes and the peace of the primitive, I should advise you to turn to almost any other part of Scotland.

Around its coasts of cliffs, reefs, and sandy bays are busy industrial towns, docks, harbours, more or less natural, refuges of fisher-folk for a thousand years; churches, castles, the ruin of what was Scotland's largest Cathedral, her first University, after many vicissitudes more flourishing than ever; and, of course, the spacious, breezy golf courses.   Inland, toward the west, are the great coal-fields—the monks were getting coal six centuries ago, and it is likely that King Robert the Bruce toasted his toes very gratefully before a coal fire on his winter visits to Dunfermline; but the land elsewhere is mostly given to farming and agriculture, with, here and there, a civic community including that of Cupar, the county town, whose Sheriff Court Records of 400 years ago may still be read.   Everywhere are the mansions and estates of families whose names are written in history, and, as well as Dunfermline, with its many Royal memories, there is little Falkland, with its Palace, partly restored, to my mind the most beautiful thing in all Fife, where kings made merry and one of them died very miserably.

You will not travel three miles over the countryside without seeing a church, or at least its square tower, with battlements, crown, or spire, showing above the trees; nor will you go far without learning the name of a saint, which may be familiar, but which will probably be other-wise, for there was a time when Fife was fairly overrun by holy men.   You will notice also, here and there, towers in miniature—pigeon cots.

Fife is not mountainous.   Walled on the north-west by the Ochil Hills, it is proud of its East and West Lomonds, the highest 1700 feet, which have a mild dignity of their own, and are worth climbing for the sake of the view.   The roads are many and good.

In the old days the people had the reputation of keep-ing themselves to themselves.   Perhaps the reputation is yet, in a measure, deserved.   The 'Fifer' is still re-garded by outsiders as an essentially canny person, by which I do not mean either parsimonious or slow.   The canniness makes for solid prosperity in the present, as it did in the past.   He is known also by his odd accent, or intonation.   It is unmistakable, and he is not ashamed

of it. Not long ago, in the lounge of a London hotel, a
visitor from these parts was heard to say: "No, sir! The
Fife accent cannot be acquired. It is a gift from God!"

Dunfermline

"A city that is set on an hill," of moderate size, old-
fashioned-looking because of its narrow streets, some of
them exceeding steep, it is mainly modern and has an
air of industry. Added to its natural advantages, the
benefactions of the late Andrew Carnegie have made it a
pleasant place to live in. A rather plain casket, perhaps,
but the jewels are there.

On an earlier page I have told of the arrival in the
Forth of the Saxon princess, Margaret, seeking a refuge
in Scotland. At Dunfermline King Malcolm Canmore
received the news, and hurried down to offer his welcome,
protection, and hospitality, afterward conducting Margaret, her brother, and sister, and their entourage to
his city. The tendency of some writers is to make a
romance of it, though my hard-hearted historian drily
hints that the union was a "maturely considered action"
on the part of Malcolm. Another tendency is to picture
the ceremony as taking place, with great pomp and
pageantry, in a cathedral-like edifice, organ pealing, and
so forth; but the truth would seem to be that they were
married in a poky little Culdee chapel, traces of which
were discovered, not so long ago, under the floor of the
Abbey, which was to be founded by their son David. As
for the pealing organ, I fancy that the wedding-guests
would have been awestricken by a concertina.

On a wooded knoll in Pittencrieff Glen are the remnants
of a building known as Malcolm's Tower, and we learn
that Malcolm built a tower here about 1066, though
probably his was a timber affair, a far from luxurious
residence for his Queen.

Margaret, however, was no sybarite. Her biography,

not altogether satisfactory, since written by her adoring confessor, Turgot, makes her a miraculous saint; but she was also a practical wife, mother, and woman of affairs—a woman of such character, indeed, that one feels she must have been, as we say in Scotland, "gey ill to live with." I can never resist the suspicion that Malcolm, with his big head, mighty arm, warrior heart, and passionate outbreaks of temper, was afraid as well as fond of her. But his causing her books, which he could not read, to be decorated with jewels is truly a pretty touch, and the motive is no affair of ours. Of those two people something really warm and human has survived the long centuries, which is more than can be said of many a King and Queen named in histories.

Concerning one of her volumes—*Book of the Four Gospels*—there is a story with a sequel so remarkable that it seems worth retelling here. The Court was on a journey, and while fording a stream the person responsible for the safety of the volume unwittingly let it fall. The loss being discovered, search was made, and at last it was found in the water, its leaves fluttering in the current. Yet there was no damage whatsoever, even to the illuminated pictures of the Evangelists and the ornamented capital letters. After Margaret died in 1093 the book disappeared, though the tale of its preservation remained with her memory. But the wonders were not ended. In 1887, nearly eight centuries later, at Sotheby's, in London, was offered for sale, from a parish library in Sussex, a little rather shabby brown volume of manuscripts. It was bought for £6 by the Bodleian Library, Oxford, where you may see it to-day—though it ought to be in Scotland. There is no doubt about its containing Margaret's 'Gospels.' On a fly-leaf Latin verses tell of their ancient ownership and adventure in the stream.

Soon after their marriage Margaret and Malcolm began

the building of a church dedicated to the Holy Trinity, the foundations of which were laid bare during recent excavations. The great Abbey Church was founded by their son, David I, in 1128, and the building dedicated in 1150. During the next century, the Abbey Church and Monastery were extended; toward the end of it the remains of the beatified Queen were transferred from their first resting-place, before the altar of the Holy Cross in the old church, to a shrine of great costliness in the Lady Chapel of the new. For three centuries thereafter silver lamps burned unfailingly before the shrine, the flames reflected in the gold and jewels, and then came the devastating hurricane of the Reformation. At this time of day one cannot fairly assess in every instance the material damage done by the Reformers, or the riff-raff that so blithely accompanied them for the fun of destruction and plunder, but Dunfermline did suffer much from the crazy crew. Out in the open, where once was the Lady Chapel, you will find a double plinth of limestone—all that survives of Margaret's shrine. Now and then a devout soul may be seen kneeling, murmuring a prayer in the name of the saint, though no relic of hers is there. In those days of destruction some pious persons removed the bones in their silver casket to a place of safety; long ago they were heard of in Spain and again in France, but to-day their place is unknown.

Of the ancient church only the nave, which makes people who know it think of Durham Cathedral, is now standing; the western doorway is one of the most splendid examples of Norman work in the land. Of the Monastery the gable of the refectory remains, with its window of seven lights, the tracery remarkably preserved. At one time there was a connection between the Monastery and the Palace kitchen of which, no doubt, the monks made use, especially when a Royal banquet was in progress.

Of the Palace ruins a portion of the south-east wall has

been ascribed to the thirteenth century, and there must have been a royal palace of sorts in Robert the Bruce's time, for his son was born at Dunfermline in 1323; but the probability is that its one-time magnificence—suggested in a glimpse from the south of its frowning wall, over 200 feet long, with its rows of Tudor windows, built on the slope above the stream—was the work of James V, who did so much for the Royal residences at Linlithgow and Falkland.   The hall on the first floor was nearly 100 feet in length.   Before James VI became King of England he and his Danish Queen favoured the Palace, and there in 1600, in an upper room, their ill-fated son, afterward Charles I, was born.   Charles II was the last monarch to lodge within its walls, and there, in 1650, with his customary delightful insincerity, put his name to the Solemn League and Covenant.   A few years after that the Palace, neglected, was on the way to ruin.

The New Abbey Church, built on part of the site of Malcolm and Margaret's Church, was opened for public worship in 1821.   Its square tower, 100 feet high, bears on the four sides of its battlements the words in huge stone letters "KING ROBERT THE BRUCE," surmounted by four royal crowns.   The Bruce died at his castle of Cardross, in the West, of a sort of leprosy, poor man, and at his own desire his body was brought to Dunfermline.   In 1818 workmen preparing foundations for the New Church came upon a skeleton in a forgotten vault.   The breast-bone had been sawn apart, and, as we were reminded at Melrose, the Bruce's heart was removed from his body, to be borne to the Holy Land by Sir James Douglas.   So, after all those centuries, back into the daylight came the mortality of Scotland's liberator. Now it lies below the carven pulpit and underneath a memorial brass bearing the hero's effigy surrounded by an inscription.

If you feel that a little 'fresh air' is now indicated you

will come across to the gardens of the Glen. Pittencrieff was once an estate within high walls. As a boy
Andrew Carnegie used to scramble up, look over the walls,
and wish it were not private property. Then he went
away to Pittsburg, became a millionaire, came home,
bought Pittencrieff, turned it into a great and lovely
pleasure park, and handed it over, endowed, to his native
city. £3000 is spent annually on music alone. There
are wonderful plant-houses and aviaries, also tea-rooms.
The seventeenth-century mansion is now a museum.
Children and grown-ups rejoice in the perambulating
peacocks and the little grey squirrels that eat from their
hands. Truly a delectable place, attracting thousands
of visitors in the summer.

In Dunfermline we never get far away from the
memory of Andrew Carnegie, yet only a curmudgeon
would hint that he has 'spoiled' the people with his
gifts, educative, artistic, recreative, hygienic. To many
people, I believe, the Birthplace Memorial and the first
home of the man himself, with their relics of his life from
its humble beginning, will prove the feature of Dunfermline. I should add that the Free Library has a
room devoted to Burns.

Loch Leven

From Dunfermline it is only a dozen miles or so to
Loch Leven, in Kinross-shire, where St Serf gave his name
to the isle which bears the ruins of a priory. But even
the devout pilgrim may turn to the smaller isle, with its
memory of Mary Queen of Scots. The tower of the Castle,
her prison for nearly a year, where she signed, perforce, the
Deed of Abdication, still stands four-square to the winds,
and a lovelier situation could not be imagined, though
Mary must have wearied of the view from her window.
In *The Abbot* Sir Walter Scott depicts it all so vividly
that he would be a brave scribe who should now attempt

to describe that last desperate adventure of Mary's, when, on a night in May 1568, with the aid of friends, she escaped from Loch Leven, only to suffer her final defeat, a few days later, in the Battle of Langside, near Glasgow. As they rowed away from the island, having locked the great door of the Castle, they dropped the keys into the Loch. In 1805 two ponderous rusted keys were found among the rushes. You may see them at Abbotsford.

Loch Leven is one of Scotland's most famous angling lochs, and the trout are of fine quality. In one season 50,000 fish have been taken by the rod, weighing nearly 35,000 pounds. The charges for boats and boatmen are not prohibitive, but one should make arrangements in advance.

Near the Loch is the quiet little old-fashioned county town of Kinross, on the Great North Road. It has a trade in linen and woollen fabrics, also a particularly nice hostelry called "The Green Hotel."

Falkland

Falkland is very old—mentioned in records of the twelfth century—albeit its most ancient relic is a stone coffin, which long ago was put to a more cheerful use as a water-trough for cattle. The thrifty Scot was once a reality.

Long before the Palace there was a castle; the foundations of its tower were brought to light by the late Marquis of Bute; and it will be just as well to remember that, if we are shown a place of gloom and told that there, in 1402, the young Duke of Rothesay, the heir apparent, was starved to death, devouring his own flesh in the process. Some one may here remark that one old dungeon is as good as another, as long as it provides the sightseer with the requisite shudder; still, it should be said that the building we see to-day did not come into being till more than a century after the death of the

HERMITAGE CASTLE, ROXBURGHSHIRE

Photo Valentine and Sons, Ltd.

[*Pp.* 117-118]

126

FALKLAND PALACE

Photo Valentine and Sons, Ltd.

luckless Prince, who, by the way, seems to have been a
far from admirable specimen, though quite a 'bright
young person' of his time.   You will find gruesome and
pathetic details in Sir Walter Scott's *The Fair Maid of
Perth*; and if Sir Walter did prefer the version of that
unreliable but entertaining old scribe, Hector Boece, to
that of austere historians, who aver that Rothesay,
though indeed a prisoner, died of dysentery in fairly
comfortable quarters upstairs, who will find fault at
this time of day with a good thrilling tale?   At any rate,
it would be a pity were tradition to be altogether ex-
cluded from Scotland's story, since tradition so often
suggests the spirit of the past in a way that a selection
of desiccated facts rarely does.   Thus, while I may not
believe that poor Rothesay ate his own fingers—a doctor
friend assures me that the thing is absurd—I have no
doubt his enemies would have loved to see him doing it.

I last saw the Palace, in its gardens, on an autumn
afternoon, when its mellowness was further mellowed by
a kindly sunshine; but rather than offer you any small
rhapsody of my own, I shall venture to paraphrase some
words of the late George Innes, a notable Fife journalist,
whose little *Guide* you ought to have if you are taking
Falkland as leisurely as it deserves to be taken.   The
existing building is part of that which once formed three
sides of a square; its front may remind you of Holyroodhouse at Edinburgh.   There is the same old-world
elegance about the trim towers, with their lofty balconies,
which guard the vaulted archway leading to a spacious
courtyard.   Here you are not entering a pathetic ruin, as
you so often do through those old archways of ours.   The
main building was saved from decay and restored by the
Bruces of Falkland early in the nineteenth century; and
great work was done later by Lord Bute, who, as Mr Innes
says, spared neither time nor money "to bring back to
the ancient pile as much as possible of its ancient

grandeur." We may not envy them their creature comforts, though we may covet some of their furnishings; but as illustrations of how the noble were housed in Scotland, three hundred or so years ago, those twelve rooms, some tapestried, some with their ceilings of emblazoned arms or allegories, were well worth preserving. And then there is the Chapel Royal, with its decorated panelled roof and walls, its oaken pulpit and Royal pew, its great screen, richly carven, and its splendid Flemish tapestries, which, if you be fond of such rare things, will charm you with their *naïveté*, as well as their colourings.

At Falkland, as at Holyrood, we are conscious of a stir among the dry bones. Impossible to stand outside that archway without seeing visions.

A winter day in 1542. A small body of horsemen rides drearily up to those twin towers, in which the mortar is not so long dry. One of the horsemen is the King, by whose will the towers were raised, a young man, not yet thirty-one, but weary of the world. Lately troubles have crowded upon him, and now he has come from that crowning shame, the incredible rout of his troops at Solway Moss. The journey has brought him through Edinburgh, and we wonder why he did not seek the refuge of his Palace at Linlithgow, so much nearer, and the comfort of his Queen there. He is sick at heart, probably sick of body as well, for a few days later he takes to his couch, to rise no more. As he lies there his mutterings betray his unhappy thoughts; he dwells on the name of his dear friend Sinclair, keeper of the Royal Standard, captured with it—supreme disaster—in the recent fight. On December 8 comes the news from Linlithgow that the Queen has given birth to a daughter. And thinking of his two little boys, who are dead, he finds neither joy nor hope in the tidings. "It cam' wi' a lass," he murmurs, meaning the crown, "and 'twill gang wi' a lass." A week later he turns his face to the wall.

Twenty years have gone, and we see the lass, now Queen, always at her happiest as a sportswoman, and her retinue, come riding out, with hounds or falcons, or maybe the weapons of archery.   But her good time, like that of her father's, is brief; and it is her son, James VI, who, in his stolid way, gets the fullest royal pleasure out of the Palace—unless his wife, Anne of Denmark, may get just a little more.   The scene is the garden, on a hot summer afternoon.   James—whom, I am sure, the courtiers and servants call 'Jamie' behind his back—is taking a stroll, cogitating, perchance, on the health of Elizabeth of England, when he comes upon Alexander Ruthven enjoying—delightful human touch!—a nap. In these days they dine early and well.   Probably James feels quite sympathetic till he spies on Alexander's person, but partly concealed by his neckwear, a ribbon, in which he recognizes—as James surely would—a recent gift of his own royal self to Anne. So he toddles off — his jealousy is not winged—to make trouble in the Queen's bower, as they call the royal boudoir. As fortune will have it, however, one of the Queen's ladies has been an observer, and now, securing the ribbon, gets there before him; so that on his abruptly demanding a sight of his gift, Anne calmly produces it from among her treasures. There are moments when even a King may pardonably scratch his head.

Falkland's town house, with its spire, was built only in 1802, but there are buildings very much older. Across the street from the Palace stands a house bearing this inscription:

KINGS FALCONER'S HOUSE

All praise to God and thanks to the
most excellent Monarch of Great Britain,
of whose princellie liberalities this is
my portione. . . .

NICHOL MONCRIEF, 1610

I

Next door is the Bruce Arms Hotel, with a stone from an older building inscribed thus:

> J.R. 6 Britain
> God saif ye King of Great Britain
> France and Ireland our soverin,
> for of whose liberalitie
> this house did I edify.

After that I felt like apologizing to Jamie.   Then my glance fell to another stone:

> B.W. 1607.   Contentment is great riches.

As you survey the surrounding scenery, with the Lomond Hills, you will almost certainly ask about the Doric column, nearly 100 feet high, perched on the Mount. It commemorates the name of the gallant Earl of Hope-toun, who, on the death of Sir John Moore at Corunna, took command of the British troops.   The Mount itself is associated with the home of Sir David Lindsay, tutor to James V, and his life-long friend, and, later, a notable pioneer of the Reformation.

St Andrews

We might equally well have started our exploration of Fife from St Andrews, and, should it be your intention to spend some days in the county, I advise you to make it your headquarters.   On the map it looks a little out of the way, yet the roads are so many and so good, the means of transport so abundant, and the attractions within the radius of a few miles so numerous, that you could not have a better daily starting-point.

Many writers about St Andrews begin by calling it "the old grey City"—a description which must surely convey to the distant reader an idea of brooding melancholy.   True, the buildings are grey, more or less—with the unfortunately prominent exception of a modern lapse

into red sandstone—and there are days when the general
aspect can be very grey indeed; but greyness is not an
uncommon characteristic of cities and towns, and the
feature of St Andrews that I would first seek to impress
on you is its brightness.   It is one of the sunniest places
in Scotland, and, I think, the sunniest place in Fife.
Often the rain-clouds seem positively to avoid it; often,
standing under a clear sky, you can see them shedding
their moisture on the valley of the Tay, a few miles away;
half-way out on the golf course you may come to the
fringe of a shower, so that your ball, dry at one hole, is
wet at the next.   The air of spring can be keen—too
keen, maybe, for some people, though invigorating to
most.   At almost any time of year you may have a
visitation of the *haar*—that condensed and chilly breath
of the North Sea, drifting over the land like pale smoke,
giving the ancient towers a strange ghostly look and,
maybe, preventing golf for the time being; but it passes,
and the sun shines again.

   With a less cheerful climate, St Andrews could hardly
have become—to use that most absurd of *clichés*—"the
Golfer's Mecca," nor yet a favourite residence for retired
professional and business men, who continue to play
their daily rounds, regardless of the years.   They see
St Andrews and—live!

   The city stands high on a slight promontory in a wide,
shallow bay—westward, a long, lovely reach of sands,
bordering the Links; eastward, sheer cliffs, with shingly
coves, and dread reefs.   Thinking of the city's fame
through the ages, you will probably be surprised by its
smallness—that is, ignoring the surrounding growths of
recent years—but I do not think you will be disappointed.
It is singularly and almost elegantly compact.   From
the west four roads lead straight to the Cathedral—
South Street, which starts from the only remaining
'port,' or city gate, tree-bordered, and so splendidly

broad that you may view the vista ending in ruined towers, without noticing the shops on either hand; Market Street, modern, undistinguished, but with its memories of the past—mainly, as far as we know, cruel ones; North Street, spacious, uncommercial, austere, beautiful with the old College Tower and Chapel, coldly vacant during the holidays, but a wonderful setting for the scarlet gowns of the students—we don't call them 'undergraduates' in Scotland—who in other ways give colour to the life of St Andrews; and lastly The Scores— *i.e.*, 'scaurs,' meaning cliffs—with modern terraces, mansions, and schools. Long ago The Scores was known as the Swallowgait and Castlegait, while the eastern part of North Street was appropriately called the Fishergait. Cutting those main streets run others, mostly narrow, sometimes mere passages, called 'wynds.'

This compactness means that you can see St Andrews in a day, though you will want several days to become acquainted.

St Andrew did not become Scotland's Patron Saint till the eighth century, previous to which veneration was paid to St Peter. There is a pretty story of St Regulus, in the fourth century, escaping from Patras in Achaia, with certain bones of St Andrew, and after a voyage of many months, landing at Muckross, afterward known as Kilrymont; but it would seem more likely that the relics were brought from Hexham Abbey, by Bishop Acca, about 730, to Kilrymont, which then became St Andrews; and that about the same time Angus, King of the Picts, heard a heavenly voice say: "I am Andrew, the Apostle of Christ, come to defend thee against thine enemies. . . . Take care to dedicate a tenth of thine inheritance to God Almighty and his Apostle, St Andrew." To some of my readers, I fear, there may be something highly suggestive of the 'canny Scot' in the saint's admonition.

It is usual, I believe, for the visitor to begin his pere-
grinations at the west end of South Street, but I have
always preferred to start in North Street, because there
I can step into the Past, which is the real St Andrews,
without the distractions of the Present.

The College Tower and Chapel are the features of the
street.   St Salvator's College was founded, in 1450, by
Bishop Kennedy, grandson of Robert III.   He was
Scotland's Chancellor and virtually her ruler for twenty-
five years, rescuing finally the Stuart dynasty from the
power of the Douglases.   The original College buildings
have gone, but their successors looking down on the
grassy quadrangle have an antique aspect; in the labora-
tories the Inquiring Spirit remains, discovering more and
more things in heaven and earth than ever were dreamed
of in the old Bishop's philosophy.   The buildings have
been officially known as the United College since 1747,
when its revenues and those of the now extinct St
Leonard's College were incorporated.

The square Tower, brooding in peace and dignity
to-day, has witnessed many a spectacle, sombre, colourful, merry, horrible—processions of monks in black or
grey, pageants of ecclesiastics in gorgeous vestments,
citizens on holiday, prisoners on the march, cruelty and
death.   In 1547 a cannon was fired from its roof at the
Castle, in which John Knox was one of the garrison.   In
front of the gateway, Patrick Hamilton for six mortal
hours sustained the torture of fire before he lifted up his
charred hands to let them fall for the last time.   His
initials mark the spot on the pavement.   The unresting
spirit of the friar who, under pressure, played the part of
his 'accuser,' still nightly haunts, lamenting, the ruins of
the Monastery, which you will see in South Street—at the
point where most of the buses start to-day.   Time enough
to declare your unbelief after you have spent five minutes
there, alone, say, at two o'clock on a black winter morning.

The Chapel, with its resemblances to St George's, Windsor, has lately been restored—not that it had reached the ruinous state. It was, of course, duly 'purged' and plundered by the Reformation mob, and some things can never be replaced. Where, for example, are the tall silver image of the Saviour, "with a great loose diadem set with precious stones," the crosses of gold set with pearls, the chalices, the monstrance? These and many other treasures disappeared in those wild times, when even the lead from the pious founder's coffin was purloined. Yet it may be that they, as well as those of the Cathedral, were reverently hidden away ere the mob broke in; there are still people who cherish hopes of their discovery, remembering that the maces of the University were lost for more than a hundred years.

In 1773 the vaulted stone roof was found to be unsafe, and it was decided to substitute a timber one. Whether by accident, or to save trouble, is an open question, but the whole mass, being loosed from the walls, was allowed to crash. The new oaken roof of that period is the one we stand under in the very beautiful chapel of to-day, with its great screen of carven stone. Everything possible has been done to have the workmanship of to-day in keeping with that of Bishop Kennedy's time. The fresh decorations have been inspired by the ancient; the 'newness,' unavoidable in so many directions, strikes no jarring note of modernity. After you have looked around, your interest will, I think, become concentrated on two things—Bishop Kennedy's tomb and John Knox's pulpit. The tomb, above the black marble slab, is an amazing piece of elaborate and delicate stone-work. One guesses how dreadfully it must have suffered from the falling roof and the rains while the Chapel lay open to the weather; yet it is still a thing of grace.

While restoration was in progress, in 1930, workmen

ST ANDREWS: CHURCH OF ST SALVATOR, NOW THE
UNIVERSITY CHAPEL

Photo Will F. Taylor   134

ON THE LINKS AT ST ANDREWS

Photo Valentine and Sons, Ltd.

came upon the vault beneath the tomb, which was opened in the presence of the Principal, Sir James Irvine, whose rule has been so happy and fortunate for the College. It had been opened in 1683, when several silver maces were found, and twice during the nineteenth century. On the first of the later occasions the floor was found to have been torn up, and the bones of the old Bishop were scattered. They were gathered together and placed in a coffin, presumably a cheap one, after a cast of the skull had been taken. Twenty years later they were placed in a new coffin, the other having given way. Now they have been reverently enclosed in a casket of lasting nature, and the vault has been sealed, in the hope that they will rest undisturbed till the end of all things. The Bishop, it would seem, was a tall man, who had once broken his collar-bone.

John Knox's pulpit has in its time undergone many alterations and repairs, but the carving remains finely preserved. It used to stand in the Parish Kirk, in South Street. There you may picture Knox, in the last year of his life, the flesh very weak, the spirit strong as ever, being helped along to the Kirk and lifted up to the pulpit —you may picture him leaning heavily on the desk, but ere he had done with his sermon becoming, as the Rev. James Melville tells in his *Diary*, "so active and vigorous, that he was like to ding that pulpit to blads"—*i.e.*, bang it to bits—"and fly out of it!" He still 'walks'—I have a sober friend who has seen him—in St Andrews. Well, his was a personality that might well survive.

The other great building in North Street is a strikingly new one—the Graduation Hall, presented to the University by Dr and Mrs James Younger. At first it suggested a youthful, if majestic, intruder among greybeards; but time will mellow its white stone, and criticism be lost in gratitude, for the Hall was very badly needed. The still larger new building behind is the men-students' residence, St Salvator's Hall, ideally appointed within—

mainly the gift of that princely giver, Dr Harkness, to whom is owing also the restoration of the Chapel.

A little farther on we turn down a short street and come upon the Castle. It is a ruinous old place, though much care has been taken to keep the walls as we see them. Only the front wall is intact. The distant building on the verge of the sheer cliff is the remnant of that which withstood the gales of centuries. Before entering the gateway look up at the windows. . . . It is March 1, 1545, and David Beaton, the astute, scheming, feared, abhorred, luxury-loving Cardinal, sits at one of them. The Castle at this time commands a clear view of the Cathedral, but the Cardinal's gaze is on something nearer—a stake and faggots, to which the preacher, George Wishart, is presently led, bound, to be burned. In the smoke rising so heavily Beaton sees only the end of his enemy; yet there, too, is the beginning of his own end. Three months pass. It is May 29, just after dawn. Repairs are being made in the Castle, and the gate is opened, the drawbridge lowered, to admit the workmen. Norman Leslie slips in with them and asks for the Cardinal. Melville of Halhill follows, then young Kirkcaldy of Grange, and John Leslie of Parkhill, and others. The doorkeeper becomes suspicious. John Leslie quietly stabs him and drops his corpse into the moat. The servants awake, but they are unarmed and unnerved. The Cardinal, too, awakes, hears the disturbance, scents danger, and seeks the secret postern. Kirkcaldy is already there, sword naked. Back to his chamber flees the Cardinal, and with his attendant strengthens the stout door with furniture. The visitors threaten to burn it down. A brazier is brought. The smoke reaches the Cardinal's nostrils. Eventually the door is opened, and he is seen sitting in his chair. He cries: "I am a priest; ye will not slay me!" But they do slay him, and afterward they hang out on the wall what is left of him for

the people to see. And the people, led by the Provost,
stare fearfully awhile, then go softly to their homes.

Now let us go in. Here was a castle, or bishop's
palace, of a sort, as early as 1200, which must have had
successors before this castle of the sixteenth century.
One reads of not a few additions, alterations, and repairs;
but it was in a bad way toward the end of the seventeenth century, when stones were taken from its walls
to repair St Salvator's.

There is a chamber on either side of the entrance, each
with a pit cut into the rock. These pits were unknown
till 1905, while the embrasures in either side of the gateway were not found till 1920. Even the great well,
50 feet deep, in the centre of the spacious courtyard lay
hidden till 1857—so who dare say what discoveries may
not yet be made? A pleasant place to linger in is the
grassy courtyard on a summer day, the blue North Sea
the background to those shattered grey walls. Here, in
the wall of the west tower, are five steps of the staircase
leading to the Cardinal's rooms; there, at the south-west
corner, is the fragment of a tower with walls 15 feet thick
—once, according to the late Dr Hay Fleming, whose
handbook you should have, one of the very stoutest
towers in Scotland; and over yonder is the Sea Tower,
with its fearsome Bottle Dungeon.

You must, of course, see the Dungeon. I first saw it
when I was a small boy, and I still remember clutching
my father's hand, for in the gloom the bent and aged
cicerone made me think of a gnome. He lowered a
lighted candle into the pit, reciting the Dungeon's horrid
story, and when my father interrupted him with a mild
question, he had to begin all over again. The Dungeon's
diameter at the surface is less than five feet, and it
expands to fifteen at the bottom, the depth being over
twenty feet. No possible escape for the poor victims of
political, religious, or personal hate! In this place they

set the body of the Cardinal, pickled in salt—and here
it lay for seven months, but whether it was afterward
given kindly burial or cast on a midden, nobody seems to
know for certain. Fallen indeed was that mighty one!
Wicked as the man surely was, Knox dishonoured himself in his glee over the murder. One may wonder if
he ever stole in beside the poor, quiet, disfigured thing in
the Sea Tower. He was captured in the castle when, a
year later, it fell to the French gunners, and the dead was,
in a measure, avenged. On a fine summer day Knox,
from the deck of the ship bearing him away to slave in
the French galleys, looked back at the Cathedral, saw
its roof gleaming in the sunshine, and prophesied that
he would return to " ding it doon."

The castle has another 'sensation'—the Subterranean
Passage, unearthed in 1879. It was not long after that
that the aged 'gnome' led the same small boy, each bearing a guttering candle, crouching and crawling, through
that burrow in the solid rock. Electric torches have been
invented since then, but even now it is an extraordinary
experience, including the descent into the mysterious
chamber at the end, during which one may imagine
the strangest things.

From the Castle, carrying on along the cliff, we come
to the Kirkhill. Here, in the shadow of the Abbey wall,
are the few remains of the oldest building in St Andrews
—an early Celtic church. An earlier church, says
tradition, stood down yonder on a rock near the end of
the breakwater, till the North Sea took a higher level
and covered it. Its successor may have been erected
here, twelve hundred years ago, and there was a church
on the hill until the Reformation. Cists and skeletons, a
Celtic cross, coloured tiles, and stained glass have been
found in the earth around the ruins; but now, for a
moment, I would ask you to turn to a modern, living
picture.

If you are in St Andrews on a fine Sunday in a University term, come to the Kirkhill immediately after morning service. It is a custom of the students, coming out of Chapel, to parade along North Street, over the Kirkhill, down to the harbour, and out to the end of the breakwater. Grey stone, blue water, the long procession of scarlet and black gowns—an episode in colour to remember.

Now, stepping through the doorway in that ancient wall, we find ourselves in the great burial ground containing the Tower of St Regulus and the Cathedral. I regret these frequent encounters with mortality, but there is no way of avoiding them in our present quest. "What a ruin!" you may say of the Cathedral, and be astonished to learn that yonder plain but noble square tower of St Regulus was standing up to the gales for two centuries before the Cathedral was consecrated. But why 'St Regulus'? Nobody knows. St Regulus belonged to the fourth century—the same St Regulus who, according to the rejected tradition, brought the relics of St Andrew to Scotland. There may still be people who would have us to believe that he erected the Tower fifteen hundred years ago; an enthusiast for antiquity went even farther in painting a picture entitled *The Landing of St Regulus at St Andrews*, his tower having arrived before him; and there are others who give it a date between 970 and 990. But the experts are pretty well agreed that it was set up no earlier than the twelfth century, which makes its building coeval with the founding of its grander neighbour. Even so, it is not the least of the seven wonders of St Andrews, having survived a thousand hurricanes, not to mention a fire in its interior. According to a drawing of John Knox's day, it once carried a steeple.

So long did it take to raise the vast Cathedral that on the day of its consecration, in the summer of 1318, a

goodly part of it was a full century old; the wall on
the east was weathered and darkened, that on the west
pale in comparison. At the ceremony King Robert the
Bruce and all Scotland's notable men were present. But
though the building itself was complete, the decorating
and beautifying went on with the years, interrupted and
partly undone by a fire in 1378. Some one, possibly the
person responsible, declared that the fire was caused by
a jackdaw, which carried a piece of burning wood to
its nest in the roof. The explanation is certainly more
credible than that of the domestic servant who saw the
jug jump off the shelf. In its prime it must have been a
magnificent sight—its length 335 feet; width, including
side aisles, 63 feet—with its central tower and eastern and
western turrets standing up in the sunshine. And what
a picture when they loomed, as their ruins sometimes
loom to-day, out of the moving clouds of *haar*. The
interior can only be faintly imagined, faintly as came the
light through the lovely carven windows with their
stained glass, many fragments of which remain to tell
the tale. You may see them in the Museum close by.

A little boy of eight, David II was crowned in the
Cathedral, along with his betrothed, Johanna, sister of
Edward III, and on that occasion there was brave feasting on the countryside. Among the dainties consumed
were 6000 eels—Scots people won't eat eels nowadays—
from St Andrews, and a couple of porpoises from Crail,
down the coast. Nearly two hundred years later James
V knelt before the High Altar with Marie of Lorraine.
But the Cathedral has its ghosts too. Patrick Hamilton
was tried and condemned in its shadows; so was George
Wishart; so also, in 1558, was Walter Myln, last of
the martyrs under the Papacy. He was 82, yet they
burned him.

Only a little longer and the last Mass had been celebrated in that temple of holiness and profanity. But

Knox did not 'ding it doon,' though he could have done
so had he wished. It seems certain that, whatever the
mob did in the way of damage and desecration, the
Cathedral of St Andrews was not destroyed, but that it
perished through neglect.

South of the Cathedral were once the domestic buildings looking upon the Cloister Garth, the Prior's house
standing a little apart. The Chapter House is to be recognized by the seats in the wall and several stone coffins,
and beside it is the Museum.

We leave by the west gate, opposite Dean's Court,
once the Archdeacon's Inn, mentioned in Parliament, in
1612, as the 'ancient manse.' To the left is one of the
antique beauties of St Andrews, the Pends. 'Pend'
means a covered passage or vault; we can imagine the
groined roof from the traces on the walls. It is supposed
that strangers and pilgrims waited in the shelter while
their requests for admission to the city were under consideration. A guest-house stood close by. At night it
is a bit gloomy between those lofty walls, and if it be
after midnight you may meet the Headless Nun. But
don't go looking for her. She may raise her veil, and
then, in the modern phrase, your number is up.

We are now at the end of South Street. The narrow
stretch immediately before us can have changed very
little since the days when Mary Queen of Scots cantered
along it on her way to the hunt. Mary liked St Andrews;
she made holiday here before the fateful clouds became
too heavy. Here is the house called 'Queen Mary's,'
where she is thought to have sojourned—it is not the
only house in South Street with that tradition. She left
no memorials, but one of her 'Four Maries' still visits a
house, which we shall pass presently, and which I shall
not indicate. 'Queen Mary's' now belongs to the Girls'
School, one of whose houses is just round the corner on
the left—'St Leonard's.' We can go round and peep

between iron bars—not into the school—but into the gloom of the long-abandoned St Leonard's Chapel. There are stones inside to interest the antiquary, and the key may, I believe, be got from the janitor at St Salvator's. The building—now a private residence—close to the chapel was once St Leonard's College. Long before that there was a hostel for pilgrims, but when pilgrimage became 'not what it used to be,' the authorities turned it into a nunnery for the aged. But, alas! the old bodies " behaved themselves " so badly that another change was necessary, and it was transformed into the College. George Buchanan, tutor to James VI, lived there, as Principal. It has undergone many changes since then, when the students had to get to their rooms along an outside gallery, there being no stairs inside. About the middle of last century the whole front was remodelled.

Coming out again into South Street, we see it expand to its splendid breadth. On the left is a row of tall houses, ancient, but modernized within and used as self-contained dwellings. In the rear each of them possesses a long, lovely old garden. Some years ago I spent the summer in one of them—said to have been occupied once by Cardinal Beaton's secretary, who must have been a fortunate person. The house is partly a tower, which contains two spacious circular rooms, their windows looking out upon the gardens. The one thing lacking was a ghost. From the study window over South Street I could see the oldest dwelling-house in St Andrews, once a hostel of the Knights of St John, now the home of a professor. It shares the traditional honour of having harboured Queen Mary. It is worth looking up at, if only to see how the positions of the windows have at different times been changed.

We come to St Mary's College, its outer aspect not very inspiring—but, please, turn through the archway into the quadrangle. South Street, being a main road, as well as the chief shopping centre, is often busy and at times noisy with traffic. To turn from it into St Mary's gives, if in a small way, the sensation experienced by stepping from Fleet Street into Fountain Court—out of the workaday racket into the peace of the past. The most ancient-looking thing in the quadrangle is a hawthorn tree, carefully, I dare say lovingly, supported by the hand of man with props. Every year I dread to find it gone; yet every year there I find it, looking like a very old lady whose limbs may be failing, but whose spirit remains hopeful and undaunted. They will tell you it was planted by Queen Mary, nearly four centuries ago.

The Town Church, founded in 1412, altered at different periods, was finally restored and largely rebuilt in 1909. It was in the old place that Knox was like to fly out of the pulpit, but he was not the only great figure to occupy it. The best remembered, though not the best beloved, name is that of Archbishop Sharp. "No man," says Mr Wilkie, in his *History of Fife*, "could possibly be as black as Sharp was painted"; but neither was he the man that his monument in the Town Church declares him to have been. He is sufficiently condemned by the fact that to serve personal ambition he betrayed the great cause he had been chosen to represent. On May 3, 1679, fresh from that betrayal, he was on his way home, with his daughter, to St Andrews and triumph, when his coach, after pistol-shots had been fired into it, was stopped on Magus Muir, a few miles from his destination, by a band of twelve men, in whose hearts seems to have been concentrated the hate of all Fife and much of Scotland. Here, in the written words of one of them, is how they dealt with him:

James Russell ran to the coach door and desired the bishop to come forth, Judas. He answered, he never wronged man. . . . John Balfour on horseback, said : Sir, God is our witness that it is not for any wrong thou hast

done to me, but because thou hast been a murderer of
many a poor soul in the kirk of Scotland, a betrayer of the
church, and an open enemy and persecutor of Jesus Christ
and his members—and therefore thou shalt die!

At last they got him, already sore wounded, to come
forth.

Falling upon his knees, he said, For God's sake save my
life ; his daughter falling on her knees, begging his life also.
But they told him that he should die, and desired him to
repent and make ready for death.

And then—well, among other things, they "haked his
head in pieces." And then—most horrible touch of all
—"they went to prayer," and returned thanks.

Perhaps you will think the black and pale marble
monument of the Archbishop, made in Holland, and
erected by his son, a disfigurement of the beautiful
church; many people do; but the late Dr Hay Fleming
gave the best of reasons for its retention in a Presbyterian place of worship: "More than a monument to
an Archbishop's memory, it is a monument to Tolera-
tion."

On the other side of the street the ruined chapel is all
that survives of the Blackfriars Monastery. It stands
in front of the Madras College, a school founded a century
ago, on the fortune of Dr Bell, a son of St Andrews.

South Street ends at the West Port, originally a barrier
with a gate, not a triumphal arch, though as such a recent
visitor explained it to a friend. At one time the houses
were built against it on either side; there were no side
arches; and a guard was in attendance. Portions of it
must be very old, but it has suffered rebuildings and
renovations, while the carving overhead on the outside,
and that of the city arms on the inside, belong to the
nineteenth century.

And now, though I have left out scores of interesting

things, let us turn from the city, go down to the sea, and get rid of the dusts of the past. A few minutes' walk, and we are looking over the Links and the sands.

It is easy to understand the quickening pulse of the golfer who approaches these Links for the first time. Since my small boyhood, when I looked with awe at Tom Morris, I have always regarded that unimposing but dignified building, the Club House of the Royal and Ancient, with something more than mere respect. In those days the members played in scarlet jackets, since when no pullovers have ever made such rich pictures on the greens.

Then, too, there was but one course, known to-day as "the Old." Now there are also "the New," "the Eden," and "the Jubilee," the last, I believe, being sometimes called "the Duffers'." Everybody, of course, wants to play on "the Old," which in summer means a ballot every evening. "The Old" starts from the Club House; the others from spots on the farther side of the Swilcan Burn, flowing so gently over its rich mud under a Roman bridge—of the eighteenth century. That long open stretch of turf, whin-bushes, and dunes, is a sight indeed for town-tired eyes, and beyond it are the Sidlaws above the Tay, and beyond them, afar, the Grampian Range—most glorious to spy on a clear winter day. Perhaps I should mention that there is no Sunday play— "the greens need a rest, as well as the folk," quoth old Tom Morris; but there is no law against your walking out on the course, finest of promenades, while explaining fully to your companion how you came to take eight to the fourth hole on Saturday.

Here there are two public putting-greens, quite level, and there is a third on the other side of the town, beyond the harbour. The Ladies' Club green, all miniature mountains and perfect turf, is situated a little way out on the Links.

K

For sea-bathing St Andrews offers abundant facilities
—pools, with dressing-rooms, under the cliffs, bathing-
machines on the sands. For tennis the same applies,
and the Scottish Hard Courts Tournament is held here
annually in August.

The malignities of the Old St Andrews are as lifeless
as its ruins. Among its places of worship, representing
most Presbyterian denominations, we find also an
Episcopal and a Roman Catholic Church, the latter on
the edge of the cliff, within a stone's throw of the Protestant Martyrs' Monument. And this reminds me to
counsel you, whatever your leanings, to go and at least
look at the little All Saints' in North Castle Street—the
gift of Mrs James Younger. It is sheer beauty; the
stains of the past are not on it.

The Countryside

I am hoping you may have time to see something
of the countryside. St Andrews, for all its antiquities,
is new-fashioned and cosmopolitan; it is certainly far less
representative of Fife than are the smaller places. Inland,
much may be seen in an afternoon's run. The network
of roads gives a wide choice, though, for myself, I should
select the following: Out to Dunino, with its old
sequestered church and, near by, stones suggesting sun-
worship; round by Cameron—whence St Andrews gets its
water—there is trout-fishing in the reservoir; on, past
the Peat Inn and Baldinnie, to Ceres—a charming small
antique set in a hollow, with village green and a bridge
once crossed by men bound for Bannockburn; and then
to Cupar, on the Eden, in sylvan surroundings, capital
of Fife, and seat of its ancient courts of justice. Cupar
has what the Scot calls a douce — meaning sweetly
sedate — look. Used to its own importance, it seems
to assume that you will recognize that importance as
a matter of course. From Cupar we may return to

St Andrews by Dura Den, 2½ miles east—a little woody ravine, which is generally regarded as the beauty spot of East Fife.   The geologist is intrigued by its yellow sand-stone and the quite extraordinary numbers of fossil fish, perfectly preserved, therein.   After that we turn into the St Andrews road—note the crossroads at Pitscottie—and presently pass Magus Muir, with its cairn, where the Archbishop was done to death.

Or we may return by Leuchars, where the Norman Church, still comely in spite of additions, looks down, a grey old dreamer, on the spick-and-span aerodromes of the Royal Air Force, and stands unheeding under the roaring bombers.   It is amazing how its decorations and embellishments, floral and grotesque, have survived the neglect of man and the violence of nature.   The original church must have been about 400 years old when the belfry, by no means an eyesore in itself, was stuck on, at the expense of the ancient roof.

We approach St Andrews by Guardbridge, so called from the bridge built by Bishop Wardlaw 500 years ago, and still the only way of crossing the river.   It is so narrow that there are nooks for foot passengers to stand in while a vehicle passes over; but it is so unusual an old bridge, that if you are in a car or bus you do not mind waiting your turn.   Time was when a stout chain forbade entrance till the stranger paid toll or supplied credentials.   The old Bishop knew what he was doing. If unwelcome persons came along and insisted on cross-ing, they could jolly well flounder through the river, while the guardians treated them as targets.

The East Neuk

Actually the Neuk is the point, Fife Ness; but the name is commonly applied to a portion of the southern promontory, on which is set a series of little old towns—the most characteristic feature of Fife.   Most of the towns are ancient Royal Burghs, so you must never call them villages. One of them, Kilrenny, got the distinction through a mistake, abandoned it in 1672, and got it again in 1707—through another mistake; but all came right in the end. Crail is the first of them. The road from St Andrews goes over the hill, not far from the sea, through Boarhills and Kingsbarns, which once deserved their names, and at the end of ten miles, down into Crail, which means 'rocky cliff.'

Crail holds its charter from Robert the Bruce, and possesses two Papal Bulls, beautifully engrossed, of Julian II and Leo X. Like the other Neuk towns, it has been laid out anyhow. The early Fifers planted their houses where they listed, and left the streets to arrange themselves, which may strike you as rather a delightful change from the formality of St Andrews. Yes, Crail is old; its folk were doing business with the Netherlands a thousand years ago. Of the beginnings of its church we do not know anything definite; in 1517 it was endowed as a collegiate church, and its western tower with the short steeple still looks down on the Marketgait. Its bell is dated 1620; but the bell in the Town Hall, with its foreign-looking tower, is a century older; there is a suspicion that it once belonged to the kirk. The curfew, as in St Andrews, is rung in Crail. Built into the church wall, where was once a porch, is an object much older—a stone carved with the effigies of animals and birds and crawling things. Once it stood inside the church; then it helped to pave one of the passages till, in 1857, a Mr Stuart, an archæologist of his day—probably regarded as a freak then—appealed successfully for its better preservation.

Not so very long ago Scots folk were reputed to possess a natural inclination for relaxing themselves among the tombs—even youth did its courting there; but now there are picture-houses. Still, for memorials in stone I can think of no country churchyard more satisfying than

Crail's. Near the entrance you will find another sort of memorial, the celebrated 'Blue Stone of Crail,' which came from the devil himself. It seems that he was picnicing on the May Island, out yonder, gloating on the ruins of those very early holy places laid low by the pagan Norsemen, when, his glance having strayed to the Kirk of Crail, he took a shot at it 'for fun'—and, if you don't believe it, look at his thumb-mark on the boulder. But Crail's 'Blue Stone' does not appear to have retained any infernal influence. In bygone times Crail folk about to leave home would kiss it to their safe return; and there is no law against kissing it to-day, if you are leaving your heart, or some of it, in Crail.

Crail has a golf course of its own, but you may go beyond it and find a better one at Balcomie, on Fife Ness, less than two miles distant. There also is the grim Tower of Balcomie; and on the way you will see another Celtic Cross, which, like that in the kirk wall, may have been one of the crosses marking the boundaries of the place of sanctuary allowed by the church.

Four miles south, *via* Kilrenny, is Anstruther—that is, Anstruther-Easter and Anstruther-Wester, Royal Burghs, though not nearly so old as Crail, divided, rather than separated, by a small river of the queer, sad name of Dreel. Anstruther-Easter sits cheek by jowl with Cellardyke, another Royal Burgh and fishing community. 'Anstruther' being somewhat of 'a mouthful,' the natives sensibly call it 'Anster.' At one time the populations of the three towns, now municipally one, stretching nearly a mile and a half along the coast, must have lived on and by the sea; and though to-day they have their land industries, the fine harbour is still an important East Coast fishing centre. A compliment to the sea may be noticed in Anstruther-Wester, where the walls of several houses have been covered in dainty, if laborious, fashion with shells. As a boy of eighteen,

Robert Louis Stevenson sojourned here, dreaming his dreams, while he was supposed to be assisting in the engineering of the new harbour. At all events, in his *Random Memories* he wrote, "History broods over that part of the world like the easterly *haar*," and he calls St Andrews "an ineffectual seat of learning." He was not, one fears, too happy in Fife.

Anstruther-Wester's kirk has suffered not so much from Reformation as from restoration; Anstruther-Easter's, though less stricken in years, looks aged enough, and rather odd too, with the little gable of the stairway turret sticking out from the top of the square tower under the spire surmounted by chanticleer. At the harbour, looking down on the Town Cross, there are lofty houses with something of a foreign look, and we are reminded of the long-ago connections with the Flemings and Hollanders.

If you go down to the harbour in the season you will probably notice the names on the fishing craft. Some are homely, others extremely classical. There was once an East Coast skipper who called his boat *Ajax*, which sounded so sweetly to the ears of another skipper that he rechristened his boat *Bjax*.

Beyond Anstruther's golf course upon the cliffs above the Billowness—a sandy patch among reefs, where they bathe—we find Pittenweem, yet another Royal Burgh and fisher haven. 'Weem' means 'cave,' and Pittenweem probably means 'hamlet by the cave.' The actual cave, or 'cove,' as the folk call it, is associated with St Fillan, but was probably used as an abode by other anchorites. It is deep, with two branches, and has a natural fresh water supply. Pittenweem's own particular saint was, however, Adrian, or Odhrain, who came over from the May Island and in due season was martyred: he is to be seen in his boat on the Burgh's Seal. The town, which consists of three streets connected by lanes, had a Priory as early as 1114, but the ivied ruins are those

of a less ancient erection. Many of the old stones went
to the building of the dower-house of the Earls of Kellie,
now the Episcopal rectory. The Parish Church was
much altered some fifty years ago; the seventeenth-
century tower remains, the most notable thing about it
being a chamber in the base, with a barred window, once
used as a place of confinement. I never pass by without
seeing the ghastly face of Janet Corphat, who, being suspected of witchcraft, was most shockingly maltreated and
murdered by the mob.

A more cheerful memory is that of Charles II's visit, on
his way to Anstruther. His grandfather, James VI, had
done the town a good turn by handing over to it the great
house of the Monastery, and had further gratified with
his sympathetic interest the inhabitants, who were then
gravely afflicted by a plague of witches; so all Pittenweem turned out in its best garments; and all the men
who had weapons furbished them up and displayed them,
in a guard of honour; and flags were flown from the
Church tower; and an *al fresco* banquet was spread for
the Merry Monarch, who must have been merrier than
ever, if he took all that was offered—"great bunns of
white flour baked with sugar and spice," ten gallons of ale,
and, if you please, seven different kinds of wine! And,
to finish up, they gave him a salute of six-and-thirty
cannons, 'all shot at once!' One could do with lots
more of such gay little incidents in Scotland's story. It
was, I am almost sure, a Pittenweem man of a much later
generation who was so taken with the bright scarlet and
white of a new barber's pole that he determined to apply
the same scheme of decoration to his cottage door;
wherefore he entered the shop and demanded a pot of
"strippit pent"—*i.e.*, striped paint. Before we pass on
let us take a look at the snug harbour—which reminds
me of something I meant to say when we started on our
tour of these little old towns: If ever you feel in want of

a moral tonic, get into talk with one of these East Coast fishermen. They are still a people living apart from the pettifoggery of modern life.

A mile or so down the coast St Monans clings to the hillside around its harbour. It is not Royal; it has more legend than history; but no place on the East Coast is quite so well beloved of the artist. Its cruciform church, which has been called a gem of middle-pointed Gothic art, is its landmark, standing on a rocky mound within reach of the sea-spray lashed up by the gales. There it was raised in 1362; nearly two centuries later it suffered severely at the hands of English invaders, but the original squat tower and choir remain among the rebuilt portions. Inside there are an ancient tomb, with a finely carved canopy, and, suspended from the roof in one of the transepts, the model of a three-masted ship, made and gifted by one, Captain Marr, a hundred years ago. Such votive offerings from seafarers were not unusual in the old days, and there is something touching in the thought of rough hands working tenderly on fragile spars and intricate rigging, all to the glory of God. Not far away, on the shore, is the ruin of Newark Castle—there are several Newarks in Scotland, the word meaning simply 'new work,' in the building sense—once the home of Sir David Leslie, one of the great Scots soldiers of the seventeenth century. The castle was still a home in the next century; therein, after the Jacobite Rebellion of 1715, a fugitive, young Lindsay, of Balcarres, an estate some miles inland, was concealed and secretly nourished by a maiden, who did not seem to mind being chaffed on her unprecedented capacity for food.

On a level sandy stretch stands Elie, which to most people to-day signifies golf, and nothing but golf. It has the reputation of a very healthy climate, especially in winter, and its sea-bathing—in summer—is an attraction. If Shakespeare did not invent Macduff, then it was from Earlsferry, next door, that the Thane of Fife made his escape, while at his castle, such as it was, a few miles away, his good wife, in order to give him a start, humbugged Macbeth. Anyway, the cave yonder is called Macduff's.

Largo's chief romantic interests are in its having been the home of that famous fifteenth-century sea-dog, Sir Andrew Wood—his look-out tower still stands in Upper Largo—and of Alexander Selkirk, whose experiences gave Defoe the material for *Robinson Crusoe*. Selkirk's house, which he bought for his father's declining years—he died himself at 47, a lieutenant in the Navy—has disappeared, but the place of it is marked, and there is a bronze statue to his memory. For the antiquarian the neighbourhood has its attractions. Green Largo Law, which rises nearly 1000 feet, a mile or so inland, was a place of pagan rites, while over at Lundin, with its very old square tower, are three great standing-stones, memorials of the sun-worshippers. This Law, like other Laws, has its tradition of hidden treasure—in its own case a gold mine—and it is not wise to make a point of disbelieving all legends. Only three miles away is Norrie's Law, to which was long attached the tale of an ancient chieftain's burial in his silver armour. Early in the nineteenth century a tinker thought he would have a dig, and lo and behold! he was rewarded with a quantity of Celtic ornaments. He got most of them safely to the melting-pot, then celebrated his good fortune in another sort of pot—and betrayed himself.

Now I am going to leave it to you, whether we cut back across country to St Andrews, or you carry on along the Forth shores to the point of our entering Fife, North Queensferry. If you decide to carry on, let me commend for your guidance *The Fringes of Fife*. The author, Mr John Geddie, explored the whole coast of Fife, and he did it on foot. He can, therefore, tell you all about

Leven, with its shell-white beach; Wemyss, with its caves, where Mary first met Darnley; business-like Kirkcaldy, with its four-mile main street and fragrance of linoleum, where Michael Scott, 'the wizard,' pursued science in the thirteenth century, and where Thomas Carlyle taught mathematics, poor soul, in the nineteenth; Kinghorn, where Alexander III, galloping home through the dark to his dear lady, was thrown and killed; Burntisland, where the astute burghers induced the invading Cromwell to repair their harbour and pave their streets; bonnie Aberdour, with its sands and children playing; Inverkeithing, where they break up ships that have served their day. . . . Yes, Mr Geddie will tell you all about them, and also many things which I have been unable to mention on our journey.

CHAPTER V

GLASGOW—THE TROSSACHS—THE CLYDE

AN American professor who, in 1819, sojourned a few days in Glasgow, recorded his warm appreciation of its preachers and teachers, its gas-works and Lunatic Asylum, and then departed, with a kind word for its hospitality. Twenty years later, an English lady, who spent a couple of months among the beauties of the Clyde, and wrote an enthusiastic little book about them, allotted but three of its 105 pages to Glasgow, and devoted them to rhapsodies on the Blind Asylum and the Necropolis, thereby, apparently, exhausting the city's charms. And the other day in London a man, to whom I had just been introduced, said pleasantly: "Ah, Glasgow! Always raining there—isn't it?"

I admit that the foregoing is not calculated to promote thrills of anticipation; at the same time, it gives me an opening, just as the *savant*, about to lecture on the lobster, was given an opening by the definition of the crustacean in Dr Johnson's *Dictionary*—"A red fish, which swims backwards." Having quoted it, "Gentlemen," the *savant* proceeded, "that is an admirable description, except that the lobster is not red, is not a fish, and does not swim backwards." Similarly, Glasgow is not essentially a joyless city; it is not lacking in the lighter attractions; and its rainfall, while healthily abundant, is not extravagantly so.

Glasgow has many memories, but most of them are in the air. Seldom can we say, as we can say so often in Edinburgh, or St Andrews: "Here is the house in which such and such an event took place." Gone, for instance, from the High Street, or thereabouts, is the mansion in which Darnley fell ill during the last days of 1566, and to which came Mary to tend him, and to persuade him to go with her to Edinburgh. That is one of the most mysterious episodes in Scottish history. Why was she so anxious to have him in the capital? Until the hour of her arrival at his bedside they had been bitterly estranged. A little while ago, he had sulked in his chamber at Stirling Castle, while, with splendour and ceremony, in the chapel, they christened his son, prince of two kingdoms. What, then, passed in the Glasgow mansion? Did Mary make it up with her husband, or was she dissembling? What was in her dark mind as they started, that winter day, in "ane chariott" upon the journey east —his last? Did she know—did she not know—of the things being planned for him at Kirk o' Field House, outside the walls of Edinburgh, where he was done to death nine days later? Stones keep their secrets, yet had the mansion been preserved, some of us might sense within its walls that same sinister thing which lurks in the Queen's chamber in Holyroodhouse.

The two most notable antiquities are the Cathedral and a fifteenth-century mansion, known as Provand's Lordship. The Cathedral marks the place where Glasgow had its beginning. The sages are still discussing whether the name means 'green hollows' or 'grey dog.' On the bank of the Molendinar Burn, now concealed in a useful sewer, tradition says that St Mungo, from Fife, built a cell and chapel, which were to become the centre of a community. In time he was made bishop; Columba, from Iona, came to visit him, and they exchanged pastoral staffs; for ten years he remained with his flock; then persecution caused him to flee to Wales; but at the end of twenty-eight years he returned, laboured for a further score of years, and died on January 13, 603. In the crypt of the Cathedral is a beautiful Gothic shrine, said to mark his grave, though the Cathedral was not raised till centuries later; but whether or no his dust be there, his name remains as that of Glasgow's patron saint.

A church was founded in 1123, and was dedicated thirteen years later. It may be that only part of it was stone, for it was wiped out by a fire. A new church, which was dedicated while unfinished in 1197, is represented to-day by a solitary pillar, with carven capital, in the south-west corner of the crypt. Beside that pillar, known as Jocelin's, are pieces of a slightly later building; but the Cathedral, as we know it, was not begun till about 1240, when Bishop William de Bondington put his whole heart into raising a monument to the glory of God and the memory of St Mungo. All Scotland, in one way or another, contributed to the work, and help came from Europe. Before he died, in 1258, Bishop William saw the crypt and choir almost completed. His successor finished the nave and, perhaps, built the north-west tower, which, thanks to certain well-meaning persons, was taken down about a hundred years ago. Little was done during a whole century, and then one important piece of building followed another—chapter house, sacristy, consistory house, and library—the last removed by the afore-mentioned well-meaners. In the beginning of the sixteenth century Bishop Blackadder brought the great work to completion—nearly 400 years after the laying of the first stone—with the rood screen, stairways to crypt and choir, the altars of Holy Cross and Madonna Misericordiæ.

Sad to say, the glorious fane was to suffer, not from the violence of the Reformers, but from the abuse and neglect of those responsible for its care. In the seventeenth century the crypt, acknowledged to be the finest in Europe, was allowed to get into a most filthy state, and for long to remain so. When the congregation who had worshipped in it removed to a church of their own, they earthed the floor to a depth of five feet and used it as a family burying-place, providing a suitable atmosphere of woe by blackening the arches and vaulting with soot, with blobs of whiting to represent tears; and to add to the gloom they built up the lancet windows with rubble. Happily, nearly all traces of that pious desecration were removed in the nineteenth century; yet the thought of it, when you look up and around at the wonder and loveliness, induces the reflection that beauty has never meant very much to the majority. The whole Cathedral, indeed, was in a sorry condition when, at last, in the nineteenth century, men's consciences awoke to the shame of it; but to-day we behold it, save for altars and images, as it was four hundred years ago. Services are held in it every Sunday.

I may say that I attempted for you a description of this noble edifice—and destroyed it. No conception of the building and the relics contained in it can be given in a page or two. I will only add that the Cathedral is *the* treasure of Glasgow, and Glasgow would be poor, indeed, without it. It stands under that mount of monuments, the burial ground known as the Necropolis, the most prominent memorial being that to John Knox, and is separated from the High Street by a spacious square, on the north side of which is the Royal Infirmary.

I can remember when the High Street was a very shabby place. I dare say the City Fathers had no choice but to demolish most of its old buildings. Happily, Provand's Lordship escaped. You cannot miss it as you come over from the Cathedral—the corner building, with the crow-stepped gables, so obviously a survival. Originally it was part of the hospital of St Nicholas, founded, in 1471, for the support of twelve aged men by Bishop Muirhead, whose arms are on the south gable. Since then it has seen and suffered many changes. At first each storey had three rooms, with large fireplaces; each room had its own access, either from an outer stair or from timber galleries. The rooms then appear to have been occupied by the master of the adjoining hospital and canons of the Cathedral. After the Reformation, when the more powerful people helped themselves to church property, the building was acquired by William Baillie, who also acquired lordship over the 2000 acres known as the Lands of Provand—hence the name—and the house was converted into one dwelling, which meant the cutting of communicating doors between the rooms. In the sixteenth century the house and lands passed into the hands of Sir Robert Hamilton, who, in 1667, sold the lands to the City of Glasgow for 106,000 merks, or nearly £6000. Twenty-five years earlier he had sold the house itself to William Bryson, who gave it a new western front and built wings to enclose the old open timber galleries. He has left his initials on the broken sundial on the south gable. A lot can happen in a hundred years, and in town houses it is usually for the worse. By the nineteenth century the old place had sunk pretty low. A water-colour drawing made by William Simpson, R.I., in 1843, shows it as a 'pub.' You will find the signboard, as well as the drawing, inside the house.

In 1906 the property came on the market, and that would have been the end of the story but for a group of gentlemen who formed a club for its preservation. Over-coming many difficulties, the club, which could not afford to buy, became tenants in perpetuity for payment of an annual ground rent of £100. In 1927 Sir William Burrell presented to the club a large sum of money, so that the house might be furnished in the manner of the seventeenth century; and now it is a treat for the lover of antiques. The furnishings include sixteenth-century stained-glass windows, early Flemish tapestries, a seventeenth-century oak cradle, Scots oak cabinets, William

and Mary walnut high-back chairs, and, notably, a score
of Scots oak arm-chairs, carved and carrying dates and,
in some cases, armorial bearings. The three principal
apartments—kitchen, tapestry bedroom, and large room
on the middle floor—are very well worth your attention,
with their creamy sandstone walls, their low ceilings
supported by great oak or pine beams, and their vast
fireplaces, not to mention the relics contained in them.
But the house has another interest. When Mary came
to see the invalid Darnley, she did not, as her letters tell
us, lodge in the mansion where he lay, and there is some
reason for fancying that she stayed as a guest in Provand's
Lordship. So, if you believe that she really penned
the incriminating correspondence known as the Casket
Letters, you may picture her, in the silence and secrecy
of night, writing the worst of them within these walls.

The house is open daily, except Sunday and Thursday,
at the following hours: in summer, 10 A.M. to 1 P.M.,
and 2 P.M. to 5 P.M.: and in winter, 10 A.M. to 12 noon,
and 2 P.M. to 4 P.M. Admission 6d.

In the High Street, too, for 400 years stood Glasgow's
University College. Poor at first, it had gathered some
financial strength when the Reformation, through the
alienation of ecclesiastical endowments, impoverished
it once more. When the Chancellor, James Beaton, fled
to France, he took with him the Papal Bulls, Charter, and
Deeds, not only of the University, but of the Cathedral,
and we may reasonably suppose that he left as little as
possible in the way of plate and cash for the Reformers.
New endowments came, however, from Queen Mary,
from the burgh, and from James VI, who also gave it a
new constitution; and for the first time a student had new
regents, or professors, for the different subjects, every
year of his course, instead of the same regent for all
subjects from beginning to end. Medicine had its first
professor in 1580, who, among other things, may have

told his students how excellent a remedy for corns was a black snail bruised and mixed with powder of samphire, while nothing was better for a stye on the eyelid than the gall of a hare mingled with honey. By the middle of the seventeenth century the University was flourishing, and two hundred years later the building in High Street had become hopelessly inadequate for its purpose. For the new buildings the finest site in the west end was secured; and in 1870 the old place, sold to a railway company, was no more. Thanks to the munificence of Sir William Pearce, a portion of the old front—the gate house—was saved and re-erected at the main entrance to the new grounds.

If you walk down the High Street you will come to Glasgow Cross, where there is a reminder of the past in the tower of the old Tolbooth, with its chimes. The Cross itself, while true to the antique, was recently gifted to the city by Mr George William Black, C.B.E., LL.D. You will not now notice the equestrian statue of William III, which was removed some years ago to a more commodious situation, in Cathedral Square, because it had become an obstacle to traffic. I am afraid that "Billy" never obtained much public regard, save on Hogmanay, when the crowd, having greeted the New Year, would discharge its empty bottles at him. There is a use for everything. Looking westward, that old-fashioned tower, with steeple, belongs to the Tron Church, and the street is Trongate, which runs into Argyle Street, one of Glasgow's longest and busiest thoroughfares, and the working people's chief shopping promenade.

We do not know when Glasgow began to develop the commercial instinct; Mungo may, very likely, have encountered on the banks of the Molendinar some 'business men' who expected him to pay his way; but it becomes manifest in the twelfth century, when we see the community, then ordained into a burgh, squabbling with

L

other burghs over trade privileges. Also, at that time
King William the Lyon gave permission for a Fair to be
held annually, in July. Should you come to Glasgow
about the middle of that month you will find its atmosphere smokeless and all the factories closed; and the
workers still refer to their summer holidays as 'the
Fair.'

Progress, if slow, was seldom violently interrupted.
Glasgow has no outstanding records of burnings and
slaughter. In the fifteenth century the University was
founded, the Archbishopric was created, and a stone
bridge was completed across the river. In the seventeenth
century one of Cromwell's officials reports Glasgow to be
a handsomely built town, and any doubts concerning the
business instincts are set at rest by the record of a pretty
piece of attempted profiteering. The occasion was the
General Assembly of 1638, so fateful to Charles I, Epis-
copacy, and the country generally. Great crowds of
visitors were expected, wherefore the citizens "did putt
on their houses and beds excessive pryces." But even
then it was not a free country. The magistrates inter-
vened, many rooms were left vacant, and—well, I suppose
it was what a modern landlady would call a 'wash out.'

Then there was the dreadful period of religious persecution; but after the Revolution of 1689 civil strife
came at last to an end; men cleared away the wreckage
of their affairs, repaired what was left, and set about
seeking new methods and markets. By the Act of
Union ratified by the two countries in 1707 Scotland
was given the right of free trade with the English
colonies, of which one of the quickest and largest results
was Glasgow's trade with Virginia in tobacco. By that
trade men grew really rich, fabulously rich, as riches
were reckoned in those days. The importers of the leaf
became known as the Tobacco Lords, and, alas! they bore
their honours most unblushingly. On the pavement in

front of the old Tontine, near the Cross, they strolled
to and fro, mightily bewigged, in scarlet cloaks.   An
ordinary citizen desiring speech must await a nod or
beck ere he ventured to approach.   Was ever human
conceit more fatuous?   And never did pride strut before
a heavier fall.   Wealth, more wealth, and then—the
American War of Independence.   The Colonies were
owing Glasgow £1,000,000—an enormous figure then—
sheer ruin for the Tobacco Lords, whose place saw them
and their scarlet gowns no more.   But other merchants
turned to other markets, and Glasgow went on advancing.
For the Tobacco Lords it should be said that their trade
meant the beginning of Glasgow as a port.   Hitherto
the shallowness of the Clyde had permitted the passage
of only the puniest craft to the town; cargoes were trans-
shipped twenty miles down the river.   Now, by various
devices, the channel was deepened till, by 1775, ships
drawing six feet could reach the Broomielaw, near the
centre of the city.   That was the birth of the Clyde as a
commercial river, and of the Glasgow you see to-day.

Socially and artistically, if we are to believe a Scottish
writer of the same period, who is usually reliable, Glasgow, with a population of 40,000 and a University, had
scarcely begun to move:

> They were far behind [Edinburgh] in Glasgow, not only
> in their manner of living, but in those accomplishments
> and that taste which belong to people of opulence, much
> more to persons of education.   There were only a few
> families of ancient citizens who pretended to be gentlemen,
> and a few others, who were recent settlers there, who had
> obtained wealth and consideration in trade.   The rest were
> shopkeepers and mechanics, or successful pedlars.   It was
> usual for the sons of merchants to attend the College for one
> or two years, . . . [but] there was neither a teacher of
> French nor of music in the town.   The young ladies were
> entirely without accomplishments, and had nothing to

recommend them but good looks and fine clothes, for their manners were ungainly.

In other words, Glasgow's 'society' was still too bedazzled by its new riches to think of much else; nevertheless, with another generation or two, Commerce was beginning to raise its cap to Culture.

A deeper river, greater ships, more and more merchandise of increasing variety—so progress continued, despite periods of depression, especially that which followed the end of the Napoleonic Wars and also that of the 'sixties. It may be that Glasgow will never again know a century like the nineteenth—that era of steam and steel harnessed and moulded to serve ten thousand new inventions. With coal and iron at her gates, all manner of workshops and factories within them, shipbuilding on her river—those were Glasgow's great years of industry. Prosperity was at its peak just before the War, and, as all the world knows, where peaks were then are pits to-day. It chances that I am writing this in an atmosphere of universal uncertainty. Civilization is at its wits' end. Yet it is the same wonderful world, and mankind is more capable than ever. What is going to happen? Well, by the time this reaches your eyes you will, perhaps, be wiser than anybody is to-day.

Not a jewel, Glasgow is set among gems. On the north side of the Clyde, it is built mostly on hilly ground; on the south, mostly on a plain. The narrow river, with its long western vista of wharves and docks, and its more open eastern view, may not attract you, but it is the waterway to a thousand and one natural delights. On either side, for miles and miles, the city lies spread, much of it sad, with that drab ugliness which designers of the past, out of the poverty of their imaginations, applied to everything connected with industry; yet brightened, here and there, with green and open spaces, preserved for the people by men of heart and vision. It is fringed by cheerful residential districts, some quite new, some built with mansions, others with cottages. West and south, one may find pleasant places to live in; one may catch glimpses as fair as are to be found in the west of London; in the splendid parks one may forget the drabness and ugliness. Glasgow is "no mean city," in either sense of the adjective. Its early industrialism left it a horrid legacy of slums and rookeries, but to have seen the improvements effected during the past fifty years is to have faith in the future.

The business part of the city that you will want to see will be, I fancy, confined to a square and several streets on the north side of the river. George Square is the heart of modern Glasgow. The whole of its eastern side is occupied by the Municipal Buildings, with their great central tower, in the style of the Italian Renaissance, built in 1889, at a cost of over half a million pounds. Not everybody at first admired their outward magnificence, made more resplendent by the art of the sculptor, though time has mellowed opinions as well as the stone, yet it hardly prepares one for the splendour within, especially of the Grand Staircase and banqueting hall. In the shadow of the buildings, its simplicity emphasized, is the Cenotaph, often the scene of ceremonial, imposing or quietly pathetic. The square is bounded on its other sides by the Head Post Office, the Bank of Scotland Buildings and Merchants' House, and the North British Hotel, once the old "George," adjacent to Queen Street Station, terminus of the L. and N.E. Railway.

The spacious pavement of the square is decorated by flower plots and monuments. By far the most striking of the monuments is that in the centre—a fluted Ionic column, 80 feet in height, bearing a giant effigy of Sir Walter Scott, set up in 1837. There are a dozen or so statues at the sides and corners, and I wonder how many of the thousands of people who cross the square daily

could, off-hand, name them all.   Frankly, I am shirking
the question when I say that they include Queen Victoria,
Dr Livingstone, Robert Burns, Sir John Moore, and
Thomas Campbell, the poet, the two last Glasgow-born.

I must not omit here one of Glasgow's most important
institutions, the Royal Technical College, in George
Street—oldest technical college in the world, and the
first 'temple of knowledge' opened to women on the
same footing as men.   Founded in 1796, under the will
of John Anderson, Professor of Natural Philosophy in
Glasgow's University, it was long known as "the Ander-
sonian."   One of its first professors was Dr George
Birkbeck, whose name remains in Birkbeck College,
London.   In Glasgow he formed a class for free instruction in Mechanical and Chemical Philosophy, which
was so enthusiastically attended by artizans that there
were 700 names on its roll—1 per cent. of Glasgow's
population then.   In 1823 this class became detached
from the College and called itself the Mechanics' Institution—a title which soon became familiar on buildings,
large and small, in all parts of the country.   Sixty years
later, however, it became joined again with the College,
which to-day, with its seven acres of floor space and two
miles of corridors, is the largest building devoted to
education in Britain.   It is not a rival to the University;
its science students may receive degrees from the ancient
institution, as though they had followed their course of
study within its walls.

Glasgow's most attractive city thoroughfares, which,
all told, will not give you much over a mile's exercise, are
Buchanan Street, Gordon Street, Union Street, St Vincent
Street, Renfield Street, and Sauchiehall Street.   They
contain, generally speaking, the best shops and warehouses, also the handsomest buildings of banks and insurance companies, all more or less new.   Glasgow, like
other commercial cities to-day, wishes that her principal

streets had been made broader; in places there is congestion, aggravated by the tramways system, in itself so
excellent. For a general survey of Glasgow the top of
a tramway car is the place. From the centre of the city
a yellow car will take you south to the splendid Queen's
Park and Langside, where Mary met her final defeat; a
green car, west, by Great Western Road, the Botanic
Gardens, and the mansions of Kelvinside, to a sight of the
hills and lower reaches of the Clyde; a white car, also
west, to Kelvingrove Park and the University. The last
mentioned is the part of uncommercial Glasgow which
you ought not to miss, even if you can spare only fifteen
minutes to walk across Kelvingrove Park, the finest, as
a scene, of the city's open spaces. Here the little river
Kelvin, flowing to join the Clyde, passes through a deep
hollow between steep, grassy, tree-covered slopes. The
eastern slope is crowned by what is still Glasgow's most
handsomely formed and proudly situated terrace, though
many of the stately mansions are now boarding-houses
and nursing-homes. On the opposite summit, Gilmore-
hill, across that green gulf, stands the main building of
the University. Glasgow has nothing more dignified.

The University was designed by Sir Gilbert Scott. No
architect could have had a more ideal site, and the building is worthy of it. Neither ornate nor severe, it stands
there, overlooking the city, with its struggling swarms,
aloof yet benevolent, grave yet not sombre. But for
their many windows, the square towers terminating the
wings might pass for those of a distant age. The same
might be said of the great central tower, which rises
150 feet above the Gothic arch of the main entrance,
were it not for the surmounting spire of open stonework,
a thing of grace that always strikes me as youthful,
though very likely it does so because I was familiar with
the tower before the spire was added. The building has
a length of 532 feet and a breadth of 295 feet. Within

are two quadrangles divided by the Bute Hall, 115 feet long, built above the cloisters, with their groined roof. The Arts Quadrangle lay open to the west until the beautiful War Memorial Chapel made the square complete. There are over 5000 students. In the north side of the buildings are housed the Library, of which the nucleus was formed in the fifteenth century, and the Hunterian Museum, bequeathed by William Hunter in 1783; both perfect treasure houses, continually enriched with the passage of the years.

As you stand on the terrace in front of the University your eye will be caught by the great, many-towered red-sandstone pile on the opposite bank of the Kelvin—Glasgow's Art Galleries, opened in 1902. Their cost was half that of the Municipal Buildings. I mention this not as a matter of pride, but by way of contrast between that year and the not so very distant past. Glasgow got its first chance in Art in 1753, when the Brothers Foulis, beloved of every bibliophile for their beautiful printing of books, set up an Academy of the Fine Arts. They received encouragement from the University and support from sundry Glasgow merchants, but, after a struggle lasting two-and-twenty years, the end was failure. Still, they had sown the seeds, and two of their pupils became distinguished—David Allan, who illustrated Allan Ramsay's *Gentle Shepherd*, and James Tassie, for his medallions. But neither found a living in Glasgow. It was not till the nineteenth century that public interest began to awake in a more or less drowsy fashion, and not till 1861 that the Institute of the Fine Arts held its first exhibition. Yet, only forty years later, Glasgow spends over a quarter of a million on a home for a collection which, in the words of an expert, is of European importance. Splendid gifts, rather than purchases, have made it so. People come from afar to look upon Rembrandt's *Man in Armour*, Corot's *Souvenir*

GLASGOW UNIVERSITY, FROM KELVINGROVE PARK

Photo Valentine and Sons, Ltd.

LOCH LOMOND

Photo Valentine and Sons, Ltd.

d'Italie, Turner's *Modern Italy,* Rubens' *Boar Hunt,* Israëls' *Frugal Meal,* Whistler's *Carlyle,* to name but a few. People remain to study the examples of McTaggart, Millet, Cox, de Wint, Maris, Degas, Pissarro, and scores of others. The collections of modern water-colours and etchings are in themselves an attraction.

Besides works of art, the Galleries harbour a Museum, full of riches for students of Archæology, Natural History, Geology, Shipbuilding, and Engineering. A Gallery has been set apart for relics of Old Glasgow, from prehistoric to Victorian times, and perhaps it holds the most fascinating display for the ordinary person, as well as the student.

And that is all I shall write about Glasgow. For so great a city it has amazingly little to offer to the sightseer, and I do not wish to be accused of scraping the platter. Yet I will tell you one thing more : world travellers have described it to me as the most 'friendly' of cities—and that is something.

The Trossachs and Loch Lomond

"The Trossachs" has long been the favourite one-day tour from Glasgow. The transport includes every means except flying—rail, motor, four-in-hand coach, and steamers on Loch Katrine and Loch Lomond. The Trossachs themselves form but a small though remarkable part of it. The Gaelic word is said to mean 'bristling territory,' and the walls of that narrow passage between Loch Katrine and Loch Achray do indeed bristle in strangely erratic fashion, with oaks and hawthorns, hazels, birches, and mountain ashes, while the lower ground is littered with queer rocky hummocks, to which trees and bushes crazily cling—altogether a work of Nature in her most rough-and-tumble mood.

> Crags, knolls and mounds, confusedly hurled—
> The fragments of an earlier world.

A visitor of a hundred years ago described the Trossachs as 'wild and horrid'; but perhaps he saw them on a grey evening.

The tour may be made with variations; it is 'featured' by the railway and motor transport companies. I prefer the original way, which means going first to Callander, because I think it keeps the best for the last; and, as I am touching elsewhere on the country between Glasgow and Callander, and on Callander itself, I now ask you to imagine the trip as having started from the latter place.

From Callander to the Trossachs the road—8½ miles— is one that might well, for our pleasure's sake, be taken slowly. Yon great mountain ahead is Ben Ledi—"Hill of God"—once, no doubt, a place of pagan worship. The streams on the left are Teith and Leny; on the right opens Leny Glen, at its entrance Leny House, seat of the Buchanans, an ancient clan of these parts. We pass through the village of Kilmahog, and since 'Kil' means 'cell' or 'chapel,' we conclude that a holy man of the name of Hog dwelt here in the dim ages. His name in the Gaelic was *Chug*, not that it sounds much prettier, but it is something to have a name of any sort on the map a thousand years after one has ended this little earthly pilgrimage.

Soon appears in its fair valley Loch Vennachar, where, long ago, I hooked—and lost—my first trout, and where, on another day, I saw a pike so enormous that it gave me a bad dream. If you remember your *Lady of the Lake* and want to see the spot where Fitzjames and Roderick Dhu had their great fight, you will, alas, look in vain for Coilantogle Ford; you will see, instead, the sluices erected to control the outflow of the Teith. A little farther on is a bosky bank known as the Wood of Lamentation, the lamentation being caused, long ago, by the ill-deeds of a kelpie inhabiting the waters. Kelpies, so common in the Highlands, were water-sprites of peculiar malignancy who, sometimes in the form of horses, often beautiful, would come ashore, with unhappy results for the human beings who encountered them. The kelpie of Vennachar appeared where a number of children were playing, took them for a nice little ride, and suddenly plunged, children and all, into the loch.

For some miles the road skirts the shore, then diverges and, running between lush growths of tree, bracken, and whin (gorse), passes the hamlet of Brig o' Turk ('Bridge of the Wild Boar') and comes down to the shore of little Loch Achray. Coleridge and Wordsworth, like Scott, fell in love with the loch. Near it stands the Trossachs Hotel, a commodious house, and thence, through the Trossachs, overlooked by Bens A'an and Venue, we go down the winding road to Loch Katrine, where, at the pier, a yacht-like steamer is waiting.

The Loch is not named after some fair lady of long ago, though I find a learned traveller, in 1811, persistently calling it 'Loch Catherine.' Katrine, I am told, is derived from Gaelic words meaning 'Battle of Hell,' which may seem absurd on a soft blue summer day; yet when the winter blasts come screeching down from the rain-shrouded, ghostly heights, to thrash the black waters into grey whirling smoke, it must be admitted that the old Gaels had a *flair* for giving a place a name. The steamer pier is in a creek; as we emerge we see, under the bulk of Ben Venue, Goblin's Cave and the Pass of the Cattle (*Bealach nam Bo*) leading to the secretive corrie, or cleft, in the hillside where the Macgregors used to conceal the herds 'lifted' from the Lowlands. Just outside of the bay is Ellen's Isle, or *Eilan Molach*—*Eilan* means 'isle'; it may have suggested 'Ellen' to Scott— rocky and woody; but you will not see the 'Silver Strand,' from which Fitzjames made his crossing. The water you are sailing on is Glasgow's water—it made your tea or coffee this morning—and some time ago the City's increasing demands rendered the raising of the loch's level inevitable. Before long, on the southern shore, you will notice Royal Cottage where Queen Victoria rested in October 1859, when she 'turned on the water' for its long dark journey to Glasgow.

It is a pleasant sail down the wood-fringed loch. Ruskin was, perhaps, artistically correct, though his criticism does seem rather smug, when he declared that the hills are too high to be perfectly sublime; but Ruskin has gone his way, and the same hills remain the delight of unnumbered people not so 'particular.'

The sail ends at Stronachlachar. If you are from Germany, you will love the word; if from England, you will say it ought to be played on the bagpipes. It means nothing worse than 'the mason's promontory.'

The loch, narrowing, extends about two miles beyond Stronachlachar to Glengyle, once a home of the Macgregors. There is an old house, with an odd window in the thick wall of the sitting-room, which Rob Roy is said to have used as a loophole for his musket. Close by— too close, I remember, for some modern guests in the house—is the family burying-ground, where Wordsworth wrote his verses on the hero. The mighty warrior, however, lies over at Balquhidder. In spite of his reckless career, he lived to be seventy-four, and all but ended with what Scots used to call a 'strae (straw) death'— *i.e.*, a natural death, in bed. He was lying there when the visit of his friend Maclaren, of Invernenty, roused him, and he demanded to be dressed in his old fighting garb. For a while, with his claymore handy, he sat by the peat fire, talking to his guest, then bade his piper play the lament *We Return No More*. While the piper was playing he passed. So 'tis said.

In Queen Mary's time the Macgregors were outlawed. A personage had been murdered in Glenartney—not, perhaps, by Macgregors, though the murderers obtained their protection. The head of the personage was placed

on the church altar; the Macgregors filed past; each
laid his hand on it, approving the deed and those who
had done it. The Government decided that the clan
should be wiped out. The Macgregors took to the
mountains and continued to thrive on the proceeds of raids
and plunderings. In the reign of Charles I they were
treated as foreigners; their children were refused
baptism; every male over the age of sixteen was required
to appear annually before commissioners and give
security for good behaviour. Yet when Cromwell came
the Macgregors turned out against him, for which act of
patriotism they were, at the Restoration, pardoned the
past, and made free men again. All went pretty well till
they joined up with the Jacobites, and in 1693 the old
statutes against them were once more put into force.
The name of Macgregor was proscribed. Rob Roy took
the name of Campbell, the ancient enemy, albeit it was
a Campbell who had succoured his wife and children
when, in his absence, they were evicted from their home:
his sons took the name of Drummond. The truth would
seem to be that the Macgregors were born rebels; circumstances made them robbers.

From Stronachlachar, by coach, passing Loch Arklet,
at the west end of which is the house whence Rob Roy
abducted his bride, the formidable Helen, we come to
Inversnaid on Loch Lomond. The Snaid Burn joins the
Arklet; there is a pretty waterfall close to the hotel,
and Rob Roy's Cave is less than a mile away. The land
here was Rob Roy's patrimony. Across the water the
Clan Macfarlane once held sway. On the islet off Inver-
uglas is the ruin of the chief's castle. Inversnaid is on
the wilder side of the loch. There is no shore road,
north or south.

Now from Ardlui, at the head of the loch, approaches
a grey-and-white steamer with a scarlet funnel.

If you have scanned the map of Scotland, you must

have observed how nearly all the lochs are long strips, never broad sheets, of water. The close setting of the mountain ranges accounts for this. Loch Lomond is about 21 miles long, and for most of its length does not exceed a mile in breadth; only toward the southern end does the width become about five miles

The steamer carries us diagonally to Tarbet. Scotland has many Tarbets, or Tarberts. The word means 'a place over which a boat can be drawn,' otherwise an isthmus. In the days of the last Norse invasion King Haco had some of his galleys drawn across country from Loch Long to Loch Lomond, about 1½ miles. To-day on both lochs steamers ply, in connection, and between Arrochar and Tarbet motors run where once the Norsemen hauled and sweated. A cutting 40 feet deep would unite the lochs. The hotel at Tarbet is a favourite with sojourners and motorists.

From Tarbet there are many fine prospects. The most memorable views, I think, are those of 'the Cobbler,' a curious formation on the ridge of an Argyllshire range westward, and, across the loch, Ben Lomond and its lesser neighbours. In the course of our sail we see the Ben in varying aspects. A monstrous mass, mostly of granite, rising into a cone, it reaches a height of over three thousand feet, with, on the north side, a precipitous drop of nearly two thousand. Toward the summit, outcrops of quartzite appear, from a distance and in certain lights, as snowy patches; not that the Ben is unfamiliar with real snow. The view from the top—bens and glens, inland and sea lochs, firths and islands, Ireland itself— is, for lack of a bigger word, magnificent. There is an old and true story of two young men so overcome by the wonder of it all that down they knelt on the summit and dedicated their lives to the service and glory of God. To the mountaineer the ascent is easy. Every year thousands of persons, with no special training, make it without undue exhaustion. Just opposite Tarbet there is a path from the shore to the summit, but the usual starting-point is Rowardennan, our next port of call, with its convenient hotel.

Below Rowardennan, whence the steamer crosses to Luss, the loch expands into an irregular triangle containing the great majority of its thirty islets, or inches, as they are called. Luss is charming in itself, as well as in its outlook on the inches. In summer it is a retreat of roses among the hills; in hot weather you might find it enervating, while on a still evening the midges, as I have been told by sensitive persons, are 'simply ferocious.' But the midges, I'm afraid, are a plague common to the West of Scotland in windless weather. From Luss it is easy to find cooling airs on the water, cruising among the islands and house-boats; a calm summer night on the Loch is an unforgettable experience. On such a night you will never suspect that these quiet waters could be savage and cruel. Yet Loch Lomond has known many a tragedy. From the mountains swoops the squall and lays the white wings low on the sudden surge. He needs to watch the weather who hoists sail out there, in spring or autumn; and summer gales are not unknown. But normally Luss looks out on a placid scene. From its comfortable hotel the fishers go after the salmon and trout; and though the loch is not celebrated for its baskets, I have known anglers come back to it year after year. Loch Lomond is—Loch Lomond. It contains an odd fish known as the 'fresh-water herring,' which is found also in Loch Eck, over in Argyll.

Rossdhu ('Black Promontory') is the home of the chief of the Colquhouns. Beside the Georgian mansion is a remnant of the ancient castle. The Colquhouns, like nearly everybody else, had trouble with the Macgregors. In 1603, in Glen Fruin yonder, where to-day the angler wanders peacefully, a bloody fight took place between the clans, and at night the countryside was gold and crimson with burning farms, while into the secrecy of the outer darkness the Macgregors drove the plundered cattle. A holiday might be spent among the islands, which are mostly high and wooded. Of the larger ones, Inch Tavanach and Inch Lonaig are near to Luss. The first had once a monastery; the yews on the second were planted by Robert the Bruce to supply his bowmen with their weapons. Over at Balmaha, whence the steamer is now proceeding, is Inch Cailleach—'Isle of the Old Women,' otherwise Nuns; south of it is Inch Murrin, the meaning of which I cannot trace. Upon it are ruins of a castle and chapel, also a row of ten boulders, set at intervals of 80 feet, another of Scotland's archæological puzzles. In 1930 this island, for long given over to nature and deer, was purchased from the Duke of Montrose by a gentleman who has cleared some hundreds of acres for cultivation, built a pretty house, a farm-steading, sundry cottages, a power house, a jetty, started a poultry farm, and laid out a golf course. The deer have been given a fenced reservation at the north end of the island. There is certainly a charm in having a little world of one's own within 30 miles of the city. (At the last moment I learn that the island has again changed hands. The new landlord, I hear, is willing to let the cottages to summer visitors.)

From Balmaha (accent on the last syllable) the steamer proceeds to Balloch, at the effluence of the River Leven, an hour by train or motor from Glasgow.

The Firth of Clyde

Fortunate is the traveller who gains his first impression of the Clyde from the deck of a ship coming in from sea, on a fine summer evening, or, if it be not hazy, in the early morning. The course is between the mountainous island of Arran, with a near sight of spectacular little

Ailsa Craig, core of a volcano, and the more distant cliffs
and sands of Ayrshire; through the narrow channel
separating Little Cumbrae from low-lying verdant Bute;
past Great Cumbrae and Rothesay Bay; on, between the
hospitable shores of Renfrewshire and Cowall, toward the
opening of Loch Long and the rugged mountains of
Argyll, grim against the northern sky; and then, with a
sweep almost abrupt, into the mouth of the river itself,
where a large town looks solemnly across at a small
smiling one, and where the eye turns presently from the
mountains and woody Rosneath to scan the long, peaceful vista of the estuary.

Yet that is but one of the many aspects offered by the
Firth of Clyde, and it is not easy to advise the visitor who
comes to Glasgow with too little time, as most visitors
do, which to choose. With ample time the ideal way
would be to have one's base in one of the coast towns,
and make daily excursions in a motor-boat of not too
light build, exploring the shores of the Firth, its lochs and
islands; or, which might be more comfortable, if less
romantic, make the voyages of discovery on the handsome steamers of the railway companies, who issue
"go-as-you-please" tickets for weekly, fortnightly, or
monthly periods at remarkably reasonable rates.

A word about the steamers. Besides the fleets of the
railway companies, there are the Williamson steamers
and the long-famous MacBrayne's *Columba*. Most of
them have their regular daily sailings, short or whole-day
trips; some have different excursions for certain days
of the week. The railway steamers start from the
companies' piers, all about an hour's train journey from
Glasgow, at Craigendoran, Greenock, Gourock, Wemyss
Bay, Fairlie, and Ardrossan. Certain of the Williamson
steamers and MacBrayne's *Columba* sail from Glasgow,
and connect with trains at Greenock or Gourock. Many of
the steamers make evening cruises and Sunday excursions.

M

Partly because it is a 'classic,' mainly because it includes so many features of the river and Firth, I am choosing the *Columba's* trip to Ardrishaig, as an example of a one-day outing. It is for you to say whether you will board the steamer at Glasgow at 7 A.M. or take train to Gourock, an hour and a half later. The hardship of rising at six on a summer morning may be mitigated by the excellent breakfast served in the saloon, which in not a few cases appears to promote a glow of conscious virtue, and the passage down the river is really worth while. Time was when passengers regarded with disfavour those narrow murky waters, and tried not to breathe, but that was before Glasgow had conquered her sewage problem, and to-day the tide, though far from crystalline, ebbs and flows without offence. For some miles the *Columba* paddles discreetly between wharves and docks and ship-building yards, sliding past, maybe, the towering bulk of a liner, or a dredger at its eternal job of keeping the bottom clear of silt; and then the river begins to broaden between green fields, though the channel for shipping remains narrow, confined by artificial banks and marked by perches and beacons. When the first little steam-boats plied here, with their draughts of four feet or so, their skippers had to watch the tide and look out for sandbanks; now and then they ran aground, to be held up for hours. Sometimes the skippers stranded them deliberately, as when they were the owners, or part-owners, and down in the stuffy little cabins some Glasgow merchants were sitting drinking claret or brandy, from which was more profit than from the passage fares.

Beyond the last of the shipyards, and all on the northern bank, are Old Kilpatrick, where St Patrick may have preached before he put out in his frail boat to tell Ireland; Bowling, with its small harbour, under Dumbuck Hill; the remains of Dunglass Castle, a Colquhoun stronghold, and beside it the obelisk to the

memory of Henry Bell; and then Dumbarton, with little
to illustrate its long story, save that solitary, lofty,
double-peaked mass of basalt, known as 'The Rock,'
which guards the Vale of Leven.

Like Edinburgh's and Stirling's Rocks, it must have
been a place of refuge and defence since ever man appeared in these parts, which was long before it looked
down on the Roman galleys and the Britons in their
canoes. It was called by the Romans *Theodosia*, by the
Britons *Alcluith* ('Height on the Clyde'—'Clutha' is
still the poetic word for the river), and by the Gaels
Dunbreatan, whence its present name. Away back in
the sixth century the Rock was the capital of the kingdom of Strathclyde, which extended south to Cumberland and Westmorland, and six centuries were to pass
ere Strathclyde itself became a part of the united Scotland we know to-day. During those and the five succeeding centuries the fortress changed hands repeatedly,
and much blood must have moistened the Rock. There
are no signs of its ever having been a magnificent stronghold, apart from its natural defences. Its interest rests
on the numerous names of historic personages associated
with it. It seems likely that Scotland's hero, Sir William
Wallace, captured at Glasgow in 1305, was kept there for
a few days, before being sent to London and his ghastly
doom. His great two-handed sword lay there till the
end of last century, when it was removed to the Wallace
Monument, near Stirling. Bruce took the castle in the
year before Bannockburn. Skipping two hundred years
of its history, we see Queen Mary, a little girl of six, embarking thence for France. She revisited the castle in
1563, and on May 13, 1568, was making for it with her
army, when they were forced to fight at Langside, near
Glasgow—the final disaster. The most extraordinary
tale of the Rock—too long to detail here—is concerned
with its capture by escalade, without loss to the attacking

party, in 1571. On a foggy night the assailants, with hooked ladders and ropes, contrived, but not without some desperate moments, to scale the 200 feet of crags, surmounted the walls, and surprised the garrison. The chief reward for attaining the summit to-day—without ladders and ropes, of course—is the view of the Clyde and Loch Lomond, and the possibility of finding the real Scotch thistle, which does not by any means grow everywhere in Scotland.

Now the scene opens up, so that we see, on the left, overshadowed by its hill, Port Glasgow—Glasgow's port before the river was made navigable—and Greenock, an important though hardly imposing town, with an out-look of great splendour. Northward, the mouth of the Gareloch, most placid of fjords, opens between Rosneath and the western end of Helensburgh, with its many fine houses and fair gardens set on the hillside, a centre for the more leisured tourist.

Greenock is associated with shipbuilding and sugar-refining, and with the name of James Watt, the great engineer, who was born there in 1736. Lovers of Burns know that his Highland Mary died of fever in 1768 at a house in Minchcollop Close, and that Greenock's is the oldest of the Burns Clubs.

Gourock in its bay, under its steep hill, is a popular summer playground. Not so long ago visitors to such places on the Clyde were left to find their own amuse-ments, but now entertainment is being more and more provided, though to a visitor acquainted with the gaieties of English watering-places it may seem modest.

Rounding Kempock Point we are on the Firth proper, and making for the shores of Cowall, for miles lined with houses, where before the day of steamboats were mere hamlets, a solitary farm, or cot. Yonder opening to the north is Loch Long; that directly ahead Holy Loch, so called, perhaps, because in the far past a ship laden

with earth from Palestine foundered in its waters; but
more likely because a holy man, with the neat little name
of Mun, made his hermitage on its shore; and just as
likely because of a pagan superstition. From its head
the road runs inland, skirting Loch Eck, and across
country among the hills to Loch Fyne—a beautiful
drive. Holy Loch is a favourite anchorage for yachts,
especially at regatta time. The headquarters of the
Royal Clyde Yacht Club are at Hunter's Quay, on the
south corner of its mouth.

Dunoon is a cheerful little town, very busy and colourful with its summer crowds. Time was when the visitors
were almost exclusively Glasgow folk; now it attracts
people from all parts of the country by its boating facilities, swimming galas, and entertainments in the Castle
Gardens. Its great annual event is the Cowall Games,
held on the last Friday and Saturday of August, a feature
of which is the march past of a thousand pipers. There
is scarcely an excursion on the Firth that cannot be made
from its pier. The round, by road, *via* Holy Loch and
Loch Eck, to Strachur on Loch Fyne, and thence by sea,
has been a favourite for generations. On the hillock
above the pier from a very early date stood a castle,
which in the fourteenth century became a royal palace
under the keepership of the Campbells, afterward Lords
of Argyll. Mary visited it in the summer of 1563, and
seems to have refreshed herself with a taste of the simple
life, for, says an old ballad:

> Now she's cast off her bonny shoon
> Made o' the gilded leather ;
> And she's put on her Highland brogues
> To skip among the heather.

But her light-hearted days were drawing to an end.

The castle has gone, and on the green slope is the
memorial of another Mary—Burns's Highland Mary, who

was a native of Dunoon, a serving lass made immortal by a song.

Our course continues along the Cowall shore.   On the opposite side of the Firth lie, close together, Wemyss Bay, a quietly attractive place with a railway pier, and Skelmorlie with a new hydro-hotel.   Rounding Toward Point we come into Rothesay Bay, thence into an inner bay in which sits Rothesay town, sheltered from nearly every wind that blows.   Like Dunoon, it caters for the people, and is thronged at midsummer.   Like Dunoon, too, it is admirable as a base for the marine excursionist, and though situated on an island only 15 miles long and 6 at the broadest, it offers attractions to rambler and antiquarian.   Electric trams run across the island to Etterick Bay, an extra playground, with its sands and dance-hall, and buses to Kilchattan Bay in the south.   Wherever you turn on this Island of Bute you are confronted with views magnificent or exquisite.   None of its own gentle hills reaches a thousand feet; its three little inland lochs, Ascog, Fad, and Quien, all south of Rothesay, have no sinister aspects.   The northern half of the island fits so snugly into a gulf in the mainland that, glancing at the map, you may imagine yourself stepping across, yet presently we shall be sailing through these straits, the Kyles of Bute.

Rothesay came into existence with the castle.   The earliest attempt at a castle may have been set up by the Norsemen, who held the fort against frequent assaults for 150 years.   It is a circular building 138 feet in diameter, with walls 26 feet high and 9 feet thick.   One of the flanking round towers remains.   You cross a drawbridge over a deep moat, and enter a vaulted hall, with a dungeon below and another hall above.   These, not forgetting the "bloody stair," are the chief remains of the ancient stronghold, and their preservation is owing to the generosity of the Marquis of Bute, hereditary keeper of the castle, and a descendant of Robert II. After the Norsemen were finally evicted it was held by the Scots for half a century, and then taken by the English, who retained it for three years. Robert III, who came to the throne in 1390, created the first dukedom in the Scottish peerage, and conferred the title on his eldest son —and so to-day the Prince of Wales is also Duke of Rothesay. As a place of habitation the castle came to its end, by burning, in 1685.

While I have been at my tale the *Columba* has been moving, and having crossed the mouth of Loch Striven has entered the Kyles at Colintraive, as sweet a little place as you could wish to see. "Some day we must go and spend a quiet holiday there," says every second person who spies it from a steamer's deck. Fortunately man only proposes, otherwise Colintraive would have the population of Glasgow. The rocks which presently all but bar our passage—the bow wave is running up them as we slip through—are the Burnt Islands, so called since 1685, when the Earl of Argyll's ammunition dumps were blown up by the garrison, scared by the approach of King James's ships. Northward Loch Riddon runs into the hills, beyond it fair Glendaruel, name known to every West Highlander, if only through the farewell song of Deirdre, "the most beautiful woman who ever lived," to whose tragic legend of a thousand and more years ago several modern, as well as old-time, poets have turned their art. At the loch's mouth the Kyles bend sharply, and we come to Tighnabruaich ('House on the Slope'), another alluring little place.

Emerging from the Kyles we have a sight of Etterick Bay, Inch Marnock, an islet whereon, in the old days, the Bute folk marooned incorrigible topers, possibly because the soil produces splendid barley, and, farther south, the noble Isle of Arran. Then rounding Ardlamont Point we are in one of Scotland's largest fjords, Loch Fyne, which has much beauty, if less grandeur than some of our lochs, and is known to artists and philistines alike for the finest herring in the world.

Our course is across the loch to Tarbert, which stands on the short isthmus between East and West Loch Tarberts. On the isthmus were once three guardian castles; the ruins of one remain in the village. Little East Loch Tarbert is a natural harbour, with an entrance that requires a good steersman, and Tarbert's business is mostly fishing. At the head of West Loch Tarbert one may embark for the big island of Islay, sailing out by the little one of Gigha, with its strangely mild climate. Beyond it the Sound of Jura can be unkind—passengers have been known to pray; but West Loch Tarbert, with its gentle hills and homes and woods reflected on the placid surface, is a dream loch, and is so in my memory of a morning, near to Christmas, when the inshore waters bore a crust of ice, and pale passengers in from the Sound thanked heaven for the still water and the voyage over.

Islay, with its domineering neighbour, Jura, is still somewhat in the background, though there are signs that it is being discovered by more and more holiday-makers —not, perhaps, a matter for rejoicing to those who have already come to regard it as their particular retreat. Without the magnificence and romance of Skye, it has attractions of its own, including a splendid golf course at Machrie, with a convenient hotel, and some fine little trout lochs. It has glorious sands, though its rocks have a sad record for wrecks. A monument and grave-yard recall the appalling tragedy of a troopship during the War. Islay's story is partly told by relics of the Norsemen and of the Macdonalds, Lords of the Isles. Jura, separated by only half a mile of water, is mainly a range of mountains, the two loftiest bens being known as 'the Paps.' The name Jura means 'Deer Island'—a better description to-day than ever it was. At the north end of the island lies the Strait of Corrievrechan, where warring tides create a 'whirlpool,' with strange tales of drowned mariners and mermaids.

The *Columba's* outward run ends at Ardrishaig ('Height of the Briars'), where one may take motor for Oban, thence train for Glasgow—a remarkable round.

Another great day's outing on the Firth is the trip to Campbeltown, *via* the north of Arran and Kintyre coast.

Inveraray

Near the head of Loch Fyne rests the old capital of Argyll, Inveraray. One of the Williamson turbine steamers will take you there, or you may travel from Glasgow by road, *via* Loch Lomond and Glen Croe. Inveraray is quiet and quaint and out of the world. It makes me think of a little old lady sitting still, with hands folded and a contented smile, while time passes on. Like an old lady, too, Inveraray stopped growing long ago. The present town was founded in 1742; an earlier town was made a Royal Burgh in 1544. It sits on a small promontory near the mouth of the River Aray, under the shadow, or, rather, benediction, of the wooded hill, crowned with an old watch-tower, Duniquaich. (*Quaich* is a drinking-cup, and maybe the man who named it thought of an inverted one.)

Inveraray has an entrance arch, a square, a main street, and a Celtic cross which may have come from Iona. In the square are the parish churches of Inveraray and Glenaray under one roof. If, on a Sunday, you enter at the south door, you will hear a service in the Gaelic tongue. Also in the square are the County Buildings, and behind them the old commodious jail. Till not so long ago the judges in their chariots arrived periodically, as they had done, through generation after generation, to hold a High Court at Inveraray, which must always have been a big thrill for the little town.

They put up at the Argyll Arms, where they had a 'cellar' of their own, which, I believe, reflected favourably on their judgment, if not their judgments.

The history of Inveraray is that of the Argylls. The first knight of the line was Sir Colin Campbell of Lochow (Loch Awe), who was dubbed in 1280. The first earl was another Colin, created in 1457. The marquisate came in 1641, and the dukedom in 1701. But we may believe that the Clan Campbell had little regard for such titles for the head of their house. To the clansmen he would be always the chief—the *MacCailean Mhor*—'Son of the great Colin.' They were mighty men, the old Argylls; they made their marks on Scotland; when they employed craft it was usually in a big cause.

The Inveraray Castle we see to-day was built about 1750. According to Sir Walter Scott, it was anything but an improvement on its "noble old Gothic" predecessor. It is a great, quadrangular building of two storeys and dormer-windowed attics, with a round, pointed-roofed tower at each corner, all built of a rather grimly grey stone; but regarded from a distance and a height, among its glorious surroundings, I should say it looks not undignified. It stands in a park nearly 30 miles round, with plantations dating from the middle of the seventeenth century, and three grand avenues.

Inveraray is the birthplace of Neil Munro, the beloved novelist, poet, and journalist, who died at Helensburgh in 1930. They brought him home by road, round by Arrochar and through Glen Croe, over Rest and Be Thankful, as the summit is feelingly called, down to Loch Fyne, round the head of the loch, by the stronghold of Dunderave, inspiration of his *Doom Castle*, and so to Inveraray, to rest under the benediction of Duniquaich. Neil Munro knew the West Highlands and the West Highland folk as no other writer has known them. He thought in Gaelic before he wrote in English, and so one gets in his books the real Highland feeling, as well as the atmosphere.

The Isle of Arran

Arran is a little world—55 miles round—of inspiring heights and brooding hollows, but the mountain giants are in the northern half, which is of peculiar interest to the geologist. That vast granite mass is surrounded by a band of slate into which it penetrates, a sign of its once molten condition, and, south and west, the slate is bounded by Old Red Sandstone, while in stretches east and north the sandstone has an edging of carboniferous rock. In Glen Dubh, near Brodick, the sandstone, changed by whin dykes, is almost quartz, white and tinted, with fine crystals of amethyst. In the southern half of the island only a little granite exists, and no slate or sandstone, the rocks being chiefly of the trap varieties. Belting the island, from 10 to 20 feet above the sea-level, is a sort of terrace, once the beach. From the shores, reaching into the grim mountains, are the green glens, watered by the tumbling torrents, white against the dark rocks, and the burns, always in a hurry, chuckling to themselves, dodging among the heather and bracken, where on a sunny afternoon you may disturb an adder in its siesta.

Arran devotees will assure you that it contains no spot so perfect as the spot they favour yearly, but I think they would agree that in the approach its fairest and grandest scene of all is Brodick Bay, with that crescent of yellow sand between its rocky horns, those three wood-portalled glens, and Goatfell, greatest of a group of great peaks, standing guard on the north. The pier and the Brodick Hotel are on the south side of the bay, a little distance from the village called Invercloy, which turns inland from the sands, and in which there are boarding-houses and villas. Do not look here for a promenade, bands, and picture-houses. The scene derives its gaiety from nature and the holiday-makers themselves in their pleasures of boating, bathing, mountaineering, tennis, golf.

Six miles north of Brodick, over a fine level road, is Corrie, a little wayside village with much charm and a favoured hotel. Compared with Brodick it is more open and bracing; yet when the east wind comes along, thanks to the mountains behind, an atmospheric cushion is created and the cold blast is diverted upward and over Corrie itself. It is the best base for the ascent of Goatfell. Two miles beyond Corrie is Glen Sannox ('Glen of the River Trout'), one of our grandest glens, glorious in its August purple. Three miles north of Sannox, on the shore, are the famous Fallen Rocks. Here a cliff has collapsed, and the scene is one of colossal ruin.

To 'put a girdle round' the island is nowadays a matter of a few hours, but the itinerary would mean more pages than are here available. I propose, therefore, to sketch a short tour of the southern and, to most people, more interesting half.

From Brodick we cross the island by the String Road. Besides a distinct change of scenery, the west side shows most of what I may call the 'unnatural' sights of Arran —for example, the prehistoric fort at Drumadoon and the Stone Circles of Tormore. The String Road goes down by the hamlets of Shiskin and Shedog ('Little Jewel') to Blackwaterfoot, on the shores of Kilbrennan Sound, with its inn and golf course, always 'full up' in the summer season. A mile or so by footpath, north of the village, is the fort, set on a columnar cliff. It must have been a tremendously strong place in its day; and though generations of the local people have removed much of the material for peaceful purposes, it is still impressive as the work of a community whose chief appliances were, so far as we know, bone and muscle.

Half a mile beyond are the King's Caves, bored by the

indefatigable sea, when at a higher level than to-day, in the sandstone cliff. One of them, says tradition, sheltered the Bruce on his return to Scottish shores from his winter exile on the Isle of Rathlin, or, as has been suggested, in Norway. He landed here, in February 1307, with 300 men. Sir James Douglas was holding Arran for him, but we may picture him in that cave as a sorely worried man. His wife and daughter were prisoners in England; Edward had just beheaded his brother Nigel and some of his best friends; and Scotland, as a people, was still more against than for him. We may picture him, too, marching across the island, possibly by the track that became the String Road, to Brodick Castle, lately taken from the English; while on the eastern cliffs his watchers kept a lookout for the twinkle of a bonfire across the water—signal that in his own earldom of Carrick, at least, they were ready to support him in one more desperate effort. On the walls of the cave are carvings, notably one of a Highland sword or claymore.

A mile and a half inland, northward, round by the farm of Tormore, we find the Stone Circles—six of them, one being double—also several monoliths, the tallest over 15 feet above ground. The stones of the circles are of both granite and red sandstone; the former were obtained from the moor near by, but the latter must have been brought from the shore, and, as they weigh up to ten tons, we are again faced with the question: How was it done? Within the circles relics have been unearthed, including cists enclosing urns, human remains, flint arrowheads, and a pin of bronze from the grave of a girl, no doubt a person of importance—perhaps a chief's young wife or daughter—but proud of her pin.

Going south we look out upon a widening sea, beyond the Mull of Kintyre, with its little satellite, Sanda Isle, away down to Ireland; then, as we turn eastward, over the water to small Ailsa Craig, with Galloway in the background, we pass through Sliddery, which is nicer than it sounds (the word means 'slow water'), and come to Lagg, with its cosy inn, one of the prettiest spots in Arran. There are more caves hereabouts. In one of them the congregation of Kilmory Kirk, who did not like the minister presented to the benefice of the parish, worshipped every Sabbath, from 1814 to 1821, when the Duke at last condescended to give them a pastor of whom they could approve. It is a big cave, but Arran's biggest is under Bennan Head, yonder, where the cliff drops nearly 500 feet.

Kildonan, reached by a road which strikes off from our highway, near Dippin, has a magnificent prospect of the outer Firth. From the square tower of its ruined castle a constant watch was kept in the days when every strange sail was a possible enemy. To-day there is a coast-guard and lifeboat station, and 'Lloyd's' reports the passing ships to Glasgow. The islet of Pladda ('Flat Island'), a mile off the coast, carries one of the most important lighthouses on the Firth.

Whiting Bay—named so naturally after the fish—is open and breezy, the scenery of its shores not wild. Glen Eaisdale (usually called 'Ashdale'), its beauty spot, conceals among its greenery Arran's greatest waterfall, also the remains of a prehistoric fort. The most notable sight is the Giants' Graves, half a mile south-west of the mouth of the glen. One of them is 20 feet by 2½ feet; it is formed by slabs of stone, the greatest weighing about ten tons.

Toward King's Cross Point, the main road cuts inland and over the hill to Lamlash (4½ miles). It was from the Point, after sighting the beacon—which was a false signal—that Bruce set sail for Ayrshire. King's Cross village claims to be the birthplace of the illustrious spider, whose persevering efforts to make good encouraged the downcast king to have another try; though, to be sure, his Majesty at that time must have been only too familiar with the insect and its ways.

From the road we look down on Lamlash Bay, so protected by Holy Isle as to form the most perfect natural harbour. It has been a haven from the days of dug-outs and coracles to these of battleships and speed-boats. Holy Isle was probably sacred, in the pagan sense, before a sixth-century Christian made his hermitage in a cave thereon. Near the cave, which has a runic inscription on its roof, is a spring for long believed to have curative properties for all diseases. The little island lies, like a couched lion, $1\frac{1}{2}$ miles offshore, is about five miles round about, and gives the impression of being much higher than it is—1030 feet. The road to Brodick is one of the most beautiful in the West.

A word about fishing in Arran. Excepting the Rosa at Brodick and the Machrie on the west side, all streams and lochs are free to the angler; and I believe you can get permission for the exceptions by applying to the factor of the estate at Brodick. With plenty of water, these two rivers offer salmon, grilse, and sea trout. "All the streams and sea pools," says my authority, Mr P. Castle, "are good for sea trout."

Arran offers much to the mountaineer, and nearly everybody climbs Goatfell ('Goat' here means either 'sacred' or 'windy'), on which the track is fairly well indicated. For Ben Nuis and the other peaks the inexperienced climber is recommended to take guidance, or all the expert advice he can get. There are difficulties and dangers which may be avoided by being not too proud. One must chance the mists, but one can count on clear weather with the wind in the north-west.

The Upper Clyde

To the antiquarian the ruin of Bothwell Castle, a few miles from Glasgow, is of special interest because of its unquestionable age, design, and construction; but even to the person who has never found "sermons in stones" it can hardly fail to appeal. Those massive round towers, with their fine ashlar masonry and walls, 15 feet thick and 60 feet high, have been standing and looking down the woody bank of the Clyde for over 600 years. It is not a case of beauty having grown up around a ruin deserted of man. In the sixteenth century there was a locally popular song, *Bothwell Bank, Thou blumest Fayre,* —and probably it was an old song then. At its full magnificence the castle covered an area of 240 by 100 feet, and its enormous strength balanced its almost defenceless position. Its long story is one of changes of ownership, punctuated sometimes in red. But the story is, more or less, the story of any other ancient stronghold, whereas Bothwell Castle itself is like none other. You would soon forget the tale, with its name-list of kings and nobles, but you will remember the sight of those brooding towers above the lovely river.

By way of contrast, go to Blantyre village, not far away, where in a one-room dwelling in 1813 was born David, afterward Doctor, Livingstone. His father was a Highlander—a Jacobite ancestor fell at Culloden; his mother was a Lowlander, with the blood of Covenanters; and it was the mingling of the two distinct strains that gave Scotland one of her really great men. Lately Blantyre has become a place of pilgrimage. In 1931 over 72,000 people came to look at the missionary's birth-place. Five years earlier the tenement containing the humble room was about to be pulled down, but, thanks to a small band of enthusiasts, the building, which is prettily situated, was purchased, restored, and converted into a National Memorial. There, among relics and pictures, you may gain an impression of the life of a man who, unlike the mighty men of Bothwell Castle, asked nothing for himself.

Fifteen miles to the south-east is Lanark, so old that it knows nothing of its beginning, though annually it celebrates its long past. There is a bell in the parish church that was ringing two hundred years before Bannockburn, and no doubt its tone was familiar to the ear of Sir William Wallace, who married a Lanark girl. Their happiness was brief. The English were in occupation then, and one day in the street a band of them started to 'rag' him. He took it good humouredly till one of them threw a foul jest at his wife. A moment later the offender was yelling and goggling at the blood spurting from his wrist, his hand being in the gutter. Wallace was quick with his sword, but the English soldiers were too many for him and his few friends. His wife opened the door of their house; he slipped in and presently escaped from the back to the countryside. So they slew the girl. Afterward Wallace did some horribly brutal things to the English—but there's always a reason.

Every year in June Lanark commemorates Lanimer Day, and rides the burgh marches, as it has done since the sixteenth century. Lanimer is a corruption of Landmarch. It is a day of festival for the town and places around. There are processions led by the Provost and magistrates, the principal character in the bright pageantry being the Lanimer Queen, a maiden chosen from the girlhood of the public schools.

Lanark has its strange old tales, but here is a strange modern one, which I heard only the other day. A gentleman coming in his car to Lanark on business brought his daughter with him. While he went about his affairs she took a stroll, and presently stepped into an antique shop. She wanted to spend just a pound, but saw nothing tempting at the price. At last from a drawer the dealer brought a string of dark beads, and eventually she bought them. They were without a clasp, and next day her father took them to a city jeweller. "What are

N

they? " he asked casually. "Black pearls," came the answer. You may imagine a pause till the customer inquired their value. "We can offer you £250." The father took them home and told his daughter. As it chanced, he was going to London that night, and next morning he showed the string to a famous firm there. The jeweller, having examined the string, fetched his partner, who was even more interested. "£800," he said, "but may I ask——" The visitor gave the brief history. "Well," said the jeweller, "these pearls have been lost for a long time. They were worn by Mary Queen of Scots at Fotheringay Castle, on the morning of her execution. And I understand the executioner was a Lanark man." Can you credit it ? And yet why not ?

Paisley

"The place where the thread comes from" is just over the Renfrewshire border, six miles from Glasgow. I mention it partly because, if I don't, some of my ancestors may come haunting me, but mainly because of its Abbey Church, lately restored. Architecture apart, the Abbey has an interest unusual in that it was founded in 1163 by Walter Fitz Alan, High Steward of Scotland, whose forebears came from Brittany, and whose blood was to go to the making of the Royal Stuarts; wherefore it forms a link, the only visible link, I believe, connecting the originator of the Stuarts and King George V.

A statue of Robert Tannahill, a poet whose memory is cherished in the West, is in the churchyard. Annually throngs attend the open-air concert of his songs on Gleniffer Braes; but the poor fellow, neglected, penniless, ended his mortal life in a stream. At Paisley Place, the shabby building adjoining the Abbey, in June 1684 was celebrated the wedding of Claverhouse ("Bonnie Dundee") and Lady Jane Cochrane. From the festivities the groom was summoned to go a-hunting—Covenanters.

THE CLYDE, FROM ABOVE GOUROCK

Photo Valentine and Sons. Ltd.

[P. 180]

STIRLING CASTLE

Photo Valentine and Sons, Ltd.

CHAPTER VI

STIRLING

From Glasgow Stirling is 29 miles by rail, 27 by the shortest road, and from Edinburgh 35. But if you intend motoring from Glasgow, I suggest that you avoid the shortest road, with all its surface excellence, for it is as dull as it is busy, and take the road that goes round by the Blane Valley, the Campsie Hills, and the outskirts of Aberfoyle with its memories of 'Rob Roy.'

The Lake of Menteith makes the double mileage worth while. It is the only 'lake' we have in Scotland. How the English word came in I have never been able to find out, yet it is the right word, for there is something southern in the little loch's tender beauty, which may have given Scott his first idea of a setting for *The Lady of the Lake.* On the largest of the three islands, Inch-ma-Home ('Isle of Rest'), wooded with chestnut trees, the seeds of which came from Rome, are the well-preserved ruins of an Augustine priory, within whose walls lie many whose names are written in Scottish history. Bruce was there three times as a guest at the Priory, and Mary as a little girl was also a visitor. The garden where she played and made her innocent daisy chains is on the southern shore, set apart by a fence. Then there is the tale of a nun who fell in love with a Highland chieftain's son, with whom she planned to elope. In the interval, however, he was called to take part in a clan fight, and being mortally wounded confessed his sin to a too convenient monk. The monk, disguising himself, went to the lovers' trysting-place and, when the poor girl arrived, drowned her in the lake. Afterward they buried her, but in an upright position, presumably to prevent her resting, on the eminence known as the Nun's Hill.

No good Scot traverses these parts without saluting the name of R. B. Cunninghame Graham, descendant of Robert II, claimant to three ancient earldoms, Scotland's most respected man of letters and Nationalist, and still, with all his fourscore years, surely her most gallant figure.

At Thornhill a road strikes off for the little village of Kippen, where there is a vine, perhaps the most fruitful in the world, its yield far exceeding that of the celebrated vine at Hampton Court—which, I am sure, is one of the last things you expected to find in Scotland. Beyond Kippen, near Fintry, is our best example of a 'mote.'

Stirling recalls Edinburgh. The Castle stands on a mount of basalt, steep at one end, and the early part of the town on the descending ridge; and though on a very much smaller scale than the capital, it has retained much of the old-world atmosphere. It was an important place long before Edinburgh, and is still important as the agricultural and commercial centre of the shire.

It comes out of the haze early in the twelfth century. A document exists showing that Alexander I, son of the saintly Queen Margaret, dedicated a chapel in the Castle. He died there, and was followed by David I, the great endower of churches, who often resided on the Rock; but it was William the Lyon who was first to regard the place as a home. Toward the close of his long reign of half a century, falling ill in the North, he yearned for the Rock and the breezes that blew upon it, and struggled painfully back to Stirling, where he died in 1214. His son and grandson saw Scotland becoming prosperous, but the good days came to an end when the third Alexander, last of the Celtic kings, was thrown from his horse in the darkness near Kinghorn, in Fife. Four years later died the Maid of Norway, his granddaughter, who was to have wed the King of England's heir, thus uniting the Crowns of the two countries, and the ambitious Edward had to seek a less easy way of becoming Lord Paramount of Scotland. There had been peace for a hundred years, but now it was to be war—Scotland's War of Independence. Stirling, not Edinburgh, was then the Heart of Scotland, and to Edward, before he had finished, the Rock must have been a familiar sight—and a cheerful one too, for when he did lose the Castle he always succeeded in recapturing it. On the last occasion, in 1304, when his engines, throwing boulders and great balls of lead procured from the roofs of churches, were battering down the walls, he brought his queen and her ladies to see the fun. Edward was certainly a great soldier, and it would have hurt him bitterly could he have seen, nine years later, the frantic flight of his son from yonder field up to the Castle gate, where he was advised to flee farther.

The connection between the Castle and the Battle of Bannockburn was closer than is always made clear. In 1314 the Castle was still in English hands, though all the other castles in the country, save two, had fallen to Bruce, whose brother was now besieging it. In the spring of the year, however, Edward Bruce—not, we may believe, from any humanitarian motives—accepted the governor's promise—given, perhaps, with tongue in cheek —that the Castle, if not previously relieved, should be surrendered to the Scots on June 24. So the coming together of the two armies on the 23rd of that month was really brought about by the hot desire of Edward II, with his 50,000 men, to relieve the garrison by the day appointed, while the Scots were there to prevent him, if possible. As it befell, they did prevent him so thoroughly that the first attempt, on the 23rd, was the last, and he was further discouraged by the spectacular fiasco of Sir Henry de Bohun's essay to settle everything at the outset by lancing the Bruce. The big battle was fought on the following day, and if Scotland may still seem a little arrogant at times about the result, she has a pretty good excuse, for, after many defeats, it was really a very great victory, which has meant more to her than the result of any other battle. Edward's forces were much the superior in numbers, but undoubtedly their size helped toward their undoing, for they were crowded between two streams, and the one half was unable to fight because of the other half being in the way.

Next day the Castle was surrendered, and Bruce, as was his way, dismantled the fortifications, lest the place should again fall into English hands—which, however, it did, not long after his death. The English held it for six years, and then, after a long siege, the garrison was starved into submission. Old Froissart tells us that artillery was employed in this siege, which would make it the first occasion of the use of gunpowder in Scotland by Scots. The 'crakkis,' as Barbour quaintly calls the cannon, were probably as troublesome to the assaulters as to the assaulted; one can imagine them 'crakking' in divers ways, and one remembers how, more than a hundred years later, James II, at the siege of Roxburgh Castle, was killed by the misbehaviour of one of his pet 'bombards,' then considered the very latest thing in guns.

It may be that there are still relics of the stonework which was standing in those days, but the oldest of the existing buildings were not raised till the times of the Stuarts, and mainly by the three later Jameses. The outer gateway, which is approached by a spacious esplanade whereon stands the National Memorial to Bruce, a mailed figure facing in the direction of Bannockburn, is only about two centuries old, and replaced an earlier entrance. It is reached by a bridge over a fosse. The inner barrier carries the initials of Queen Anne, though it was merely repaired in that lady's reign. But the Keep,

now before us, opened its gates to James IV, of whose
four towers two have disappeared. History suggests a
scene with that archway for setting, the persons being
his widow, Margaret Tudor, her two boys, and emissaries
of the Regent Albany, come to demand the custody of
the children. Margaret, however flighty she may have
been, did not lack pluck. There she stands, facing the
emissaries, listens to their persuasions and threats, and
then ends the interview with a signal that brings down
the portcullis between them. Later, however, Albany
beat her by appearing in person at Stirling with 7000 men.
One of the boys was James V, and he grew up to build
the Palace which, as you will see presently, is the finest
thing in the Castle.

Meanwhile, passing through the tunnel-like gateway
we come to the Parliament House, which seems to have
been a James II erection, probably designed by Cochrane,
the luckless architect who, with others of the King's
'upstart' favourites, was hanged from the bridge at
Lauder by the reasonably angry nobles. The dignified
mass of stone and mortar, with its noteworthy oriel
windows, has survived much ill-usage. To the north of
it, below the old Mint—money, by the way, was coined in
the Castle from the days of Alexander III, and there is a
queer tale of James IV and an alchemist (this James could
be sadly credulous) who claimed to possess the secret of
transmutation—you will see another tunnel, an entrance
to the Castle till the end of the fifteenth century.

Though he died young, James V got much out of life,
and one of his more worthy enjoyments lay in the building of palaces. You may picture him on a fine morning
at Stirling—a slim man, long-faced, with a big Roman
nose and a moustache covering the corners of a mouth
that was probably humorous—watching the builders and
sculptors and, very likely, having a joke with them.

The Palace forms a quadrangle, the courtyard of

which is known as the Lions' Den. Two at least of the Jameses kept a menagerie. The building is a mixture of the Gothic and French Renaissance, the masons having been brought over from France. Between the windows are niches with pillars carrying statues, more or less damaged, but there is a fairly well-preserved example at the north-east corner, said to portray James himself as the 'Gudeman of Ballengeich.' The building was never quite completed; the west side shows that more was intended. The bars were put on the windows when the kidnapping of the young James VI was a possibility. Its use as a barracks has not improved the interior, but several grand fireplaces survive, also one or two of the original iron-studded doors.

To read the story of Stirling then is to people the Palace with ghosts. The invisible population of Holyroodhouse is not larger nor more distinguished. It would be interesting to know the thoughts of each member of that gay throng who attended the christening of the child fated to bear the crowns of the two kingdoms; to know how Mary looked on that occasion, while Darnley sulked in his own apartment, and what the two were thinking of each other; yes, and to hear the whispered remarks of the guests upon the Queen of England's gift, the christening basin—three hundred ounces of gold. The actual christening took place in the chapel hard by, which was rebuilt later, with no particular elegance, by the subject of the ceremony. By many generations it was used for anything but worship, but as I write I learn that it is now to recover dignity as the Castle Museum.

West of the chapel is the building containing the apartment known as the Douglas Room, which, had not fire destroyed most of it in 1855, would have been the oldest complete structure within these walls. Yet the original chamber remains in the restored house, and had you been standing meditating in the archway under its dormer window, on a February evening in the year 1452, you would have been disturbed by the sound of a scuffle above, and then startled by the thud of a body, very bloody, at your feet. That was the end of the supper-party given by James II to William, Earl of Douglas.

It is not a pretty story. James suspected the powerful earl of disloyalty, yet thought to win him over from his alliance, which might lead to a rebellion, with the Earls of Crawford and Ross. He invited Douglas to come to Stirling, and under a letter of safe-conduct Douglas came. The first interview seems to have passed pleasantly enough; on the following day king and earl dined amicably together. But at supper that night, James raised the vital question. "Will you," he said in effect, "break your bond with Ross and Crawford?" Now Douglas too was descended from a king, and his answer was an unqualified "No." Whereupon James, in the one foolish and passionate act of his brief career, whipped out his dagger and, crying "Well, this will break it!" struck twice at his guest, wounding him in the neck and chest. The courtiers added their four-and-twenty strokes and stabs, and then dragged the dread thing into the ante-room and got rid of it by the window.

Let us quit horror for a while and take a survey from the ramparts of the Douglas Garden. Afar are the scattered peaks of the Highland hills; below stretches the rich Carse with the silvery-blue serpentine windings of the Forth, which hereabouts makes $12\frac{1}{2}$ miles of a journey through $5\frac{1}{2}$ miles of land. Across the valley rises the shrubby Abbey Craig, on which is perched the Wallace Monument in the form of a baronial tower, with a crown, 220 feet high. The Monument is reached by a winding path; a winding stair goes up to the battlements; it harbours a magnificent statue of the hero, also his mighty sword, which lay for centuries in Dumbarton Castle, and other memorials. In that valley now watered by the Forth was once, very long ago, a sea loch, which must have been deep, since whales came into it. Their bones have been found and along with them the primitive flensing implements used by the early inhabitants of Scotland. The view from the Castle walls is full also of historic interest. For example, the narrow bridge down yonder, dating from the fifteenth century, marks the site of the timber one which in 1297 helped to give Wallace his greatest victory by collapsing while packed with the enemy. South, within a loop of the Forth, stands the square tower of Cambuskenneth Abbey, where lies the dust of the unwise, unsoldierly, yet not cowardly, James III—his portrait in the Scottish National Gallery gives him the longest face you could wish to see—slain after the Battle of Sauchieburn, not far away. In his flight from the field he fell from his horse at the door of a Bannockburn mill, and was badly hurt and stunned. The miller and his wife, not recognizing him, carried him indoors. Regaining consciousness, he asked for a priest. "Who are you?" then inquired the miller, and James answered in these pathetic words: "I was your King this morning." The goodwife flew willingly to the door, calling, "A priest for the King!" Presently came a man, outwardly a holy one. "Give me the Sacraments," said James, though hoping he might yet recover. "That will I do heartily," returned the other, and with a blade, till now concealed, gave him swift passage.

I am sorry I cannot point to the spot on the Rock where James IV and his Court witnessed what must have been the first attempt at aviation in Scotland, by the alchemist, Damian, who had evidently determined to do something desperate to regain the Royal favour. On a pair of wings of his own invention, he declared, he would fly to France. An historian says that he sprang boldly from the battlements; while a writer of fiction avers that a courtier cut short his hesitation by giving him a shove off. Be that as it may, he went plump on the rocks and broke a leg. James, who was always lenient toward people of that sort, pardoned the fiasco, accepting the aviator's plea that all would have gone well had he used eagle's feathers instead of hen's.

In Stirling Town are at least three buildings which you ought to see. First, the parish church, which harbours two congregations. The nave belongs to the fifteenth century—some say earlier; its oaken roof has been said to be "the finest open-timber roof of the Middle Ages possessed by any church in Scotland." The lower half of the tower belongs to the same period; the upper half—a tower upon a tower—to the next century, when the choir, which is higher than the nave, was built. The upper tower has been twice under fire, from the Castle, in 1651 and 1746, and bears marks of misdirected shots. Regarded sidelong, the differences in height and style between nave and choir make for an ungainly whole; but from the purely archæological point of view each portion is a delight. Moreover, in St Andrew's Chapel you will find a beautiful Antiphonary, bound in wood and brass, of the fifteenth century.

At the top of Broad Street stands Mar's Work. With its semi-hexagonal towers flanking the wide, arched gateway and its elaborate, many-windowed frontage, it must have appeared a splendid place when the Regent Mar and his lady gave their house-warming in 1570. On the towers are two mottoes which I venture to give in modern spelling :

> The more I stand on open height,
> My faults more subject are to sight.

> I pray all lookers on this lodging
> With gentle eye to give their judging.

And yet it has been hinted that Mar plundered the stones from Cambuskenneth Abbey.

But wait a moment! On the rear of the house is a third motto:

> Espy, speak forth and spare not.
> Consider well I care not.

Which does suggest that the Regent had his truculent side.

In Castle Wynd, a street sloping up to the fortress, you will find what has been called, and truly, I believe, the finest example of an old town house left in Scotland—Argyll's Lodging. It was begun in 1632 by the Earl of Stirling, courtier and poet—to whom James VI presented a great part of North America, including Canada, and who died in poverty—and was completed by the Marquis of Argyll nearly forty years later. Forming three sides of a quadrangle, with staircase turrets ending in sharply pointed roofs in the angles, crow-stepped gables, carved chimneys, ornate windows, and a broad, low, pillared doorway, it is as pretty an old-world residence as one could wish for one's own. While now it serves as a hospital, its antique features, including fine fireplaces, have been respected.

Dunblane

About six miles north of Stirling, *via* Bridge of Allan, a pretty residential place, with a spa and a mild climate, is Dunblane, just over the Perthshire border. Of Dunblane it has been written, "Dirty Dunblane, let us pass it by!"—but that was about 1650. To-day its cleanliness is unquestioned, including the streets of the town, which are narrow, twisting, and steep, and its air is considered of the healthiest, as witness the big hydro-hotel on the hill. St Blane founded a church in the eighth century, and in the twelfth David I endowed the Cathedral, but his work remains only in the lower stages of the tower. The nave belongs to the following century. The western front is particularly admirable. In 1633 Archbishop Laud observed that it had been a handsome church "before the Deformation." After that event the choir was used as the parish church, and the nave remained more or less a ruin for 300 years. Toward the end of last century it was successfully restored. Close by runs the Allan, which I am told would be a really good salmon river were the poaching stopped. Anglers, by applying to the local association, may fish for salmon and trout for a few shillings a year.

CHAPTER VII

AYRSHIRE—GALLOWAY—DUMFRIES

Ayr and the Poet

AYRSHIRE has fine roads, rich rural scenery, a splendidly varied coast, a brisk, healthy climate, and a long history; but, should you ask a fellow-traveller his main reason for going thither, the answer will almost certainly be "Burns" or "Golf."

If it be Burns who draws you, let us begin with Ayr, a cheerful town, with a real 'county' atmosphere. I have still to meet the holiday-maker who cares a button for municipal statistics, so I shall merely say that Ayr is big enough to have a theatre, an entertainment pavilion, three picture-houses, a racecourse, with four meetings in the year, and several commodious and good hotels. Like all the towns and villages on the Ayrshire coast it has a magnificent outlook, while its countryside is a land literally flowing with milk—and, for all I know, honey too—though in these days the farmers do not make a song about it. If you wander over that countryside, knowing anything of the poems, you will realize how generously the Poet's genius was nourished upon its soil.

Ayr is in Kyle, the middle of the three old divisions of what is now the shire—Cunningham and Carrick being the others. Kyle, if it does not mean 'woods,' was perhaps called after Coil, who, in Scotland's tribal days, may have been the monarch of convivial tastes destined to acquire immortality in a nursery rhyme. In Ayr Sir William Wallace began his campaign for freedom by burning the quarters of the English garrison, garrison included; a few years later, after Bannockburn, the Scottish Parliament met in the kirk to confer upon Bruce and his heirs for ever the succession to the Crown. During the three following centuries Ayr must have known many alarums and excursions; for when the Ayrshire barons were not fighting against the English they were, like the Highland clans, fighting among themselves. In 1560 it is recorded by the parish minister that the citizens were not safe in their own streets. A century later Cromwell was responsible for the building of the fort, some fragments of which remain, and, as was his way, put the kirk to secular uses for his military. However, it should be added, he partly defrayed the cost of a new kirk, in which you may worship to-day, and in the yard of which are some curious epitaphs.

But Scotland had seen the last of military strife, and had emerged, still hopeful, from half a century of extreme depression, when Burns came into it, on January 25, 1759. The Ayr he knew was a town in process of recovering its prosperity; how low it had fallen we gather from the words of the distinguished tourist who, early in that century, came to spy more than the land—Daniel Defoe:

> It is now like an old beauty, and shows the ruin of a good face, but is still decaying every day ; and from having been the fifth best town in Scotland it is now the fifth worst.

Burns must have been familiar with a great many interesting things since removed. As somebody once remarked of another town with a long story, "It's all sites and no sights"—not that Ayr is destitute of antiquities. The Auld Brig, crossing the river Ayr, is the most ancient, though we may hesitate to believe that, with its four lofty arches, it was standing there 650 years ago. Raised about 1500, confirmed by occasional repairs, it carried its years bravely till 1892, when its stability became doubtful. The alarm went forth; from Scotsmen everywhere, led by the late Lord Rosebery, responses were received; and the sum of £11,000 ensured its safety. Now it looks good for a few more centuries. If you know the poem *The Twa Brigs*, you will look for the New Brig, built while the Poet was still in his teens. In the poem the Auld Brig assures the New that it will still be 'a brig' when the other is ' a shapeless cairn '—a true enough prophecy, since the New Brig, seriously damaged by floods, had to be rebuilt in 1877.

In front of the railway-station are two striking monuments: the first, by Sir Thomas Brock, in memory of territorials of the Royal Scots Fusiliers killed on active service; the second, by G. A. Lawson, of Robert Burns, one of the finest statues of the Poet in Scotland.

In the High Street you cannot miss the Tam o' Shanter Inn, with its thatched roof and large sign depicting the departure of Tam on his famous midnight ride. Dr Robert Chambers tells us that Tam had a prototype, a farmer in Carrick, whose wife was a very superstitious woman. One night, riding hazily home from Ayr, Tam lost his bonnet, with his money in it, and in order to quench his wife's wrath, which she had been 'nursing to keep it warm,' pulled himself together, and set her shuddering to a terrible tale of witches seen on the road. As I write, negotiations are in progress toward making the old place the town's property, thus preserving it for all time. A sight of the interior makes it easy to picture the opening scene of *Tam o' Shanter*—the snug room on a stormy night, the buxom landlady, and Tam, with his crony, the Souter, getting merrier and merrier until the hour strikes when he must face that drenching, darksome journey on a road whose reputation is ghostly.

Nor can you miss the Wallace Tower, over a hundred feet high, standing out on the pavement, holding in a

niche a statue of the hero. Farther down the High
Street is the Kirk Port, with ancient archway, and
beyond it the Kirk itself, already mentioned. The Town
Buildings, built in 1820, are also in this thoroughfare,
their steeple being Ayr's fairest ornament.

A little way south of the High Street, at the foot of
Cromwell Place, rises the old tower of the church of St
John's, commonly called Fort Castle. The remains of
the real fort are close by. We are now near the Low
Green, the Esplanade, and the sandy beach, with their
most splendid outlook, though not quite so extensive as
the prospect from the end of the pier running out from
the harbour. Thence, looking north, you scan the coast
of a great bay—a coast carrying a succession of golf
courses, all more or less famous: Prestwick, with three
clubs—the rather exclusive Prestwick and St Nicholas
and the more cosmopolitan St Cuthbert—also the new
municipal course; Troon, with two private and four
public courses; Gailes, with two; Irvine and Bogside.

To Largs

A refreshing run may be made from Ayr, through the
above pleasant places and Ardrossan and Fairlie, to Largs
—one of Glasgow's oldest and most popular holiday resorts. Historically its chief fame lies in its having been
the site of the Battle of Largs in 1263. The battle, I'm
afraid, consisted largely in the throwing of stones at the
storm-beaten Norsemen, with their broken ships, on the
beach, Haco's galleys having suffered, if in a smaller degree,
what Philip's galleons were to suffer three centuries later.
It was the end of the Norsemen in these islands. Largs is
nicely sheltered by the Great Cumbrae, with its solitary
town of Millport prettily situated on a bay at the south
end. The island is only ten miles round; but the Millport
minister of a century or so ago did not measure the importance of a thing by its bulk, for on the Sabbath he was

o

wont to pray for "the inhabitants of the Great and Little Cumbraes and those of the adjacent island of Great Britain."

To Girvan

Looking south from the pier at Ayr, across the sands, we see, on the verge of the cliff, Greenan Castle, an object photographed on my boy's memory, and one which, I fancy, you will remember as long as you remember Ayr. I have found no story about Greenan; but the ruin, gaunt against the sky, is weird enough to suggest some rare tales of horror. It is visible at closer quarters from the coast road to Girvan—a magnificent run of 22 miles, mostly high above the sea.

A more commanding ruin is Dunure Castle, farther south, especially if viewed from the shore. In 1570 Earl Gilbert Kennedy, the owner, had a tiff about lands with Allan Stewart, commendator of Crossraguel Abbey, some miles inland; and, having waylaid and seized him there, brought him to Dunure, where in front of the great kitchen fire he caused him to be roasted *and* basted until the required signature was obtained. A little way beyond Dunure, from the sandy Bay of Culzean (pronounced without the 'z'), the road strikes inland toward Maybole town, which has a few interesting old buildings and is within two miles of the remains of the Abbey. Coming back to the coast we pass Culzean Castle—not a ruin, but a splendid eighteenth-century erection, the home of the Marquis of Ailsa.

Presently we are in the village of The Maidens— alluring name, but, alas! once more, the Maidens are only rocks. Almost next door is Turnberry. On the Point, where blazed the false yet fortunate signal which, as you may remember, brought Bruce over from Arran, is an honest lighthouse. The name Turnberry, however, if you ever look at railway posters, will raise visions of one of Scotland's most attractive golf courses and a luxurious hotel.

All this time we have been coming nearer to that strange lump of granite, Ailsa Craig, and Girvan, a prosperous town, with a reputation for health-giving breezes, is the place from which to visit it—a trip of ten miles. The rock is roughly three-quarters of a mile long, half a mile broad, and more than a fifth of a mile high. The climb to the summit is stiff; the upper part is, or was, a small forest of giant nettles. The Craig carries a lighthouse, and, in spite of the presence of human beings and a powerful fog-horn, swarms with birds, mostly serious solan geese and funny red-nosed puffins. Many a man, who has never been within three thousand miles of Scotland, has touched it with his hand in manipulating a curling-stone of Ailsa Craig granite.

Alloway

From Ayr the pilgrims go to Alloway—by motor or on foot—Alloway, birthplace of Burns. A hamlet, rather than a village, all its importance in the eyes of the world rests in a lowly whitewashed wayside Cottage, with a thatched roof. Perhaps the exterior of the Cottage is kept a little too spick and span; one does not feel that it looked so when the little boy arrived, during a winter tempest, more than a century and a half ago; yet realism is not everything, and one is thankful for its preservation—its remarkable preservation—considering that it was for long a tavern before being bought by the trustees of the Monument, in 1880, for £4000. The interior is furnished as in the day of Burns' parents. The kitchen is the scene of *The Cotter's Saturday Night*, though it could have been only a memory to the Poet, whose home it ceased to be when he was seven. But with that poem in mind, it is easy to picture him there, as a small boy, sitting with his people, dreaming in the firelight or candlelight. Reverence is a word that may look like becoming obsolete; yet reverence is very evident among the visitors to this room, many of whom are in Scotland for the first time, some having come from the ends of the earth. There is also a museum furnished with relics of the Poet.

The Monument, a short walk distant, was erected in 1820, and consists of a triangular base, a Corinthian cyclostyle, and a cupola surmounted by a tripod. In the grounds surrounding it is a grotto sheltering stone effigies of "Tam o' Shanter" and "Souter Johnnie," the work of James Thom, the untutored sculptor of near-by Tarbolton.

Alloway's Auld Kirk is quite near. When Captain Grose, the artist, came here for material for his big book on Scottish antiquities, he and Burns became friends, and Burns asked him to make for him a picture of the Kirk. Grose agreed on condition that in return Burns should write a poem involving witches. Burns composed *Tam o' Shanter*, all in one day, though not without great pains, and in the open air. Grose contrived to give the ruin a really 'haunted' appearance, so that we can almost believe, while looking at his drawing, that the fuddled Tam, on horseback at yonder gable window, did actually behold the unholy revels of the witches described in the poem. We must remember, too, that in Burns's day witchcraft was not a thing of long ago. As late as 1722 a witch was burned in Sutherland, and it was not till 1735 that the statutes against witches, applicable to England as well as Scotland, were repealed—with the strong disapproval of many Scottish ministers.

Near the gate of the Churchyard lies the dust of Burns's father, and such are the ways of souvenir-hunters that the original stone was long ago removed in bits.

The Auld Brig o' Doon, a single arch, steep and narrow, was old in Tam's time. In the course of recent repairs a cobbled roadway, deep under the existing one, was laid bare. It would be over those cobbles that the Poet makes the frantic farmer urge his terrified mare, before the flying witches, to reach the keystone of the bridge:

> There, at them thou thy tail may toss,
> A running stream they dare na cross.
> But ere the keystane she could make
> The fient a tail she had to shake.

Of the Doon itself, enough to say that at this point, in its sylvan surroundings, it affords one of the fairest of scenes in Scotland.

Mauchline and Kilmarnock

Eleven miles out of Ayr is Mauchline, with its many Burns memories. There he was married in 1788 to Jean Armour, and you will see the house where they lived awhile in one room. "Poosie Nancy's" tavern, scene of *The Jolly Beggars*, is still there. Happier monuments, however, are the National Memorial, with its tower, and the Cottage Homes for aged working folk, raised by the Burns Association. A mile and a half from Mauchline is Mossgiel, the farmhouse where he spent four years and wrote much.

Commercially Kilmarnock is Ayrshire's most important town. While its burghal motto is the sober one of *Virtute et industria*, its past was not always peaceful, especially during Covenanting times. This is a typical churchyard inscription:

> Here lie the Heads of John Ross and John Shields, who suffered at Edinburgh, Dec. 27th, 1666, and had their Heads set up in Kilmarnock.

The pilgrim, however, will visit Kilmarnock because of the Burns Monument in the Kay Park, with its museum containing many relics, including a copy of the first edition of the poems, known as the "Kilmarnock," many manuscripts, and the McKee collection of Burnsiana.

Galloway

A general survey of Galloway may be made in a few days; to gain a fair knowledge of it would take months. In old buildings alone it has, for a tale like mine, most embarrassing riches, and I can direct you to only a few of the more remarkable.   The most helpful and beautiful and handy book I have found on this part of Scotland is *Highways and Byways in Galloway and Carrick*, by the Rev. C. H. Dick, whose grace of style I used to admire and envy in our old college days.   For the tourist who wants to know 'all about' Galloway, without reading a dusty work, it is the book—a study of twenty years.

Coming down by the shore road from Ayrshire we pass through the charmingly placed fishing village of Ballantrae, with its castle of Ardstinchar and wonderful sea prospect, and climb up the hill to enter Glen App. The Glen has a church—not ancient, but, as they proudly told me, the smallest in Scotland—which has lately been beautified to the memory of a girl, daughter of a shipping magnate, who ventured to fly the Atlantic, and was heard of no more.   Thence we come down to the green shores of Loch Ryan, with their caves, and through the village of Cairn Ryan into Stranraer.

To most people Stranraer is merely the port from which one takes the short cut to Ireland on luxurious steamers; but it has other virtues.   Lying snug at the head of the loch, it owns a solitary antiquity, a sixteenth-century castle, preserved.   With nearly all Galloway on its right and the Rhinns on its left, it offers a fine base for excursions.

The Rhinns—once an island and a freakish performance of Nature, which you will find repeated in the Island of Mull—deserves a chapter to itself, if only for the

queer stories connected with it. Let me tell you only
two. In the year 1710 the minister of Stoneykirk—*i.e.*, St
Stephen's Church—had in his flock two lairds who were
at enmity. He sided with the one, but continued to pay
pastoral calls at the house of the other, though, being
aware of the bitter resentment there, he was, for a time,
careful to refuse any tangible token of hospitality. One
day, however, the housekeeper, after a discussion on
spiritual matters, offered a glass of wine which he, being,
perhaps, very 'dry,' accepted. Shortly after leaving the
house he was observed to be "swelling visibly," and, a
little later, the villagers were further intrigued by the
spectacle of buttons flying from his waistcoat. They
followed him, and presently experienced the crowning
thrill of seeing him fall down, dead. Apparently the
Rhinns folk had their own methods of dealing with such
emergencies. Instead of summoning the authorities, or
even a leech, they simply stood him up against a convenient dyke, propping him there with his own walking-
stick, to await the arrival of his man-servant. The rest
of the tale is disappointing. There was no murder trial,
the Presbytery concluding that death was due to an act
of Providence. But one goes on wondering about the
buttons.

The other story is much older. Long, long before
Scotland had discovered whisky, she had a beverage
drawn from the heather—heather ale—the secret of
which was held by a family of a Galloway clan. When
Niall of the Nine Hostages and his men came over from
Ireland, a thousand or so years ago, they coveted the
secret. They fought for it—fought till of the Galloway
clan were left only five—a father, his three sons, and a
traitor who had informed Niall concerning the ownership
of the recipe. At last the father and sons, fighting
bravely, were driven to the verge of the cliff forming the
Mull of Galloway, the most southerly point of the Rhinns,

and of Scotland. There the Irish leader, who seems to have wanted the recipe very badly, bade his men pause, and announced that the four might have their lives in exchange for the secret.

"Nay," answered the old man, with a swift glance at his eldest son, named Trost, "I have no wish to live dishonoured, and my younger sons shall not do so. Yet my eldest son may live—if he choose."

So they killed the father and two younger sons, and then Niall called to Trost: "Tell me the secret, so that you may go free."

"Not to you, who are a stranger," Trost replied, "but to Sionach, there, who is of my own race, will I tell it. So may I lessen the disgrace. But Sionach must come to me—close to me—so that none but he may hear my words."

"Go forward, Sionach!" commanded Niall, and the traitor moved forward, unwillingly enough, toward the cliff's edge.

"Nearer!" cried Trost, throwing down his weapons. "Do you fear an unarmed man?"

At that Sionach took courage and went up to Trost, who clasped him in his arms and plunged over the cliff.

And that is why, when you come to Scotland, we shall, very regretfully, be unable to offer you any of our celebrated heather ale.

The popular place on the Rhinns is Portpatrick, on the western shore, the nearest point to Ireland—a pleasant little old-world village set in a rocky cove, under cliffs, on one of which is magnificently placed a great hotel, much frequented by golfers. It possesses a seventeenth-century church, with an odd round tower, which may, at one period, have been a watch-tower or lighthouse. A little way south of the village, perched on the point of a lofty promontory, is Dunskey Castle—a really impressive ruin. Time was when Portpatrick did a considerable

shipping business with Ireland—a print of 1815 shows
it as a busy haven—and we know of distinguished passengers, like Mrs Siddons and Keats. For years the
Irish mails were sent thence to Donaghadee; a dock was
built, alongside which trains could be run; but in 1873
the whole thing was abandoned and left to the winds and
waves. You can see—indeed, it is one of the sights—
how the breakers have dislodged and made sport with
the huge blocks of masonry.

From Stranraer let us go east, by Castle Kennedy,
Dunragit, and Glenluce, to Newton-Stewart. The
stately ruin of Castle Kennedy, set between two little
lochs, stands in one of the world's most beautiful landscape gardens, which, I believe, is open to visitors on
Wednesdays and Saturdays. Near by is the modern
Castle of Inch, home of the Earl of Stair. At Dunragit
we are in the centre of a land flowing with cream and
fresh butter—at all events, they flow continually from
the great creamery there to all parts of the kingdom.
This is certainly not the Grey Galloway of Samuel Ruther-
ford Crockett and John Buchan, and when you come to
Glenluce, about four miles by road from the great Luce
Bay, you will see how very green grass can be, especially
around the old Abbey. That is because, centuries ago,
the monks riddled all the soil. To-day the rent of these
lands runs high. The Abbey, situate in a broad vale,
girdled by low hills and trees—the monks had eyes for
beauty as well as abundant crops—was founded toward
the end of the twelfth century, and was one of the three
Cistercian houses in Galloway. It escaped the heavier
blasts of the Reformation, and the chapter house, its
roof supported by an octagonal pillar 18 feet high, is
almost intact, while considerable portions of choir, tran-
sept, and cloister walls, also of two little chapels, still
stand.

A short run, by road or rail, across the moors brings

us to Newton-Stewart, on the Cree, prettily situated in a deep hollow. The town is not old, but across the river is the village of Minnigaff, with things in its church to delight the archæologist; and in the surrounding country-side are joys for artist and antiquarian alike—such a plethora, indeed, that I must refer you to Mr Dick.

Less than 10 miles north of Newton-Stewart, Glen Trool—sad-sounding word, though it means only 'stream'—with its loch, presents Galloway's finest piece of inland scenery. The glen is narrow and deep; the loch, fringed by pine woods, is walled by Galloway's greatest hills, steep green slopes topped with bare preci-pices. Here one feels out of the world; and so, perhaps, felt King Robert the Bruce when, as Barbour tells, he took refuge for a season in Glen Trool, and passed much of his time in deer-hunting. But somebody carried the news of his hiding-place to the Earl of Pembroke, at Carlisle, who lost no time in despatching a mounted force that should trap him in the glen. The Earl, however, was not the only one to be well served by spies, and the King received tidings of the enemy's approach. The Scots were poorly equipped, but in such a place Nature may become an ally. All night long a party of the King's followers laboured and sweated on the top of Mulldonach Hill, and by dawn had edged the summit's verge with massive granite boulders; while the remainder lay low at the head of the loch. Day brought the in-vaders, but already Nature was against them, and they had to leave their horses before they reached the foot of the loch. As they advanced, the way became harder and harder; no thought of marching in good order; they scrambled along the lower slopes as best they might. At last they came to a place where only single file was possible. On one side of the track, if such it could be called, Mulldonach rose precipitous; on the other side the land fell almost sheer to the loch.

Easy to imagine it when you are in the glen. For a while no sound, save the soldiers' calls and curses, and the rattle of stones dislodged by their stumbling feet. Then, like a knife thrust into each of them, the sudden note of a hunting-horn! There is a brief hush in the hollow, then yells from above. And down comes the granite—a bombardment that would break the nerve of the bravest. Panic—and the King's men are up with their bows and arrows, picking off those who have not been smashed or drowned. At the head of the loch is a spot called the Soldiers' Holm, where the poor devils, or some of them, were buried. Bruce died in 1329. The six hundredth anniversary of his death was marked by the raising of the Memorial Cairn at the head of the glen.

There are other graves in the neighbourhood. Among the trees on the south-west of the loch is a monument to six men who died there on a Sunday morning in 1685. With others they were at their worship when Captain Urquhart and his dragoons came upon them. . . . There are many such graves in Galloway. The dust of Covenanters is a part of it. It is an old story, but even at this time of day the subject may still suggest controversy. To some of us the Covenanters, with all respect to their courage, may appear as stiff-necked and aggravating psalm-singing people, while the dragoons did only their duty; to others the dragoons' was a foul duty, while the Covenanters stood for Scottish freedom, as surely as did Wallace and Bruce. So we might argue within four walls, out of the abundance of our bookish knowledge; but at the graves in those lonely open spaces the tragedy comes close, so close that we see the blood on the heather and hear the weeping of those who have stolen back to seek their beloved dead; and if we have any admiration for brave men we shall be silent, setting it all down to "man's inhumanity to man."

Beyond Glen Trool, northward and eastward, are the

wildest regions of Galloway, and of Carrick too—great
solitudes, homes of the otter and fox and still, maybe, of
the eagle—soundless, save for the bleat of sheep or the
melancholy cry of the curlew and croak of the raven;
where you might wander on ninety-nine days without
meeting a soul, and on the hundredth the man would be a
shepherd. Until lately some of the Galloway shepherds
and their families lived lives of inconceivable remoteness
from the world, but now they have their 'wireless,' and
what it means to them no town-dweller can appreciate.

Here, indeed, is Grey Galloway, and the names of
some of its features are gloomy, if not ghastly—for
example, the Murder Hole of Loch Neldricken—there is
another Murder Hole up at Loch Doon—Loch Enoch,
Loch Dungeon, Cauldron of the Dungeon, and Black
Water of Dee. At the west end of the first loch, under
the loom of the hills, a few yards from the shore,
surrounded by sedgy shallows with boggy bottom, is
a deep black circular pool which, had it been situated
in the West Highlands, would surely have been the
reputed abode of some horrid monster. It has no
legend, but, should you view it on a dull day, you will
easily imagine something unpleasant. Loch Enoch, in
its bed of ice-ground granite, high among the hills, has
the curious feature of an islet containing a small loch
of its own. They say that the trout of Loch Enoch, if
they still exist, are deformed—lower fluke of tail and
under fins partially rubbed away by contact with the
granite particles.

The Cauldron of the Dungeon—'dungeon' suggests a
castle, but here, I believe, the word has to do with 'rock'
—is a broad waste of moorland, with small cheerless lochs
and unhappy streams, almost completely shut in by
callous mountains. Looking down upon it you have a
scene of desolation where, in certain lights, Nature seems
to hate Humanity. In the *Gallovidian Encyclopædia*

Mr Taggart writes of the five large hills that lie beside one another "and gradually rise, the one a little higher than the other." Toward sunset "the shadows of these hills on the level moors below seem like the fingers of an Awful Hand." Here you will meet hawks that scream and threaten, goats gone wild, croaking ravens. The only human abode is a shepherd's cot, six miles from the nearest road. If you are making an exploration of the Cauldron and the strange places around it, or fishing in the burns, you may find yourself in danger of being over-taken by darkness; if so, it will be wise to seek hospitality of the shepherd and the comfort of his peat fire for the night. Here you are always on the verge of adventure, and you may want a stout heart as well as stout boots.

From Newton-Stewart you may run south to Wigtown, rather an austere little place where, in 1685, they put to death two women Covenanters, tying them to stakes on the shore of the Water of Bladenoch, and letting the rising tide do the rest. In the churchyard you will find their graves, with quaint, pathetic inscriptions. One of the women was in her sixties, the other in her teens, and it would seem that they met death with equal fortitude.

Only a dozen miles south of that place of crime, at Isle of Whithorn, marked by the ruins of a chapel, on the site of St Ninian's *Candida Casa*, Christianity first set foot in Scotland.

From Newton-Stewart, once more, let us go across country to New Galloway, about 18 miles, on a very good road, which used to be a very lonesome one. The name New Galloway is a little confusing, since it stands not for a district but a village, and a superior one. About seven miles out of Newton-Stewart, in the wildest of spots, we pass a monument to the memory of Alexander Murray, D.D., who began life as a shepherd boy and became Professor of Oriental Languages in the University of Edinburgh.

New Galloway—the railway-station of that name lies five miles to the south—is close to Loch Ken, which, to my mind, is Galloway's loveliest, as well as its largest, loch.   There is a fine view of it, with wood-sheltered Kenmure Castle, from the golf course, one of the best in the south.   In the castle is preserved the head of a pike which weighed 72 lb.   Anglers may care to hear its story. One day in the year 1750 or thereabouts the laird remarked to his bailiff, John Murray, that he didn't believe the loch contained anything but minnows.   A day or two later, Murray, while watching some ducklings on the surface, saw them disappear, one after the other.   So he baited a strong line with a duck, started fishing, and eventually got a bite.   He landed a pike as long as himself, killed it, carried it on his back to the castle and dropped it at the laird's feet, with the blunt remark, "There's your minnow!"

Burns visited the castle—which is not a ruin—and while riding away from it, over the hills, in a thunderstorm, received his first inspiration for *Scots Wha Ha'e.*

Less than two miles east of the village, at Balmaclellan, was the home of Robert Patterson, prototype of Scott's 'Old Mortality.'   While his wife kept a school there, he went about the country on his white pony, with mallet and chisels, erecting stones to the memory of martyred Covenanters and recutting the worn inscriptions on existing memorials.

Kirkcudbright (pronounced 'Kirkoobrie'), beloved of artists, is sweetly set on the Dee, a few miles from the Solway Firth.   It is the sort of country town that one likes at first sight—quiet, roomy, wholesome, mainly modern, yet fortunate in the survival of ancient landmarks in its very midst.   The greater part of the beautiful Tolbooth is very old; the steeple may have been built of stones taken from Dundrennan Abbey, about five miles to the east; the Mercat Cross dates from 1504; and the walls of Maclellan's Castle are not much younger. And if you desire more antiquities, without leaving the town, there is the Stewartry Museum in tree-lined St Mary's Street.

A feature of Kirkcudbright is the Embankment Walk, locally called 'the Bank.' Or you may take a short stroll to St Mary's Isle, which is a peninsula, where once stood a priory, and, later, the Earl of Selkirk's mansion, in which Burns composed his best-known *Grace before Meat*:

> Some ha'e meat and canna eat,
> And some wad eat that want it ;
> But we ha'e meat and we can eat,
> Sae let the Lord be thankit.

Of Dundrennan Abbey, first of Galloway's Cistercian houses, the remains, Norman and Gothic, are fragmentary, but there is much for the visitor who dotes on carved stones. To most of us, however, Dundrennan is associated with Mary, Queen of Scots no more. There, on May 15, 1568, in flight from the Battle of Langside, she spent her last night in Scotland—and one may hope that she slept well, after the long day's ride. On the morrow she took boat across the Solway, to yield herself to the tender mercies of Elizabeth.

If you can stay a while in Kirkcudbright—the leading hotels are the Royal and the Selkirk Arms—you should visit the Solway coast, especially at Auchencairn and Colvend, and also make the trip to Gatehouse-of-Fleet and Creetown. The coast scenery between these two places is particularly fine, and there are several castles, if Nature be insufficient. Among the caves in the cliffs is one known as 'Dirk Hatteraick's,' the name of the smuggler in *Guy Mannering*. Smuggling, in the old times, must have been the occupation of a goodly number of the inhabitants of these coasts—maybe they lived by taking in one another's contraband—but I fear that in our sophisticated day tales of smugglers have no 'kick' left in them, even for schoolboys. Here, however, is a tale of a Galloway cave, though not of smugglers, which, so far as I know, is Scotland's gruesomest. If you have already heard of Sawney Bean you may not want to read it.

In the reign of James I all Galloway and, as time went on, nearly all Scotland, was thrilled, horrified, and puzzled by the mysterious disappearances of travellers from a stretch of country near the coast. The travellers set forth, never arrived, and the searchers found no traces. Innkeepers and others were suspected, and some of these unfortunate wretches were roughly tried and executed. But the disappearances continued—continued, in fact, for the space of more than a generation. Then, on a summer evening, a farmer and his wife, she riding pillion, were returning home from a fair, when they were ambushed by a band of horrible-looking beings, of all ages. The farmer sought to charge through them, but some of them seized and tore his wife from the horse, and before his eyes slit her throat and—drank of the blood; after which they proceeded to cut her up. Though fighting like a fury, the farmer must soon have suffered a like fate, had not a party of people, also returning from the fair, appeared in sight. Whereupon the horrible band fled, taking with them the body. The countryside was roused; the king himself was summoned. Yet for a time it seemed as if the murderers had disappeared as completely as their earlier victims. Bloodhounds were obtained, and the hunt was extended to the shore, under the cliffs, with their many caves. The hunters would have passed a cave which, as was obvious, was flooded at high water; but now the tide was low, and suddenly the hounds became excited. The hunters proceeded

into and up the cave, which was of such depth that they
were, at last, thinking of turning back, when, in a great
chamber, dimly lit with smoky wicks, they came upon
Sawney Bean, his woman, and their progeny of twenty-
five years. The habitation was a storehouse of human
apparel, weapons, money, and so forth, of horse accoutre-
ments, and of all manner of merchandise. But it was
more than that; it was a *larder*. On the rocky walls
were plenteous supplies of food, in the shape of human
limbs, smoked, or pickled in brine. For, you see, Mr
Bean and his large family were cannibals. . . . For the
credit of Galloway I ought to say that the father was
not a native. He had come from—but, no, I had better
suppress his original address. To conclude, the dreadful
crew, forty-eight in all, counting grandchildren, were
taken to Edinburgh, thence to Leith, where the males,
their hands and feet amputated, were bled to death, and
the females burned. They died cursing and swearing.

Now we are making for Dumfries, and, if you can choose
your route, let it be the longest of the three possible
routes—the road that goes round by Dundrennan, north
to trim, granite-built Dalbeattie, then south to Kipp-
ford, east along the coast to Kirkbean, and north once
more, by the estuary of the Nith, to New Abbey, under
the great hill of Criffell. Thus you will see a part of
Kirkcudbrightshire, very varied in scenes and sights,
and I shall be able to end my little sketch of Galloway
with a happy impression.

New Abbey

Most strangers, I dare say, visit New Abbey from
Dumfries, only 7 miles away; but they miss something
by not arriving at it from all the grimness and sadness,
in the spiritual sense, of Galloway. History, when one
comes to think of it, is so largely a record of man's
inhumanity, that one rejoices in the gleam of human

P

tenderness that has lingered through the ages at New Abbey.

To-day New Abbey is a village, but the name belonged originally to the neighbouring monastery, and was so used by the monks who came to occupy it from the older Dundrennan Abbey. Its later and present name you shall know shortly. In the year 1233 the Lady Devorgilla of Galloway, a maiden of the highest lineage and of great wealth in lands, both in Scotland and England, married John Balliol, Lord of Barnard Castle, Durham, and of vast estates in Northumberland and France. A marriage of convenience, no doubt, but for all that a love match. Their Galloway home was Buittle Castle—its ruin, or that of a successor, remains on the banks of the Urr, near Dalbeattie. These young people had come into the world in a wonderful century, for all over Europe a great revival, religious and intellectual, was in progress.

They had been married some twenty years when Balliol, as the result of a quarrel with the Bishop of Durham, was condemned to the penance of being "publicly whipped at the door of Durham Cathedral" —a mere form, one supposes—and to pay the fine of "a sum of fixed maintenance to be continued for ever to scholars studying at Oxford." Devorgilla could, and did, take her share in the second part of the punishment —and that was the beginning of Balliol College, Oxford. Later they founded a monastery of Grey Friars in Dumfries, and built a bridge across the Nith there: they also established a monastery of Black Friars down in Wigtown. To-day you will find nothing of the religious buildings, but you may still walk across the bridge—of which, however, I should add, there is no authentic record till 1426.

In 1268 John Balliol died—perhaps alone—in France, whither he had gone on business. Devorgilla lived on for a score of years, during which she saw to the building of the Abbey, and then—but let the old Chronicler tell it:

When John Balliol died, Devorgilla had his dear heart embalmed and enshrined in a coffer of ivory, enamelled and bound with silver bright, which was placed before her daily in the hall, as her sweet silent companion. At her death she desired the relic to be laid upon her heart when sleeping in the new Abbey, which she caused to be built. Hence it received the name of Sweet Heart Abbey.

As such it is known to-day, a ruin, but not an abject one; the upstanding square tower and nave alone save it from that, while of walls and arches, gateways, windows, and carvings there is so much left that any attempt at description in this cramped space would be vain. A full and very entertaining illustrated account by Mr Wentworth Huyshe is published by Robert Dinwiddie, Dumfries (1s.), and should be in the hand of the visitor.

Dumfries

Said Tobias Smollett: "If I was confined to Scotland, I would choose Dumfries as my place of residence." I once met a popular lecturer who said the same thing (applause) of every town in which he lectured. Nevertheless, Dumfries has received its share of merited compliments since the novelist's day. Set on hilly ground, amid rich country, where the winding Nith makes a great bend, and on one of the L.M.S. main lines, it is the largest town in the south of Scotland. Viewed from the air, its extent is enlarged by its neighbour Maxwelltown, which though separated by the river, and until 1930 municipally apart and in Galloway, is now one with it and included in Dumfriesshire.

For a town so old—it was a Royal Burgh in 1190—it is poor in antiquities. Its only truly ancient landmark is 'Devorgilla's Bridge,' which, whether of the thirteenth or fifteenth century, must have been one of the wonders of

Scotland in its day. With the banking and consequent narrowing of the river, the original nine arches were reduced to six, and now, approached by a flight of steps, it is used for foot traffic only. Of Devorgilla's other benefaction, the White Friars Monastery, nothing remains; probably it would never be mentioned now but for the fact that in 1306 Bruce, aided and abetted by Roger Kirkpatrick, slew the Red Comyn before the High Altar. One wonders if poor, pious Devorgilla turned in her grave, for, the sacrilege apart, Comyn was her grandson and Bruce her kinsman.

The existing buildings that may be called 'old' are the Parish Church, St Michael's, built about 1745, and the Midsteeple, once the Town House, at the bend of the High Street, erected some fifty years earlier. Burns worshipped in the church, and his funeral procession— the greatest visible tribute he had ever received—started from the Midsteeple. In the High Street, too, north of the Steeple, is the Hole in the Wa', an inn established in 1620, the present owner of which possesses, I understand, a remarkable collection of Burns relics.

As in Ayr, Burns is the paramount memory in Dumfries. In the High Street, south of the Steeple, is the Globe Inn, where sometimes he forgot his cares; and if we go down that thoroughfare and turn into Shakespeare Street, thence into twisting little Burns Street (formerly the Mill Brae), we shall see the place where he finally escaped them. To anyone who knows his life, the sight of that small two-storeyed house in that drab, little street means a lump in the throat. The house is in the care of the Dumfries Burns Club. You may see the room where he died, on July 4, 1796, arranged as nearly as possible as it was in his lifetime; also a number of relics. In the Globe Inn, too, are relics, very personal—his chair, punch-bowl, and toddy-ladle; and in a room upstairs, scratched on a window-pane, are two verses, precious because of the hand that wrote them. The inn is the scene of the Club's annual dinner on his birthday.

He lies in St Michael's Churchyard, in a mausoleum of Grecian temple design, erected in 1815. His statue stands at the top of the High Street.

You will like Dumfries for itself—a pleasant town, awake yet not aggressive; with just enough of the old-fashioned to relieve the modernity; with several handsome buildings, including the Academy, where J. M. Barrie was once a pupil; with its noble river, on which you may go a-boating to Lincluden Abbey and other fair scenes; and its two fine golf courses, so choicely situated that if you have a keen eye for beauty you will probably play rather badly.

Caerlaverock Castle

Of all the many old places in the shire none impressed me quite so much as Caerlaverock Castle, on the Solway, about eight miles south of Dumfries. An ingenious person has sought to derive the name from the Welsh *caer*, meaning 'fort,' and *laverock*, Scots for 'skylark'; but I cannot say that those grim walls hint, however faintly, at feathered songsters, though doubtless they witnessed many a lark of another sort in their day. The earliest building of which I have been able to learn was the one captured in 1300 by Edward I, and recaptured twelve years later by Bruce, who had it levelled to the ground. Before long a new castle was erected, only to meet with a similar fate, in 1356, from Sir Roger Kirkpatrick, the idea being to take no chances of the English gaining a foothold. Nevertheless, we read of Sir Roger being in residence in 1365 at Caerlaverock, presumably Castle No. 3; he was, in fact, stabbed to death there in his bedchamber by his friend and guest, Sir James Lindsay, a lady being the inspiration.

Outwardly most of the existing castle is of the fifteenth century—the heavy corbelling of the parapets tells us that; yet it is interesting to learn from a poem written in honour of Edward's victory in 1300 that the general plan of that time has been repeated in subsequent buildings. This repetition was, no doubt, determined by the site—roughly, a three-cornered rocky island, in a marsh, which was converted by the raising of a great mound into a shallow lake. The poem informs us that the castle was shaped like a shield, with a tower at each corner, one of the towers being double and containing the gateway; and so it is to-day. The walls, in fact, form a triangle, and so much of them are standing and the towers are so intact that the whole has been said to present the most splendid example of an ancient fortress in Scotland. A gangway takes the place of the old drawbridge, and you enter the narrow, lofty gateway, under the Maxwell crest, with its motto, "I bid ye fair." Internal alterations, improvements, and decorations were being made until the seventeenth century; and you may still ascend a handsome stair to the Grand Hall, where you will see that the old builders had an eye to beauty as well as to strength. But strength was surely the first consideration, as witness the walls which, in 1640, resisted bombardment by the Covenanters for three months. When the garrison, by order of King Charles, surrendered, it was the end of Caerlaverock as a place of defence or habitation. Archæology apart, Caerlaverock, in its lake on that grassy mount, overlooking the Solway, is a 'picture' well worth going to see. Sir Walter Scott thought so much of it that he made it the model of his Ellangowan Castle in *Guy Mannering*.

In the Shire

Ecclefechan ('Church of St Fechan'), birthplace and burial-place, under a very modest stone, of Thomas

CAERLAVEROCK CASTLE, DUMFRIESSHIRE

Photo Valentine and Sons, Ltd.

AN OLD COTTAGE IN THE WESTERN HIGHLANDS
Photo Alexander B. Beattie

231

Carlyle, is 17 miles east of Dumfries. His house, a plain two-storeyed building, with a wide archway in its front, stands in Main Street, and harbours many intimate relics. The fine memorial, his statue, was set up in 1929. On Repentance Hill, near by, is an old beacon-tower, on which they used to keep watch for the approach of the English, and burn a signal fire, when necessary.

Lochmaben, an ancient burgh, 10 miles northward of Ecclefechan, stands amid seven little lakes, on the largest of which is a fragment of a castle, once the most impregnable in these parts, which may have been the birthplace of Robert the Bruce. The Castle Loch is noted for its vendace, a white fish found nowhere else in Britain, though I believe it is known in Ireland, at Connemara. It is, they say, a great delicacy, but not to be captured by ordinary lures. The angler will, however, find plenty of other fish in these lochs and neighbouring streams. In past winters the Castle Loch has been the exhilarating scene of the International Curling Match between England and Scotland.

Lincluden Abbey, over the Galloway border, may be reached by water from Dumfries; but the two miles' road to it is equally beautiful. Burns knew it well, more than one of his finest poems seem to have been inspired there. Pennant, the eighteenth-century tourist, admired the carved stone-work of the ruin, which has been described as "the richest example of decorated work in Scotland."

For forty miles of charm and interest I commend a run north to Thornhill, returning by Moniaive.

To Glasgow by Lanarkshire

If you are motoring from Dumfries to Glasgow you may do so by proceeding beyond Thornhill and through the Dalveen Pass, one of the impressive breaches in the rather mild Lowthers, into the Upper Ward of Lanarkshire. There you will make contact with the River

Clyde, in the shadow of the Leadhills. At the village of the same name—the highest in Scotland—lead mines have been worked for a thousand years. The soil is so charged with the metal that poultry, I am told, cannot thrive. There is gold, too, in the Lowthers, though to-day it would not repay the seeker. At one time, however, the yield was £100,000 a year. The crowns of James V and his queen were made of it, as were that monarch's famous "bonnet pieces," about the size of sovereigns.

Elvanfoot, Crawford, and Abington are roadside villages on the next ten miles of a bracing, sometimes bleak, countryside, which sojourners like very much or not at all. The scenery generally has been described by one who did not like it as "undistinguished." The great highway between the West of Scotland and England runs through it, also a main line of the L.M.S. Railway.

It is worth while, after passing Abington, to digress westward for a mile or two, to see antique, pretty Douglas village, also the Kirk of St Bride, so carefully preserved by the Earl of Home. The Kirk harbours two strange memorials—silver caskets enclosing the hearts of the "good" Sir James Douglas, slain while conveying the heart of the Bruce toward Palestine, and of another famous Douglas, "Archibald Bell-the-Cat."

In the approach to Glasgow much 'black country' may be avoided by taking the road on the left, beyond Lesmahagow—an old saint is to blame for the name—and going round by the breezy uplands of old-fashioned Strathaven (pronounced "Straven"), with its striking ruin of a fifteenth-century castle, and then by East Kilbride into the south side of the city.

CHAPTER VIII

A DAY IN THE WEST

WERE a summer stranger to come to me, in Glasgow or Edinburgh, saying, "I have one day. How can I make the most of it?" I should reply: "If you don't mind getting up early, you can, between dawn and dark, see all Scotland, in the sense of her natural characteristics; you can look upon her fairest firth, several of her loveliest lochs, her widest moor, her noblest mountains, some of her kindliest or grandest glens, one at least of her wildest rivers, and a group of her most remarkable isles of the sea."

The journey means over 300 miles on the railway, and I am aware that many people nowadays regard the train as the second-best means of seeing a country. In Scotland, at any rate, that notion can be cherished to the point of prejudice. We have, indeed, several stretches of line which in scenic outlook are immeasurably richer than the roads leading to the same destinations, and one of them is the West Highland Railway, a section of the L.N.E.R. The train starts from Glasgow at 5.45 A.M.; from Edinburgh at 4.30; from London, King's Cross, at 7.30, the previous evening. At Glasgow and Edinburgh you can buy a ticket to include meals on board.

The line runs close to the Clyde till it reaches Craigendoran, starting-point of the red-funnelled railway steamers, where it diverges from the Helensburgh line. As it ascends we look down the Firth to Cowall and the Holy Loch. Presently, among woods, we are above the placid, low-hilled, almost land-locked Gareloch, anchorage for ships out of commission, surely the most reposeful scene in the West; yet, within a few minutes, beyond the moorland above Garelochhead, we have a glimpse, a warning, of something sterner—the ragged crest of Ben Arthur. Quite suddenly we emerge from the moor, at Whistlefield, above the meeting-place of Loch Long and Loch Goil, in their deep, narrow channels among the mountains of Argyll. You might look on that scene a hundred times and never see it twice the same, for it changes as changes the season, the light, and the wind.

For a mile or so we travel along the heights of Loch Long, looking over at the lofty rugged range, named by some antique humorist 'Argyll's Bowling Green,' then swing into Glen Douglas. Here, as at so many points on the journey, the track itself, in its windings and undulations, is fascinating to watch. Glen Douglas, with its legend of King Arthur, is too smooth and shallow in its far stretch toward Loch Lomond to be impressive, except in the feeling of melancholy lonesomeness suggested by a solitary farm and clump of trees in the foreground. But soon we are back at Loch Long, looking up at Ben Arthur ('The Cobbler'), and beyond it Bens Ime, Vane, and Vorlich, all over 3000 feet high, all very 'stern and wild.' Yet down yonder, at the head of the loch, is the sweetest, homeliest of glens, with the flowery village of Arrochar sheltering near its mouth. Here were once the lands of the warlike Macfarlanes, whose battle-cry, "Loch Sloy," was inspired by a tarn among the hills; and war is still represented on Loch Long by a torpedo-testing range. Across the water is Glen Croe, where the road with its dangerous bends at the summit, 'Rest and Be Thankful,' winds among the hills to Loch Fyne. There is another road to Loch Fyne from Lochgoilhead, with the cheery name of Hell's Glen.

Just when you think the train is going to descend upon Arrochar it turns east and slips across the wooded neck of land to Tarbet on Loch Lomond. Even if you have

already seen Loch Lomond in the Trossachs tour, you
will be glad to find its waters and the Ben over yonder in
another aspect. Through the woods, but nearly always
within sight of the loch, we come to Ardlui, near its
head, a dream place, for all that it has a modern hotel.
The loch ends in the arms of Glen Falloch, where Nature
is at first sedate, but soon displays herself in rough-and-
tumble moods, the Falloch River being a rare spectacle
when in spate. Long ago, in the dawn of an Easter Day,
I walked through Glen Falloch, deeming it the last word
in wild beauty, yet seeing not half the wonders I was to
see years later—from the window of a railway carriage.
Away down yonder runs the slatey-grey road, a dull
ribbon through a glory of colour; up here is the railway
track, rising higher and higher along the mountain side,
with the advantage of the eagle over the sparrow.

There is an old tale concerning three men of Atholl
who came to Glen Falloch on clan feud business against
one Duncan Dhu, whom they did not know by sight.
They came on Duncan engaged in splitting the trunk
of a great tree by means of a wedge. After some chat
Duncan agreed to lead them to the man they wanted, if
they would first help him to finish his job. Willingly
they got their grips on the edge of the cavity, whereupon
Duncan knocked out the wedge, and they were trapped—
easy game for Duncan's axe. The only feud to-day is
against foxes—with tails.

Still far ahead, Ben More ('Great Peak'—there are
many Ben Mores in Scotland) rises into view, a majestic
cone; marvellous on a winter afternoon, the white summit tinted by the sunset glow. In some ways, for this
part of Scotland, winter is the time.

At 7.30 there is a halt at Crianlarich, set deep among
the mountains on the edge of Strathfillan, amid streams
and lochs abounding in trout. Here our line crosses by
a viaduct the L.M.S. line and also the road to Oban.

Meanwhile you must be ready for breakfast, and, as we
sit down, the real climb begins. When the first restaurant
car came up here, an old Highlander said to a traveller
who was making a great song about the comfort of it:
"Comfort! You with your eating and drinking in a
railway train! It is a great wonder that Ben Doran did
not fall down upon you!" We shall see Ben Doran
('Mount of Storms') presently.

For a few miles the track skirts Strathfillan, while the
L.M.S. line runs almost parallel on the other side. On
the left you may gain a glimpse of the ruin of a very
ancient chapel, known as St Fillan's. Fillan was one of
the first missionaries to come from Iona to the mainland.
He must have been, as a fellow-traveller once put it,
'some saint.' While residing in Fife he translated
certain of the Scriptures, and when evening fell his left
hand became illuminated, so that he did not need to light
a candle. A similar tale is told of St Machar, of Aberdeen. About a mile along the road from the chapel is
the Holy Pool to which, long ago, the sick of body came
eagerly, while those with "minds diseased" were brought,
willy-nilly. The method of dealing with a mental case
was, to put it mildly, peculiar. Bound hand and foot,
the unfortunate was dropped in. If he returned to the
surface bearing one of the big pebbles from the bottom
he was declared to have miraculously recovered, and the
pebble was added to the recording cairn hard by. If he
failed to bring up a pebble they tried a second treatment,
and took him along, still bound and dripping, to the
chapel, where they laid him on a slab for the night. If
in the morning he was found to have freed himself from
his bonds—St Fillan having driven out the devils—he
was cured; if not, his case was accepted as hopeless.

In the neighbourhood, at Dalrigh, soon after his coronation in 1306, Robert the Bruce fought a battle with the
Macdougall of Lorn, whose forces were much superior.

Bruce, though defeated, sustained a gallant rearguard action, during which he was attacked by three of the clan, the chief and his sons, all very strong men. He slew the sons, and, when the father flew at him and grappled, slew him also. But the dead hands would not let go, and to free himself he had to let them have his mantle, along with the brooch that fastened it. The Brooch of Lorn, as it is called, is still a treasure of the House of Macdougall.

We come to Tyndrum ('House on the Hill Ridge'), a favourite centre for anglers and mountaineers, whose Royal Hotel, among its fir woods, I saw burning, one evening in August 1931. A new and finely equipped house is expected to be ready by Easter 1933. Meanwhile guests of the Crianlarich Hotel, under the same ownership, have the privilege of fishing the waters in these parts. You can fish for salmon on the River Orchy for 10s. a day. The Fillan is good for trout; so is little Loch Lyon, which yields baskets of from 20 to 30 lb. Mountaineers have a grand choice of peaks; to attain a summit is to stand on the roof of Scotland.

The scene grows wilder. Over a thousand feet up we cross the boundary between Perthshire and Argyll, Scotland's great watershed—those torrents ahead will ultimately mingle with the Atlantic; those behind with the North Sea—and approach one of the 'sensations' of the line. Under the shadow of Ben Doran, whose steepness emphasizes its great height, is a glen which no engineering could get across. So the line had to be carried up one side and down the other, and even then two viaducts of dizzy height were necessary. It is known as the Horse Shoe Bend, and after unnumbered journeys I still find a thrill in watching, from the window, the engine taking the curves at the viaducts.

Coming out of the glen, blackest of hollows on a wet winter night, magical with the moonlight on the snow, we turn north to Bridge of Orchy ('Tumbling Stream'). Glen

Orchy, with its winding water, runs south to Loch Awe, and the road that thus far has remained, more or less, in sight of the railway strikes away from the line, first north by the Black Mount toward Kingshouse, then west, down through Glen Coe, to Ballachulish and Fort William. By midsummer 1933 there should be a new and splendid road, replacing a rather dreadful one. The golden eagle is known here. I have heard of one hovering closely over a shepherd, presumably in the hope of getting his collie.

Loch Tulla, skirted on the south by the new road, good for trout and salmon, lies low beneath the railway, and beyond it we scan the Black Mount deer forest covering 80,000 acres. The word 'forest' may seem odd for an almost treeless expanse; but we are, and have been, since we left Loch Lomond, travelling through a land that, a thousand years ago, was covered with woods—the ancient Caledonian Forest. Assuming that this is a summer journey, it is unlikely that we shall see any deer; but in winter, during hard weather, they come down from the mountains, close to the line, too famished to heed the sight and sound of the train. North of the loch, adjoining a farmhouse beside the Tulla Water—a strangely unprotected situation for a stronghold—stands the ruin of Achallader Castle. Late in the seventeenth century it was the scene of a clan battle; cairns mark the graves of the slain.

Through Crannock Wood, a remnant of the forest, with its fine old die-hards of fir-trees, we come to Gorton and enter the loneliest stretch of the journey—15 miles across Rannoch Moor. No road runs through this waste of peat and boulders, heather and wild growths, dark pools and deadly bogs; a sad-coloured expanse in winter, save when the sun shines on the far-flung sheet of snow. It is a desolation that you can feel, yet a desolation of extraordinary dignity, as you gaze across it, westward, to the mountains of Glen Etive and Glen Coe.

Rannoch Moor comes into *Kidnapped*; no writer has
given so illuminating a description of it as Stevenson.
Here is another marvel of this railway's construction.
How was a track to be well and truly laid over such a
morass? The answer seems simple when you know it.
Countless tons of brushwood were sunk in the peat, to be
preserved by it as a safe foundation for as long, at least,
as railways are likely to run. Dig into the peat and you
come on the stumps of the ancient firs. The pine-oils
are still in them. A dried splinter burns with a clear,
bright flame. Such splinters have supplied the evening
light in many a shepherd's cot. The author of *Mountain, Moor, and Loch* gives a picture of an old shepherd,
over Kingshouse way, burning splinter after splinter to
give his wife light for her spinning-wheel; and I have
heard of a famous preacher who did his youthful studying by means of this economical luminant.

At Rannoch we have a road again, running due east
to Loch Rannoch, seven miles away. To the north Ben
Alder overhangs Loch Ericht, which I have heard described as the abode of gloom; and it can be dreadful up
there, though not always so. Both lochs are noted for
cannibal trout which run up to 25 lb.; Ericht is most
easily reached from Dalwhinnie, on the Great North
Road. Near to the line, on the west side, is Loch Lydoch
(or Laidon), connected with Loch Rannoch by the Gauer
Water, bluest of blue lakes on a fine day, a sapphire in
the rudest of settings. The sheet of water farther west is
the Blackwater Reservoir.

Two miles beyond Rannoch, also on the left, is small
Lochan-a-Chlaidheimh—pardon my introducing such a
'mouthful,' but my map spells it so, though the pro-
nunciation is something like Lochan-a-Clive—'Little Loch
of the Sword.' In its centre three counties meet—Perthshire, Argyll, and Inverness-shire—and it has a story.
Toward the close of the fifteenth century the Camerons

and Atholls had a dispute over their boundaries, but, instead of making war, the two chiefs agreed to meet alone by the loch and talk it over. Lochiel, head of the Camerons, was on his way to the trysting-place when he met an old woman who, with veiled hints, so roused his suspicions that he collected sixty-five of his clan, instructing them to follow secretly and conceal themselves in the heather. Later, at the lochside, Lochiel saw the Earl of Atholl approaching, all alone, and was ashamed of himself—but not for long. The negotiations did not proceed too smoothly, and at last tempers gave way. At a signal from the Earl twenty men of Atholl sprang from the heather, where they had hidden themselves in advance of the meeting. But Lochiel had his signal too. He turned his cloak to show the scarlet lining, and the sixty-five Camerons appeared. The odds were too great; Atholl grinned and shrugged. Then raising his sword he kissed the blade, and flung it into the loch, renouncing his claim, and declaring that the land should be Lochiel's for as long as the sword lay in the depths. But there's a sequel. In 1826 a boy fishing in the loch hooked up a basket-hilted sword and took it to the minister of the parish. Consternation among the Camerons! Was the land to go back to Atholl? "Not at all!" said one of their wise men, and had the sword returned to the loch.

At Corrour, where the line reaches its summit, 1350 feet up, there is a fine view of Ben Nevis overtopping its mighty neighbours in the west, and then we descend to Loch Treig—well-named, if the word really means 'desolation.' I have seen the sunshine on it, but never have I seen Loch Treig look gay. Sullen it lies, or stirring with wrath, under the dread heights of its western shore. The train cuts down and along the slope of the eastern side. Before long—perhaps by the time you read this —the lower part of the track will have been raised some

30 feet, for, with the reinforcing flood to come from Loch
Laggan, Treig is going to be deeper than ever, so that its
controlled waters shall flow more strongly through the
tunnel, 15 miles long, bored under the mountains, to provide greater power for the Aluminium Works at Fort
William. What will happen to the trout-fishing on this
famous loch? Will nine-pounders continue to delight
anglers? The river Treig, which used to pour from the
northern end to join the Spean, was a mere trickle when
I saw it lately, its bed obscenely exposed. And the splendid Spean itself—what of its trout and salmon in the
future? But man must be served.

At Tulloch, where the Spean comes rattling down from
Loch Laggan, we find again a road—by which we might
go right across Scotland—and the line turns sharply westward. The scenery changes. We are among trees and
meadows in Glen Spean, among the Braes of Lochaber,
that countryside which inspired the best known of all
Highland laments, *Lochaber No More*. From Tulloch
onward there is a temptation to keep watching the
amazing Spean on the left, with its white cataracts, its
sheer falls, its black, horribly smooth, swift-moving
depths in channels so narrow that one feels one might
leap across—if one had the courage; but if we look to the
right we may see, athwart the hillside, one of those
'Parallel Roads' which are certainly among the Seven
Wonders of Scotland. There are more of them in Glen
Roy, the mouth of which we shall pass presently, and if
the air be clear we may be quick enough to glimpse them.
In the hope that some day you may view them at closer
quarters, I shall try to describe them as I saw them last,
on a February afternoon, when it was so warm in the glen
that my friend and I lay down on the heather to regard
them.

Glen Roy ('Ruddy'), near to Roy Bridge station, is
very narrow and very deep. The road runs high up on

Q

its western slopes. It is not a good road. We were driven by a man who knew the way, yet there were moments when he did not like it any more than we did. But when, rounding a bend, we came in sight of the extraordinary thing, a few risks did not matter. Athwart the hills, east and west, about half-way up their faces, were three clearly defined lines, precisely parallel, and as perfectly straight as if they had been drawn with the aid of a ruler. The two upper lines were, as we afterward learned, separated by some 80 feet; the lowest was about 200 feet farther down. When we got up to the lowest—a moderate climb—we found ourselves on a terrace, or shelf, in the hillside of varying breadth up to 50 feet. The 'Roads' are not always easily recognized by climbers; their visibility at a distance is accounted for by the colour of their vegetation being somewhat paler than that of the vegetation above and below.

What are they? For long they were regarded as artificial; the Highlanders thought they had been made by an earlier people for hunting purposes. In 1817 Dr MacCulloch, pioneer in Highland geology, advanced the theory that they were the beaches of an ancient lake, and as time went on other geologists expanded the idea. A scientific explanation would require several pages, and here it must suffice to say, in the words of the late Professor J. W. Gregory, that the

'roads' of Glen Roy were formed by a lake which was produced in consequence of a lateral glacier projecting across the glen near Roy Bridge, and another across the valley of Glen Spean. Lakes thus formed naturally give rise to stratified deposits and parallel roads, or beds of detritus at different levels.

In other words, the glacier arrested the drainage of the valley, and as the glacier shrank, the lake in the valley sank to lower shores.

At Roy Bridge is Keppoch House, old-time seat of the

THE 'PARALLEL ROADS' OF GLEN ROY

Photo David Donald

242

LOCH SHIEL: PRINCE CHARLIE'S MONUMENT

Photo Robert McLeod

MacDonells of Keppoch.   There is a truly gruesome tale
hanging here, but I shall keep it for another and more
appropriate place.   Across the railway from Keppoch
House is the hill of Mullroy (*Maol Ruadh*), scene of the
last of our clan battles—fought between the MacDonalds
and the MacIntoshes in 1689.   (The MacDonalds and
the MacDonells are of the same clan.)   Beyond this
place, on the right, you may notice on the heath several
cairns.   They are known as 'resting cairns'; they mark
the spot where funeral processions, which sometimes had
many miles to travel, halted for rest and refreshment.
The stones in a cairn record the number of mourners.

Three miles on lies Spean Bridge, a small village in a
pleasant position, with an hotel which I have found good.
Near by is High Bridge, one of the celebrated General
Wade's constructions, at which, on an autumn night in
1745, the first shots were exchanged between Prince
Charlie's men and King George's.   About here the
Spean turns north and, game to the last, as good as leaps
down the long steep hill, amid birches and oaks, to lose
itself in the River Lochy, in the Great Glen that all but
splits Scotland in two.   Almost by the same course a
little train descends toward Gairlochy and the Caledonian
Canal, thence up the glen to Fort Augustus—a run of
only an hour, yet an hour full of beauty and romance.

From Spean Bridge it is downhill to Fort William, with
Ben Nevis rising on the left, the highway on the right.
By the roadside you can hardly miss seeing two more
'resting cairns,' and if you keep watch on the same side
you will presently have a glimpse of the hoary old towers
of Inverlochy Castle, where a battle, famous in Highland
and Covenanting history, was fought in 1645.   (You will
get a 'close-up' view ten minutes hence, when the train,
resuming its run, comes out of Fort William on the
Mallaig line.)   The Marquis of Montrose at Inverness, at
the other extremity of the Great Glen, learned that his

enemy Argyll was at Inverlochy with a strong force. It was winter; but Montrose, instead of leading his men by the open glen road, made a truly remarkable forced march among the snowy mountains and surprised the vanguard of the Campbells, eventually winning a great victory. Scott tells the story of the fight in his *Legend of Montrose*. The Campbells fought bravely, though their chief, whose physical courage seems to have been less than his moral, preferred to watch the struggle from his *birlinn* or galley, anchored off-shore, and accordingly lost prestige—yet it may have been that he was ill. There was present an equally 'canny' person, who, however, as we shall learn later, could not be suspected of cowardice. He was Ian Lom ('Bald John'), bard of the Keppochs, who had guided Montrose through some of the worst mountain passes. When bidden by his chief to join in the fray, he replied, "No, no! For if *I* am killed, who can sing of your victory? "

Fort William is the first town we have seen in a hundred miles. By no means imposing, it is important as a centre, for, excepting Oban in the south, there is no town nearer than Inverness, some 60 miles away. Facing the west, it lies stretched along the shore, under the great Ben, near the head of Loch Linnhe ('Enclosed Sea-loch'). It has one long principal street, with many shops, and its residential parts are charming. Fort William's population used to be about 2000, but, thanks to the Aluminium Works, it has increased considerably. Its situation makes it ideal for anyone who would explore the Great Glen, Glen Nevis, which some of us consider *the* glen of Scotland, Glen Coe, and the lands on the farther side of the loch. Oban is distant about three hours by steamer; the sail is one of the finest in the West.

The town received its present name when the fort was built in 1690; before that it was Maryburgh, and before that again, Gordonsburgh; but though founded so long ago it has, in itself, no antiquities; even the fort has disappeared. Its feature is the Ben.

'Nevis' probably means 'sky-touching,' yet I remember my disappointment when, long ago, I had my first sight of Scotland's loftiest mountain (4406 feet). You may experience a similar feeling, so let me explain that Ben Nevis suffers from the proximity of his lesser, yet mighty brothers, two of them within a mile of him, so close, in fact, that in effect they form one mountain. It is only by ascending one of the lesser brothers that the full savage magnificence of the big one is realized.

In 1883 an Observatory was established on the summit, and did most useful work till 1904, when funds gave out. The Observatory, however, involved the making of a pony track, which ever since has simplified the ascent. Within recent years 'freakists' have reached the top by motor-car and motor-cycle. But even the pony track may be lost in foggy weather, or when under snow; every now and then one hears of skilled mountaineers having been in difficulties; and, of course, only skilled mountaineers, or novices in their company, should attempt the less beaten tracks. Well into the summer the higher cliffs are icy, and the fresh snows may come with September. On a clear day the view from the summit is a rich reward; but I should say that the summit is pretty often 'capped,' even when the sunshine is blazing below. In Fort William you can buy a booklet giving useful instructions for the climb.

Imagine that I have been telling you all this while we have been taking the air on the platform and enjoying the fair prospect of Loch Linnhe during the allotted ten minutes. I must not omit mention of Fort William's Museum, with collections of Highland and Jacobite relics.

The train sweeps round the head of the loch to Banavie —accent, please, on the first syllable—meaning 'white or clear water.' Here we have the best lowland view of

the Ben. Banavie Locks are the starting-point for the
solitary passenger steamer plying on the Caledonian
Canal to Inverness. There used to be several steamers
daily. The coming of the motor doomed the traffic. In
those days Banavie's roomy hotel was busy. When,
later, it got burned out they did not think it worth while
to rebuild. So there stands its shell, melancholy monument to progress. But a merry old tale remains. An
American guest in the hotel was consistently scathing
about the Scottish scenery. Rannoch Moor was nothing;
Loch Linnhe was less; as for Ben Nevis, it was a mere
pimple compared with the Rockies. At every meal this
jibing went on till the patriotic Scottish waiter lost his
head. Mad for revenge, he procured a live lobster and
placed it in the guest's bed. That night there was
violent ringing, and when the boots attended in the dim
light, the American, having danced off some of his agony,
said solemnly: "You may not have our prairies and lakes
and mountains, but I allow you have the biggest fleas I
ever encountered!"

At pretty Corpach, which you would never guess means
'graveyard'—the burial ground of Kilmallie near by—
the hill-waters of the Canal enter the brine of the loch.
The Canal, designed by Telford, was begun in 1803 and
not fully finished till 1847, when it had cost three times
the original estimate. It provides a lovely, if leisurely,
passage to Inverness.

From Corpach the route lies along the side of Loch Eil,
really a continuation of Loch Linnhe, the two joining
at right angles. After all the wildness we have come
through, Loch Eil provides a peaceful pause. The slopes
beyond its usually slumbering waters are gentle and
dotted with crofts. The region has many memories of
the Camerons, whose lordship dates from the fifteenth
century. They did not sustain that lordship without
fighting for it, and whatever the tale may be—there is

none brief enough to repeat here—one senses honour as well as courage. Nor ought we to think of the old chiefs as barbarians. They got more than their wine from France. Their sons were sent thither for education, and in the sixteenth century, wrote Bishop Lesly, the women of Lochaber were

> clothed with purple and embroidery of most exquisite workmanship, with bracelets and necklaces on their arms and necks, so as to make a most graceful appearance.

If Sir Ewen Cameron in 1654, disarmed in a desperate struggle with an officer of General Monk's army, did bite a piece out of the Englishman's throat—well, it was his life or the other's; and when, later in the same fight, an English soldier levelled a musket at him, one of his clansmen rushed forward to receive the bullet.

From the head of Loch Eil we cross a strath and ascend through a gorge to the viaduct that crosses the Finnan, flowing from the glen of that name into Loch Shiel. The viaduct stretching between two very deep cuttings was constructed of a concrete made of the material dug from the cuttings, mixed with cement. There are twenty-four arches, and from the middle we look down 110 feet. When it was being raised, people declared that it would prove an eyesore amid such scenery. Nothing of the sort. Sailing up the loch, one sees a thing so delicate that the fairies might have built it. For us it provides an unforgettable vista of the loch reaching far to the south-west between the steep slopes of noble mountains. Here we are in the Clanranald country, and the Mac-Donalds of Glenaladale, whose mansion stands on the west side of the loch, trace their ancestry back to Somerled of the Isles.

The loch forms a boundary between Argyll and Inverness-shire, and for centuries it formed also a boundary between religions. When the wave of the

Reformation surged northward it failed on the southern shore of Loch Shiel. On the other side there are districts in which it would have been hard to find a Protestant till the coming of the railway. As you look down you will see on the near shore an erection that suggests a lighthouse, with a statue on top—Prince Charlie's Monument. There he came on an August morning in 1745 to inaugurate the campaign by raising his standard. He expected to find an army of clansmen awaiting him, but the glen was empty, save for the small band who had come with him. About two o'clock, however, Lochiel, with 600 or 700 Camerons, came over the hill, marching in two lines, three deep, and upon the mound down yonder the aged Atholl unfurled the banner and, supported by a man on either side, raised it to the breeze. A little later the pipes were heard, and Keppoch appeared with 300 MacDonalds. Thus the beginning of the great adventure, which for a little while was to succeed so brilliantly—there was a week when London shook in its shoes—only to end in utter disaster—an adventure undertaken by those Highland chiefs and their clansmen, half of whom were barely armed, out of sheer loyalty, altogether against their better judgment, however much Charles may have believed in his lucky star. It was folly, but the folly that only a fool would laugh at. A few months later Charles was a fugitive, chased from corrie to corrie in these mountains by King George's redcoats; there was a Government reward of £30,000 for his capture; he was any clansman's prisoner; yet none betrayed him. That is a thought to carry among those bens and glens.

A little steamer plies up and down the loch daily. For the angler there are salmon, sea-trout, and brown trout; and my brother, who used to fish there, told me of eels that made him feel shuddery—five-footers, thick as a man's arm. He saw some of them caught and kicking on the heather. The loch extends almost to the sea, the

connection being made by the River Shiel. Near the
end of the loch is a green islet with the ruin of St Finnan's
Chapel. On what was once the altar stands a small
square bronze bell, one of three known in Scotland,
maybe of the period of St Columba. Once the bell disappeared—taken by an enthusiastic collector of souvenirs.
Whether conscience revolted, or the outcry somehow
reached him, I cannot say, but after a season the bell
came back. The hotel at Glenfinnan station is the
Stage House. Its guests have boats and fishing free.

Beyond Glenfinnan the line rises amid the hills, their
harshness somewhat relieved by heather, bracken, and
occasional trees, and the train positively wriggles round
corners. Then it turns down to Loch Eilt, with its tiny
islands, each with a fir-tree or two, runs along its shores,
and climbs once more till—lo, we are looking down on a
sea-fjord, studded with rocks—Loch Ailort. There is an
inn near the station, and if you would dream amid the
wildest loveliness, Loch Ailort is the place. Yet soon
after leaving the loch, still ascending, we come to a patch
of bleakness, which is emphasized by the glimpse upon
the hillside of a lone little chapel, and never a dwelling
in sight.

Make ready while the train is passing deep-sunken
Loch Dubh, said to be swarming with giant eels, for the
appearance of Loch-nan-Uamh ('Loch of the Caves'),
on the left; for if you are ready—and may the weather
be clear!—you will have one of the rarest glimpses in the
West—the Loch itself, and beyond, in the open sea, the
isles which are as strange as their names—Eigg and Rum,
also little Muck.

Into Loch-nan-Uamh sailed the French frigate bearing Prince Charlie—without his promised army and
munitions, but debonair, gallant, and sanguine, and in
fine physical trim. On the deck, before long, gathered
the chiefs, all seeking to persuade him against the fated

enterprise. But well Charles knew how to deal with brave men. "Let Lochiel," he said, "stay at home and read of the doings of his Prince in the newspapers." That was enough for a Cameron. Lochiel went home to raise his clan, and the others followed his example.

And out of Loch-nan-Uamh, little more than a year later, sailed another French frigate, bearing away the same Prince, now a fugitive, who had taken so much and given so little.

Having crossed three viaducts, all affording glorious views, we pass among the woods and wild flowers of Glen Beasdale, where there is a sort of story-book station, with a station-mistress who looks as if she loved it, and come out upon Arisaig, with its dwellings prettily scattered around the bay. Here Nature squanders her wealth of form and colour on moor, mountain and loch, open sea and islands. To Arisaig ('House in the Bay') the spring comes betimes; in few parts of Scotland do the birds nest so early, and the fuchsia flowers in May. The hotel, close to the beach, is roomy and of good report. There is sea and loch fishing, and motor-boats may be hired.

The train dives through two cuttings, and then, suddenly, there opens a particularly fine view of Eigg, with its spectacular *sgur* (scaur, or precipice), also the mountains of Rum and those of the south end of the great island of Skye. If it be very clear we may even descry North Uist, in the Outer Hebrides. Under Eigg's *sgur* is a cave of ghastly memory. In the sixteenth century 200 MacDonalds sought refuge in the cavern, the mouth of which was partly covered by a waterfall, from the MacLeods of Skye. The MacLeods turned aside the fall, kindled great fires at the mouth, and suffocated the lot. A few minutes more, and we are at Morar ('Place of the Great Water'). Morar has the whitest sands in Scotland. When the sunlight falls on the shallows the colours are exquisite beyond words. It has also our deepest inland loch, which is separated from the shore by a mere furlong. The railway viaduct crosses the falls.

Loch Morar, set amid the starkest of mountains, was once the crater of a volcano. Its greatest depth is 1007 feet. You will find no such depth in the North Sea, and you must go many miles from land—out beyond St Kilda—to find it in the Atlantic. There are dwellings here and there on Loch Morar's shores, but it is a lonesome place. You do not wonder, as you walk by it or sail on it, at the old tales of strange, uncanny things rising from its deeps. Superstition is not dead. 'Morag,' one of the creatures, huge and shapeless, is said to bulge from the surface when a MacDonald or a Gillies is about to die. Frankly, I should not ask to be out there alone in a small boat on a black night, or—which might be worse for the imagination—in the late dusk. I have no personal knowledge about Loch Morar's 'fearfulness,' but I could tell of other lonely Highland lochs, along the shores of which some Highland friends of mine, who fear nothing that moves by day, would never walk solitary by night. You would understand it, too, if you made a stay in one of those little places.

I cannot remember whether it can be seen from the train, but on a wooded knoll near to the station there stands a great black cross. It was set up in 1889 by Bishop Angus Macdonald, first Bishop of Argyll and the Isles after the restoration of the Scottish Catholic Hierarchy, to commemorate the fact that for more than 200 years the district of Morar—'Blessed Morar,' as it is called—had been the centre of Catholic life in the Highlands of Scotland. The first time I saw the great cross was in winter, when the mountains were white. As a sign amid those wide open spaces it is more impressive than a cathedral.

We are nearing the end of the run. From the white sands of Morar, passing through a valley, we come to the cruel coast of Mallaig and its barren hills. Mallaig is an important spot—terminus of the railway, port of the steamers plying to Skye and the Outer Isles, haven for fishing craft—but no one could call the village beautiful. It seems to have been flung down anyhow when the railway came along. Nevertheless, its outlook is superb; and just round the corner is Loch Nevis, loveliest of fjords, and, next door, Loch Hourn, at times the most forbidding. For exploration by motor-boat Mallaig, as a base, would be hard to beat. Skye, the Sound of Sleat, with its lochs and islands, and Eigg, with its singing sands, would—given fair weather—provide material for a very long holiday. The Marine Hotel (unlicensed) runs trips by well-appointed sea-going launches. The Station Hotel, which also hires motor-boats, is so grandly situated that there is danger of your spending the day at a window, wondering which delight you will choose.

Well, it is less than six hours since we left Glasgow, and we have gained at least an impression of Scotland. We shall gain another impression on the return journey; we shall see everything in a new aspect and in a different light, for the West Highlands in the morning and after-noon are not the same. Meanwhile we have 2½ hours to spend. We can spend them in Mallaig, or we can go back now to Fort William and spend them there, taking the later train to Glasgow, where, I believe, you will sleep well.

CHAPTER IX

OBAN—MULL—STAFFA—IONA—GLEN COE

From Callander to Oban

WHILE to the extremely active person the air of the trim and cheerful hill-sheltered little town may be over-soft at midsummer, the average holiday-maker finds it good to breathe. Under broad-shouldered Ben Ledi, Callander sits by the Teith, a little below where the Leny, dancing down from Loch Lubnaig, tumbles into it on its way to swell the Forth at Stirling. In a fair setting, with still fairer surroundings, Callander is tempting, primarily, as a centre for the exploration of southern Perthshire, and of Stirling and Dumbarton shires, and its 18-hole course is one of the finest inland. The best trout-fishing is on lochs Lubnaig and Vennachar; the salmon-fishing on the former is first-rate in the spring; and there is sport to be got in hill lochs and burns—permission for all to be obtained from the proprietors. The Town Council, however, has leased a stretch on the Teith, and one can fish for salmon and trout throughout the season for 6s.; for trout only, 3s. The Ben offers a fairly easy climb; the more distant view includes Edinburgh and the North Sea, Ben Nevis and the Cairngorm Mountains; enthusiasts go up in the middle of the night to greet the sunrise.

Seven miles from Callander, on the banks of the Teith, is that splendid antiquity Doune Castle. Never a hopeless ruin, much has been done toward its restoration, and to-day it stands as one of old Scotland's most majestic strongholds. The buildings form a square nearly 100 feet across; the walls, 10 feet thick, are 40 feet high, the

253

towers nearly 80 feet, and all seem set there for ever. The main parts of the building were erected toward the end of the fourteenth century for the first Duke of Albany, Regent of Scotland. His son succeeded him in both titles, but within two short years made such a mess of things that James I, soon after returning from his captivity in England, had him executed, along with his two sons and the aged Earl of Lennox, on the 'heading hill' at Stirling. The castle then fell to the Crown, and in course of time James IV presented it to his Queen, the sober-faced but alluring Margaret Tudor, who for her third husband chose Henry Stewart, a descendant of the original owner, through whose son it passed to the Earls of Moray.

Unlike so many old strongholds, this castle has much to show within its walls, not only in gloom and mystery, but in illumination of the domestic past. Here, for example, we learn that the food was passed from the kitchen to the hall through 'dresser windows,' and that the hall was reached from the courtyard by an outer stair, roofed over, for the gentry then would no more have thought of entering by the ground floor, which was cellarage, than they would dream to-day of entering their town-houses by the basements. Moreover, at Doune there are two halls, the Great Hall over 60 feet long, and the smaller Baron's Hall, which has been beautifully restored. During the fifteenth century, in the face of rudeness and brutality, civilization was advancing, one of the tokens of that advance being an increasing desire for privacy. The ancient custom of dining on a dais in full view of the uncouth retainers was becoming distasteful to the lords and ladies, and to the seclusion of a 'withdrawing-room' was added that of a lesser hall or dining-room. James I had come home from his English captivity with ideas of English refinement, as well as an English wife, and the lump must have been fairly well leavened by the time his great-grandson came to the

throne. So we can picture James IV and his buxom
'Maggie,' in a dark velvet gown, cut low and square, and
edged with pale colour, with her heavy gold necklet, her
long chain and pendant, her Madonna-like coiffure half-
covered by a dark cap, also relieved in front by a pale
band, the "poke of it hanging down her back"—you can
picture them dining or supping in the Baron's Hall, and
maybe, if there are no guests, sulking or squabbling.

Every castle has its tragic stories, but Doune provides
a little comic relief in the tale of the Queen, the Tailor,
and the Ferryman, which, incidentally, supplies the
first suggestion I have discovered in Scottish history
of a 'tailor-made.' Imagine the aforesaid Margaret one
morning in a fine tantrum, because Master Spittal, the
local tailor, had not arrived at the castle according to
appointment. It was not altogether Master Spittal's
fault. He had set out in good time, but on arriving at
the ferry—there was then no bridge over the Teith—he
had found himself without a bawbee in his pouch; and
the ill-conditioned knave of a ferryman had refused to
carry him on trust, even on her Majesty's business. My
veracious chronicler does not tell how the matter ended,
so far as it concerned Her Majesty, nor—most unfortunately—does he give any particulars of the new garment
and its price. The point, however, is that Master Spittal,
despite the emptiness of his pouch, was a man of sub-
stance, and he proceeded without delay to defray the
cost of a bridge, thereby not only discomfiting the ferryman, but making his own name famous for all time. In
the bridge you see to-day is only one of the original stones,
but on that stone you will find, I think, the effigy of a
pair of shears.

From Callander the road and railway ascend through
the narrow Pass of Leny to Loch Lubnaig. Scott
describes it in *A Legend of Montrose*, also in *The Lady
of the Lake*, where young Angus is racing up the

glen, bearing the Fiery Cross, symbol of war and a call to arms for every able-bodied clansman. Lest a reader should, quite naturally, picture a torch-like object flaring in the darkness, I may say that the Fiery Cross consisted of two sticks charred and dipped in goat's blood. It is the poet in Scott that declares how "Ben Ledi saw the Cross of Fire" which " glanced like lightning up Strathyre." The cross was borne by runners in relay fashion, each of whom, as he sped onward past a cot, would shout any necessary instructions.

Strathyre in its green nest among the hills is a pretty village, with an inviting hostelry. The verdure continues beyond Balquidder village, two miles off the main road, on the shores of peaceful Loch Voil, where rests the dust of the restless Rob Roy, Helen his wife, and several of his sons.

Bleak Glen Ogle leads us to verdant Glen Dochart, the Macnab country, and Loch Dochart, one of the loveliest of little lakes, lying under the loom of Ben More, with the ruin of a Campbell stronghold on a woody isle. On a winter night, long ago, when the loch was frozen, the Macgregors stole across the ice, surprised the slumbering garrison, and left not one to tell the tale. So we come to Crianlarich, with its good hotel, busy with anglers, mountaineers, and motorists.

As a young man, on a summer night I used to take the 10 o'clock train—not too comfortable in those days—from Glasgow to Oban, simply for the delight of meeting the morning up there. At Crianlarich it might be only a glimmer, but as the train slipped through Strathfillan, past Tyndrum, with Ben Odhar across the valley, and the tarn of Lochan Bhith, the glimmer was growing. In Glen Lochy, under lofty Ben Lui, the dawn seemed to hesitate, but when we came down into the great hollow holding Strathorchy, Dalmally, and the eastern arm of Loch Awe, morning was already there.

Loch Awe—it is likely that the word means simply 'water'—is one of our show-places, though for consistent beauty it is hardly to be compared with Loch Lomond.

Where the Orchy falls into the loch, on a small rocky peninsula, once an island, stands Kilchurn Castle, a mere shell, yet with its environment one of the most entrancing sights in Scotland. The oldest part of it may have been erected about 1440 by Sir Colin Campbell, but the south side belongs to a hundred years later, and the north was built by the first Earl of Breadalbane in 1650. It was a residence till 1740, and Hanoverian troops occupied it in 1745, but that must have been the beginning of the end.

At Loch Awe station is an hotel, and a pier from which a launch plies to Ford, at the far end of the loch, calling at Taychreggan, Port Sonachan, both with hotels, and other places, as required. From Ford one can reach the Ardrishaig–Oban road. The loch contains salmon, seatrout, brown trout, pike, perch, and *ferox*. "Be guided," says Mr Castle, "by the local ghillies, who know the best bays to fish, according to wind and weather."

From Loch Awe, following the shore of the loch's western arm, we enter the Pass of Brander, one of the most forbidding defiles in the country. Below, on the left, is the ever-narrowing, darkling water, beyond it a steep, grey, scree-littered hillside; on the right Ben Cruachan (accent on the 'Cru') rises nearly 3700 feet— though it was once under the sea, shells having been found on its summit. Its lower slopes are wooded, its upper ones bare and lumpy, showing a ruddy sort of granite, and its top is split into two cones. It dominates the other mountains for miles around, its nearest rivals being Bens Lui and Doran. Where the loch ends, the River Awe flows from it into the gorge, stealing softly at first, then rushing headlong among the rocks, with a pause here and there in a pool, on its brief five miles'

R

and Loch Awe, which got its name from a ruler of part of the early Scots kingdom of Dalriada, which ended about the ninth century. The vision of those days is very vague, but we know that the Macdougalls became Lords of Lorn in the twelfth century. One of their memorials is ivy-clad Dunollie Castle, perched on a promontory a little way beyond the end of the esplanade, looking down upon the mansion of the descendants of its one-time lords. Among the treasures in that mansion is the famous Brooch of Lorn, which, along with his cloak, the Bruce had to abandon in the combat, near Tyndrum, in 1306. Some years later the Bruce met the Macdougalls again, this time in the Pass of Brander, administering a disastrous defeat, and presently took from them their chief stronghold, the Castle of Dunstaffnage, of which more presently. He did not, however, recover his useful ornament, of which we hear again, more than three centuries later, in the Castle of Gylen, over in Kerrera. In 1647 that stronghold was assaulted and taken by a force sent to punish the Macdougalls for their adherence to the cause of Charles I. This time, to the dismay of the family, if not the whole clan, the brooch disappeared. Now it seemed lost for ever; but in 1826, at an auction sale in London, it was discovered by Captain Campbell of Loch Nell, who purchased and restored it. The brooch is round, rather less than five inches in diameter; eight jewelled obelisks surround a central setting containing a large rock-crystal. The setting is removable, and covers a cavity which once contained some sacred relic. Unhappily there are romance-killers who will tell you that it is of sixteenth-century workmanship.

A mile beyond Dunollie are the Ganavan Sands, with bathing facilities and a nine-hole golf course in a glorious situation. Oban's eighteen-hole course, Glencruitten, is on the hill, about half a mile from the town.

Of Dunstaffnage Castle, four and a half miles north of

Oban, only the shell remains; but my expert, who is
extremely severe upon those irresponsible scribes who
play lightly with centuries and exaggerate accordingly,
readily allows that those grey walls, with their slightly
projecting angular towers, may well have been standing
when Bruce evicted the Macdougalls. Moreover, we know
that Bruce did not destroy, but gave the stronghold, which
must have been almost new then, to the loyal Campbells.
We have, therefore, an example of a thirteenth-century
exterior which I do not think can be equalled in Scotland.
The castle is set among trees on a promontory at the
mouth of Loch Etive, looking out upon the Firth of Lorn,
the Island of Mull, Loch Linnhe, Lismore, and Loch Nell.
The walls, 68 feet high and 9 feet in thickness, enclose the
remains of buildings, some much less ancient, some not
ancient at all, and a court 80 feet square. The entrance
is by a stair against the eastern wall. You can go up to
the battlements, where are (or were) three brass cannon,
the largest of which, though inscribed as made in Amsterdam, belonged to Spain. It was, in fact, recovered from
the wreck of a galleon, one of the ill-fated Armada, sunk
in Tobermory Bay, over yonder in Mull.

With Dunstaffnage is associated a slab of stone more
celebrated than any monument in the country. When
the Scots came over from Ireland to found the western
kingdom of Dalriada they brought with them *Lia Fail*,
the Stone of Destiny. Some say it was the seat of justice
of Gathelus, a contemporary of Moses; others that Jacob
dreamed his dream, at Bethel, with his head pillowed
upon it. Anyhow, in the course of time it was borne by
the Scots, descendants of the Egyptian princess Scota,
on their journeyings from Egypt, through Spain, to
Ireland. For centuries it served in Ireland as a coronation-seat; and then, in the fourth century, Fergus I, King
of the emigrating Scots, took it, along with his other
treasures, to Iona, and, for all we know, Columba may

have used it for *his* pillow.   Having rested in Iona for a
century or so, it was brought over to Dunstaffnage, where
it remained, a witness of many royal ceremonials, till 850,
when Kenneth II had it transported to Forteviot, his
capital, in Perthshire.   Later it was removed to Scone,
and in the Abbey there, according to the chronicle of
Fordun, served as the coronation-seat of our Scottish
monarchs till, in 1296, Edward I, on one of his successful
invasions, took a fancy to it, and caused it to be conveyed to Westminster Abbey.   Edward seems to have
been as superstitious as any untutored Scot, for at first
he thought of a shrine for the Stone.   Then he had it
fitted into a chair of bronze, and, later, into that chair
of oak on which all English and British sovereigns—
except, I think, 'Bloody Mary'—have since been
crowned.   And Dr MacCulloch hinted that the stone came
from the same quarry as the stones of the Castle!

Mull and the Way to Iona

We come out of Oban Bay by the north channel.   Clear
of Kerrera, our course is north-westerly across the Firth
of Lorn to the southern tip of Lismore, with its lighthouse.   In that narrow passage to the Sound of Mull the
shallow water, with disputing tides, babbles noisily.

Mull is a grand island, though hardly as spectacularly
so as Skye.   The two are as different as the musics of
Beethoven and Wagner.   Unlike Skye, it is not in the
high favour it deserves.   Yet Mull's turn will come.   It
appeals especially to the real explorers, those who travel
afoot.   A land of brooding mountains, mysterious moors,
glens of rather solemn beauty, far-reaching sea-lochs, it
is some thirty miles long, twenty-five at its broadest,
while to follow its ragged coast-line would mean covering over three hundred.   Ben More, the loftiest peak,
over 3000 feet high, is a remnant of the volcano which
spouted up the stuff that formed those amazing columns

in the south of the island, also the wonder isle of Staffa,
Ulva, and its lesser neighbours.

Flint barbs found in the soil tell of primitive inhabitants, but most of Mull's history known to us is that
of the Macleans, who gained their footing through the
marriage of one Lachlan with a daughter of John Macdonald, Lord of the Isles, in 1366. The Macleans, who
were a clan as early as 1250, claim descent from an Irish
king a thousand years or so earlier. So proud, indeed,
were they of their ancient origin that when a stranger
ironically inquired of a clansman how his ancestors had
contrived to survive the Flood, he received the haughty
reply, "The Macleans had a boat of their own."

The steamer passes between the lighthouse and a rock
known as 'The Lady's.' As it enters the Sound there
appears, high on a headland, Duart Castle, the custody
of which was given to a Maclean by a Lord of the Isles in
1390. I was reading about that castle the other day in
a book quite recently published, and found it described
as "a ruin"—which, as you will see, it certainly is not.
The mistake is pardonable; I should be making it now,
had I not chanced only last year to renew my acquaintance with Mull. Then I looked up to see once more the
old familiar, deserted shell—and lo, it was wearing a
roof, while wisps of smoke were floating from its chimneys!
The writer of a book of this sort should always be prepared to be told that some ancient landmark, which he
has taken great pains to describe, is no longer visible;
but a resurrection, such as that of Duart, may well catch
him napping. What had happened in the interval was
this: Sir Fitzroy Maclean, chief of the clan, purchased
the place of his ancestors, who were dispossessed in 1691,
restored it, and made it his home. Unhomely enough
the great tower appears on the verge of that steep cliff,
and you may wonder what the ghosts think of the central
heating and electric light.

The Sound has an average breadth of about two miles. The land on the northern side is Morven—'Big Mountain,' not that the hills are so great as others in Argyll. Here and there on its shores may be spied a ruin, or modern mansion, or farm. It is not exactly desolation, for one is never long out of sight of human signs; none the less, to some of us there is melancholy in those great stretches of rock and heather. The Mull coast is more cheerful, perhaps because its habitations are more frequent. Just beyond Duart is Craignure village, and, a dozen miles farther on, pretty Salen, each with an hotel. From both places roads wander across the island to Phionphort, on its southern promontory, whence plies the ferry to Iona.

Ten miles farther, and we come to a place whose fame has been sung to the world, if only by Scottish comedians, who may never have seen it. Its name has, perhaps, a 'funny' sound, though it means 'Well of (the Virgin) Mary.' Since the beginning of ships, mariners, fleeing from the wrath of the outer seas, have blessed Tobermory Bay, sheltered by Calve Island—a haven of still waters when the Sound, a few fathoms off, is yeasty white.

The old village is sweetly hidden among trees, up on the hillside. The little town stands naked on the shore, a single row of shops, dwellings, hotels, churches, and a distillery. In such a setting there ought to have been designed the prettiest little town in all Scotland; but those who founded it, toward the end of the eighteenth century, were thinking of Tobermory as a great fishing centre. The traffic did not come, and Tobermory has gone on dreaming ever since. Once, about fifty years ago, it looked like waking up. If not fish, said somebody, what about tourists? Why not a tourist centre, like Oban? Well, yonder on the cliff above the pier, that big building, the Western Isles Hotel, with its many vacant windows, gives the sorry answer. Still, things

will happen when Mull comes into its own, like Skye.
The change has, in fact, begun. I learn that the hotel
is to be 'restored' and made ready to welcome visitors
in the coming years, when its high windows will no
longer look blindly upon the charms of the West. Of
the existing hotels is the good old Mishnish—the correct
title, I assure you, not only at two in the morning, the
word being the name of the district, meaning "fruitful
promontory."

If Tobermory has acquired fame beyond the music-
halls, it is mainly because of the treasure hunt that has
been going on, with long or short intervals, for more than
300 years. In the autumn of 1588 a Spanish ship sank
in the bay, which, since then, like many a gold mine, has
swallowed more wealth than ever came out. The ship
is believed to have been the *Florida*—some say the
Florencia, but that may have been the name of her commander—one of the pay-ships of the Armada, laden with
silver coin. This is the story—the one that seems the
most reasonable of those I have heard. In 1588 Scotland,
a separate kingdom, was not at war with Spain, and the
Florida, luckier than many of the scattered fleet, came
into the bay to receive a friendly enough reception from
the Macleans and other inhabitants of the coast. She
remained until her commander judged that it would be
fairly safe to venture upon the high seas, and meanwhile
was provisioned by Maclean of Duart. Payment, however, was not forthcoming, and Maclean sent his factor
to collect it. The factor coming on board was made
prisoner and sent below; sails were hoisted and the
anchor was raised. The ship was under way when the
captive, having found means of reaching the powder
magazine, revenged himself by applying a light. It was
a splendid explosion. Part of the deck, with people on
it, went planing ashore, like a magic carpet. For some
distance the stricken ship sailed on, spilling cargo as she

went, then filled and foundered. The chests of silver coin may still be in the mud. Cannon, swords, plate, and other interesting things have been brought up; and a nest of silver coins was, not so long ago, found in the clay—somebody's little hoard in a purse long since rotted away.

From Tobermory our course becomes westerly, across the wide mouth of Loch Sunart, which, winding away eastward toward Loch Linnhe, separates Morven from Ardnamurchan ("Height of the Great Headland"). To some people these districts, along with Ardgour, Sunart, and Moidart, seem rather remote; but for that very reason they may appeal to other people. Though I last saw their rugged charms through a three-days rain mist, I would fain return, if only to behold again the broken grandeur of Castle Tirrim on its sea-girt rock in Moidart, Loch Sunart and its islets, Ardnamurchan and its terrifying coast—most westerly outpost of the Scottish mainland.

Staffa

But now we turn south—no land between us and America, save the islands of Coll and Tiree; the first bold and rocky, the second so low-lying that from one side of it the waves may be descried leaping above the shore of the other. And so, mid seascapes that are of Scotland's most glorious, down by the little Treshnish Isles, Gometra, Ulva, where Thomas Campbell found inspiration for *Lord Ullin's Daughter*, to the wonder of Staffa.

Staffa—'Isle of Staves or Pillars'—has a formation somewhat similar to that of Giant's Causeway, over on the north of Ireland, though the pillars are less regular. Geologically, it is thus described by an expert:

> Conglomerated tufa forms the basement; columnar basalt is arranged in colonnades, which form the façades and the walls of the chief caves; and amorphous basalt, overlying the columnar basalt, is pierced here and there by ends of columns and by angular blocks.

The oval island, about $1\frac{1}{2}$ miles around, and 144 feet at its highest, is roofed with the richest verdure. It is walled by cliffs, but there is a beach where boats can land in moderate weather. The steamer does not allow too much time; to make a complete survey one would have to stay in Iona, Ulva, or Mull, and come over by motor-boat. The outstanding features of this phenomenon are the Herdsman Rock, the Great Colonnade, the Cause-way, and four of the sea-carved caverns—Clam Shell Cave, Mackinnon's Cave, the Boat Cave, and Fingal's Cave.

The Clam Shell Cave has oddly bent columns on one side. Mackinnon's, with its great gaping mouth over-hung by pillars, is spacious and easily reached dry-shod. The Boat Cave, as its name suggests, demands that its visitors come afloat—and in still weather. While only 12 feet wide and 10 feet high, it is 150 feet in depth, and its entrance also is overhung. The spectacle of all is Fingal's Cave. Fingal, or Fionn, was the mighty hero of the Gaels in the third century, glorified in the poems of the bard Ossian, his son.

Queen Victoria, with the Prince Consort and children, visited Staffa in 1847, and it must have been what Victorians used to call 'Queen's weather,' for the barge from the yacht entered Fingal's Cave—and that may not be done every summer day. I quote Her Majesty's simple words, which are more illuminating than some of the grandiose stuff that has been written about the scene.

> The appearance it [Staffa] presents is most extraordinary, and when we turned the corner to go into the renowned Fingal's Cave the effect was splendid, like a great entrance into a vaulted hall ; it looked almost awful as we entered, and the barge heaved up and down on the swell of the sea. It is very high, but not longer than 227 feet, and narrower than I expected, being only 40 feet wide. The sea is

immensely deep in the cave. The rocks under water are all colours—pink, blue, and green—which had a most beautiful and varied effect.

Often the swell rolling into the cave is fearsome, as is its noise, though less so than the noises in some of the other caverns. A walk has been cut on one side of the gulf, protected in some measure by a cable held up by iron stanchions; but it is not a path on which to take liberties. At high tide one should be prepared for the arrival of an extra big roller. Tidal waves are not unknown. I can remember reading in the morning paper of the sudden, tragic end of three members of a party caught by such a wave.

Staffa is uninhabited. Once a sturdy shepherd undertook the care of sheep fortunate enough to be placed on that luxuriant pasture. I cannot say how long he kept his post, but a time came when his nerve broke. It was not the solitude nor whatever silence he may have known; it was the sounding of the swell in those caves— the mutterings, moanings, groanings, and boomings in the night time that finished him. I dare say he began to hear things not of the sea, and to see things not of the earth; and Ulva, with its human beings, four miles away, might as well have been at the other end of the world.

Iona

The musical word Iona, with which the Macdonalds, once Lords of the Isles, still sometimes name their daughters, seems, alas! to have been but an old mistranscription of *Ioua*, as it was distinctly written in the most ancient manuscripts. The name in the sixth century was the exceedingly easily spelled one of *I* (pronounced 'Ee'), meaning simply 'Island.' *I*, however, appears to have been too easy for the succeeding generations of scribes, whom one can figure scratching their tonsures ere they satisfied their passion for originality by writing it *Ii, Ia, Io, Hi, Hii, Y, Yi,* etc.

There is a Gaelic proverb which says that if a man goes once to Iona he will go thrice; and we know that Dr Johnson, during his visit, slept in a barn, on straw, and made no complaint. Also there are many people, not Highlanders nor philosophers nor yet pilgrims, who return to it year after year. Yet, when you see it for the first time, you will probably wonder why. There are many isles of the West more remarkable in appearance, more attractive in aspect, than Iona—3½ miles long, 1½ broad, its greatest height, Dun-I, only 327 feet; rocky, though neither bleak nor barren. Approaching it, without knowing its name, you might regard it as an unconsidered trifle shed by its great neighbour Mull. What, then, is the attraction, its history apart? I think one must live on it a while to understand.

I got an inkling of the charm when, as a youth, I spent some weeks upon it. In those days nearly every tourist in the West called at Iona, but few people had discovered it as a place for a summer sojourn. There was, indeed, only one other guest at the Columba Hotel—an old gentleman, an Englishman, who had come for many years, and who, not long afterward, passed from its peace to an even deeper one. He knew and loved every foot of the ground, and with great good nature appointed himself my guide. Iona then became a world in miniature, with many interesting and beautiful features of its own—features unsuspected by the hurried visitor. Then came home to the island a young man, Alec Ritchie, in whose company—though it was before the day of motorboats—I discovered its delights from the mariner's point of view. The memory has an added interest in the fact that Mr Ritchie was then conceiving the idea of his beautiful Iona jewellery, inspired by old Celtic designs, which was destined soon to go all over the world, and,

incidentally, like other fine and successful things, to be
'cribbed' by smart commercial people, with no bright
ideas of their own. Mr Ritchie has further served his
miniature world by writing an illuminating little *Guide*.

There are various tales, but it will be enough to say
here that in 563 Columba, a man of noble lineage and
an exile from Ireland, landed at Port-a-Curraich ('Bay
of the Coracles'), on the west side of the island, and
proceeded to found a monastery, the buildings being of
wattle. The monks were of three classes: the elders
devoting themselves to religious and literary exercises,
the younger serving in the monastery and on the land,
and the youngest receiving instruction. All were under
vows taken at the altar; they wore white robes, with
hoods of unbleached wool covering their heads, which
were shaven from ear to ear. We know that Columba
was a man who spared neither his body nor his intellect.
During thirty-four years his labours on the island were
interrupted only by arduous missionary journeys.

None of the world's great men has left a more shining
name, but of his life we have no tangible memorial, unless
it be that heart-shaped stone, unearthed in recent times,
which may have served as his pillow.

On the day before his last he went up the little hill
overlooking the monastery, and from the summit, with
uplifted hands, gave his pastoral blessing to all, adding:
"Small and mean though this place is, yet it shall be held
in great and unusual honour, not only by Scotic kings and
people, but by the rulers of foreign and barbarous nations,
and by their subjects; the saints also, even of other
churches, shall regard it with no common reverence."
On the following day, at evening, he went alone into the
church. Though it was mid-June, darkness must have
filled early the little, small-windowed place. Yet his
servant, Diarmid, coming to seek him, beheld a great
illumination which, however, faded as he approached.

Groping his way, Diarmid came upon the old man lying
before the altar, and summoned the monks.   They were
just in time.   A benediction in the flutter of a hand, and
Columba departed, aged 76.

In time stone buildings replaced the wattle ones, but
it is small wonder that none of these early erections
remain, except, maybe, as traces.   The Norsemen came,
burning, destroying, slaying; five times, at least, between
795 and 986, they came, those gallant Vikings, to murder
defenceless monks.   Yet it may be that the monks sometimes struck back, for at Port-a-Curraich is a Viking's
grave—a 'ship-barrow,' 50 feet in length.   There are,
west of the Port, the *Laithrichean*, or foundations, the
Culdees Cell between Dun-I and Dunbhuirg, a hill-fort
on the latter, and the Glen of the Church in the middle
of the island—all very ancient remnants; but the oldest
walls standing are those of the Chapel to St Odhrain, or
Oran, which may belong to the late eleventh century.
The Nunnery and Cathedral are more than a hundred
years younger.   The cruciform Cathedral, with its low,
square tower, was a ruin, though preserved, when I first
knew it.   To-day it is fully restored as a place of worship.
It stands apart from the village, on the bare moor, near
to the sea, austere yet friendly.   Recently a bell was
gifted by a young man who had noticed the lack of one;
and I expect that city people who like not church bells
at home will be affected differently on Iona.   To hear a
bell's note sing out over the sea is a revelation.

Early kings—fifty-two of them, all told — princes,
bishops, Highland chiefs, lie buried there.   Once Iona
possessed many Celtic crosses;   now there are few, including St Martin's, which is 14 feet high, in front of the
Cathedral.

Of all the queer tales of those ancient times that of
Columba and his disciple Oran is surely the queerest.
There are two versions, both worth retelling, and you

can judge which seems the truer. Soon after landing on Iona Columba said to his disciples: "It is permitted that some one of you go under the earth of this island to consecrate it." If there was a general hesitation we need not wonder; but Oran arose quickly and answered: "I am ready." Then said Columba: "O, Oran, you shall receive the reward of this: no request shall be granted to anyone at my tomb, unless he first asks of thee." So they buried Oran, and he went to the Good Place.

The other version is as follows: They buried Oran alive, in order to placate some fiend who was in the habit of undoing at night all the good Columba did by day. At the end of three days they dug him up, and behold he was still alive—very much so, for he forthwith began to tell them all of his great discovery in the darkness; to wit, that there was neither God nor devil, neither heaven nor hell. Whereupon Columba, deeply shocked, gave instructions for his immediate reburial—for good.

In summer Iona's daily event is the arrival of the steamer from Oban. The landing-place is on the narrow Sound that lies between the island and Mull. We go ashore by boat, a very short trip, and walk up to the village on our way to see the things I have been trying to tell you about, and many others. I mention the tiny village, because, despite the tourist traffic and holiday sojourners, it remains in some ways unsophisticated. One little instance: A lady entered the shop and asked for a pair of shoe-laces. With a pleasant smile the merchant replied: "We are not keeping them." "But in a shop like this," said the lady, "that seems rather extraordinary." "Ah, well, you see, ma'am, we used to be keeping shoe-laces, but they were always getting sold out."

"There is a legend dear to the Celtic heart," writes Miss M. E. M. Donaldson in her *Islesmen of Bride*, that at his last hour the Gael will find himself upon a western shore, looking toward the sinking sun. Swiftly over the sea of gold will come to him a white galley. Without rudder, sail, or oars, the vessel will be drawn in to the shore solely by the great longing that is in the heart of the beholder to be borne thence by her to the mystic island of all desire—Tir-nan-Og—the Land of the Ever Young.

One does not need to be a Gael almost to behold it, standing on Iona's little hill, Dun-I, looking out to the other isles of the sea, toward sunset.

Glen Coe

With the completion, in 1933, of the new road between Bridge of Orchy and Ballachulish the anxieties of not a few motorists on the mountain route to Glen Coe will have vanished. Visitors coming to Scotland in their cars will probably choose it, especially if starting from the Lowlands on a tour with a destination north of Fort William; or they may make it their route to Oban, with the idea of returning south by the road described in an earlier part of this chapter—or *vice versa*.

In pre-motor days the pilgrim to Glen Coe usually travelled from Oban by steamer to Ballachulish, thence by coach, and this, I think, is still the most attractive, though maybe not the most exciting, way. In the two hours' sail up Loch Linnhe one enjoys the lesser lochs, islands, and mountains as they can never be enjoyed from the land; and if more variety be desired, while time must be considered, one can return to Oban by road, or by rail, from Ballachulish.

So let us take the steamer—no open sea on this trip. Crossing to Lismore we may meet the swell coming in from the Sound of Mull, but soon we are in the lee of the long island in the narrow Linn of Lorn. To the east lie the mountainous districts of Benderloch and Appin, between them Loch Creran, with Eriska Isle in its mouth.

s

Appin is Stewart country.   The scene of the most vivid of the many vivid episodes in Stevenson's *Kidnapped* is set near Duror, yonder.

The coast here has the most extraordinary contours— like a half-solved jig-saw puzzle.   In the shallows of little Loch Laich, as we near Shuna Isle, on a low rock stands Castle Stalker, roofless, but still foursquare to the gales, though the walls were raised by Duncan Stewart of Appin in the reign of James IV.   The Royal Arms are to be seen above the doorway.   Viewed from the shore against a dull sky it is as stark and grim a thing as you may see in the Highlands;   spied from a little way up the hillside, through the trees, the weed-fringed rock shows its shamrock shape, and, if the sky be smiling and the water laughing, you would wonder why somebody does not restore the jolly old place, as Duart has been restored, and live in it.   Shuna has the fragment of a castle which, they say, was never completed.

Ballachulish lies under Ben Vair, on Loch Leven— another of those sea-lochs which Nature stopped short of making inland lakes.   Ballachulish means 'Village on the Straits,' and across the straits is North Balla-chulish, whence the road winds past charming Onich to Corran, and then in pleasant level stretches along the side of Upper Loch Linnhe—which also just escaped being a lake, as witness the narrows at Corran—to Fort William.   A ferry, carrying motors, crosses the straits, but the road to Kinlochleven, with its aluminium works, and round the head of the loch, has lately been recon-structed, and its extra twenty miles or so are well worth the fuel.

About three miles up the loch from the pier, and beyond the slate quarries, the Glen opens.   The old road enters by the thatched cots of Carnach and Bridge of Coe, near to which is a Celtic cross of red granite, erected in 1884 by Mrs Archibald Burns-Macdonald of

Glen Coe, a direct descendant of MacIan, to commemorate the Massacre. The place of the tragedy is in the vicinity of Clachaig, two miles farther on, whither the road goes quietly among fir-trees—Nature's way of 'breaking it gently.' The new road is a little way south of the old.

Coe, or Cona—to use the name familiar to Ossian—means 'narrow'; but the solitary syllable, with its mournful cry, seems singularly appropriate now. The valley is known also as 'the Glen o' Weeping,' which reminds me to mention Marjorie Bowen's novel of that title, a colourful, poignant rendering of a dreadful story. I should not wonder if the name was there long, long before the Massacre. It might well have come from the first man, with a sense less crude than that of mere animal fear, who strayed into the shadows of those mountains and their desolation. He would, of course, be fearful, too, as many have been fearful since, for those mountains are so lofty and steep, so barren and cruel, that coming to the Pass, beyond the sullen little loch, and hearing the sob of the winds in the corries, he would feel himself in the depths of a place abhorred of the gods; he would fancy the stone monsters closing in upon him. Charles Dickens thought it "perfectly terrible." "The Pass," he wrote, "is an awful place. There are scores of glens high up which form such haunts as you might imagine wandering in, in the height and madness of a fever." Macaulay, after seeing it both in sunshine and in rain, declared it to be "the very valley of death." On the other hand, just to show how different people may see the same thing differently, I quote from Dorothy Wordsworth:

At Kingshouse, in comparing the impressions we had received at Glen Coe, we found that . . . we had been prepared for images of terror, had expected a deep den-like valley with overhanging rocks, such as William has described in his lines upon the Alps. The place had nothing of this character, the glen being open to the eye of day, the mountains retiring in independent majesty.

Yet there is a gloom in Glen Coe that the sunshine does not dispel; its very shimmer on the wet rocks is sardonic. The sun is no ardent lover here, rather a heartless deceiver. As often as not, it is only a tepid gleam through broken clouds, or a pallid glimmer beyond the vapours trailing their skirts over the heights. There are three peaks which might well be called the Weird Sisters. Only once have I seen them naked, and they then seemed to hate the blue sky. Buchaille Etive, at the head, though the first word means 'Shepherd,' is a threat in stone. To name all those crowding heights would be to make only a strange list of "sound and fury, signifying nothing," unless you could spend a week or two among them with a map and compass. Enough to call them the Mountains of Glen Coe. As such you will not forget them.

The scene of the Massacre is, as I have said, near Clachaig, where there is an inn, on the old road. It is a sombre enough situation, beside the unhappy Coe, though cheerful compared with the Pass beyond. Very briefly, here is the tale:

By 1691 warfare in the Highlands had come to a lull, but the chiefs who favoured the return of the Stuarts, expecting help from France, were restive, and many flatly refused to take the oath of allegiance to King William. At midsummer the Earl of Breadalbane, described by contemporaries as possessing a fox's cunning, a serpent's wisdom, and an eel's slipperiness, had a meeting with the chiefs at Achallader Castle, near Loch Tulla. Some of the chiefs took the bribe, others refused, and all remained disaffected. At the end of August was issued a proclamation threatening "the utmost extremity of the law" for those who should not take the oath by January 1, 1692. This proved more effectual than the bribery,

GLEN COE IN WINTER
Photo Robert McLeod

THE TAY AT ABERFELDY

Photo Alexander B. Beattie

[P. 288]

and by the day appointed the oath had been, more or less reluctantly, taken by all the chiefs, excepting two, MacDonell of Glengarry, who had openly strengthened his stronghold, and MacIan of Glen Coe, who in the past had made himself obnoxious to the Government.

He of Glen Coe, however, had decided, on the last day of the year, to pledge himself, and had gone to Fort William to do so, only to be told by the military people there that the formality could be executed only before a sheriff. There was no sheriff nearer than Inveraray, the country was under snow, and it was January 6 before he could make his affirmation there. Still, it was accepted, duly registered, and a certificate dispatched to the Privy Council in London.

In London town sat Sir John Dalrymple, otherwise Lord Stair, Under-Secretary of State, and King William's very dutiful servant. He did not believe that all the chiefs who were taking the oath intended to keep it; he believed that nothing short of making a frightful example of one or two of them would cause the others to maintain it. Accordingly he was more and more disgusted as name after name came in; but when MacIan of Glen Coe's did *not* come in, he made no secret of his satisfaction. Here was a fit and proper person for the making of a frightful example! And then, after all, arrived the certificate from Inveraray, to spoil everything. Yet where there's a will there's a way, even if it must be a crooked one. The Privy Council was induced to reject or ignore the certificate. King William, who did not read everything too carefully, and who had lately put his signature to "letters of fire and sword," was not told about it. Dalrymple was free to go ahead, and he went ahead. His apologists have said that he really wished for a peaceful settlement. If so, why did he place the matter in the hands of two officers whose people were hereditary foes of the Macdonalds—Major Robert

Duncanson and Captain Robert Campbell of Glen Lyon
—with instructions for "extirpation"?

On February 1, Captain Campbell entered the glen,
with 120 men, mostly Highlanders, at his back, and
exhibited a Government order for the quartering of his
troops. Hidden against his breast, warming his heart,
was the dire Dalrymple order. MacIan had nothing to
fear; he had taken the oath. His people received the
soldiers with what hospitality they could afford, and for
twelve days treated them as honest men. It is inconceivable that all those six score soldiers could all the time
have known why they were there. One pictures Glen
Lyon and Drummond, late on the night of the 12th, giving their underlings their orders and something—maybe
a good deal—to drink.

When you come to this part of Glen Coe, close your
eyes for a minute, forget that it is a summer day, and
imagine——

It is between four and five on the morning of February
13, black and bitter cold. Glen Coe is under snow. But
though so early, here and there lights flicker. Glen Lyon
and Drummond, with their men, are astir betimes,
weapons in their hands. First blood comes from Mac-
Ian himself—they shoot him as he gets out of his bed;
they treat his wife so brutally that within a few hours
she, too, lies dead. The alarm is raised; the wretched
defenceless people, half-naked, deeming that all passes
will be guarded by other bodies of troops, make for the
mountains. But now there is plenty of light, for the
thatches are flaring, and the butchers can get on with
their business. One may hope that some of them had
compassion, since the number of the slain was small in
comparison with the number of the slayers, and more
than a hundred escaped to the inhospitable hills. And
one may guess at the thoughts of Glen Lyon and Drummond when, at last, in that smoky yellow glare, walled

in by shuddering darkness, they carefully counted their victims—thirty-four men, including a patriarch of eighty, two women, and two children. Only thirty-eight! One can hear the curses of the gallant gentlemen. From their point of view, as it would be from that of my Lord Stair, the Massacre had been a dismal failure.

Not so long ago a traveller, overtaken by night in the glen, heard the crying of a child. He sought to reach it, but it was always a little way ahead. At last he came to a cot, knocked eagerly, and when the door was opened by the shepherd, cried :

"There is a child——"

"Ay, ay," said the shepherd, "there is a child, but you cannot be doing anything, for it has been crying since long, long ago."

In Glen Coe, even on a summer day, it is not hard to believe things like that.

CHAPTER X

THE HEART OF SCOTLAND

Perth and Northward

In the course of our journeys in the West—to the Trossachs, to Oban, and to Fort William—we saw Perthshire in its wildest and, to some of us, most romantic aspects; yet we covered less than one-third of the broad shire owning the richest variety of inland scenery in Scotland, of which it forms the splendid heart. Scenery apart, it is a land for the farmer, the shepherd, and, with its moors, rivers, and deer forests, the sportsman.

The name Perth may be a corruption of Bertha, a traditional town, two miles up the river, which was washed out, along with its dwellers, by a great flood in the year 1210. At all events, Perth is very old, and was Scotland's capital before Stirling, which had the honour before Edinburgh. To-day it is a modern, cheerful place of some 35,000 inhabitants, with a long history, though not very much to show for it.

In its earliest days it was known also as St John's Town, in honour of St John's Kirk, one of the very earliest stone churches in Scotland, and now, after many vicissitudes, Perth's oldest surviving building, lately restored to serve its primal purpose and also as the county's War Memorial. Its ancient stones must have witnessed many a strange event, though none stranger than that of May 11, 1559, when John Knox, the day after he was outlawed at Stirling, arose in the pulpit and preached a sermon that fairly put the fat of fanaticism in the smouldering fire of the Reformation, which forthwith blazed up. His hearers, after bringing down the images and doing other damage, rushed forth to sack and destroy the neighbouring religious houses, in which pleasing task they were cheerily assisted by the ever-ready mob.

An object of their fury was the Blackfriars' monastery, which has an ugly memory of its own—the murder of a king, first of the ill-starred Jameses.   As a practical monarch, seeking the general good of his country, though by no means neglecting his own, James may merit a certain admiration, but he sacrificed popularity by beginning his reign with a tax of "twelve pennies in the pound," and by sternly putting his nobles "in their places."   In 1437 he came to Perth as president of a council gathered to receive an envoy from Rome.   The castle being under repair, he found quarters in the Black-friars' convent, just outside the town-wall.   And then—

The King and Queen are about to retire.   Alarming sounds are heard.   "The door!" cries the King; but lo, it is seen that the bar is missing, removed by some traitor's hand, whereupon quick-witted Catherine Douglas, the Queen's lady-in-waiting, heroically thrusts her arm through the staples.   Soon the fair arm is broken; but meanwhile the King, by a secret trapdoor, has disappeared into a cellar.   There he curses himself and his favourite game of tennis, for until a day or two ago the cellar had had an opening to the convent garden, and he had caused it to be built up, because the tennis-balls *would* keep popping into it.   Sweating, he hears the stamping, the clatter of arms and tongues overhead, and expects every moment to be discovered.   But the noise dies down . . . the footfalls become fewer . . . suddenly a door slams, and there is silence. . . . After a while he comes up, pale, yet maybe smiling, for, though a little man, he is sturdy and no coward.   He is help-ing to tend the brave Catherine when, once more, the assassins, who have been lurking at hand, return—and now it is the end.

We know that James VI was a golfer, and Perth likes to think that he played on its North Inch, as well as at St Andrews.   Perth does not, however, like to think that its North Inch course less abundantly merits the title 'Royal' than the course of Dornoch, in the far North, which received the title after King Edward VII had blandly viewed it from a distance.   Anyway, it is pleasant to picture James—who would, no doubt, consider our plus-fours most unfashionably long—following his ball of feathers with a stiff timber club over that magnificent stretch, now part of a fine public park.

There is a South Inch also, crossed by the Edinburgh road through an avenue of trees, its most prominent, though not most cheering, sight being the General Prison for Scotland, the oldest part of which was built for the confinement of French prisoners in Napoleon's day. The word inch here means 'island,' and there was a time, as you may learn by examining the slopes above the banks of the Tay, when the river—or was it the sea?—flowed at a higher level than now.   A water-surrounded inch remains in Moncrieffe Island, which carries a very delightful 18-hole course on splendid turf, three miles long, though all the hazards, owing to the flat ground, are artificial.   A newer course, with natural hazards, will be found on Craigie Hill, which, like the island course, is only about ten minutes' walk from the city.   While near the river, let me tell the angler that he can have free fishing during the season for trout, and in the autumn for salmon, over a two-and-a-half miles stretch, from the top of the North Inch downward.   As to other fishing waters, Mr P. D. Malloch, of 26 Scott Street, is always willing, I believe, to give information and expert advice. The river, too, is excellent for boating.

Long before James's day Wallace and Bruce had exciting experiences in Perth, and in 1396 on the North Inch was staged a little battle which might well have

become a model to warring factions of the future. The
cause of dispute has been forgotten, but the heads of the
Clans Chattan and Kay, instead of sending round the
Fiery Cross, very sensibly decided to settle it in a match
of thirty a side. Everybody thought it a grand idea.
All the best people, including King Robert III, were
present, and the Perth folk took a holiday. Just before
the hour an unfortunate hitch, as a modern newspaper
reporter might say, occurred. One of the clansmen,
having lost his courage, plunged into the Tay, to seek
safety on the other side. But there were sportsmen in
Perth, and one of them, Gow Chrom, the bandy-legged
smith, offered himself as a substitute; and then all the
gladiators formed up and gave a grand display, hacking
and hewing till only nine were left alive, one of them
unwounded. He was the aforesaid Gow, and we learn
all about him and his sweetheart in Sir Walter Scott's
The Fair Maid of Perth. An old house known as
'The Fair Maid's' stands at the corner of Curfew Row,
and is open to visitors.

The Salutation Hotel, in South Street, was there when
Prince Charlie came to Perth in 1746, and contains the
room where he lay. Its spacious dining-room, with the
great, high, arched window and musicians' gallery, is
worth seeing.

When that excellent English tourist, Pennant, visited
Perth in 1769 he went up Kinnoull Hill, an easy climb,
and also Moncrieffe Hill, whence he beheld "the glory
of Scotland." Assuredly he beheld one of Scotland's
glories when he looked down on the wide, wooded Strath
of Gowrie, with the ever-broadening, winding course of
the smooth-flowing (the meaning of the word) Tay;
beyond Abernethy, with its ancient round tower, and the
Ochil Hills to Fife; away over fertile lands to the Bens
of the West and the Grampians in the North. To-day
a road, almost as smooth and winding, goes down near

the river, by an occasional old-world village, to Dundee. Elcho Castle, a ruin preserved by being reroofed a century ago, may be glimpsed on the river's bank; and just under the hill, in the woods, you have a contrast in the modern Castle of Kinfauns. Kinnoull Hill, precipitous on one side, is interesting to geologist and botanist. In the gully known as the Windy Gowl the echo repeats itself eight times.

Concerning the tower on the verge of the precipice, I had to ask many people before I discovered its story. In the eighteenth century the ninth Earl of Kinnoull, with his friend and neighbour landowner, Lord Gray, was sailing up the Rhine. They did not think the Rhine a finer river than the Tay, but they did greatly admire the baronial castles on the heights. So, when they came home, the Earl built the tower on Kinnoull Hill, and his lordship built one on his own Gray Hill, a mile to the east. On the top of Kinnoull you will find also a stone table. It was set up by the same Earl, who was so fond of the view that he often dined there. In 1924 the hill was gifted to the city of Perth by the late Lord Dewar.

Scone

"Crowned at Scone." So begins the tale of the reign of many a Scottish king, but the tidy little town of Scone, two miles out of Perth, was not the scene of the ceremonies. Of the original Scone, which lay a mile or so to the west, only its Cross, surrounded by noble trees, remains. It was in this old Scone that, after sundry removals, the Stone of Destiny lay for three centuries, till Edward I took it away to Westminster.

Scone's Abbey and Abbot's Palace were destroyed in 1559—a direct result of Knox's sermon in Perth—and only traces remain. Possibly much of the material was used in building, on the Boot (or Moot) Hill, in 1624, the

Parish Church, of which the aisle survives to-day. About the same time a new palace was begun by the Earl of Gowrie; but James VI, who owed him several bad turns, took it, along with other property, and presented it to David Murray, of the Tullibardine family, afterward Earl Scone and Viscount Stormont, who completed the building, of which, however, only a gateway stands to-day. The present palace, a conventionally castellated edifice, was set up by the Earl of Mansfield—the Stormonts had succeeded to that title—in the beginning of the nineteenth century. It harbours many treasures of old furniture, including a bed belonging to James VI and curtains worked by his mother, Queen Mary, while prisoned in Loch Leven Castle. The old place of coronation may now be that of the music gallery, though I am inclined to the theory that our kings were crowned on a hillock in the neighbourhood.

Scone, by the way, is one of those funny words of ours which are so apt to bother the stranger. In the twelfth century it was written 'Scoone,' and is still pronounced 'Skoon.' The scone of the tea-table is, however, pronounced 'skon,' not 'skone.' You may care to remember this if, in the course of your tour, you should want to inquire whether they bake good scones at Scone.

To the motorist Perth provides a base for the exploration not only of the whole shire, but of Fife, Angus, Kincardine, and parts of Aberdeenshire and Invernessshire. The roads are good; their scenery is seldom dull. For a day's 'special' golf, St Andrews is reached in an hour or so, by road or rail, and Gleneagles in half that time. Nobody in Scotland thought anything of Gleneagles—'Glen of the Church' (Gaelic, *Eglais*—French, *Eglise*)—till some bright brain of the railway company conceived the idea of a perfect golf course and a monster luxury hotel. Even should you despise golf you ought to see the course.

Crieff as a Centre

Crieff, seventeen miles from Perth by the direct road, is an important little town, sunnily situated on a steep slope in the fair valley of the Earn. Many tourists choose it as a centre instead of Perth. It has a big hydro and several good hotels.

Crieff's most prominent natural feature is the Knock—the wooded hill that rises above the town, along the brow of which is a favourite walk, and from the top of which you behold one of the finest landscapes in Scotland.

If you love a garden you will go to Drummond Castle, three miles south. The ironwork gate, wrought in Italy more than two hundred years ago, opens on an avenue a mile and a half long. The original castle, built in 1491 —Queen Mary spent a Christmas there—was wrecked in Cromwell's day, and all but destroyed forty years later. Partially rebuilt in 1715, it was then garrisoned by Government troops, but in 1745 was again laid low, by order of the Jacobite Duchess of Perth, lest Government troops should reoccupy it. Once more rebuilt in part, in 1822, it is now used mainly as an armoury, and contains a collection of old Scottish weapons. The modern castle, a little way off, is undistinguished, but the gardens under its south walls make it noteworthy among all such places in the kingdom. Covering ten acres on a steep slope, they are laid out in the Italian, Dutch, and French fashions.

From Crieff a highway and railway run due west into the Perthshire we saw on the road to Oban. The highway skirts the fine estate of Ochtertyre, with its mansion perched above the little loch, and its ruined fortalice on a promontory. At Ochtertyre Burns wrote *Blythe, Blythe and Merry was She*, but "she" was not a local girl. The road continues through Comrie—in the neighbourhood of Glenartney, celebrated by Scott—a sedate little town amid scenery of the wildest and tenderest, the chief sight being the 'De'il's Cauldron'—a fearsome chasm on the river Lednock.   You would hardly guess that placid Comrie has a reputation for earthquakes, which it owes to its situation on the great line of 'fault' separating the Highlands and Lowlands.   The quakes, however, though more frequent than in any other part of Scotland, are most politely performed.

Five miles beyond Comrie, St Fillans is daintily set in stern surroundings under Ben Vorlich, at the eastern end of Loch Earn.   The loch offers good trout-fishing.   Road and railway continue along its shores—or you may make the seven miles' trip by motor-boat—to Lochearnhead. Thence, if motoring, you may be tempted to carry on through Glen Ogle to Killin, run down the side of Loch Tay to Kenmore, and return to Crieff by Aberfeldy and the Sma' Glen.   I am going to touch now on the district enclosing the three last-named places, for it lies nearer to Crieff than to Perth, and is surely the finest of all the fine outings you can take from the former.

The Sma' Glen is a defile made impressive by its narrowness rather than by the height of its hills.   The ground above the Almond, which runs down to join the Tay, opposite Scone, was traversed by the Romans, whose progress was doubtless spied by the Caledonians in their fort on Dunsmore Hill.   Possibly the track they made remained to give hints to General Wade, who, in 1762, constructed the road of which traces remain.   In the pass of the glen, under frowning steeps, not far from the stream, is the great stone reputed to mark the grave of Ossian.   Tradition has buried the bard in several places, but in this place has been discovered evidence of, at least, the burial of somebody; for when some of Wade's soldiers, in an idle hour, moved the stone aside, they found bones and, of all things, money.

On the eastern hillside, in the face of the Eagle's Rock,

gapes the roomy Thief's Cave, in which Alastair Bain, for long prosperous in the sheep-stealing business, took shelter. The night was chill, Alastair was hungry, and his wits were weary. Thoughtlessly he lit a fire and proceeded to roast one of his recent captures. An enemy spied the dancing light; a band of enemies came softly upon him. Trapped, he was taken supperless to Perth, and in due season hanged—the close of many a hungry Highlander's career in those good old times.

Through Amulree, quaint village favoured by anglers, we carry on north to Aberfeldy, which is surrounded by some of the loveliest scenes in Scotland, notably the falls of Moness, where Burns was inspired to write *The Birks o' Aberfeldy*, the hamlet of Weem, near to which is Castle Menzies, ancient seat of the clan chiefs, and the Tay, as viewed from the woody hillside at many different points. At the town the Tay is spanned by a Wade bridge, with a line of poplars at one end. Dorothy Wordsworth thought the bridge "ambitious and ugly," but I hope you may disagree with her.

Kenmore has been called Scotland's model village; it is certainly a trim little place. Burns left some verses inscribed over a mantelpiece in the Kenmore Hotel. The gates of Taymouth Castle, once a home of the Breadalbanes, now a great hostelry, open on the village square. The castle, built between 1801 and 1842 on the site of an old-time stronghold, is

> a magnificent pile of four stories, with round towers at the angles, extensive wings on either side, and a massive central quadrangular tower, forming an airy pavilion, 150 feet high. The interior is fitted up in most princely style. The pleasure grounds comprise a circuit of 13 miles.

Yet it is not, I assure you, necessary to arrive in a Rolls Royce, the valet following in a Daimler with the money. As a friend said to me, "I just pulled myself together at the gates, walked up with my little suitcase to the castle, pulled myself together again, stepped in, asked for a room —and was happy for a fortnight after." Recently on this estate were unearthed five Greek coins of the second or third century B.C. How did they get there?

At Kenmore the Tay emerges from its loch, which stretches westward for over fourteen miles between heathery or grassy hills. Ben Lawers, all but 4000 feet high—a cairn on the summit raises it above that height —is the loftiest of the Perthshire mountains, and perhaps the most inviting in Scotland. Climbers usually start from Lawers Hotel; the ascent is not difficult—it may be done on a pony—and the view from the top rivals that from Ben Lomond. The loch is famous for its spring salmon, ranging from 20 to 50 lb.; the fishing is open to guests of the hotels situated at a number of points along its shores. There is a road on either side of the loch, and in summer a steamer plies between Kenmore and Killin. Killin has lost something of its old-world character—thanks to slates and corrugated iron, which have replaced the thatch—but of its surroundings the not always enthusiastic Dr MacCulloch has written: "The most extraordinary collection of extraordinary scenery in Scotland—a perfect picture gallery in itself." Among the attractions are the six cataracts of the Lochay; the falls of the Dochart; the green islets in that river, on one of which, in the old days, members of the wild Clan Macnab came finally to rest; also the gloom-surrounded ruin of Finlarig Castle, which, if not haunted, ought to be, and by many a grisly ghost; and the grave of the great Celtic warrior, Fingal.

North of Loch Tay lies Glen Lyon, one of our longest glens, where Nature is at her most aloof in brooding majesty. There are depths in the glen that never know the winter sunshine. It may be reached from Killin by a mountain road, which leaves the loch road at Morenish

T

and climbs over the lower ridges of Ben Lawers, touching a height of 1800 feet above sea-level; but the easier way is from Kenmore, by Fearnan, a few miles up the loch, or round by Coshieville, near to Garth Castle, originally a lair of the notorious Alexander Stewart, Earl of Buchan, who, though of the fourteenth century, is still remembered as "the Wolf of Badenoch."

Near the head of the glen Meggernie Castle shows a high square tower, with peaked roof, of the fifteenth century. You come upon it through a wonderful lime-tree avenue. It is the centre of a great sporting estate. But to most of us the human interest of Glen Lyon is in Fortingall, at the eastern end, a village of light-brown cottages roofed with dark-brown thatch, thick and shaped about the upper windows, so that, in a way, one is reminded of Devon. How old is Fortingall? In the churchyard, with its sculptured stones, is a yew-tree, a mere broken shell; yet still flourishing, I believe, in its scion of about two hundred years of age. The tree itself was ancient when, a hundred years before Agricola came, Rome sent an embassy to Scotland, which was received by King Metellanus, at Fortingall. It would seem that the embassy made a stay, and one of the ambassadors became father of a son. And the boy grew up to bear the most unhappily famous name in the world's history—Pontius Pilate. So runs the strange legend.

Some ten miles farther north lie Lochs Rannoch ('Bracken') and Tummel ('Plunging Stream'), linked by the river of the latter name. Loch Tummel is really an expansion of the river, which hurries on eastward, then southward, to join the Tay. The mountains here are dominated by Schiehallion, over whose name etymologists differ. Some say "Hill of the Caledonians"; others, "Maiden's Breast." Perthshire has nothing lovelier to show than Loch Tummel and the Tummel Valley. The vista, as seen from the hillside, of the loch, with its wooded bays and promontories, lying between gentle slopes, and Schiehallion looming in the west, is unforgettable.

Loch Rannoch is a larger loch, nearly ten miles long. Kinloch Rannoch, at its eastern end, has long been known to fishers—the cannibal trout are famed—and now the motor has made it accessible to many people who can be happy without ever wetting a fly. The road proceeds along the shore of the loch and continues a few miles beyond to Rannoch station, on the West Highland railway, where it ends abruptly on the margin of the Great Moor.

Now we can return to Crieff by the way we came, or from Kinloch Rannoch make our way east to the Great North Road. But the Great North Road requires a place to itself, and I ask you kindly to imagine yourselves back in Perth, from which point I shall begin the attempt to describe some of its features.

The Great North Road

In July 1728 General Wade, the remarkable Irishman who served the British Government so well, and Scotland better than she knew, wrote from Blair Atholl to the Right Hon. Henry Pelham:

> I am now with all possible diligence carrying on the new road for wheel-carriages between Dunkeld and Inverness, of about 80 measured English miles in length.

Only 15 miles were then completed; but by the autumn of the following year the work seems to have been about finished, and he was making plans for the road through the Sma' Glen. In August 1730 Duncan Forbes, the Lord Advocate, wrote from Perth to a friend:

> I have visited Mr Wade at his roads, which go on with all the despatch and success imaginable. The Highlanders

begin to turn their heads and hands to labour, which in a
little time must produce a great change upon the face, as
well as the politics, of the country.

Never was truer prophecy.

Throughout the hundred-odd miles the new road,
which cost about £8000 a mile, and the railway run near
together, and, of course, there are days up yonder, even
in summer, when the train passenger is not to be pitied.

At Birnam and Dunkeld, 15 miles out of Perth, delightfully set beside the Tay, among the wooded hills, you
have the feeling of being at once in Highlands and Lowlands.   Tradition points to the site of a Pictish fortress
called Duncaledon ('Hill of the Woods'), from which
the present name is derived.   Columba had not been
seven years on Iona when one of his missionaries built a
cell at Dunkeld, which was the beginning of a monastery;
and in 815, after the massacre of the Iona monks by the
Vikings, Dunkeld became the religious centre of Scotland.
The Cathedral dates from 1318.   In 1560 it was 'purged,'
to use a favourite word of the Reformers; in 1689, along
with Dunkeld House, it was held by the lately formed
regiment of Covenanters, the Cameronians, against
Highlander troops 5000 strong, or four to one.   The
siege lasted from the August dawn till dark; the commander of the defenders, Lieut.-Col. William Cleland,
fell early in the fight, but his men carried on, and, when
the musketry fire from the houses of the town became
too hot for their patience, parties with torches on pikes
made sallies, and were so successful that only three
houses survived the flames.   In the end the Highlanders
abandoned the task and retired, whereupon the Cameronians threw up their bonnets and sang praises to the
Lord.

The Cathedral is a ruin, save for the choir, the earliest
part of the building, fully restored in the beginning of the
present century, after intermittent repairs, by the late

THE HEART OF SCOTLAND 293

Sir Donald Currie, and used as the Parish Church. Of
the interesting monuments not the least is the mighty
stone effigy of that fourteenth-century terror, Alexander
Stewart, "the Wolf of Badenoch," in all his warlike
array. One may be permitted to wonder how the statue
of such a person got there, and imagine the ghost's ironic
chuckle, since he it was who, in 1390, gave the town of
Elgin and its wonder Cathedral to the flames. Near by
is Dunkeld's only ancient house, one of the three left
by the Cameronians—the Dean of Dunkeld's mansion.
Besides its Cathedral, Dunkeld, in the old days, had
several chapels, one dedicated to St Jerome. Alack for
the poor saint, his name became corrupted to 'St Jorum!'

The bridge across the Tay, a fine example of Telford's
work, completed in 1809, joins Dunkeld with Birnam—
and the name Birnam connects Scotland with Shakespeare, though Birnam to-day is a modern village, nicely
laid out, with an hotel of size so solemnly impressive in its
Saxon-Gothic architecture that you may feel like taking
off your hat before you enter, and a railway station
that is almost an ornament. The station serves Dunkeld
also. It has not been discovered that Shakespeare
visited Scotland, but he must have known the geography
of these parts before he wrote *Macbeth*. Probably it was
the woods of Birnam *Hill* that came to Dunsinane,
another hill, about 12 miles to the south-east, on the top
of which are remnants of a fortress, perhaps Macbeth's.
"This castle hath a pleasant seat," says King Duncan, on
his arrival at Inverness; "the air nimbly and sweetly
recommends itself unto our gentle senses." He would
have said the same at Dunsinane—after climbing the
necessary 600 feet. There was a vitrified fort on the top
long before Macbeth's day. In 1857 was unearthed a
beautiful double-serpent ring in bronze.

Pitlochry rests open and sunnily under Ben-y-Vrackie
('Speckled Mountain'—the effect of the heather against

the grey rocks). From a mere clachan or hamlet it has grown to be one of Scotland's most fashionable resorts of sojourners and tourists, with a hydro and large hotels. Without a history of its own, it is in the midst of historic scenes. Behind it is the pretty village of Moulin, and beyond that the hamlet of Kinnaird, where Stevenson wrote three of his shorter stories—*The Body-snatcher*, *The Merry Men*, and *Thrawn Janet*. He worked in an upper room of the cottage, and on the night he finished *Thrawn Janet* he read it to his wife, and so terrified her and himself that they came downstairs, holding hands, shuddering like a pair of children.

Of all the scenes near Pitlochry the most historic is the Pass of Killiecrankie, a name that suggests a wild dance —of witches and warlocks, indeed—although it means simply 'Wood of the Aspens.' But it might well have had a name of sterner omen, this gorge, through which brawls the Garry, the reckless river that, with a few placid intervals, descends a thousand feet in its course of 22 miles. All Glen Garry is full of wonder, though perhaps it attains its grandest at Struan, nine miles north, where, among other things, if the water be low, we may see the salmon, several at a time, leaping ten feet to get up the fall. Through richly wooded country we enter the Pass overlooked by Ben-y-Vrackie, which must have witnessed many a black deed in the old days,. for here was a happy hunting-ground of brigands.

About noon on July 27, 1689, General Hugh Mackay, for King William's Government, rode into the Pass from the south, with some 3000 foot and four troops of horse, marched through it, and proceeded to take up his position on the steep slope of a hill beyond its head, with the Garry in his rear. He had not completed his arrangements, however, when Graham of Claverhouse, 'Bonnie Dundee'—Lely's portrait shows a stately, breast-plated cavalier, less handsome of face than haughty—

THE PASS OF KILLIECRANKIE
Photo Alexander B. Beattie

IN OLD ABERDEEN
Photo Alexander B. Beattie
[*Pp.* 317-321]

295

who had raised the standard of the exiled James VIII,
appeared with his Highlanders, about 2500 foot and a
squadron of cavalry, and occupied the higher slopes of
the same hill. Mackay thereupon "pushed forward his
main body to a terrace midway between his antagonist
and the haugh, forming them there in battle-line, three
deep, his horsemen in the rear." Then for some hours
the armies stood facing each other, silent, waiting for the
dazzling sun to set. It was touching the mountain-tops
when Dundee's Highlanders, who had cast off plaids and
brogues, made the first move, coming down the hillside
at a trot, which developed into a charge. As they neared
the foe they fired off their pistols, for which they had small
respect, and took to their broadswords and axes; Mackay's men let off their muskets, each throwing a solitary
leaden ball, but before they could fix their bayonets, by
sticking them into the muzzles, the Highlanders were
upon them, hacking and hewing. In two minutes they
were broken, and driven pell-mell down to the Garry.
What a sight, the redcoats and tartans in that headlong
flight and pursuit! Meanwhile, Dundee—you can see the
gleam of his cuirass in the farewell rays of the sun—had
taken his place at the head of his cavalry. It seemed to
him that they hung back. Standing up in his stirrups, he
waved his sword above his head, encouraging them to
follow. And with the raising of his arm his cuirass was
lifted a trifle, exposing an inch or two of his left side.
There the bullet got him—some say a silver bullet, for his
enemies, the Covenanters, regarded him as in Satan's
care—and his death turned the victory into disaster for
his own party. They carried him to Blair Castle, at Blair
Atholl, and later buried him in the churchyard there.

Blair Atholl ('Plain of the Pleasant Land') is well
named. The castle during its centuries of existence has
had many distinguished visitors, friendly and otherwise,
including Mary Queen of Scots, the great Marquis of

Montrose, Cromwell's soldiers, 'Bonnie Dundee,' General Wade, Robert Burns, and Queen Victoria.   The Atholls have ever been noted as hosts.   When James V, about 1529, visited the Earl, on sporting business, he was entertained in a handsome lodge built for the occasion in Glen Tilt, at the foot of massive Ben-y-Gloe.   The holiday at an end, James was riding away when shouts from his men caused him to look round—and lo, the lodge was in flames!   "Only our Highland hospitality, your Majesty," explained the smiling Earl.   There is a modern tale of an Atholl who also smiled on his guests, if perhaps a trifle slyly.   The Duke invited to lunch a party of Socialists who had been thundering in all sincerity and sentimentality against the wicked waste of the good land sacrificed to the sport of the idle rich. After lunch he took them for a walk.   On the top of a little hill he halted and waved his hand: "Gentlemen, yonder is my deer forest.   Will each of you kindly accept the gift of a small-holding, the sole condition being that you live on it?"   His guests looked upon the miles of lumpy, heathery, rocky, boggy ground, and all its desolation, and perhaps they smiled too.

Beyond the Falls of Bruar, Glen Garry, and little Loch Garry we come to bleak Dalnaspidal, where, long ago, as the name implies, was a hospice for travellers—probably a hovel, yet a truly welcome shelter in the winter. In its neighbourhood are standing-stones and cairns, marking, maybe, the graves of mighty men slain in battle, but, more likely, those of poor devils perished in the snow.   You don't want to be up here with a car in a blizzard.   It is thrilling enough in the train.

To the old inn at Dalwhinnie, on a night in October 1861, came Queen Victoria and the Prince Consort, in the course of one of their *incognito* expeditions.   They supped on a fowl, whose condition suggested that it had welcomed death, and tea.   You will find more generous

fare in the present hotel. Loch Ericht, famed for its
cannibal trout, running up to 25 lb. lies a mile away,
under Ben Alder. In that mountain was the memorable
'Cluny's Cage,' in which Prince Charlie found a temporary refuge, and which Stevenson describes in *Kidnapped*. The loch, one of Scotland's wildest scenes, has
been linked with Loch Rannoch under the Grampian
Electricity Scheme, but without detriment, I am told, to
the fishing.

Through Glen Truim we cross the Spey, which has its
origin in a lonely tarn, some 20 miles westward—the
tarn in which a sober shepherd beheld a trout that could
—as he was prepared to declare, if he met his Maker that
very night—have devoured a sheep. Across the bridge
at Newtonmore, the place for a hardy holiday, a road
strikes south-west and runs by Loch Laggan—lovely
scene of more trout stories—to Tulloch, Spean Bridge,
and Fort William.

Kingussie's smart little town stands happily, about
800 feet above sea-level, in the lee of the Monadhliath
Mountains, with a clear view of the Cairngorms. Meaning 'Head of the Pine-wood,' the name is pronounced
'Kingucey.' It is justly proud of itself, its situation, its
facilities for anglers, and its 18-hole golf course, which
owes something to the advice of Braid and Vardon.
Obviously, it is a choice centre for excursions, and one of
the most interesting sights in the Highlands is less than
a mile away.

Ruthven Barrack was built and garrisoned by the
English Government just after the 1715 rising. On a
green mound, which suggests an ancient mote, on the
south side of the Spey, the great building stands isolated,
gaunt and roofless, pretty much as Prince Charlie's Highlanders left it, after firing it, in 1746. They had compelled the garrison to surrender, but as they numbered
300 and the garrison only thirteen, there was not much to

make a song about. Against artillery, even the artillery
of those days, the place could have had small chance.
Long before the barrack's day a castle stood on the
mound, a fortress of the Comyns, the rivals of Robert the
Bruce. Later it became the chief stronghold of "the
Wolf of Badenoch," whose memory is for ever cropping
up in these parts. He had another lair on the island in
Loch-an-Eilan, to which, for its perfect beauty's sake,
come annually many visitors from all parts. It lies 14
miles north-east of Kingussie and a few miles south of
Aviemore, another of the airy mountain villages that
appeal to people who prefer something decidedly bracing.

Here we are in Clan Grant territory. The clan slogan,
"Stand fast, Craigellachie!" refers to the great rock above
Aviemore. At this point the railway forks, a line striking north-east to those favourite Speyside places, Boat of
Garten—once a ferry—and Grantown, thence away into
Moray. Grantown is comparatively modern, well laid
out, with a fine square. It was founded by Sir James
Grant in 1766, and a hundred years later Queen Victoria
and the Prince Consort by an *incognito* visit, afterward
described in her Majesty's *Journal*, made its name, and
its fame has been increasing ever since. They used to
say that if one wanted to live among nonagenarians
Grantown was the spot; and I know of a man with a well-
to-do maiden aunt there who declares that the climate
is "intolerably healthy." Indeed, I think it must have
been in the neighbourhood that the traveller came upon
the aged man sitting by the wayside and weeping bitterly,
who on being sympathetically questioned replied:
"Father scolded me." "But why did he scold you?"
asked the stranger. "For playing tricks on Grandfather."

Through the valley of the Findhorn and across a
stretch of moorland we come to Moy. Moy Hall, among
the trees beside Loch Moy, is the seat of Mackintosh

of Mackintosh. The name Mackintosh is writ large in the long history of the Highland clans, and Moy has its own tales. To Moy Hall in February 1746 came Prince Charlie, in advance of his army, to be hospitably received by Lady Mackintosh, known as Colonel Anne, because of her gallant spirit shown in raising the clan, while her husband remained loyal to the Government, whatever his secret feelings may have been. This visit of the Prince had, however, come to the ears of Lord Loudon, commanding at Inverness, who made plans for a rich capture. But the Jacobites there got wind of my Lord's scheme, and a boy and girl were dispatched by different routes to warn his Highness. One of them arrived in time, yet the Prince's escape would have been hardly assured but for the wit of Donald Fraser, the Mackintosh blacksmith. With four companions he took up a position in a pass, a mile or so from Loch Moy, placing his men some distance apart, and there, in the dark, they awaited the coming of the redcoats. Loudon, however, was taking no chances, and instead of sending a mere detachment he came himself, at the head of 1500 men. Nevertheless Fraser held his ground, and when the troops drew near enough he shouted, like a commander, "The Mackintoshes, Macgillivrays, and Macbeans to form in the centre; the Macdonalds on the right; the Frasers on the left!" and thereupon five muskets went off in five different places. Panic seized the redcoats, who thought the whole Jacobite army was upon them, and there was a frantic flight for Inverness.

Within a few miles of our destination we have one of the finest prospects in Scotland—the waters and shores of the Moray and Beauly Firths, the mountains of Ross and Cromarty, with giant Ben Wyvis in their midst, the Great Glen reaching away to the west, with, perhaps, a glimpse in the blue distance of the domed peak of Mealfourvonie ('Mountain of the Cold Moor'), and in front, above the trees, the homely, hospitable smoke from the hearths of Inverness itself.

It is the same view from the train, which reminds me that the last time I beheld it, about 5.30 on a fine summer morning, a fellow-traveller persisted in telling me the story of the American gentleman and the mackintosh. The American gentleman was fishing in these parts, accompanied by his pretty daughter. One afternoon, when the weather looked like breaking, he said to his ghillie: "Angus, do you think you could find a mackintosh for Miss Harper?" With a shy, sidelong glance at the girl Angus replied: "No, sir, but maybe I could be finding her a Macdonald."

The Road to Aberdeen

A colourful fifty-mile excursion from Perth is afforded by the road running north through the Scone estate, the bright little burgh of Blairgowrie, Glen Shee, across the Grampians by the Devil's Elbow, and over the Aberdeenshire border to Braemar.

Scone we have seen. Some miles beyond it is the Tay's chief fall, and farther on, on a lofty point of land, Stobhall, the sixteenth-century mansion of the famous Perthshire family, the Drummonds. If you remember the wonderful gardens at Drummond Castle, Crieff, you will recognize them here in miniature. In the old days two of the Drummond daughters became consorts of kings: Margaret Logie, of David II, son of the Bruce; Annabella, of Robert III; and there were expectations of another Margaret becoming queen of James IV. James, indeed, went so far as to ennoble her father, who then built Drummond Castle. But the royal favour was not followed by good fortune. The three Drummond daughters died one morning after breakfast, while the son, implicated in the burning of the Murrays in their kirk at Monzievaird, near Crieff, was taken to the scaffold.

Where the Isla, from the neighbouring county of
Angus, reinforces the Tay in the most turbulent passage
of its career is the ruin of Kinclaven Castle, founded by
Malcolm Canmore, and for long a favourite residence of
kings, and of Sir William Wallace, who took it out of
English hands. Presently, on the Lansdowne estate, we
travel for more than half a mile in the shade of a beech
hedge, almost a hundred feet high, planted two centuries
ago by Lady Nairne. In the neighbourhood lived that
other Lady Nairne whose Jacobite songs will survive the
memories of many kings and queens.

Beyond Blairgowrie ('Plain of the Wild Goats'),
taking the sunshine under the southern slopes of the
Grampians, centre of a great fruit-growing district, notably of raspberries, we travel uphill, more or less, for 25
miles. Through the gorge of the Ericht, with the
mansion of Craighall looking down from a sheer cliff,
we come into Glen Shee. You can decide for yourself
whether Shee ought to mean 'hill,' 'peace,' or 'fairies';
but I vote for the fairies, since it is well known that long
ago they were most active in these parts. For instance,
if you started to build a house on a spot sacred to their
affairs, you would wake up in the morning to find the
foundations removed, and this would be repeated till you
apologized and chose another site.

The Spital—*i.e.*, inn, or 'change-house'—had periods
of big business in the old days, for here was one of Scotland's great drove-roads for the transference of herds of
cattle between the North and the South. A road for
wheel-traffic was made to the plans of Wade, after his
retiral, and another by Telford eighty years later, and
you will appreciate the difficulties of the engineers,
especially when you come to the 'hairpins,' known as the
Devil's Elbow. At the summit, near the Cairnwell Pass,
the only possible gap in the Eastern Grampians, guarded
by the great, grey, baldheaded *Maol*, you are 2200 feet

above sea-level, on the highest road in Britain.   Even in
the late spring you may be looking on snow a thousand
feet below you, while in winter the road may be blocked
for months.   Yet, if the road be open then, what a
spectacle you may have, east and west, of the mass of
Byron's "Dark Lochnagar" and the bens of the Cairngorms, all in white! The way down is easy.

At Braemar the road turns east, wandering through
the Dee Valley, over some 60 miles, to Aberdeen.   But
Aberdeen, as is quite natural, expects that every visitor
to Scotland will 'do' Deeside from Aberdeen, so I shall
leave that fine part of the country to a later chapter.

CHAPTER XI

ANGUS AND KINCARDINESHIRE

THE revival of the original name, that of an early king, is so recent that, unless your map be recent too, you will read "Forfar" across the county lying between Perthshire and the North Sea. Smaller than its neighbour and no rival in natural grandeur, Angus has yet an importance and attractions of its own and, for its size, a big share of the story of Scotland, along with many remains of the country's earliest civilization. A land largely fertile and raising a world-famous breed of cattle, its possessions include Dundee, in point of population Scotland's third city; old Arbroath, with its abbey; Forfar, the county town; Glamis Castle, girlhood home of the Duchess of York; Kirriemuir, birthplace of J. M. Barrie; beautiful Montrose and Carnoustie, known by name, at least, to every golfer.

Dundee

To many people the word Dundee, thanks to two indefatigable firms, one local, the other in London, may suggest nothing but pots of marmalade and tins of cake, while to the city man it may stand only for jute; yet Dundee has many industries, including shipbuilding and engineering, is a considerable seaport, and, though not magnificent in itself, is most splendidly situated at the foot of the Sidlaws on the Tay.

From Perthshire there are side-doors to Angus, but Dundee is the main gateway. You may come to it by the L.N.E. Railway, over the two great bridges, or by the L.M.S. *via* Perth; and I have friends who extol the sea-trip from London, made every Wednesday by the D.P. and L. Shipping Co.'s steamer. The motorist approaching through Fife is comfortably ferried across from Newport in fifteen minutes. There is, however, for most people a thrill in the approach by the Tay Bridge.

The bridge, while longer, is not the spectacle of the towering Forth Bridge; none the less it is one of Scotland's wonders, and it arose out of a great disaster. In May 1878 the first Tay Bridge was opened for passenger traffic; in June 1879, so secure did it seem, Queen Victoria travelled over it; and on the Sunday night after Christmas, in the same year, at the height of a hurricane, it—broke. The train from Edinburgh, with some seventy passengers, steamed down to the bridge—there was one man bound for Dundee who, I have heard, alarmed by the gale, alighted at Leuchars Junction—and proceeded upon the single track into the screaming darkness. . . . Over in Dundee the railway officials waited—and waited. Some of them thought they saw, out yonder, brief flashes. At last the stationmaster took a lamp and went out on the bridge, crawling on hands and knees because of the blast. And so, in time, he came to the gulf. Only a little spaniel escaped, swimming somehow to land. . . . The present bridge, with its double track, is sturdy enough. If you look down, over the rail, on the east side, you will still see the remains of the slim piers that supported its predecessor, and marvel at man's hardihood.

Dundee has known the presence of many kings and queens, greedy, needy, or gracious, but, oddly enough, it is of the visitations of two of the queens only that we find visible memorials. The Royal Arch at the harbour, where until but a generation ago the Arctic whalers used to rest their stout hulls between seasons, commemorates the visit of Queen Victoria in 1844. Nearly 300 years earlier Mary Queen of Scots marked her visit in an unexpectedly practical fashion, finding fault with the overcrowded state of the common graveyard, and directing that a new one should be laid out, farther from the centre of the town. The new one became known as the Howff—the word means a place of resort, as often as not applied to a public-house—for, apart from its obvious purpose, it was frequented by the old Dundee craftsmen discussing the country's affairs and their own. No longer a place of burial, though the old stones remain, it is still the Howff, a much appreciated, if not precisely gay, open space in the midst of the busy city. Many a royal person has left a less useful memorial, though perhaps I should add that Mary improved the same shining hour by fining Dundee to the tune of 2000 merks for, more or less, its zeal in the cause of the Reformation.

The city's most ancient landmark is the Old Steeple in the Nethergate. There is, by the way, a hint of age in street-names like Nethergate, Overgate, Seagate, Cowgate, and Murraygate. The fifteenth-century steeple is really a massive battlemented square tower. Sir Gilbert Scott, who restored it, thought it "one of the noblest" towers in Britain. It is 156 feet high, contains a beautiful little hall, with a lofty groined roof and some finely carved sacred figures. Adjoining it are three parish churches, all under one roof, and there was once a fourth. The three are comparatively new, St Clement's having been restored, St Mary's and St Paul's entirely rebuilt, after a disastrous fire in 1841. Near by is the old Town Cross.

The Nethergate runs into the spacious High Street, of which the Town House was, until lately, the feature. Designed by William Adam, it was only 200 years old; yet it had served its day, and, as I write, is being demolished—a pity in the picturesque sense for Dundee.

Dundee University College, affiliated to St Andrews, is modern, and was founded on the benefactions of wealthy citizens, notably Dr Boyd Baxter and Miss

U

Baxter. In Dundee the name Baxter, like that of Caird, stands for philanthropy. The city is well provided with parks, and has a spacious esplanade at its west end.

Dundee has no great course of its own, but the electric tram takes the golfer speedily to Monifieth, and it is only half an hour in the train to Carnoustie, or to St Andrews and Scotscraig over in Fife.

One can hardly mention Dundee without Broughty Ferry, the breezy burgh a few miles down the river, residence of many citizens and a very popular place in summer. As well as its holiday attractions, it owns a sixteenth-century castle which is not a ruin; at any rate, the Government, for reasons of coastal defence, repaired much of it half a century ago, and a most picturesque object on its promontory it appears.

Angus

Angus is small enough to be easily explored from any of its towns, of which I shall take the inland ones first. And here I should say that in going into Angus we are entering a part of Scotland which, so far as its people are concerned, is more Scottish, in the widely accepted significance of the word, than any part of Scotland that we in these pages have yet visited. It is neither Lowland nor Highland; more than the Tay separates it from Fife. It is the Scotland of Barrie, though not of *Mary Rose*, and of Violet Jacob in her prose and verse.

Odd how trifles stick in the memory! I had forgotten that Forfar was one of the favourite residences of Malcolm Canmore and Queen Margaret; but I associate my first arrival at the town, many years ago, with a railway porter's voice drearily proclaiming "Farfar," and a boy's shrill calling of "Farfar Rock," a celebrated sweetmeat flavoured with cloves, whence the inventor, the late Mr Peter Reid, derived a fortune, which he turned to philanthropic purposes, presenting his native town with a fine park and hall. Malcolm's palace is supposed to have stood on Castle Hill. The Reid Park extends along the lower slopes of Balmachanner Hill, on the crown of which stands Forfar's War Memorial, a square tower.

Forfar has plenty of serious history, but let us, for a change, glance at some of the brighter items. In the seventeenth century two sons of the Provost who had emigrated to Sweden and prospered there sent home a fine bell for Forfar's Parish Church. When the bell arrived at Dundee, the nearest port, the Dundee authorities, declaring it to be far too good a bell for wee Forfar, refused to hand it over, and an unseemly wrangle took place on the quay, the tongue being torn from the bell and flung into the river. Eventually Dundee offered to give up the bell if Forfar purchased the land over which it would have to be carried, between the river and the boundary-line of the burgh. It was a terribly stiff price, but Forfar was bent on having its bell, and the sum being paid, the prize was carried home, where it was received with great acclamation. The enthusiasm appears, however, to have soon evaporated, for the bell remained tongueless for a hundred years.

Then there is the tale of the cow and the stirrup cup. A brewer's wife set a vessel of fresh brew to cool at her door, and a neighbour's cow came along and drank it. The brewer's wife took the neighbour to court, but lost her case, the judge pointing out that "by immemorial custom, nothing was ever charged for a standing drink or stirrup cup," and that the cow had taken the drink standing at the door. The cow's condition is not recorded.

At a Forfar inn two gentlemen and a farmer started dicing. The farmer lost everything, even his clothes. In desperation he wagered his splendid teeth. The gentlemen, now deep in their cups, bet a fortune that he would not lay them on the table. Whereupon the farmer produced the 'set,' and presently departed, a rich man.

Kirriemuir, five miles away, Barrie's "Thrums," where you will see the house of his birth, with the "Window," and where you will feel very much in Scotland, stands high, commanding a view of Strathmore, and, northward, a great expanse of glens, mountains, and little lochs. From Kirriemuir a road runs five miles south to Glamis (pronounced 'Glahms').

Of the castle, the name of which became so familiar with the marriage of its daughter to a prince, Defoe wrote:

> It is one of the finest built palaces in Scotland. When you see it at a distance . . . it looks not like a town, but a city.

He did not greatly exaggerate. It is a magnificent edifice in a magnificent situation.

> The central part is a great square tower, whose top is gained by a flight of 143 steps, and from which project three wings ; and the whole exterior is profusely adorned with sculptures, battlements, corbellings, pinnacles, pepper-box turrets, and the like.

It was Patrick, first Earl of Strathmore, who came with his family to Glamis in 1670, and proceeded to change the tumbledown old fortalice he had inherited into the lordly place we see to-day. In his *Book of Record* he wrote:

> It is hardly possible by any description I can now make to give any impression to my posterity of what this place was like when I first began my reformations.

Sixteen years later, he says, "I have made it a strong and comely structure," adding:

> There is in the Gardin a fine Dial erected, and howsoon the walks and plants are layed out, there will be statues put into it, and there is a designe for a fountain in the Boulin-green.

The Lyon sundial is still there, presenting, they say, some eighty faces to the sun.

Glamis, of course, has its legends. For example, there is a secret room in which the fourth Earl of Crauford and his boon companions, because of a hasty vow, are doomed to play dice till the Day of Judgment. Sir Walter Scott as a young man passed a night in the castle, and afterward wrote:

> It contains a secret chamber, the entrance of which must only be known to three persons at once, viz., the Earl of Strathmore, his heir apparent, and any third person whom they may take into their confidence. . . . I was conducted to my apartment in a distant corner of the building ; and I must own that as I heard door after door shut, after my conductor had retired, I began to consider myself too far from the living, and somewhat near to the dead.

It is recorded of Brechin, on the South Esk, that it was 'a great city' in 990, and no doubt Kenneth II so considered it when he dedicated it "to the Lord" in that year. Unlike many towns that boast extreme antiquity, Brechin has something tangible to prove it. Its Round Tower was possibly there when Kenneth made his vows, or was built in commemoration. We have only three of these round towers in Scotland—at Abernethy, near Perth, on Egilsay, in the Orkney Islands, and here at Brechin. The idea of the round towers came from Ireland, where there are scores. They were not towers of defence; they had chapels attached, for they were raised by the Culdees, meaning "Servants of God." The Brechin tower is somewhat younger than that of Abernethy. It is a graceful thing, rising from a square foundation, tapering to a height of over 100 feet; but the conical top is a late addition. The entrance doorway with its sculpturing is nearly 7 feet above the ground; inside the tower is divided into seven stories, the topmost lighted by four windows.

Six miles north of Brechin, Edzell offers excellent golf, superior hotels, bracing airs, though mild in winter, and many natural attractions. Edzell Castle, once the home of the Lindsays, a family so old that its name has been spelt in about eighty different ways, still presents a bold though broken front to time and tempest. In the old carnivorous days its menus included oxen roasted whole.

The Angus Coast

Of Carnoustie, enough to say that it is modern, sunny, sandy, crowded in summer, and that its golf course is good enough to have been chosen for the Open Championship of 1931.

It was of Arbroath, I think, that the old lady on her first arrival remarked: "It puts me in mind of a place I've never seen before." I leave you to evolve her meaning. It is a place, busy yet leisurely, of some 20,000 inhabitants, standing between the sea, whose murmur or roar you hear in the midst of the town, and a country-side rich and beautiful.

The Abbey, in the High Street, founded at the close of the twelfth century, was dedicated to St Mary and St Thomas à Becket, so foully murdered in Canterbury Cathedral, which the church, when completed, resembled. Only fragments remain, but they are large and splendid fragments, sufficient to move the imagination to picture the old Abbey in its glory. That glory began to depart after the Reformation; by the seventeenth century the place had become a public quarry; so the wonder is that so much is left, a landmark still to mariners, as it was to them 600 years ago. To the Scot the Abbey has a peculiar significance, for there, in 1320, was signed Scotland's Declaration of Independence addressed to the Pope.

> It is not glory, it is not riches, neither is it honour ; but it is liberty alone that we fight and contend for, which no honest man will lose except with his life. . . .

Arbroath (contraction of Aberbrothock) seems to have

been the Fairport in *The Antiquary* of Sir Walter Scott, while quaint little Auchmithie, three miles north, was his Musselcrag. It was an abbot of Aberbrothock who, according to Southey's poem, caused a bell to be hung on the Inchcape Rock, better known now as the Bell Rock, 15 miles out from the coast. A death-trap to mariners in the Middle Ages, so it remained till the beginning of the nineteenth century. In a terrible winter gale, in 1799, over threescore vessels came to grief thereon. The story of the construction of Robert Stevenson's lighthouse, which remains in all its stateliness to-day, is real romance. The difficulties were incredible. Until the foundations were completed, it was a case of dodging the sea all the time—spells of only an hour's work were common, of four hours, rare. The pit prepared for the foundations was flooded by every tide. The whole job took four years. The tower is 115 feet high, including the lantern; the thickness of the walls ranges from 7 feet to 1 foot.

From Arbroath, in whose neighbourhood are interesting old castles and mansions, we go up by Lunan Bay, with its lovely singing sands, to Montrose, one of the sunniest and driest places in the kingdom. Its sunshine and rainfall records for 1930 are better than, for example, those of Southport, Scarborough, and Llandudno. Though the name means merely 'Flat Promontory' it might well mean something much more charming, as you will probably opine as you approach the town, with its most elegant steeple, set on a peninsula lapped by the waters of the North Sea, the river South Esk, and the tidal basin. Arrived, you will probably own that the town lives up to its delightful situation. Though the older buildings suggest conservatism by quaintly presenting their gables to the street, Montrose, with its broad avenues, parks, and gardens, is essentially fresh and modern. Even in 1773 Dr Johnson allowed that it was "airy, well built, and clean." It is old enough to have been sacked by the Norsemen, and much of its early history is that of other towns in Scotland—warfare of one sort or another. From its port, in 1330, Sir James Douglas set out on his ill-fated journey to the Holy Land, with the Bruce's heart in its silver casket; and, nearly four centuries later, the 'Old Pretender,' after his brief, disastrous campaign, took ship for the Continent. When the Duke of Cumberland, after crushing the Rebellion, came to Montrose, he found the boys making bonfires in honour of the fugitive Prince's birthday, while the ladies paraded the streets in white gowns, wearing white roses. The Duke was not amused; he degraded his officer who had gallantly and, one presumes, metaphorically winked at the ladies and their doings, and threatened to have the boys whipped at the Mercat Cross. A more genial visitor was Robert Burns, who had relatives there. Some of his ancestors lie in Glenbervie Churchyard, over in Kincardineshire. His visit is commemorated by a monument. You will like Montrose, with its sea, sands, and sunshine, and its two 18-hole courses.

Kincardineshire

In the whole stretch of Scotland's eastern coast the sight of sights is surely Dunnottar Castle, near Stonehaven, 22 miles north of Montrose, 15 south of Aberdeen. In ruins—ruins that suggest a small city rather than a mere fortress—it crowns a prodigious mass of conglomerate rising 160 feet above the beach, separated from the mainland by a chasm which makes it almost insular. He was a very early man who first fancied the site for a place of defence; we know that it was used as such more than twelve centuries ago. Viewed, as it should be viewed, at a distance, from the shore, when its shattered walls and broken towers stand clear against the sky, it forms a picture not likely to be forgotten.

The flat summit of the rock, 4½ acres, carries a battle-mented wall enclosing buildings of various ages, the oldest, excepting the chapel, being a square tower of the fourteenth century, while some belong to the late six-teenth century. At one period the chapel was, queerly enough, the church of the parish, and had a graveyard attached. There is also a forge, where they may have made arms and bullets, and a peaceful bowling-green. Sir William Keith, Great Marischal of Scotland, built the earliest part of the castle, and Keiths enlarged and held it till 1652, when it was surrendered to Cromwell's troops, after a siege of eight months. Colonel Morgan had fancied he was besieging a strong force, but only thirty-five men marched out, with all the honours of war.

It was during the siege that the Regalia of Scotland, which, earlier, had been sent to Dunnottar for security, and which Cromwell was most anxious to obtain, were spirited away to a safer place. There is a pretty tale of the minister's wife with her servant, who were permitted to visit the castle, concealing and carrying the crown, sceptre, and sword through the besiegers' lines. She and the minister were awarded £2000, but they died too soon.

Within recent years much was done for the castle's pre-servation and repairment by the late Lady Cowdray, who also provided a carriage-way to it, and a new gatehouse and gateway. Inside you will find, among her other good deeds, that the ancient tower has been saved from collapse, while the dining-hall has been restored.

Stonehaven, another fresh and sunny holiday place, looks out upon a bay, a mile and a half north of Dunnottar. It has been Kincardine's county town since 1600. Stone-haven has flourished without sacrificing all its ancient landmarks. It has its Old Town as well as its New, and would probably have had more of the Old to-day but for the Marquis of Montrose's visit in 1645. The oldest building is the Tolbooth, on the north pier, at the

harbour. Its lower part was used as a prison till 1767.
Likely enough, it was never without prisoners. The
little county had its own public hangman, whose duties
were not confined to capital punishment. Besides his
rope, he had his branding-irons and other implements.
No doubt, too, his duties included the ducking—three
times over the head—in the harbour of scolding women,
which may have given him some popularity with a
section of the male population. He had a free house
and croft and peck of meal per week, with an extra
gratuity for executions. Some of the ways of making
an honest living were almost as queer then as now.

An English army surgeon coming to Stonehaven in
1746 could find lodging only in the house of a doctor, of
the name of Lawson, who kept a public-house. The
surgeon did not at all object to the 'pub,' but he com-
plained bitterly that all his victuals were flavoured with
the dust of wormwood, sage, and other medicinal herbs.
Stonehaven can entertain us better to-day.

Burns visited Stonehaven in 1787, the year after the
publication of his poems. His father was a Kincardineshire man, who left the farm of Clochnahill, four miles
from the town, to seek a better living first in Midlothian,
then in Ayrshire.

Kincardineshire is so small that much of it can be seen
in an afternoon. An entertaining round may be made
as follows: south by Fordoun—birthplace of one of our
early chroniclers, whose "carefully manipulated fictions"
are a nice seasoning to the broth made from the dry bones
of history—and by Laurencekirk to Marykirk; then
north, on a secondary road, to ancient Fettercairn—joy
of the antiquarian, with its sculptured stones and weems,
or earthhouses; then over the hill of Cairn o' Mount,
rising to 1488 feet, with its gradients of 1 in 5—delight of
the sporting motorist; on to Banchory (on the Aberdeenshire bank of the Dee), and back to Stonehaven direct.

CHAPTER XII

ABERDEEN AND THE NORTH-EAST

OFTEN in Glasgow—sometimes in Edinburgh, the Old Town apart—you may wonder if this is Scotland; in Aberdeen you will never doubt it. Arriving from Glasgow, at any rate, you find yourself in an entirely different atmosphere, in both meanings of the word. Without being a day less modern in material things than the southern city, Aberdeen yet retains some of the essence of the past, which before long gives the visitor a sense of the old-fashioned. Yet in that there is a friendliness, as there is also in the kindly native weakness for diminutives, like 'mannie,' 'doggie,' 'boatie,' and so forth.

It is quite true that the Aberdeen people are 'careful.' That, indeed, is one of the reasons why they can afford to be so genuinely hospitable. It is an intelligent carefulness—the carefulness that helped to make Scotland a worth-while business partner for England; the carefulness, too, that other parts of Scotland have got to relearn, now that the bill for lavish display, proud extravagance, sheer waste, is due. A recent sojourner summed up Aberdeen in the word 'capable,' adding that on his return to earth, a thousand years hence, he would expect to find the city still there, abiding as its granite, flourishing in its sanity, while all the other cities lay in dreary, bankrupt ruin. Incidentally, 95 per cent. of the population is of Scottish birth.

Every considerable city has its river, but Aberdeen has two rivers, neatly named Dee and Don, lying spread between them and looking out upon a broad bay. It is of the Dee that one hears more often, just as one more often hears about the prettier sister. Yet the Dee is the useful river, too, holding in its mouth the harbour and docks, where the trawlers continually come and go, and greater vessels ply their trade to Northern Europe. Long, long ago Aberdeen was doing business with the Baltic in ships that were mere pieces of impudence to the North Sea. In Sweden, Russia, and Poland to-day are people whose far distant ancestors were of Aberdeen. In Poland, about the sixteenth century, were 30,000 Scottish families.

Had the city been built closer to the sea much of its charm would now be wanting. As it is, a spacious Esplanade stretches for very nearly two miles from Don to Dee, on one side of which is the sandy beach with its bathing-machines and tents, on the other the Links, with their facilities for golf, putting, cricket, bowls, and tennis. Here, too, is the Corporation Bathing Station, with private baths, salt or fresh, and in the vicinity are the Dance Hall and Restaurant, the Beach Pavilion for vaudeville entertainment, and the Amusement Park. If you have been thinking of Aberdeen as a city of long faces, a walk on the Esplanade will undeceive you. Perhaps I ought to mention that Aberdeen's weather, while mostly sunny, is generally pretty bracing. The summer visitor should come prepared for freshness rather than great heat.

Aberdeen, with a population only a few thousands under Dundee's, comprises two towns, the Old and the New. While the Old certainly looks much the older, it is not certain that the New is the newer, though it did not begin to assume its remarkably new appearance till early in the nineteenth century. Both have very distant origins. Together, to-day, taken all in all, they make a dignified and beautiful city—beautiful in the approach from the south, which in itself is decidedly bleak and forbidding, beautiful in vistas of broad streets and buildings ancient and modern.

For a general survey you should have the Corporation's *Handbook* (free), and take a Corporation bus on its tour round the two towns.

Aberdeen stands on, and is built of, granite. Until you behold it you cannot realize what that means. It means streets that ever look clean (and are clean) and buildings that rarely grow dingy. The effect is chilling or cheerful, according to the weather, but always splendid. It is mainly a light grey granite—you will find a quarry, 300 feet deep, within the city's bounds—which in places, under the electric light, is all a-sparkle. The pink granite you occasionally see comes from Peterhead, farther north. Incidentally, the newcomer who walks much is advised to wear stout shoes.

Aberdeen's modern pride is Union Street, about a mile long, running west and east across the city. Midway in its course it crosses by a Telford bridge the little valley of the Denburn, in which runs the railway. From the bridge, looking north, you have a particularly fine prospect in Union Terrace and its gardens. The handsome modern County and Municipal Buildings, finely situated at the eastern end, have a tower 200 feet high, from the top of which you may take a view of the city and surroundings, at the cost of the climb. Among the municipal treasures are a suit of armour supposed to have been worn by a provost slain at the Battle of Harlaw in 1411, also paintings by well-known Aberdeen artists, including George Jamesone, known as 'the Scottish Van Dyck,' who died in 1644.

Near by, in Castlegate, is the seventeenth-century Mercat Cross, which has seen strange things in its day, including executions and the pageantries of temporal power. By way of contrast, the great building at the end of the street is the Salvation Army Citadel. The city's motto is *"Bon Accord,"* originally the watchword of Bruce's army which, for a time, cleared the place of the

English.   You will come across it frequently as the name
of a street, newspaper, hotel, and so on.

Aberdeen's University is younger than St Andrews,
but older than Edinburgh's.   King's College, in the Old
Town, was founded by Bishop Elphinstone in 1494.   The
square-buttressed tower with its fine lantern spire, surmounted by crown and cross, built in 1515 and rebuilt
in the following century, is, with the adjoining chapel, the
oldest remaining part.   In the chapel the canopied stalls
and choir-screen are the only perfect set spared to the
country.   But for the pluck of the principal and his
armed men the beautiful carvings would have come
under the 'purging' of the Reformers.   The chapel,
whose colour decorations are modern, contains also a
pulpit of the sixteenth and a bishop's throne of the early
seventeenth century, besides a black marble monument,
uninscribed, to the saintly and statesmanlike founder,
and a blue stone slab in memory of Hector Boece, the
first principal, and one of our early historians or, as
some will have it, 'story'-tellers.   The later parts of the
College, which is devoted to Divinity and Arts, though
not in keeping with the early, are architecturally interesting.   The library, with its 150,000 volumes and
priceless treasures, such as the Pope's Deed of Foundation and the Salisbury Missal, is housed in a modern
building opposite the chapel.

There is much that is antique and lovely in Old Aberdeen, including the Town House.   Half a mile north of
King's College, St Machar's Cathedral, the only granite
cathedral in the world, raises its twin towers and short
conical steeples, guarding the entrance under the high
seven-lighted window.   Nearly a thousand years before
they were raised by Bishop Gavin Dunbar in 1530 the
site had been consecrated by Machar, a missionary from
Iona.   Columba had instructed him to go north through
the land of the Picts till he came to a place where a river

made a curve like that of a bishop's crozier; and, sure enough, the Don does so here, as you may see by looking toward it from the north-east side of the cathedral. So saintly was Machar that, if need be, his left hand gave out illumination in the darkness. Great damage was done in 1683 by the collapse of the central steeple and belfry. The cathedral is, however, no mere ruin. Services are held in it every Sunday, and it is open on weekdays. Its most striking feature internally is Bishop Dunbar's emblazoned panelled oak ceiling.

The University's other college, the Marischal, for Science, Medicine, and Law, is in New Aberdeen, about a mile due south of King's College, and easily reached from Union Street. The present Marischal (pronounced Marshall) is a modern building, but the college was founded on the site of a Greyfriars' monastery just a century after King's, and was a separate university till 1860. Its founder was George Keith, Earl Marischal of Scotland—you may remember the Keiths of Dunnottar Castle. His somewhat truculent motto, adopted when his wife expressed her fears of public opinion upon his appropriation of Church lands at the Reformation, was, "They have said. What say they? Let them say." You may read it in the vernacular and old-world lettering inside the doorway leading to the Mitchell Hall and Tower.

The Marischal College is built in the Gothic Perpendicular style of a pale grey granite, which in the sunshine assumes a silvery whiteness. Thus far its situation has been unworthy of its magnificence and grace, and the city is at present greatly improving matters by the demolition of some old and interesting, if rather squalid, buildings. The college was built largely on public subscriptions, ranging from the princely gifts of Dr Charles Mitchell, his son, Mr Charles W. Mitchell, and Lord Strathcona, to the modest silver coin of some poor Scot.

The Mitchell Tower rises to a height of 260 feet. As I write, this morning, Aberdeen is in a ferment of delight and indignation because an unknown student in the blackness of the winter night scaled the tall, slender spire and affixed a skeleton effigy to the very tip. Even pranks are well done in Aberdeen. A small charge is made for admission to the tower and the hall, which seats 1300 people and has been described as "a noble room, like some old guildhall on the Continent." Within the quadrangle, previous to the last extension, stood the Greyfriars' Church. Its removal being necessary, a new church was built outside, and with such architectural skill and sympathy that it stands in complete harmony with the College buildings.

New Aberdeen's antiquities are to be found mainly in the East and West Churches, which, under one roof, occupy the site of the very ancient Church of St Nicholas, near the Union Street Bridge. Considering its size, Aberdeen is, as a friend expressed it, remarkably free from statues. Of the half-score named in the Corporation *Guide* I may mention Queen Victoria, at the corner of St Nicholas Street, King Edward VII and Robert Burns, in Union Terrace, and Wallace, in front of His Majesty's Theatre, a truly glorious effigy in bronze, by W. G. Stevenson, R.S.A.

There are a hundred things which I must perforce omit, but I recommend you to get up early one morning and go to the Fish Market, near the harbour. There are mornings when the trawlers land over a thousand tons, and among the catches you are almost certain to see unfamiliar faces—a giant skate, kingfish, catfish, perhaps a great sturgeon, or maybe a shark. But don't get in the way of the buyers. It was in Aberdeen, long ago, that a salesman shouted angrily at a too inquisitive stranger, "Keep back, man, keep back, and let the fish see the folk!" In the same market, too, a famous ventriloquist said to a fish-wife carrying an enormous cod: "Excuse me, madam, but is that fish fresh?" "Fresh!" she cried indignantly; "it's new fae the sea!" Whereupon, to the poor woman's consternation, the cod exclaimed: "Liar! I've been here a week!"

When you are in Old Aberdeen you will probably go along to see the Brig o' Balgownie over the Don. Failing that, you are sure to see it on a postcard, or chair-cushion, or maybe a tea-cosy, for surely no bridge was ever so esteemed. With its single Gothic arch, high above a deep, dark pool, in truly picturesque surroundings, it is the oldest bridge in the North, having been built early in the fourteenth century by Bishop Cheyne, who was friendly to the English, though he eventually took pardon from Bruce, and so may have built the bridge as a sort of penance. It has associations with Byron, who tells us how impressed he was by an antique prophecy regarding it:

> Brig o' Balgownie, black's your wa';
> Wi' a wife's ae son and a mare's ae foal
> Doon ye shall fa'.

They say he was once observed, when riding toward the bridge, to dismount and lead his pony across.

Every sojourner in Aberdeen goes over to Girdleness and the rocky Bay of Nigg ('Nook'), south of the Dee. There is a great lighthouse at Girdleness—the Girdle is a sunken rock—and if you have never been inside a lighthouse you can gain admission here. Nigg has a parish kirk of pre-Reformation origin and a Fishery Research Station.

Deeside

I have met people who declared the Dee to be the finest river in Scotland—Britain—Europe—the world! So let me leave it at that. But I should like to say that the meek little word 'Deeside' has always seemed to me deceptive, suggesting, as it does, nothing more impressive

x

than a lover and his lass wandering hand in hand on the woody bank of a purling stream, or an elderly couple taking their ease in their little garden, "the quiet waters by." Certainly to the stranger in Aberdeen, where he hears it uttered every other hour, the word cannot convey the slightest hint that by traversing Deeside he will ascend into a country growing wilder and wilder till at length, on the shoulder of Braeriach, one of the heights of the Cairngorms, over 4000 feet up, he comes upon the Dee beginning its lusty career of nearly a hundred miles through some of the bleakest and boldest, and also some of the bonniest, scenes in Scotland.

The railway to Ballater runs most of its 40 odd miles near to the river. If motoring, you should begin with the road on the south bank of the Dee, crossing by the Old Bridge, completed in its original form in 1527. Since then it has known many reconstructions and repairs, and its width has been doubled; even so the shades of Bishops Elphinstone and Dunbar, who projected and saw to its building, may still point to this or that feature, muttering, "Mine!"

High on the slope at Blairs the Roman Catholic College of St Mary's holds among its treasures a portrait of Mary Queen of Scots. Just before her execution at Fotheringay she gave to one of her attendants, Elizabeth Curle, a miniature, from which the portrait was painted. Near the village of Culter, where they make paper, Culter House, across the water, is reminiscent of a gallant who had his shoes shod with silver before attending Mary's wedding to Darnley. Of Drum Castle (glimpsed from the railway) the older part, the tower, was given by the Bruce to his armour-bearer, Sir William Irvine. Another ancient stronghold, in the lovely wooded part toward the Bridge of Feugh, is Crathes, which you may know by the carved figure in three-cornered hat and gold-laced coat on top of the building. The Aberdeenshire family of the

ABERDEEN: BRIG O' BALGOWNIE

Photo Will F. Taylor

BRAEMAR AND THE CAIRNGORMS
Photo Alexander B. Beattie

Burnetts has been there for six centuries. Near the bridge, which is old, the Feugh, always a busy river, frantic in spate, falls gladly into the Dee.

Presently, crossing the river, we come into Banchory, where the Dee, whose waters, because their bed is nearly always hard, are singularly limpid, runs like silver over pale stones. Banchory, perhaps the prettiest spot on Deeside, is modern, a favourite resort for health and holiday, bracing, yet sheltered from the cold winds, and a centre for motorists, trampers, and mountaineers. In the neighbourhood are relics of Scotland's early inhabitants, in the form of cairns, sculptured stones, forts, and notably crannogs, or lake-dwellings, discovered in the draining of a small loch. From Banchory the railway—there is a road too—takes a turn round by Lumphanan, where Macbeth met his end. Circumstantially the old chronicler Wyntoun tells how

> O'er the Mounth they chased him
> Intil the woods of Lumphanan;
> This Macbeth slew they there
> Intil the woods of Lumphanan.

Our road runs over the antique-looking Potarch Bridge and through the village of Kincardine O'Neil—there seems to be no explanation of the Irish touch—where the valley is fertile, albeit the mountains are becoming more massive and grim—to Aboyne, which also has a Hibernian tang, though, freely translated, it means "the place where the white cow took a drink." Set amid pine-clad uplands, the village has the distinctive charm of being built around a spacious green, where every autumn its games are held, drawing strong men from all parts of the country. Less than a mile away, Aboyne's low-lying, moated, many-turreted castle, mostly modern, is interesting as the home for centuries of the Huntlys, one of whom, the Marquis, was beheaded at Edinburgh in 1649 for loyalty to Charles I. A few miles north of Aboyne are the ruined castles of Corse and Coull. Coull, which must have been a stately place, belonged to the Durwards, and when a Durward died the bell of the neighbouring kirk rang of its own accord. A friend from the South, to whom I mentioned this mysterious occurrence, remarked rather drily that it was "the best lie he had heard in Scotland," and he had heard some good ones.

Now the mountains are beginning to close in on the river, and at Ballater, on its small strath, we are surrounded by them—to mention only three, Craigendarroch, cone-shaped, with wooded slopes; magnificent "dark Lochnagar," which may still be whitely crowned; and prodigious Morven ('Big Nose'). Ballater, terminus of the railway, came first into notice through mineral wells in its neighbourhood, but has flourished on its own attractions. It is a modern little town, with some fine buildings, shops, and private houses, also three hotels. Busy all summer, it becomes 'fashionable' when Royalty is at Balmoral.

Balmoral Castle, nine miles west, midway between Ballater and Braemar, was built for Queen Victoria and the Prince Consort, who were already familiar with the district, in 1855. Of granite, in the Scottish baronial style, it consists of "two blocks, connected by wings, with a massive tower to the east," on which there is a clock. The grounds are beautiful, and in summer are open to the public on two days a week; not, however, when Royalty is in residence.

By the roadside, immediately after the fifty-first milestone, you will notice the Cairn of Remembrance, a memorial of the Clan Farquharson. It has a curious, pathetic significance. Here was the gathering-place of the clansmen bound for battle, and the disbanding place afterward. Each of those who assembled gave a stone to the cairn; each of those who returned took a stone from it. There was usually a sorry pile left. Five miles onward, Craig Clunie rises almost sheer from the glen. In a cleft, 600 feet above the road, known as the Charter Chest, were hidden the Invercauld title-deeds and other documents after the Jacobite Rebellion of 1715. Invercauld himself may have hidden there while the redcoats made merry in his house, which stands on a green terrace, half circled by the Dee, in the expansion of the glen. Invercauld House had a beginning in the fifteenth century, but has known much rebuilding and enlargement. Here the Jacobites held council in 1715, when the Earl of Mar sent out the summons to the clans. It is a noteworthy building in a countryside noted for stately mansions and castles.

Nearing Braemar we pass Braemar Castle, very spectacular and in keeping with its surroundings, yet unromantic, in that while still new it was leased in 1748 to the Government, who used it as a barrack. A much older Braemar Castle has almost disappeared.

Braemar village, properly Castletown of Braemar— Braemar being the name of the district—and originally called St Andrews, 1100 feet above the sea, lies amid scenery that really merits the word sublime, in an amphitheatre of the Grampians, dominated by the Cairngorms group, which culminates in Ben Macdhui. The Cairngorms, joy of mountaineers, and, once in a while, sorrow of those who bade them "good climbing," are in their fierce, glorious, or sullen savagery indescribable. They can be terrible in their desolation, woeful where they are most wonderful. There is a place, a pass near the beginning of the Dee, that makes Glen Coe, as somebody once put it, seem merry and bright. But Braemar, as every one calls the village, rests happy and healthy in wooded shelter on both sides of the Clunie Water, with its two palatial hotels, the Fife Arms and Invercauld Arms, the latter on the mound on which, in 1715, Mar raised the Jacobite standard. It holds its great annual

Highland Gathering in September, when the pressmen are busy with pencil and camera, paying more attention, it may be, to the royal and other distinguished spectators than to the champions of the caber, the stone, the pipes, and the dance. It is the social event of the year in the North, and the day of the tartans. If you want to see how the kilt should be carried—and how it should not—come to the Gathering.

In the summer of 1881 a young man came to Braemar, and wrote a book in a house called "The Cottage," at the south end of Castletown Terrace. His name was Robert Louis Stevenson, and the book is *Treasure Island*.

The Buchan Coast

The coast stretching northward of Aberdeen is mostly cruel, and there are rocks that might inspire bad dreams, especially when the North Sea lies grey and sullen, yet it offers infinite beauty in a blue calm and immense splendour in a white storm. On its 60 odd miles are but two towns, with a number of fishing havens. Let us take a few glimpses.

Golf courses, not cathedrals, make places famous nowadays, and the name Cruden Bay must be familiar to thousands to whom almost any other name on this northeastern promontory would be strange. Two miles of fine, firm sands provide an interlude between dramas of terrible cliffs, basalt in the south, red granite in the north, and within them stretch the links, overlooked by the railway company's hotel. Time was when the golfer off his game might have found distraction in going to look up at Slains Castle, on its almost insular headland, high above Port Errol, the neighbouring village. It was not a ruin; it was, in fact, barely a century old—but what a situation! From the drawing-room and library windows one saw nothing but sky and ocean. Anything dropped thence went into the sea. I am told that a carriage-way ran round the building till a fall of rock removed it.   And now all is gone.

Some miles farther up the always interesting coast we come to the Bullers of Buchan.   Dr Johnson visited the place in 1773, and while he writes of a single 'Buller,' his description has never been bettered for clarity.   So I venture to quote part of it.

> It is a rock perpendicularly tabulated, united on one side with a high shore and on the other rising steep to a great height above the main sea.   The top is open, from which may be seen a dark gulf of water, which flows into the cavity through a breach made in the lower part of the enclosing rock.   It has the appearance of a vast well bordered with a wall.   The edge of the Buller is not wide, and, to those that walk round, appears very narrow. . . . We, however, went round, and were glad when the circuit was completed.

There is a tale of a man who, in his cups, laid a bet that, mounted on his horse, he would take the round at a gallop.   He won his bet, but, on surveying with sober eyes the scene of his triumph, died of the reaction.   Dr Johnson was fortunate in having calm weather, which allowed him to examine the interior in a boat.   On the other hand, he did not witness the Bullers playing up to their name, which means either 'boilers' or 'roarers,' otherwise we should have had a vivid account from him of that cauldron in its fearsome turmoil.

Of Peterhead, most important of the coast towns, with a population of about 14,000, I hesitate to write, since I have seen it only under abnormal conditions—in the first winter of the Great War.   I came to it in the grey of a fiercely bitter morning, to look upon a raging sea intermittently blanketed by snow squalls.   The lifeboat had just returned with some half-drowned men, and there was news—not printed till years after—of a trawler having rammed and sunk a submarine—the first feat of the kind.

Nearly all the fishermen were away on mine-sweeping or
patrol business, and all work going on at the spacious
harbour was war-work.   Peterhead looked bleak enough
then; easy to believe that one was standing on Scotland's
most easterly point; and it was not the hour to be asking
questions as to how it looked in holiday times.   The other
day Canon Wilkinson, with a personal knowledge of many
years, wrote of it thus:

> On the edge of a treeless land, a brave old town that has
> thrown itself adventurously out into the arms of the North
> Sea, its feet tethered to the mainland, but brain and body
> grappling eagerly with the thing it loves best, and to which
> in soul and spirit it belongs.

'Brave' is the word!   Bravery was singing through
the snow squalls of that winter morning.
Places, like people, receive rather than acquire reputations.   Because Peterhead is a notable fishing-port and
has in its vicinity a great convict prison, no end of
people in Scotland figure it as a town strewn with fish-
bones and brooding in hopeless melancholy, whereas it
is sweet and clean, even with a full harbour, and as
cheerful in its calm way as any.   Built mainly of its
own pink granite, it has a character of its own.   We do
not know what the Old Chevalier thought of it when he
landed at its harbour on Christmas Eve 1714, and at its
cross was proclaimed king, but we need not doubt that
the cockles of his heart were abundantly warmed for the
time being.   It is interesting, now and then, to consider
the people as well as their environment, and of this community on the most easterly part of Scotland Canon
Wilkinson's words are illuminating:

> A douce, kindly, neighbourly folk, not easy to move,
> but resolute in their definite purposes, very patient up to
> a point, but after that very downright and unyielding;
> proud of their town and its history, so educationally keen

that their schools are the finest of the county, . . . and in
religious matters manifesting a tolerance and comradeship
that have their roots not only in the hearts of the people,
but in the history of the place.

You will not, I hope, take the foregoing to mean that,
as a Scottish community, Peterhead is unique.

Away back in 1576 Alexander Fraser of Philorth, "in
the name of the Father, Son, and Holy Ghost," built a
little harbour on the north coast, and the town that grew
up around it, at first called Faithlie, was soon, and very
properly, renamed Fraserburgh.   A man of ideas was
this ancestor of the Saltouns, and though the scheme
was never completed, he obtained a charter to found
a university, and raised a building for it.   Yet Fraserburgh was for a period a university town, for when the
plague came to Aberdeen in 1647 King's College came
to Fraser's building.   To-day the harbour is one of the
most commodious in the North, while the town, with its
10,000 people, is a well-built, pleasant place.   Fraser
Castle, a square, four-storied tower built in 1570, stands
not far away on Kinnaird Head.   On this tower, in 1787,
was erected one of Scotland's earliest lighthouses, wherefore Alexander's memory is surely a fragrant one.   Near by
on a sea-crag is the massive erection known as the " Wine
Tower," which is all that is known about it.

Should you be motoring back to Aberdeen I suggest
that you first carry on along the coast to Banff, and then
take one of the three roads south, preferably the one that
runs through Huntly and Alford, so that you may come
into Aberdeen by the Don Valley.   Huntly, in the land
of the Gordons, is a good example of a northern country
town, with its fine, spacious square, and Huntly Castle,
a well-preserved ruin, is worth seeing for its dungeons
and doorway alone.   The town is the centre of a most
interesting district for the explorer, and the angler too.

Banff strikes many strangers as a funny name, but it is

easier to pronounce now than 800 years ago, when it was spelled 'Banb.' My etymologist allows that it may either commemorate an Irish princess or mean 'sucking-pig.' You will think of the princess when you see Banff's sands and links and its fair prospect of the Moray Firth. It has a long story: its castle, now a fragment, was the last northern fortress to remain in English hands after the Battle of Bannockburn; its surroundings offer much to the explorer. Its old neighbour, Macduff, across the mouth of the Deveron, has a fine harbour in a situation singularly pictorial.

Aberdeenshire has more roads than all the Scotland to the west and north of it. Inland it is studded with little towns, villages, and castles, each with its tales and anti-quities, which I am compelled to leave for your own discovery.

Moray

In olden times Moravia, or Moray ('Beside the Sea'), whence comes the surname Murray, included what is now Nairnshire, and there was a saying to the effect that the region enjoyed forty days more of summer than the rest of Scotland. Because of its fertility, perhaps, its people were too busy with their farming to be very keen on fighting. For centuries their country was regarded as fair game by the Highlanders, who harried it continually. As late as the middle of the seventeenth century we find the Chief of the Camerons explaining to the Laird of Grant that in 'lifting' the cattle of the Laird's tenant at Moynes he had been under the impression that the tenant was a Moray man, and that, as everybody knew, Moray was "the land where all men took their prey."

Elgin, on the river Lossie, is one of our most cheerfully pleasant county towns, dignified by the presence of a cathedral still splendid in decay. Mainly modern to-day, it was still old-world at the visit of Dr Johnson, who in

THE HARBOUR, MACDUFF, BANFFSHIRE

Photo Alexander B. Beattie

330

GLEN SHIEL AND LOCH CLUANIE, ROSS-SHIRE

Photo Alexander B. Beattie

[*P.* 345]

his practical way found fault with the *piazzas* of the houses in the High Street, because they kept the light from the ground-floors. The *piazzas* are gone; only three of the seventeenth-century houses remain, much altered.

On the green Lady Hill, with its monument, a Tuscan tower, commemorating the benefactions to agriculture of the last Duke of Gordon, was once a castle, in which, some say, King Duncan breathed his last, after being wounded by Macbeth in a hut in the vicinity. Duncan may not have been distinguished in his life, but few monarchs can have died in so many different places. The castle, a favourite residence of the earlier Scottish kings, was visited more than once by that keenest of English tourists and collector of souvenirs, Edward I. What a guide-book he might have written! Elgin has two crosses, the Muckle Cross, a replica, in the Market Square, near the Grecian temple, which is the Parish Church, built in 1828, and, at the east end of the street, the Little Cross, perhaps at one time a boundary mark. Close by is the Elgin Literary and Scientific Association, with its store of Moray and Jacobite relics, including the only existing copy of the Proclamation offering £30,000 for the Prince's capture, also an amazing collection of fossils from the Lossiemouth quarries; while aloof from the thoroughfare is the old Greyfriars' Abbey Church, restored by the Marquis of Bute.

Elgin's chief pride is the cathedral, founded in 1224. Twenty years later, and again in 1270, it suffered badly from fire, but such misfortunes meant only bigger and better building, including the magnificent entrance and the two noble western towers, till it became "the glory of the whole land." Once more, in 1390, it was given to the flames, this time deliberately by Alexander Stewart, Earl of Buchan, "the Wolf of Badenoch, and his wyld, wykked Helanmen." The Church had excommunicated him—either for helping himself to its lands or for wife-desertion—probably both—and this was part of his revenge. The King, however, caused him, for once, to eat humble pie by forcing him to take part in the costs of restoration. Nearly twenty-five years were spent in making repairs and redecorations, after which the grand edifice enjoyed a century of peace. In 1506 the great central tower, 200 feet high, either fell, or threatened to do so, and was not completely re-established till 1537. For a few years longer the cathedral stood firm in its perfection, and then—the Reformation. In 1568 Scotland's Privy Council, in desperation for money, had the cathedrals of Elgin and Aberdeen stripped of their lead roofings, which were shipped for Holland, to be sold there. Hardly had the vessel cleared the mouth of the Dee when she foundered, to the holy joy of thousands. But Elgin's cathedral was left unprotected from the weather, the leisurely but sure destroyer, and from man, who can be swift and savage. In 1637 the rafters of the choir collapsed, and three years later a band of Covenanters, led by the minister of Elgin, tore down and smashed up the picturesquely carven rood-screen and woodwork. Cromwell's soldiers, too, are credited, a few years later, with the destruction of the splendid western window. The walls stood bravely for another half-century, but on Easter Sunday 1711, as if weary of the cynical neglect, the great central tower crashed down upon nave and transepts. After that the place was a public quarry, till in 1807 Mr Joseph King of Newmill succeeded in getting an enclosing wall built and a keeper installed—the enthusiastic John Shanks, who during his twenty-five years of office removed 3000 barrow-loads of rubbish and unearthed the whole ground-plan of the building. Later, through the exertions of Mr Isaac Forsyth, the Crown authorities were wakened up and did their duty. It is interesting to learn that the walls and towers which have survived the outrages of Nature and man are mainly the work of the very early builders.

Enough remains—including the western towers and principal entrance, St Mary's Aisle, and the Chapter-house—to make it one of the most impressive ecclesiastical ruins in the country. You will find its tale most entertainingly told in a little book by Mr H. B. Mackintosh, M.B.E., *Pilgrimages in Moray*, published by the *Courant and Courier*, Elgin.

Elgin has its own golf course, while the famous Lossiemouth course is some five miles away. There is free fishing (sea and yellow trout) on the Lossie and on waters not distant.

Lossiemouth, Elgin's port, looks out on the broad Moray Firth toward the mountains of the far north, rejoicing in its sands, fantastic rocks and caves, its golf course, its ever-growing popularity, and its fine weather; also, one cannot doubt, in the fame that has befallen it as the home of the Right Hon. J. Ramsay MacDonald. There are mornings when the newspapers have more to say of Lossiemouth than of Edinburgh or Glasgow.

Midway between Elgin and Lossiemouth is the ruined Bishop's Palace of Spynie. A bishop was there as early as 1203, but the square tower belongs to the fifteenth century. It was built by the sturdy Bishop David Stewart, by way of retort to the Earl of Huntly, who had threatened to pull him out of his "pigeon-holes." 'Davie's Tower' measures 60 by 36 feet; its 9-feet thick walls are 60 feet high. The little loch near by was, until partially drained, a sea inlet, which came close to the palace walls.

With Elgin or Lossiemouth as a base, and Mr Mackintosh's little book for guide, the visitor who is out not merely for play can spend a full and varied fortnight. For the motorist the ways are many. He can explore along the coast, smiling at the very 'Scotch'-sounding names of the fishing-havens, such as Buckie, Portessie, Findochty, Portknockie; he can go down into Aberdeenshire, Nairnshire, Inverness-shire; and he can make the grand tour of the Spey Valley, with all its natural and human interests, by Grantown and the Great North Road to Inverness, and back through Nairn. There are people who say of the Spey what other people say of the Dee, and I am not saying that either river is finer than the other. But the Spey is a truly splendid river, the fastest-going in Scotland—a mad, sad, bad, glad river, traversing scenery that changes with the minutes. You will, I think, catch the spirit of it, if before making the excursion you read Miss Wendy Wood's *The Secret of the Spey*—not a 'guide book,' bless it, but a revelation of beautiful things and strange, which few of us could have discovered for ourselves.

I must not leave Moray without touching on Forres, on the Findhorn, which is nearly as old as Elgin, and whose name Shakespeare introduces into *Macbeth*. Its Castle Hill appears to have carried a building at one time; and my conductor—not a Moray man, I hasten to say—instructed me that the ruin on it was that of Macbeth's castle—another death for poor King Duncan; but I now learn, with gratitude, that the existing stones are only two centuries old, and comprise the beginnings of a private residence of a gentleman whose purse proved to be smaller than his ambitions. A truly remarkable relic in the neighbourhood is Sweno's Stone, our finest piece of Celtic sculpture. Of grey sandstone, it stands 23 feet above ground and 12 feet below, carved on both sides with designs of priests and warriors, with much ornament, reminiscent of the design in *The Book of Lindisfarne*, the famous manuscript of the seventh century. The Trafalgar Monument on Cluny Hill was one of the first memorials to Nelson erected in the kingdom. The hill also carries a modern hydro. Forres, with its roomy streets—it has a fine Municipal Building and a striking, if not ancient, cross—is an attractive town, but, as a matter of fact, I remember it most gratefully for its sparkling air.

Forres, as its name implies, is near the water—less than two miles from the sea, or, rather, the lagoon at the mouth of the Findhorn, to the west of which lie the Culbin Sands. At the wind's will those sands in the past have blanketed thousands of acres of Moray's most fruitful land—in places to a depth of 100 feet.   The trouble seems to have begun in the twelfth century—at least, that is the earliest we hear of it.   Much has lately been done by the planting of bent-grass and afforestation to stay the movement; but an ancient town and harbour, and ships and their cargoes, lie buried yonder, while the mouth of the river opens two miles away from its original place. Even now, the sand stirs at a breath, and on its surface the breeze works the strangest of patterns.

Nairn

By its position on the Moray Firth Nairn enjoys what may be called a bracing mildness of climate.   The sun is kind not only by day, but in its going down bestows gifts of glory. Dr Johnson found the ancient royal burgh in "a most miserable state of decay," but that was a long time ago.   The town is crossed by the old imaginary line dividing the Highlands and the Lowlands, and in early days it was Gaelic on one side of the line, English on the other. As lately as the Doctor's visit the ancient division existed, for he heard the Gaelic and smelt the 'peat reek' of the Highlanders.   To-day Nairn is a spick-and-span little town, laying itself out for the pleasure of holiday-makers.

Cawdor Castle on its rock among the woods, a few miles from Nairn, is not a ruin; it is the Past alive. Even the drawbridge over the moat is there, before the ancient gateway; the weather-beaten towers stand firm; and indoors are fine old furniture and tapestries.   Smoke rises from its hearths, for it is still a home. We shall be admitted in the absence of the family, provided we have obtained permits from the Estate Office, in Nairn's High Street.

Cawdor belonged to the Calders—descendants, perhaps, of a brother of Macbeth. A Calder, seeking a site for a stronghold, was advised in a dream to load an ass with gold and let it go whither it would. After some wanderings the ass lay down under a hawthorn-tree on a prominence beside a stream. "This is the place for me," quoth Calder, and anon his men were clearing the ground for building. But they spared the hawthorn-tree. "The trunk of the tree," says Mr Fraser Tytler,

> with the knotty protuberances of its branches, is still shown in a vaulted apartment at the bottom of the principal tower. Its roots branch out beneath the floor, and its top penetrates through the vaulted arch of stone above, in such a manner as to make it appear, beyond dispute, that the tree stood, as it stands to-day, before the tower was erected. For ages it has been a custom for guests in the family to assemble round it, and drink " Success to the Hawthorn "—in other words, " Prosperity to the House of Cawdor."

Macbeth, you remember, was Thane of Cawdor, and you will behold the room in which—let me whisper it this time—he murdered King Duncan—about 500 years before the castle was built.

A few miles west of Cawdor lies Culloden Moor, or Drummossie, scene of the last battle on British soil. On the way to it we pass the ruin of Dalcross Castle, reminiscent of the crafty Lord Lovat, who, after the defeat, found refuge for a while in a secret chamber in Cawdor Castle, but in the end came to the block on Tower Hill.

The battle was fought on April 16, 1746—5000 weary, half-starved, disheartened Highlanders, many irked by wounded pride and a gnawing clan jealousy, against 8000 fully equipped Government troops, well-fed, trained to the musket and bayonet, with superior guns and gunners. And yet the Highlanders *might* have won had there been no wounded pride, had they been unleashed a little earlier. The English commanders, at least, had a strong dislike of their mode of fighting—one shot from the musket, as a matter of form, the casting away of that weapon and all impedimenta, and then the wild, reckless, dreadful charge, with only targe and thirsty steel, that lopped off limbs and split heads to the collar-bone.

To-day part of the Moor is under cultivation; there are plantations of trees not in existence in 1746. The road crosses the battlefield. Midway we come to the great Memorial Cairn and the lowly mounds, graves of the Highlanders, who were buried in numbers together, as far as possible according to their clans. If you pause at the Cairn, with your back to the road, you will be looking across the space that lay between the armies, and toward the great boulder at the grave of MacDonell of Keppoch, who died very bravely.

It is one o'clock on a cold spring day. Snow and hail squalls sweep the Moor. The armies are drawn up, each in two lines, with reserves in the rear, about 400 yards apart. On your right are the Government troops, in lines of three deep, the soldiers "in tri-cocked hats, long coats, sash belts, from which a sword depends, and long white gaiters buttoned up the side. . . ." The dragoons, "their long loose skirts flying behind as they ride," wear trunk square-toed boots thrust in massive stirrups, and carry, in addition to their swords, huge holster-pistols and carbines. Each regiment has two flags. At intervals stand the officers, sword in hand, and a little way in advance the drummers, beating a tattoo. On your left are the Highlanders, with muskets and broadswords, their tartans sadly the worse for wear, for they have been in retreat for months, living from hand to mouth. Many are nodding from the weariness of a long night march.

The Prince and the Duke ride along the lines, addressing

Y

their men.   After that, for a while, each side seems to be
waiting for the other to begin; then at last, as a hail squall
drives in the faces of the Highlanders, the Duke's batteries
open fire—and the shooting is good.   The Prince's guns
at once respond, but half of them are manned by men
who are not gunners; the heaviest are 4-pounders; most
of the balls fly high.   The Prince has taken up his
position on a stone, a little in the rear.   A ball throws up
the soil at his feet and kills his groom.   The Duke is
watching from the second line of the right wing of his
army.   Each side still waits for the other to advance.
The Highlanders, no longer nodding, clamour for the
command to charge.   The Prince sends out the order,
but his messenger goes down to a cannon-ball.   Snow
comes, blowing blindingly in the faces of the clansmen.
Worse, the Duke's batteries are now firing grape.   It is
too much for Highland flesh and blood—and temper.
Without orders, the MacIntoshes break forward from
the right centre; the Frasers, Stewarts, Camerons, and
Atholl-men on their right, the MacLachlans and MacLeans
on their left, follow.   Unhappily they become massed
together, making a grand target for cannon and musket,
and suffer dreadfully ere they can get to work with the
claymore.   Almost every chief and man in the first rank
goes down; the Government bayonets are dripping; yet
they burst through the first line, fling it aside, so to speak,
and make for the second.   But now a deadly fire is concentrated upon them; as a body they are hopelessly
shattered; the spirit goes out of them; they are finished.
Yet some stagger on to the waiting bayonets.   Yonder
they are lying, three and four deep, where friend after
friend has fought over a fallen fellow-clansman.

But what of the Highlanders' left wing, the right having
been broken by the enemy's fire?   What ails the Mac-
Donalds that they suffer the fire, motionless, save for
gestures of rage?   Whose blame is it that the Mac-

Donalds, whose place in the line of battle has, ever since Bannockburn, been on the right, should now be on the left? None but a Highlander can comprehend the enormity of the insult. And so they stand fast, a man dropping here and there, till they see the other clans give way. Yet not all of them, for see—MacDonell of Keppoch, pistol in left hand, sword in right, makes to lead the charge. He takes a few paces—a musket-ball brings him down—a clansman lifts him up, imploring him, now that all else is lost, to keep his life. "Take care of yourself," says Keppoch, and again goes forward—to receive a second ball—and death. His is only an instance of the stark, unyielding courage, which some may call the blind folly, of these Highlanders. . . .

In forty minutes the battle was over and—the real carnage began. No quarter for the fugitives, no mercy for the wounded, on that day or the next. No discrimination. People who had come from Inverness to 'see the fun' were cut down by the dragoons. It is estimated that, while the Government army lost 310, including wounded, over a thousand Highlanders were killed—or murdered. The Duke of Cumberland had his qualities—Macaulay extols his bravery and honesty, and our own historian, Hill Burton, is satisfied that he acted from a sense of duty; but the word 'Butcher' is part of his chief title as long as his name is remembered.

Yet no bitterness lasts for ever. On a day in 1930 a military ceremony took place in the Crown Square of Edinburgh Castle, in the shadow of the Scottish National War Memorial. To the sound of the pipes came the colour parties of the Atholl Highlanders, to that of the fifes and drums those of the King's Own Royal Regiment, the successor of Barrell's regiment, part of Cumberland's army. Each brought colours once carried in enmity at Culloden, which, after a brief service, were laid, side by side, in the Scottish National Naval and Military Museum.

CHAPTER XIII

THE GREAT GLEN TO INVERNESS

ONCE in the springtime, on a hillside, not far from Fort William, a little boy, gazing up Gleann Môr nan Albin and across Scotland, said to his companion:

"Daddy, is heaven away at the end, yonder?"

"No," answered Daddy, busy lighting his pipe; "only Inverness."

The reflection is cast not on the capital of the Highlands, but on Daddy, who on many a clear day had looked up Glen More, without ever seeing anything but moor, loch, mountain, and sky. One childish fancy is worth a lot of geographical knowledge. I can think of no inland vista in which the distance gives a sensation so baffling. The tremendous, undeviating cleft, mountain-walled, through which two seas are joined by the links of loch and canal, all but splits Scotland in two. Were it possible to open all the canal locks at once, the North of Scotland would be, for a moment or two, an island. The eye searches till the mountains fade into the sky. Sight can do no more; there is nothing except for the imagination. And, after all, heaven is always "away at the end, yonder."

About 60 miles stretch between Fort William and Inverness—the last big lap of the Glasgow–Inverness Road, *via* Glen Coe, the reconstruction of which will be completed in 1933.

From Fort William, in the summer months, you have the choice of going to Inverness by water. It is the leisurely way, and from the deck of the elegant steamer, starting from Banavie Locks, you have many lovely prospects which cannot be enjoyed from the road. You can also go half-way through the glen, to Fort Augustus, by rail. Road and rail go first up to Spean Bridge, then down the wild, wooded gorge of the headlong Spean to the moors above Gairlochy and Loch Lochy, after which they continue, with small deviations, close to the water. Gairlochy, a cluster of white houses that glow in the sun and glimmer in the dusk, has no particular history, except that near by Prince Charlie twice crossed the river, first as a hopeful hero; a year later, as a fugitive. To the little place, however, hangs a tale.

In the long ago a storm-wearied wayfarer, overtaken by darkness, knocked at cot after cot without obtaining a single response. At the last cot he wailed in a breaking voice: "Are there no kind Christians here?" This time a reply came smartly enough: "Na, na, we are all Camerons here." In justice to the notoriously hospitable clan I must add that a similar story is attached to two old families in the south of Scotland, and that it was a south of Scotland writer who fastened it on the Camerons!

A little way beyond Gairlochy the Canal opens into Loch Lochy, which can look very black in winter, under white steeps and leaden skies, but not altogether bleak even then, because of the thick woods over yonder, at Achnacarry, home of the chief of the clan, Cameron of Lochiel—a peaceful place to-day, though one of alarums and excursions in the past. The castle was burned after Culloden; little of it remains by the side of the present mansion. Scenes here have been described by Miss Broster, with her gift for creating Highland 'atmosphere,' in her novels *The Flight of the Heron*, *The Gleam in the North*, and *The Dark Mile*. The real Dark Mile is an avenue of plane-trees between the loch and Achnacarry, and near the house is another fine row of trees, with a story. In the summer of 1745 Lochiel was occupied in the peaceful business of beautifying his grounds when tidings came of the arrival of Prince Charlie in Loch-nan-Uamh. Hurriedly the seedlings of the trees were thrust into a trench to await attention till a more propitious time. Lochiel, sacrificing everything on the altar of loyalty, raised his clan, followed his Prince, was severely wounded at Culloden, was a fugitive among the mountains for six months, escaped to France, and died there. Sixty years passed before the forfeited estate was restored to a Cameron, but the seedlings had survived and flourished!

Sheltering Achnacarry from the north rises the noble Clunes Hill, in the Glas Doire Mor range, all sombre bens, cleft by corries, riven by torrents, strong contrasts in their nakedness to the slopes opposite which, thanks to afforestation, will one day be clothed. From the Great Glen, east and west, open lesser glens, leading to other glens—so many that I doubt whether there is a man who has explored them all.

Until the cutting of the canal, separating Loch Lochy and pretty little Loch Oich, there was a strip of land, scene of the Battle of the Shirts, fought between Macdonalds and Frasers in 1544. The beginning of the trouble was the old, old one—an insult to Highland pride. In detail it makes a fine tale, unfortunately too long for this page. In the fight 300 Frasers and a somewhat greater number of Macdonalds took part. It began at noon, on a baking day in July, and as the struggle proceeded the combatants cast off nearly all their garments. An old ballad says that firearms were used, but they could have mattered little. The real business was done with broadsword and Lochaber axe, and when a man became too weary or sorely wounded to wield either, he carried on with the dirk. The spectacle would have delighted the ancient Romans, though it might have scared their gladiators. One must believe that the clansmen enjoyed it. Two men would pause by agreement to take a drink from the burn, and then renew their slashing and hewing till they fell down, side by side, or in a last gasping grapple.   One account, perhaps exaggerated, says that only one Fraser survived, who died on the following day. Certainly not more than a dozen of both clans saw home again.

At this point the road crosses the canal bridge to the western side of Loch Oich, and presently you will see by the roadside, opposite a white cottage, a curious monument—a stone shaft topped by a hand grasping seven heads transfixed by a dagger.   In a small cavern beneath the monument is a well, which is known as 'the Well of the Seven Heads.'

Again the story—that of a wicked uncle—is too long in its graphic particulars, but here is the skeleton.   Up at Keppoch, at the opening of Glen Roy, the chief had died, leaving the affairs of the clan in charge of his brother, Alastair Buidhe, till such time as the elder of his two sons, then being educated in Rome, should be of an age to assume the chiefship.   Alastair, crafty and ambitious, then made it his business to create an atmosphere of dissatisfaction and distrust against his brother's house, and succeeded so well that, soon after they came home, the young men were very foully murdered, seven persons, a father and his sons, being directly implicated.   For a time it looked as though no vengeance would be taken, and but for one man the matter might have rested. He was John Macdonald, otherwise Ian Lom, bard of Keppoch, the same who would not fight at Inverlochy, lest by his death there should be none worthy to sing the victory.   Ian Lom, at the risk of his life, strove to have justice done.   The man who ought to have acted was Glengarry, whose castle we shall see shortly, but he would not take the risks.   At last Sir James Macdonald of Sleat, in the Isle of Skye, a distant kinsman of the victims, sent his brother and a party of men to see what could be done. Ian Lom led them to Inverlair, near Tulloch, where dwelt the murderers, all in one house. They had looked for possible danger from Glengarry, and a watch had been set in that direction, but now they were taken in their sleep, dragged forth, and slain. From the seven bodies Ian Lom removed the heads. His resentment against Glengarry was still bitter. Placing the heads in a willow basket, he slung it on his back and set off through the mountains for the Great Glen. At last he came to the well. While he refreshed himself he may have had the idea of refreshing the heads also. At any rate, he washed them in that cold, sweet water. A little later he reached the castle, confronted Glengarry in his hall, and after reproaching him—and Ian had a biting tongue—laid the trophies at his feet. This is not a mere legend. Not so long ago an enthusiastic seeker after truth dug up the mound at Inverlair, in which the murderers were said to have been buried. He found seven skeletons—all lacking skulls. The monument was raised and the inscription composed by Colonel Mac-Donell, last Chief of Glengarry, in 1812.

Invergarry Castle, like so many others, was burned in 1746, but it had known fire and destruction on several occasions before that. It is a gallant old ruin on the 'Raven's Rock,' above the loch. That rock and broken stronghold, and a few square yards in Kilfinnan Church-yard, were all that remained of the once wide estates of the Glengarrys to the last chief, Colonel Alastair Ranaldson MacDonell. All else had been, perforce, sold. Sir Walter Scott wrote in his journal:

> He seems to have lived a century too late, and to exist
> in a state of complete law and order, like a Glengarry of
> old whose will was law to his sept. Warm-hearted, gene-
> rous, friendly, he is beloved by those who know him.

He died in 1828, and was borne shoulder-high to his grave, still like a Glengarry of old, with the pipers playing in front of a long procession of clansmen. There was a great thunderstorm that morning, which was so dark that the coffin was carried forth in the glare of torches, and as they approached Kilfinnan the bearers had to ford a swollen stream waist-deep. Almost they were being carried away when the eldest son shouted the ancient slogan, and the passage was completed in safety.

In this district, 200 years ago, was a population of 10,000; to-day it is about 500. The emigration was not made from choice. Some years ago at a railway station I saw a fellow-passenger buy a book called *The Man from Glengarry*. It is a very good story, but my companion had not expected it to be about Canada, where the exiles had founded a new home, with the old beloved name.

At Invergarry, with its charmingly situated hotel, a road strikes westward, wandering wonderfully among the hills, through Glens Garry, Loyne, Cluanie, each with its loch, also Glen Shiel, toward the three sea-inlets, Loch Duich, Loch Long, and Loch Alsh, under the mountains known as the Five Sisters of Kintail—surely one of the wildest and loveliest scenes in the West. At the meeting-place of the three lochs, on Eilan Donan, stands a castle, long time a desolate ruin, but lately restored by Colonel John Macrae-Gilstrap, and now, once more, a home. In 1539, so strong were its walls and situation, the castle was held by two men and a lad against a fleet of galleys. On another occasion from its battlements fifty heads looked down, but they were heads without bodies. The road continues by Dornie to Kyle of Lochalsh, the port for the Island of Skye, less than a mile across the water, and from thence a road runs northward across country to Inverness.

Meanwhile we make for Fort Augustus, set where the glen widens, at the head of Loch Ness, stretching far into the north-east. In spite of its two trains a day, its daily pleasure steamer in summer, the not infrequent passage of fishing and cargo craft through the canal, the motor traffic between Fort William and Inverness, and a well-appointed hotel, the little place always strikes me as a retreat. You have only to step a short way along the shore and dwell on the glorious vista of the loch to fancy yourself not of the world. The occasional quiet note of the sweetly toned Abbey bell, drifting over the water, may even encourage the fancy.

There was a fort long before the place got its existing name, built by the Frasers as a bulwark against hostile clans. You will find a fragment of it in the garden wall behind the Lovat Arms Hotel. The later fort was raised during the Jacobite unrest, and now the monastery of the Benedictines stands in its place, only some bastions and a dungeon or two being preserved in the nineteenth-century building.

After his victory at Culloden the Duke of Cumberland came to Fort Augustus. The story of his stay there makes ugly reading—a long list of needless brutalities, many of the most revolting description. The Highlanders were not assassins. Only once was his life attempted, and it was left to a peaceable travelling merchant to fool the mighty conqueror at last.

The merchant's name was Roderick Mackenzie, to whom fate had given a close resemblance, of which he was aware, to Prince Charlie. It chanced that he came into Glenmoriston, a few miles down the loch, when the red-coats were hot on the scent of the fugitive. A detachment, coming suddenly upon Mackenzie, simply let fly at him. As the poor merchant lay dying, he gasped, "Villains, you have murdered your Prince!" Amid jubilation the officer in charge had the head cut off and took it to the Fort. There was, you may remember, a reward of £30,000. At the Fort the head was shown to a prisoner who, knowing what the respite would mean to his Prince, promptly declared the features to be his. Then the Duke, with the ghastly token, set out for London, triumphant.

LOCH DUICH AND THE FIVE SISTERS OF KINTAIL

Photo Alexander E. Beattie

IN GLEN AFFRIC, INVERNESS-SHIRE

Photo Alexander B. Beattie

The same glen, with its great beauty of form and colour, holds a less tragic memory in the tale of the Seven Men of Glenmoriston, who, after Culloden, solemnly bound themselves never to relinquish their arms or make peace with the Government.   Their homes in ashes, their cattle gone, their land laid waste, they lived in a cave which you can see in the mountain-side, and carried on a sort of guerilla warfare.   For three weeks they sheltered the Prince, doing what little they could for his comfort. In disguise, one or other of them would venture into the outskirts of the Fort, hoping to secure some choice morsel for the guest; and it is recorded that once, at least, the seeker was so brilliantly successful that he had the honour and delight of presenting to His Royal Highness a pennyworth of gingerbread.   And they might so easily have earned the £30,000.   One may wonder if Charles, in his dingy latter days in Rome, remembered, among other incidents of his great adventure, that pennyworth of gingerbread, and saw in it, perchance, a symbol of the devotion, not only of the seven men of Glenmoriston, but of thousands of rude, uncultured, faithful Highlanders.

I should mention here that from Fort Augustus a road runs on the other side of the loch to Inverness—an old Wade road, but largely reconstructed.   Its chief attraction is the magnificent view from the elevation at Glendoe. Once it was the Falls of Foyers, whose glory has gone into the making of aluminium.

Perhaps the most striking sight not of nature in all our journey is the ruin of Castle Urquhart, on the promontory off the glen of the same name.   A huge structure containing the work of several periods, it has much to offer to architect and archæologist.   The promontory —ideal place for a stronghold—has been fortified since the days of William the Lyon.   In the thirteenth century the Durwards and Cumins held it.   Edward I took it twice.   Bruce sojourned in it.   As a royal castle it knew several governors, but in 1506 it was given to the Grants, in return for their services against Macdonald, Lord of the Isles, and is still their property. It appears to have been abandoned in the eighteenth century, and is now on the schedule of the Ancient Monuments Commission. Tradition says that a treasure is buried in one vault and, of all things, the plague in another. Which is in which?

Through Glen Urquhart a road runs up to Glen Affric, which I have heard many people declare to be the most beautiful glen in Scotland. Much, of course, depends upon the atmosphere and light at the hour of visitation; but to enter it on a still, clear afternoon in September, preferably after rain has charged the torrents, and to stand beside its shining loch, amid the solemn majesty of those cleft and corried towering mountains, the soiled and sorry world shut out, is to wonder whether such sheer beauty of holiness can indeed elsewhere exist. Undoubtedly it is one of the really important excursions you should make from Inverness, from which there is another road to make the run a circular one.

Inverness

There is a tale of Columba sailing down Loch Ness, miraculously in the teeth of the wind, on his way to convert the Pictish King Brude. Probably the meeting took place not at Inverness, but on Craig Phadraig—a mount, with a vitrified fort, rising solitary near the end of the loch. Within the fort may have been the royal mud and wattle palace of the monarch who, to begin with, supported by his Druids, haughtily refused an audience, ordering the gate to be shut against the visitor. On the gate, however, Columba made the sacred sign, whereupon the bars flew back, the gate opened of its own accord, and His Majesty became gracious. Not so the Druids, who foresaw the end of their power and prestige as priests, magicians, and politicians. It was no small thing to be a druid. Even a king had to wait for his druid counsellors to say the first word, and they had the last. But Columba changed all that.

Macbeth's 'Castle of Inverness,' where Shakespeare places the murder of Duncan, seems also to have been outside the town, to the east; but we do know that Malcolm Canmore built a fortress on the Castle Hill, in the centre of the town, where one stronghold succeeded another till 1746, when the last was blown up by Prince Charlie's Highlanders. The nineteenth-century castellated pile of red sandstone, in the style of the Tudor period, now occupying the site, is the County Buildings. In a way it is typical of Inverness, which is modern, with little to show for its long and frequently stirring existence and the procession of historic personages who have passed through it. But you will like it none the less for that.

Near the meeting-place of the Moray and Beauly Firths, it stands on both banks of the broad, swift-flowing, limpid river Ness, its eastern portion partly on a wooded terrace. They were wise men who decided that three of this fair river's bridges should be suspension ones. Its islands, not far from the town, are connected with the banks and with each other, to form a public pleasure wood and garden, of which Inverness is, not unreasonably, very proud. So beautiful, indeed, are the situation and surroundings that the town itself can quite well afford to be rather plain, with streets somewhat narrow for the activities of its 23,000 inhabitants, often reinforced by throngs of visitors from the great shire and its distant islands, and of holiday strangers from the South. In those streets you will never forget that you are in the Highlands. Yet you will not hear the Gaelic as often as the English—the Inverness English has been admired since Defoe's day—nor see the kilt worn as a matter of course.

The Cross, before the handsome Gothic Town Hall in

the High Street, is a composite of not very ancient and almost modern workmanship; its chief interest lies in the slab of bluish stone set at its foot. The stone may have been the coronation-seat of the Macdonalds in their mighty days as Lords of the Isles, but for many generations it provided a halting-place for women fetching water from the river. They set their buckets on 'Clach-na-Cuddin,' as the stone is called, and did what women usually do in moments of relaxation. But the stone was more than a gossip centre; it was the hub of old Inverness—and the world; the heart, as it were, of Invernessian sentiment. It is, I believe, still—in name at least—the last. If lost in, say, the Desert of Gobi, you should meet an exile from Inverness, just say to him, "Clach-na-Cuddin," and he will, almost certainly, offer you his last drop—of water.

Among the Town Hall's possessions is a portrait of Flora Macdonald, heroine of the Highlands, the girl who by her wit, as well as her courage, took Prince Charlie out of an exceedingly tight place on one of the Outer Isles. The hunters were near, and none could leave the island without a permit. Flora, then on a visit to her brother, heard of the Prince's predicament, saw him (for the first time) in his wretched hut—where he used to sit smoking an old clay pipe, held together with thread—despaired at first, and then, with her friends, conceived a plan. A letter was sent to Flora's home, in Skye, saying that she was returning, with a new maid, Betty Burke, and a permit was obtained for 'Betty,' for whom Lady Clanranald and Flora made haste to prepare suitable garments —"a flowered linen gown, a quilted petticoat, white apron, and mantle with a hood." On a stormy night, June 28, they made the crossing of the Minch in a six-oared boat. After eight hours' hard rowing they were about to land at Vaternish Point, when a party of red-coats welcomed them with a volley. Crossing the mouth

of Loch Snizort they found a safer landing-place, and
came to Monkstadt, home of Sir Alexander Macdonald.
While the Prince waited, Flora went in to whisper the
news to Lady Margaret, only to learn that the house had
already a distinguished guest—an officer in a regiment
encamped in the vicinity. Nevertheless Flora, though
inwardly dismayed, dined bravely with her ladyship and
the guest, while Macdonald of Kingsburgh, her kinsman,
then visiting at Monkstadt, slipped out with provisions
for 'Betty.' As soon as they could decently depart,
Flora and Macdonald, with their charge, set out for
Kingsburgh House; and it is recorded that Charles gave
a very poor performance as a maid. At Kingsburgh
Charles spent the night, enjoying so much the luxury of a
real bed that he lay till one o'clock on the following day.
Yet danger lurked around Kingsburgh, as elsewhere, and
at midnight, poor prince, he was once more on the run;
and he and Flora Macdonald met no more. Before he
departed, Flora, by permission, took a lock from his hair.
Because of that, and because the linen sheet on which he
had lain was carefully preserved, to be, at last, her shroud,
there is a temptation to cheapen the romance by the
importation of a 'love interest.' But in those days a
lock of hair was the commonest of souvenirs, and there
is Highland sentiment which is not amorous. Flora was
duly arrested and shipped south to the Tower. London,
however, proved far from heartless; the Prince of Wales
visited her in prison, from which she was shortly re-
leased, to be treated as a heroine. Four years after the
adventure she married her kinsman, had a large family,
spent some years in America, and eventually returned to
Skye. There, in 1773, Dr Johnson had the good fortune
to meet her—"a woman of middle stature, soft features,
gentle manners, and elegant presence."

Besides her portrait, Inverness has a memorial on the
Castle Hill. From this position you can, in a measure,

appreciate the beauty of the town's situation, but a much better view-point is on *Tom-na-hurich*, the tree-clad little hill, shaped like the upturned hull of a ship, which lies beyond the river and the public park. The Cemetery on its slopes is a lovely resting-place.

Mary Queen of Scots in 1562 paid a visit to Inverness, but Lord Gordon was in rebellion, and his seneschal refused to admit her to the hospitality of the castle, wherefore she had to spend the night in a house still standing in Bridge Street. Next day Lord Gordon instructed the seneschal to open the gates, but despite the apology, it was not long before his head was looking down from the battlements.

In Church Street, opposite a seventeenth-century building known as Dunbar's Hospital, stands the High, or Parish Church. The tower is older than the main building, erected about 1770, and there are parts probably older than the tower. The Gaelic church near by possesses an oaken pulpit which began its career in Holland, in 1642, as the rostrum of an auctioneer, and came to Inverness in 1670—one wonders why. It was given to the church in exchange for the use of a couple of pews, which suggests the naturalization of a Dutchman with a large family.

Its latitude considered, Inverness has generally a kindly climate; the cold easterly winds belong almost entirely to spring. The ill-starred Banquo was not far wrong when, in response to the lyrical Duncan, he said: "I have observed the air is delicate." All the same, you want to be prepared for something ruder than the South of England, more especially as you may be going still farther north. An eighteen-hole golf course at Culcabock overlooks the Moray Firth, and it is no great run by road, or rail, to Nairn, while Lossiemouth will surely draw the enthusiast.

The antiquarian with a taste for the mysteries will

find a feast in the circles and standing-stones at Clava, six miles east of Inverness; but it is a dreary spot for a picnic.

While there is some free fishing in the Ness, so many of the Inverness-shire waters are strictly preserved that anyone meditating an angling holiday should make inquiries well in advance. It is usually a case of choosing an hotel, often in a rather remote spot, which owns fishing rights. Mr Castle, in his little book *Where to Fish in Scotland*, says of Whitebridge Inn on the Foyers, near Loch Ness, 10 miles from Fort Augustus:

> For a real fishing holiday this is the best centre I can name in Scotland. A river at the door, many good lochs all within four miles, and boats free ; ghillie, 8s. a day.

z

CHAPTER XIV

TO THE ISLANDS OF THE WEST

THERE are no weary ways to the Isles. The way from Inverness proceeds by, to begin with, Beauly Firth and Beauly town, with its priory and its bonnie wooded river on whose bonniest reach Mr Compton Mackenzie, most picturesque figure in Scotland's national life to-day, has his island home on Eilean Aigas, among, I am sure, only the best of good fairies; then Dingwall, county capital, on the Cromarty Firth, one of the world's finest natural harbours; and Strathpeffer, very prettily set at the base of Ben Wyvis, mild sport for the mountaineer, in a sheltered vale watered by the Peffery's "bright, beautiful stream." It was not, however, a fair setting and surroundings that put Strathpeffer in the way of becoming a favourite and fashionable resort; its fame was founded in 1777 on its medicinal springs, sulphurous and chalybeate, though to-day it does not wholly rest on these. Still a village in name, its rusticity has given place to big hotels, modern houses, and shops far from countrified. A panorama of the surrounding country, gemmed with little lochs, is obtained with small exertion from Knockferlie, whose summit carries one of the most complete examples of vitrified hill-forts.

Amid the mountains, by a succession of lochs, uphill and down, road and rail continue to Auchnasheen, desirable spot, but best known as the place from which a road strikes toward Loch Maree and Gairloch, without question two masterpieces of Nature unsurpassed in the West. Of the vista from Glen Docherty of Loch Maree and its seven-and-twenty wooded islets reposing under the heights, Ben Slioch paramount, a visitor once observed that it was enough to make a true poet or artist commit suicide. You will perhaps be informed that 'Maree' is a variant of 'Mary' (the Virgin), but the name commemorates St Maelrubha, a missionary from Bangor, Ireland, in the seventh century. The loch was once of the sea, being connected with it by Loch Ewe. The trout are plentiful; the hotel at Talladale has a good name. The place has its legends, more or less tragic, some with a suspicious resemblance to the folk-tales of other parts of the world. Unromantic but interesting is the fact that, centuries ago, iron was smelted here by men from Fife. Their works have gone, but their east-coast names remain on the countryside.

Into Gairloch, eight miles past Talladale, in pre-motor summers came every other afternoon the scarlet-funnelled steamer from Oban. To the passengers it was the exquisite ending to a long day's sail amid wonders of sea and shore. Looking ahead, they beheld the blue, isle-studded loch rimmed with yellow sands and many-hued rocks, and beyond, the trim row of white cottages, the well-named old mansion of Flowerdale, and the woods and heather under the mountains; looking back across the shining sound, the heights of northern Skye, and westward, over the Minch, in dim blues and purples, the distant forms of Lewis and Harris. From the land Gairloch is a delight, but from the sea its gentle beauty comes as a surprise in that grim coast. Loch Torridon, a few miles southward, for example, is altogether savage. At Gairloch, after the War, Mr Lloyd George met the Irish plenipotentiaries to discuss the Home Rule settlement. Peace is always in the air here. The hotel has nearly a hundred rooms—not that that means many to spare in the season.

Skye

Pardon the digression—my only opportunity of bringing Loch Maree and Gairloch to your notice. Our way from Auchnasheen is through Glen Carron to Loch Carron, its upper reach almost landlocked. Within the sheltering point is Strome Ferry, its deserted piers giving it an air of melancholy. Time was when it was a fairly busy port, terminus of the railway. A few miles onward, its successor, Kyle of Lochalsh, has developed from a mere township into a fair-sized village, with banks and a L.M.S. railway hotel. Here less than a mile of water separates Skye from the mainland, and at times the tides run fiercely. The village opposite, with the long, low, white hotel, is Kyleakin, *i.e.*, Strait of Haakon, or Haco, that Norse king who, on an autumn evening in 1263, anchored here his armada of galleys, sailing south later to meet disaster on the Clyde. That, however, did not prevent marriage between a chief of the MacKinnons and a Norse princess, who is remembered as "Saucy Mary." A weirdly upstanding fragment of their Castle Moil remains on a rocky mound, near Kyleakin. Mary, they say, added to her pin-money by stretching a chain across the strait, lowering it only after each vessel seeking passage had paid her toll.

A ferry plies between the shores, towing when required a barge for motors. If you have a car it is well to wire "Stationmaster, Kyle of Lochalsh," in advance. Do not, however, expect transportation on a Sunday. Skye is still 'particular' about the Sabbath. Some of us write unkindly letters about it to the Press; others of us 'take off our hats' to Skye.

From Kyle of Lochalsh the steamers coming from Mallaig sail for Broadford and Portree, in Skye, Isle of Raasay, and the Outer Isles.

At this moment I should be happier if I knew less about the island. My mind goes back to the time when I covered all its roads, mostly awful, on a gig, getting down at the hills to ease the poor horse, which was as glad as I to reach a hospitable inn in the dusk or, maybe, in the

blackest darkness—for it was mid-winter and the weather
not good.   Yet I saw Skye then as I have not seen it
since, nor shall see it ever again.   I saw it slowly, wherefore the memories are too many for my present purpose.
I still believe that Skye should be taken slowly; that if
time be limited one should see a little and see that little
long.   None the less I sympathize with those who say:
"There are the roads—not bad ones; here is a car, let's
be moving!"

If you can take Skye slowly you may come to learn
something of the West Highlander, doing so more easily
than in many other parts of the Highlands, and to know
him is to understand better many pages of Scotland's
story.   The world knows him well as a fighter, but he
is friendly, kindly, courteous, with a charm of manner
which the Lowlander, speaking generally, has not.   The
Lowlander calls him lazy, but the Lowlander, who is
often lazy, does not understand leisureliness.   Laziness
is a deliberate thing, more or less; leisureliness is mainly
a matter of native climate, certainly not of a slow-work-
ing brain.   He is proud, but not with the cheap pride
of arrogance; his is a pride that is easily offended,
almost childishly so, not a pride that wittingly offends.
The Lowlander, who does not always differentiate between
proper pride and self-conceit, and whose name is only
a label, calls him 'clannish' and scoffs at his unyielding
clutch on the past; the Highlander continues quietly to
despise the Lowlander as poor in all but material things.
It is an experience to the Lowlander, if he be sympathetic,
to find himself in a social gathering of Highlanders.   He
will not be made to feel an outsider, yet he will feel a
foreigner—not merely because of the language, for he
will become aware of sentiments which have no life in his
own more 'business-like' existence.   The Highlander is
not without craft—craft which served him well in the old
fighting days, and which, I think, he still feels justified in

employing, in milder doses, against the Lowlander. It is, indeed, sometimes hard to say how much of it is simple guilefulness, and how much guileful simplicity, and even the Lowlander who has been deceived is, often as not, constrained to smile.

I offer an anecdote. A friend seeking family holiday quarters took a cottage in an outlying part of Skye, in response to an advertisement which mentioned, as extra attractions, "fishing, boating, golf." On the bright morning following his arrival, after breakfast, delighted with everything, feeling fit for anything, he inquired of his genial landlord as to the golf. After some consideration the landlord replied: "Yess, yess; there iss a golf. I will be showing you the way to the place." Having gone along a mile or so of lonely road, they arrived at a field on the steep hillside, where the rough growth was a foot deep. Here the landlord paused to reflect. At last—"Yess, yess; there wass a golf, and I will be finding it for you." He proceeded to poke about the field, muttering, "There wass a golf, there wass a golf." Then suddenly stopping short, on a note of triumph, he exclaimed: "I wass sure there wass a golf—and here iss the hole!" I say nothing about the 'boating' and the 'fishing.'

If you are meditating a holiday on the island, let me counsel you to read *The Misty Isle of Skye*—a book as long as this, yet without a page too many. The author, Canon MacCulloch, as rector of St Columba's Church at Portree, spent many years on the island, and the book's sub-title, "Its Scenery, its People, its Story," is well justified by the contents, which are excellently illustrated. It will surely cause you to decide to visit Skye; and you will come to the island with that understanding and sympathy which make enjoyment of a new country almost a certainty.

And now for some poor words of my own. Skye is the

second largest of the Scottish islands. Its name in Norse and Gaelic may mean 'winged,' and on the map it has several 'wings,' though Ossian, the ancient bard, called it "Isle of Mist." Its coasts are so indented that no spot on it is more than four miles from the sea. It is not all fiercely wild: there are, indeed, exceedingly tame, if not depressing, stretches of moorland, also green and kindly glens. Trees are scarce, save where they have been planted about mansions. There are no large lochs or rivers, but many of both, and the rivers swell tremendously in flood. Rain falls often, though often one does not notice it. Within recent years Skye has known finer summers than any other part of Britain. Mists— blankets or bridal veils—come and go. Without mist, Skye would have a wonder less; for when the Atlantic vapours lie low on the mountains you behold the strangely carven peaks and pinnacles towering above the fleecy grey like the stupendous city of a dream. You may get really wet days, even a cloudburst, but, often as not, the summer rain is kindly, warm, almost imperceptible in its falling—and how unspeakably lovely is the succeeding sunshine on the foam-streaked mountainsides, while the lowlands, refreshed, exhale in the warmth their earthy scents and fragrance of bog-myrtle! You will never after smell myrtle without a thought of Skye. Enough to add that its worst weather has not prevented Skye from becoming favourite among the Western Isles.

If possible, see what you can of Skye, to begin with, from the water—sailing first, if you have started from Kyle, into Broadford Bay, which you will remember afterward by the great blunt cone of Ben-na-Cailleach and the more distant mighty, rugged Blaaven; then out between the isles of lofty Scalpay and little Pabay, looking north to the wide gape of Loch Carron; round into the Sound of Raasay Island, on which Dr Johnson

had quite a good time; past the mouth of Loch Sligachan
and the majesty of the Coolins; and, at last, into the Bay
of Portree ('Haven of the King'—James V), with cliffs on
right and left, and Skye's little capital perched high ahead.

The arrival of the steamer in the evening is Portree's
daily event. The steamer means newspapers and mails
and "the return of the native," temporary or otherwise;
also, in the summer, strangers. Perhaps if the steamer
arrived early in the day Portree might be different. As
it is, except, maybe, at the very height of the holiday
season, the visitor, strolling through the streets ere midday, might imagine that he had come "to a land where it
was always afternoon." Portree, Skye's only town, has
about 1000 inhabitants and plenty of shops, but its
business is done without bustle and in a peculiarly dis-
creet fashion. It makes no desperate effort to entertain
its visitors; it has no 'objects of interest,' excepting the
beautiful Episcopal Church of St Columba, with its great
memorial window to Flora Macdonald. Yet it has its
own social activities, with a leaning to literary subjects,
and Canon MacCulloch allows that it does wake up for a
shinty match, and becomes excited at the prospect of
a dance. Generations of sportsmen and tourists have
passed through it, but only within recent years have
holiday sojourners filled its hotels. Skye became popular
almost in a night. I remember when people would exclaim, "Skye! Why, it's always pouring there!" And
now their sons and daughters swear there is no place
like it. You may not believe me if I say that Skye has a
magical quality; so I shall merely suggest that, apart
from its scenery and history, its charm may lie in the fine
freedom and healthy adventure which it can still offer
to a sophisticated age.

The tourist may make Portree his base for the whole
island, though Skye is well furnished with hotels and inns,
some in outlying places. Portree, at any rate, is the base

from which to explore the north and west.   A road, never far from the coast, goes right round the northern 'wing.' Had Skye no wonders of its own, this journey would still be wonderful.   All the way northward you are looking across the sea, over Rona Island toward Lochs Torridon and Gairloch and the far-flung mountain masses of the Mainland, and then, having turned westward, toward the Outer Isles, with the dominating mountains of Harris, dreaming upon the horizon.   But Skye will often bring your eyes back to herself.   There is, for instance, not many miles out of Portree, the Storr, with its appalling precipice, and its Old Man—an amazing spire of rock, 160 feet high—to which you may climb, though I hope you will view it from the sea also.   Strange things, horrid and tragic, are said to have happened up there, and in the dusk you can well believe it.   Then there is Staffin, with its blue bay and green islet, and, above it, the still more amazing Quirang, which is, I believe, the English way of spelling *Cuith-fhir-Fhinn*, meaning, roughly, 'the pit of the men of Fingal.'   Actually, it is a mountain, rising 1800 feet above the sea, steep everywhere, but almost sheer on the north-east side.   A sort of crater in the summit, in which several thousand men might lie, gives it its name.   The summit is roughly walled with a natural rampart, breached in places, where you may enter.   One of the breaches, steep and narrow, is overhung by 'the Needle,' a point of rock 120 feet high.   In the vast crater rises 'the Table,' a mass of rock 300 feet long, with a 'cloth' of grass almost brilliantly green.   All around is chaos of rock once tormented by fire and earthquake— altogether a nightmare of Nature.

The road turning west crosses a stretch of moor by Kilmaluaig hamlet, and brings us to the broken shell of Duntulm Castle, once the principal stronghold of the Macdonalds, Lords of the Isles.   Set on a mound at the cliff's very edge, its windows look down into the sea, and

out of that situation came the tragedy which ended the
castle's existence as a home, late in the eighteenth century.
From one of the windows a nursemaid, playing with a
little Macdonald, let the child fall—and the grief-stricken
family abandoned the ancestral walls, which have been
allowed to crumble ever since.

Two miles south by Score Bay, with its pillared and
caverned cliffs, is the old churchyard of Kilmuir, where
Flora Macdonald lies under a massive piece of granite and
a great white Iona cross, a landmark to mariners. Three
thousand people attended her funeral, and by the law of
Highland courtesy all had to be given refreshment.

Presently we are passing through a green plain of
splendid fertility—old Pennant described it as "laughing
with corn"—on our right the gulf of Loch Snizort, across
which on that summer morning in 1746 came the six-
oared boat bearing Flora and the disguised Prince. Later
you will have a glimpse of Monkstadt House, where they
first sought shelter; but in these few miles are a hundred
things to interest and delight. Charming is the first
sight of Uig Bay far below, its village in a deep, green
hollow—trim cottages and gardens, kirks, an hotel, and
to the north a cluster of crofts whose colours, sober and
blithe, change with the light. Thither the road falls,
only to rise again, and we look across the loch to the
cliffs of Vaternish, and out of it to the peaks of Harris,
and beyond the western moors to Macleod's Tables, the
two flat-topped Healavals, standing alone; then down
and over some miles of moorland, rather grim, where the
basalt bulges from the heather. A few miles more bring
us to Kingsburgh; but the house where Charles slept so
well, and later Dr Johnson and Boswell, is no more. Now
the ever-changing scene is bright again, the loch shining
below, the land coloured with crofts, little woods,
patches of wild flowers. Looking back, you can still see
Harris, and far ahead, dimly, the long, ragged ridge of

the Coolins. And so it goes—to every moment its gleam
of pleasure or flash of wonder, its sigh of melancholy or
touch of wistfulness—till we come once more into Portree,
unaware where the moorland ends and the town begins.

Were Skye the flattest, dreariest of isles, it would still
be distinguished by its possession of what is almost certainly the oldest inhabited house in Scotland—Dunvegan
Castle, on the west side, 24 miles by the shorter road
from Portree. Visitors are admitted on certain days
of the week. Seat of Macleod of Macleod, twenty-fourth
Chief of his line, whose ancestry goes back to the Norse
kings of the Isle of Man, its foundations may possibly
contain stones of a fort that stood on the rock a thousand
years ago, though the oldest part of the castle belongs to
the thirteenth century. Observed from the sea, with its
square, uncompromising tower, flat battlemented roof,
narrow windows, all without the slightest hint of ornament, it surely looks the starkest, most unhomely building in Scotland. Almost the same may be said of the
main front, the severity of which is mitigated only by the
hospitable doorway. In other words, Dunvegan Castle
has been preserved without being spoiled. The building
really embraces two castles—thirteenth and fifteenth
century—which were not joined till 1780, following the
suggestion of Dr Johnson, who had been a most apprecia-
tive guest of the chief seven years earlier.

The approach is by a fine avenue and a stone bridge
over the gap, once one of the castle's defences. Much of
the interior has of necessity been modernized. The old
baronial hall has become the drawing-room, its windows
in the 9-feet thick walls looking out upon the loch. Amid
its comfort and refinement it is not easy to picture the
scene enacted within the same walls in 1552. The tale
leading up to the incident must be omitted; enough to
say that Ian Dubh (Black John), guile in his heart, had
bidden eleven Campbells of Argyll to a banquet, at which

each Campbell was placed between two Macleods. The feast was over, the drinking was about to begin, and before each Campbell guest a servant placed a cup. And the cup was filled with blood. It was the signal, and the dirks of the Macleods were ready.

In the tower is the Fairy Room, for there was a chief who married a fairy-woman. After a time—twenty years—she was summoned back to Fairyland, and could not choose but go. But she left behind her a little silken garment, which came to be known as the Fairy Flag. Thrice it might be waved to bring help were the Macleods in dire extremity, but with the third waving its virtue would depart. Twice in the past it has been waved: once in a desperate fight with the Macdonalds, again when an unborn heir was in danger. Of yellow silk, with an embroidery of red spots, it has long since faded; the material is grown so frail that you feel it would part at a touch. There are other tales, equally miraculous, of the origin of the 'Flag,' which lies in a case in the drawing-room beside the Dunvegan Cup, a vessel of dark wood on four legs, 10 inches high, heavily decorated with silver, once with gems. For long its origin was a mystery, but now it would appear to have been a gift to a Macleod, long, long ago, from a friend, O'Neil, in Ireland. There also is the celebrated Rory Mor's drinking-horn of the twelfth century—the horn of a great ox, or perhaps a urus. It is a huge thing. When a chief came of age he proved his manhood by grasping it, brimming, by the mouth, the horn being curved about his arm, and emptying it at a draught. Dunvegan has many treasures, artistic and literary, including letters of Sir Walter Scott, once a guest in the castle, as well as warlike. The country and coast around is rich in strange natural features, notably the extraordinary pinnacles rising from the sea, known as Macleod's Maidens.

Nine miles south of Portree is Sligachan, at the head

CASTLE MOIL, KYLEAKIN, SKYE
Photo Alexander B. Beattie

LOCH CORUISK, SKYE
Photo Robert McLeod

of the sea-loch and in the glen of the same name, under the sometimes almost overwhelming menace of the monstrous, craggy, savage-toothed Coolin (miscalled Cuchullin) Hills. Here the word 'wild' is too tame. There are fifteen peaks over 3000 feet high, but the marvel is in their fearsome formations. It is not the heights of our Scottish mountains that matter; it is their effect. You ought not, if a novice, to think of attacking those peaks without a guide. Danger lurks among the rocks and swoops in the sudden mists.

Sligachan can be a dreadful pit of gloom; and it can be a hollow so delectable that even the Coolins seem no longer malevolent. I remember coming down into it in that long-ago winter journey. All day it had rained, but now, in the dusk, it was clearing; the mists were melting into the air, which already held a presage of frost, and the Coolins, white-crested, loomed out, very black and forbidding. A solitary gleam peeped kindly from the inn—more hospitable light than the hundred brilliant windows of a Grand Hotel. A homely supper, a glowing hearth, a 'crack' with the host for an hour or two, and at last—blessed memory of real creature comfort—a large toddy, followed by a feather bed, and firelight flickering in the room. In the night came snow, but with morning the sun shone. Could this be gloomy Sligachan? Yet you do not need to come through the hardships of winter to see as great a change between one hour and the next. The inn has grown into a modern hotel, and, by all accounts, an excellently conducted one.

Beyond the Coolins where they go down into the sea, due south of Sligachan, in an inland abyss lies Coruisk, the loch that never smiles. The name means 'Water Cauldron,' but it is the coldest-looking cauldron that ever was. There are several ways of getting to it. For those who would reach it without effort the steamer makes a cruise from Portree and Broadford, *via* Mallaig, to Loch

Scavaig, every Thursday. There the steamer anchors, and its boats convey the passengers to the barrier of rock, only a furlong broad, that dams Coruisk from the sea. Scavaig itself is worth the voyage, but, if possible, Coruisk should be seen from above also. There are several ways from Sligachan, none of them quite easy, the worst of them an adventure. You will want the company of some one who knows the way; at least, I do not advise you to seek it out for yourselves, though the Canon's chapter, explaining the most picturesque route, might enable you to do so. Nor shall I attempt to describe Coruisk itself, lying—under a curse, one might fancy—sunless, at the bottom of those awful steeps, heathered in some places, bald in others. Despair in the depths, desolation on the heights. Great men have described it, and their words are pictures—till you behold the scene; then the pictures fall into words again. I am inclined to think that the most suggestive and most lasting word-picture is the one which burst from the tourist who, gazing downward, suddenly shuddered and exclaimed, "What a d—d awful inkpot!"

Before leaving Skye—reluctantly—I must just mention Broadford—a restful place in itself and a convenient centre, marked by the great blunt cone of Ben-na-Cailleach ('Old Woman'), on whose summit was buried the home-sick Norse woman who desired to lie in the track of her homeland's wind. Dr Johnson and Boswell enjoyed two jolly evenings in Broadford. On the second occasion a young and pretty matron sat on the Sage's knee and kissed him, while Boswell unwittingly acquired a headache on whisky. One can still obtain satisfactory, if less pronounced, hospitality in the village.

I am aware that I have told you next to nothing about Skye, but I will tell you one thing more. If you come to Skye you will not 'rather like' it. You will either dislike it or love it very much.

The Outer Hebrides

One large island, several small, and scores of tiny ones,
they extend for 130 miles—a great broken, sometimes
low, sometimes lofty, barrier—nothing between them and
America, save some scattered islets and skerries, St
Kilda, about 40 miles distant, and Rockall, lone peak of
a submarine mountain, 200 miles out in the Atlantic.
Though no great distance from the mainland, they are
still hardly known to the dwellers there. The steamer
traffic is, indeed, rather less than it was fifty years ago.
The visitors who fail not are the anglers.

But while the holiday-makers who sojourn on the
Outer Hebrides are few, some thousands sail every
summer from the Clyde to look at them.   These trips
take about a week; the routes are calculated to give the
tourist an extensive impression of the West Coast, its
sea and isles.   The steamers are not large—trade require-
ments apart, handy vessels are necessary for the nego-
tiating of many of the ports—and, as the berths are
usually fully booked during the season, the prospective
passenger may do worse than pray for fine, quiet weather.
Yet I have never heard anybody admit that the trip was
otherwise than enjoyable.   Much of the Outer Isles may
be seen, too, by taking the shorter sea passages from
Mallaig or Kyle of Lochalsh.

For some centuries the Norsemen held sway out there;
their memory survives in a large proportion of the place-
names.   Long before the Norsemen, however, there were
people who have left solid memories, such as the famous
Stone Circle of the Sun Temple at Callernish, in Lewis,
and there are fragments of early Christian buildings in
many places.

Commercially, Lewis is the most important part.   Its
town of Stornoway, with 4000 inhabitants, is well built
and prosperous-looking—a scene of great activity during

the herring season. The late Lord Leverhulme, who, by purchase, became owner of Lewis at an age when most men are thinking of curtailing their work and responsibilities, promoted various large schemes, not all successful, but all directed toward improving the island's trade and agriculture. Had he begun younger, or lived longer, some of the difficulties might have decreased or disappeared; for he expected too much of the natives, apart from the business community, and never was better justification for the old platitude, "There are things that money cannot buy."

There is not very much for the motorist in Lewis. The roads are quite good, but he would cover them in a day or two. The most adventurous run is down to Harris—at least, it seemed adventurous as I knew it, when cars were less efficient than they are to-day, and the steep hills were rather like gravelly water-courses, with frequent pebbles of a few pounds weight to give variety. Yet Harris, if you do not land there from the steamer, should certainly be visited from Stornoway. It is splendid in its barren heights, if at times pathetic in its barren lowlands, where I have seen crofters scraping the available soil into ridges several feet apart, in order to obtain depth for their sowing. There are no trees, except at the hotel, in Tarbert, and some miles down West Loch Tarbert, where there used to be a whaling-station, around which my Norwegian friends planted some thousands of baby ones brought over from their own country. Many perished at the outset, but many also survived to make all the difference to the scene. If you climb a little way up the hillside there, and the day be clear, you will spy St Kilda away in the west, a lonesome little peak, wearing, very likely, a cap of cloud, gay or sombre, as the sun decides. If you continue by the road that winds and heaves above the loch, and from which the views are glorious, you will come at last to the Atlantic itself and, in a rocky bay, to a modern castle in which Sir James Barrie spent a summer, not very long before 'Mary Rose' came into being.

The little town of Tarbert stands, like a Tarbert on the mainland, between two lochs on the narrow isthmus which connects North and South Harris. The word 'Harris' means, broadly, 'high,' as are its mountains, and in certain lights the greyest things you ever saw. Yet they do not repel, rather do they fascinate; and for anyone to whom stark nature is sufficient for a week or two Harris is the place. With a motor-boat, especially on West Loch Tarbert, one may discover a new world.

If you come to Harris by sea, from the east, you will pass in the Minch the lone cluster of rocks known as the Shiant ('Fairy') Isles, where Mr Compton Mackenzie has his second island home. Basaltic, treeless, yet rich in verdure, they present the strangest shapes, which change with every angle of view, and should you spy them in the dusk or early dawn, you will not wonder at the old West Highland ideas of supernatural creatures, benevolent or very much otherwise.

Rodil, once a holy place, at the southernmost point of Harris, is the motorist's Land's End. Before him is the broad sound, with its scatter of islets, reefs, and shoals, and beyond it, reaching south, a long string of islands, small, whose intercommunication is by boat, save where they are so close that one may ford the gap at low water. Lochmaddy, in North Uist, has an hotel, an anglers' hostelry, for the island has no particular attractions besides its plenteous trout, but Lochboisdale, away down in South Uist, has, unexpectedly, a very good golf course. It is said of the skippers of the steamers trading with these Hebridean ports that at night they smell their way about, and if you glance at the map you will almost believe it. I have suggested, rather than told, things about these Outer Isles, but I will end with something definite about Castlebay, in Barra, almost the farthest

2 A

south of them. In the bay, on a rock, which it completely occupies, stands, ruined but bravely, Kismul Castle, principal stronghold of the MacNeills. In the old days, when the chief was ready to sit down to midday dinner, a clansman would appear on the battlements and shout—in the Gaelic, of course—words which may be freely translated thus: "Take notice, all the world! The mighty MacNeill is about to dine!"

St Kilda

The air of mystery and wonder which has so long enveloped the name St Kilda is to be explained by the island's isolation, rather than by its remoteness, for it is only 40 miles from the most westerly point of North Uist; and its isolation is to be explained equally simply by its commercial unimportance. With its evacuation by the remnant of its never large population in 1930 it became less important than ever, though for a few days then it received more attention from the Press than it had known in all the preceding century. St Kilda, the name, has always been a puzzle, for "no sich person" can be traced. The old name, which was used by the natives, is Hirta, and there was a period when they could not pronounce the consonant 'r,' so it is just possible that Hirta became 'Hilta,' which, being spoken gutturally, some early visitor mis-heard as 'Kilda.' St Kilda is actually a group of four islets—Hirta, Soay, Borreray, and Levenish—and some stack, or needle, rocks. It has the highest perpendicular precipice in Britain; yet, while the rock scenery is very remarkable, you might be disappointed if you had come direct from Skye.

The only inhabited part was the great upsweeping hollow above the bay, in the south-east of the main island, guarded on either side by terrible rocks, but open to winds which, often enough, made a landing impossible. The village, as one sailed into the bay, looked rather a desolate little place—a crescent of grey stone, zinc-roofed cottages, known as The Street—the old thatched ones were destroyed by a gale in 1861—a small kirk, a manse, and one or two other buildings, also a little graveyard. Besides their crofts, the people had their sheep, distrib- uted among the islets, while from the sea-birds that swarm in myriads, particularly the fulmars, they derived a considerable part of their 'income' in oil and feathers. The intrepid and skilful methods of the bird-hunters on those fearful crags and precipices would have been a revelation to the visitors who saw the men only at their cottage doors or lounging on the beach.

But it was a poor life, cut off from the world for about eight months of the year, save for the chance call of a trawler. One may believe that the older people were truly sad as they were borne away from their island, but for the younger people, who had had glimpses and tastes of a wider, fuller life, St Kilda was become impossible. At the end the population had dwindled to about 30— which meant not enough men to do the work. When I knew it the population was between 70 and 80, and had remained at that point for many years; but even then the community had apparently become too limited in variety for some of its members, not necessarily for the young ones. In Harris, in 1913, I met a St Kilda man— an elderly man with a patriarchal beard, and a widower —who had come to the mainland, as the St Kildans regarded the Outer Isles, in search of a wife. At the outset he was quite hopeful, prepared to take any lady, from twenty years of age upward; but months later I learned that, having pursued his quest in many places, he had returned home—alone. I am sure it was not the good man's fault, and if you go out to see St Kilda, now with its 'deserted village,' and the sea-birds in full possession, you will understand the point of view of the spinsters and widows of the Outer Isles.

CHAPTER XV

THE FAR NORTH

THE title may seem to savour of extravagance, but even at this time of day the Scotland north of Inverness is to a great many people, Scots included, a distant country. In pre-motor days it was 'at the back of beyond'—most of it known only to sportsmen, some golfers, and venturesome tourists, including intrepid cyclists. The man returned to, say, Edinburgh from a cycling holiday, able to say in a convincing tone that he had been to John o' Groats, was more than a hero: he was a prodigy. The map explains much. Not a thin black line of railway in all the western half, nor in the north, until you turn east to Thurso! Look, for instance, at the roads running west and north from Lairg, the outpost of the railway, in Sutherland—nothing much to the motorist, but serious considerations to the traveller behind two horses—though, as a matter of fact, they could be very jolly roads. Still, at best, they meant a long, rough journey, and the ordinary person planning a holiday never dreamed of taking them.

In these northern counties—Ross and Cromarty, Sutherland, Caithness—are wide, roadless expanses, of 'no use' to anyone but the sportsman and, maybe, the hardiest tramper. That is at least suggested by the fact that Sutherland, our fifth largest county, is almost the smallest in point of population—only ten persons to the square mile. At the same time, in variety and magnificence of scenery, it is by far the richest of the three, though the others are far from poor.

To the motorist who does not look for fairly good roads

all the time, and who is not perturbed by the prospect of an occasional ' I in 5,' or even ' I in 4,' I would commend an extensive tour planned by my friend Mr Inglis Ker, in his *Scotland for the Motorist,* under the heading "Fort William to John o' Groats." The route lies up the Great Glen to Invergarry, thence across country to Dornie on Loch Duich, thereafter up the north-west and along the north coasts to the aforesaid John o' Groats—a total distance of 362, mostly wonderful, miles. A few years ago this run would have been unthinkable, but the roads generally have been improved. Meanwhile let us look at the east side, starting from Inverness.

Immediately north of Inverness is that singular piece of land, its shores washed by the Beauly, Moray, and Dornoch Firths, known as the Black Isle, whereas it is pleasantly green, and is not an island. But the soil is exceptionally dark-coloured, and even Sir Walter once called a promontory an island. Redcastle, in its south, like Dunvegan Castle, Skye, is "almost certainly" the oldest inhabited house in Scotland; Fortrose, on the eastern shore, has an ancient cathedral, its chapter-house restored and very sensibly used as the meeting-place of the local town council. The geologist will turn north to little Cromarty, on the sharp tooth of land in the mouth of the Firth, birthplace early in the last century of Hugh Miller, a stonemason who filled his mind with learning and literature, studied the rocks around him, wrote books about them that won the admiration of the world, and eventually became editor of an Edinburgh paper. His old home remains to house his collection of mineral specimens and manuscripts. Another famous son of Cromarty was Sir Thomas Urquhart, who, when not on military service—he fought for Charles I at Worcester —found time to translate Rabelais.

The word 'firth,' recurrent in these parts, suggests the Norsemen, and the name Tain, the town on the southern shore of the Dornoch Firth, is a corruption of *thing*, 'a place of assembly.' Tain was for long a destination of royal pilgrims—James V came barefooted—to the shrine of St Duthas, of whose chapel a fragment remains. At the chapel, in 1306, the wife and daughter of Robert the Bruce were captured by the Earl of Ross and delivered to Edward I; within it, a century later, a Macneill of Sutherland burned a Mowat of Caithness and his followers, who had sought sanctuary. This burning of a church containing enemies is not unique in the annals of the really good old days.

The golfer will be more interested in the town on the other side of the Firth—Dornoch, where, in 1630, there were

> the fairest and largest linkes or green feilds of any pairt of Scotland, fitt for archery, golfing, ryding and all other exercise. They do surpass the feilds of Montrose or St Andrews.

All the same, a hundred years ago those 'linkes' were to be let at 41 shillings a year. But it is another story to-day, and Dornoch needs no advertisement here. I am told that enthusiasts there in June play three rounds a day, and manage it nicely without getting up early— thanks to the sun's late hour for retiring. Don't, when you come for the first time to the seventeenth hole, let the stone there put you off your game. It commemorates the burning of a witch in 1722—the last crime of that sort committed in Britain.

In August 1930 Dornoch, a pretty little town, with an unexpected 'southern' look, celebrated with pageantry its tercentenary as a royal burgh; but its story is much older. Its Parish Church is part of its thirteenth-century Cathedral, which was burned in 1570 during a clan squabble, and afterward partially restored. It was further restored early in the nineteenth century, that era

of muddle-headed architects; but their worst disfigure-
ments have since been removed. Age is represented also
by the surviving tower of the episcopal palace opposite,
and by the castle, a finely preserved old place. Dornoch
has no industry, except golf; it fills its little coffers in
the summer and folds its hands in the winter. It owes
much of its modern fame to the railway company, whose
commodious hotel overlooks the links.

The country immediately behind is Sutherland's front
garden, beyond which lie the wilds, in parts more curious
than impressive, for the mountains rise not in ranges but
in solitary heights, giving the land a queer, lumpy appearance. Not far inland, at Clashmore, is the modern
Skibo Castle, in which the late Andrew Carnegie spent his
summers for twenty years—an enormous mass of towers
and turrets, almost appalling when you attempt to count
the windows, wondering whether the millionaire phil-
anthropist ever found time to see the insides of all the
rooms. Another imposing, and an altogether statelier,
home is the Duke of Sutherland's, Dunrobin Castle, near
Golspie, a few miles up the coast. I have seen visitors
from the south look at these palaces in their splendid
grounds, with expressions that exclaim, "Are we really
in the North of Scotland, that poor, benighted, backward
country?" Dunrobin Castle, though most of it is nineteenth-century, had its beginning seven or eight hundred
years ago, and is another claimant for the distinction of
being the oldest inhabited house in Scotland. In the
park are two brochs. Brochs were old when castles, in
our comprehension of the word, were new. The idea of
the brochs seems to have come from the Mediterranean.
There are similar stone works in Sardinia; and Mr Mackenzie, in his *Scotland : The Ancient Kingdom*, infers
that some of our Caithness examples may have been
standing in the days of Alexander the Great. The broch
people, he says, were "agriculturists, stock-rearers,

hunters, and fishermen. . . . They practised the crafts
of spinning and weaving. They made ornaments of
gold"—which exists in Sutherland—and

> manufactured articles of bronze, iron, and lead. For body
> paint they used a red ore or iron still found in Caithness.
> Portions of " red keel " (hæmatite) discovered in brochs
> suggest that the Pictish ladies used lip-sticks.

The excellent road winds on to Brora—another Norse
word—old-world, but with sundry thriving industries
and a splendid golf course, also grand scenery, good
autumn sea-trout and brown trout-fishing—the Brora
is one of the great salmon rivers, but is strictly preserved
—and several good hotels. People book their rooms in
Brora a year in advance. On the way to Helmsdale,
close to the road, is a well-preserved broch.

Helmsdale, Sutherland's only eastern port, and its
district are interesting in many ways. The ruined
castle's tale is of Isobel Sinclair, who in 1567, intending
to do away with the heir to the earldom, poisoned instead
the Earl and Countess, and her own son as well. Four
centuries earlier a lady, with the not over-melodious
name of Frakark, made herself so obnoxious by her
political intrigues, that Sweyn, the Viking, had to burn
her, along with her women, in her house at Borrobol.
Within easy distance are ancient remains—hut-circles,
burial and chambered cairns, relics of the Stone Age,
and so forth—sufficient to give the archæologist a
busy, happy holiday. There is a nine-hole course, free
trout-fishing, excellent sea-bathing. Up the river lie
the Kildonan Goldfields—never a payable proposition,
though for centuries the presence of the metal has been
a lure. It was in these parts that the last wolf in Sutherland, some say in Scotland, was killed toward the end of
the seventeenth century.

Caithness

Two miles beyond Helmsdale, high up at the Ord, we pass into Caithness. Between this point and Wick lie a number of fishing havens, none doing so well as they once did, but each with distinctions, historic and antique. The paramount feature of the Caithness coast is its rock scenery, tremendous and terrific, in places grotesque and almost horrifying. The recent stories of Neil Gunn, *The Grey Coast* and *Morning Tide*, have their settings here among the fisher communities; the remarkably fine description of a storm in the latter book poignantly reminds one that fish have a price not quoted in the market.

Of the Caithness capital, in its bay, Stevenson wrote:

> The plateau broke down to the North Sea in formidable cliffs, the tall out-stacks rose like pillars ringed about with surf—the coves were overbrimmed with clamorous froth, the sea-birds screamed, the wind sang in the thyme on the cliff's edge ; here and there small castles toppled on the brim. . . .

He was writing of the time when healthy Wick had made "another boy" of him.

Wick is the most important place, with its 8000 people, north of Inverness, and you should see it and its harbour when the summer herring fishing is on. Otherwise it is not a show-town, though many strange things in relics and rocks lie at its doors. One of Stevenson's toppling castles, the 'Old Man,' a tower of very early workman-ship, has its perch within a mile of the town, a landmark to mariners; and there are others overlooking Sinclair Bay, to the north, in one of which, with the cheery name of Girnigoe, in 1576, a father imprisoned his son, who, after being half starved, was allowed hearty meals of salted beef, but no water, whereby he perished miserably. At Keiss, also with its castle, are some Picts houses, which have been excavated. Wick's golf course (18 holes), with a marvellous outlook, is situated along the shores of Sinclair Bay.

To John o' Groats it is 16 miles over a good road. The old thrill of attaining that once remote and often lonesome spot is no more. You will find there a commodious hotel and perhaps a score of cars. But the thrill of the indescribable seascape remains, as you look across the Pentland Firth to the Orkneys. The view should be taken from Duncansby Head, a mile or so to the east. The Pentland Firth, with its warring tides lashed to frenzy by the gale, can be wicked, very wicked. I have still a memory of it, from the deck of a cargo steamer, in the grey of an August morning in 1901, when—but no, you may be thinking of a trip to the Orkneys, and the Firth is not always in a vicious humour.

The House of John o' Groats stood near the present hotel. The last news of it is found in the writings of a clergyman at the beginning of the eighteenth century:

> John Grott's House, the northernmost house in Scotland ; the man who now dwelleth in it and keepeth an inn there is called John Grott, who saith the house had been in possession of his brothers for some hundreds of years.[1]

So John is not a myth, but whether he was a Scot or a Dutchman is not quite certain. Most of the tales make him a Dutchman, de Groot, who had seven male relatives. They celebrated each anniversary of their arrival in Scotland with a gathering and a feast, but always quarrelled as to who should occupy the head of the table. At last John, a man of peace, found a way of satisfying everybody. He built an octagonal house, with eight doors, and furnished it with an octagonal table, and at the next gathering each relative entered by his own door and took the seat at what was to him the head of the table. The table seems to have been in existence in the

---

[1] By " brothers " he meant, no doubt, his family.

eighteenth century. The beach here, in the sunshine, is dazzling—strewn with cowries, called locally 'groatie buckies,' which, I have heard, are not found on any other coast of Scotland.

In the Thurso ('Thor's River') neighbourhood the cliff scenery becomes sublime. Scotland's most northerly town, well built and picturesque, has a long history. Though the ancient Church of St Peter is now far gone in decay, it was serving its purpose at the close of the eighteenth century. The interior was then panelled with wood, with crude carvings, one of which depicted Abraham, clad in kilt, hose, and a long surtout, about to sacrifice Isaac, while an angel looked on with what appeared to be the greatest amusement. On a Sunday in 1649 a notorious freebooter, Donald Macalister, whom steel and lead could not injure, attempted to fire the church while service was in progress; but the congregation—who carried arms, by the way—got out in time, and one of them successfully shot Donald in the ear with a silver button snipped from the laird's coat. Our Scottish Sabbaths have not always been dull.

From Scrabster, across the bay, the mail-steamer runs daily to Kirkwall, capital of the Orkneys, taking, weather favourable, about three hours. The more distant Shetlands enjoy a regular service from Aberdeen—16 hours. It is, I regret, not possible in this book to discuss these two groups of most amazing islands—amazing alike in their forms and in their innumerable monuments and relics of the past, many of which are better preserved than those of a similar nature on the mainland. I may remark that in Shetland particularly, though the islands came into Scotland's possession five centuries ago, the natives are still Norse at heart. If you are interested, a request addressed to the "Town Clerk of Kirkwall, Orkney Islands," or of "Lerwick, Shetland Islands," will bring you the official guides.

As already mentioned, there is no railway west of
Thurso, and when I was there last the road was not in
condition for the car of the period.   So for the 40 miles
stretching between Thurso and Tongue I would refer
you to Mr Inglis Ker's *Scotland for the Motorist*.   My
visit to Tongue was made more recently by the road
from Lairg, round by Loch Laxford in the west and
Durness in the north.   I still cherish the memory of my
first sight of Tongue, so unexpectedly kindly, with its
woods and fields and beautiful calm bay, after the long
stretches of harsh and rugged scenery.   It was worth
the journey, too, to behold Ben Loyal (*Laoghal*), whose
name, if it does not, ought to mean 'Champion,' for it
is Sutherland's most glorious mountain.   People go to
Tongue mainly for the fishing—salmon, sea-trout and
brown—and its hotel seldom has vacancies; but there
is a nine-hole course, and it is a cheerful place generally,
though some declare that Altnaharra, beside Loch Naver,
under Ben Clebrig, 10 miles south, is lovelier.   William
Black, the Scottish novelist, once in every tourist's bag,
so to speak, is, I fear, almost forgotten.   He was a keen
salmon-fisher and used to stay at Altnaharra Hotel.   One
of his novels, *White Heather*, too pretty a tale for to-day,
had its beginning on Loch Naver.

Now if you have come to Tongue from the east you
will probably think of going south by Lairg.   The road
by Loch Naver to Lairg is the shorter one—37 miles; that
by Durness and Loch Laxford is 96 miles, and has its ex-
citements.   On the way to wind-swept Durness, where in
March 1932 was caught a 7½-lb. trout containing a lady's
wedding-ring, you are still in a human world; beyond it
you cross the most desolate corner of Scotland, with Cape
Wrath a dozen miles away.   It is not much of a road to
the Cape, which well deserves its name, but a young
friend, lately returned from a push-cycling tour, tells me it
was worth the extra miles, while the men of the great

lighthouse that casts its beam across nine leagues of open sea were glad to see him; and I have just noticed that the Keoldall Hotel, Durness, advertises "Car for hire to Cape Wrath." Having crossed the corner, you come down to Rhiconich and Loch Inchard, where the angling and the deep-sea fishing are excellent. The scenery here suggests an earthquake. Then on, over the hill amid no end of little lochs, to Laxford Bridge. 'Lax' is Norse for salmon, and you may see one or two fighting their way up the river. Loch Laxford is one of the really remote places in Scotland. There are dwellers on its shattered shores who, I am assured, have never seen a horse. At Laxford Bridge the road turns inland, and throughout its 38 miles to Lairg you are running, with scarce a break, on the banks of long, narrow lochs, the last, Loch Shin, by far the largest, though not the fairest.

Lairg is small to be the hub of Sutherland, but what there is of it is good, including the hotel. The angler predominates, and the motorist is more and more making it a base. One of the favourite runs is to Lochinver, though it has some rather tame stretches. As you come through Glen Oykell the detached, conical mountains of the West bob up, or so it seems, in the oddest fashion. A favoured angling centre is Inchnadamph—it means nothing worse than 'the pasture of the ox'—at the east end of Loch Assynt, in the shadow of massive Ben More of Assynt, noted for its salmon, trout, and *ferox*. This Ben More is the peak of Britain's oldest mountain, and the loftiest in Sutherland. The road skirts the fine loch for about nine miles. On a peninsula is ruined Ardvreck Castle, stronghold of the Macleods of Assynt, to which the great Marquis of Montrose, defeated at last, was brought, starving, on the last day of April 1650. Three weeks later he was hanged at Edinburgh. The hoary, abject ruin by the roadside is that of a mansion destroyed by fire about the end of the eighteenth century.

In distant days I came to Lochinver by sea from
Glasgow, the red-funnelled, clipper-bowed steamer moving cannily into the rocky haven where the village lies
snug. It was Lochinver's weekly wake-up, and the
Gaelic flowed strongly while the stout ferry-boat lay
alongside—for every member of the steamer's crew, including the skipper, was a West Highlander—receiving
much merchandise, but, as a rule, only a person or two.
It was a scene which is still typical of some of the little
rock-bound ports of the West. The passengers, most of
them taking the week's cruise, hung over the rail, watching the unloading operations and those who disembarked
—perhaps an angler, his fussy anxiety about his rods
being treated with that paternally patient politeness of
which only a West Highlander is capable; possibly a
lady bound for some 'big house,' with no end of luggage,
very courteously assisted down to the boat; and maybe
Mary Macleod, come home on holiday from service in
Glasgow, assisted just as courteously, but welcomed
heartily or chaffingly—very happy, though terribly
embarrassed under the eyes of the watchers. At last
the boat, piled high with hampers, sacks, packing-cases,
and parcels, was pushed off, waves and farewells were
exchanged, the *Claymore* picked her way to sea, and
Lochinver had another week to think it over. For a long
time, however, Lochinver has had its pier and its big
Culag Hotel, formerly a lodge of the Duke of Sutherland's, and it has developed in other ways. The barren-
ness of the district only emphasizes the riches of its
ever-changing colours on moor and water; and to those
aloof mountain-peaks, so fascinatingly stark and strange,
the departing guest must turn again and again for
another last look. He will never forget, at least, Suilven,
the 'Sugar-loaf.' Yet this part of Scotland does not
please everybody. "Nothing but scenery!" was the
remark of a dissatisfied tourist.

If you are now making for the south you cannot do better than turn down to Loch Broom ('drizzling rain' —but not always), the wide fjord with its mouth full of islands, and with Ullapool, most important village of this coast, on its inner reach. Old Ptolemy knew about Loch Broom, but its only fame rests on its loveliness. Nowhere are Nature's grandeur and tenderness more wonderfully blended; its chief guardian, Ben More of Coigach, is at once the most strikingly shaped and colourful mountain in the north-west. For a last memory of the West Highlands I could not wish you a fairer. Ullapool was established by the Fishery Society in 1788, and much was done for it in the following century by the proprietor, Sir James Matheson of Lewis. Called 'village,' it is really a little town, trimly built, attractive, with a sometimes busy harbour.

The road skirts the loch shore into Strathmore, with its lively river Droma, and continues west, between Tom Ban and the towering Sgurr Mor, by the Glascarnoch Water, almost to the foot of Ben Wyvis—which will not be new to you. There it turns south to Garve, on the Dingwall and Kyle railway, near to Strathpeffer, only an hour's run from Inverness—our starting-point for the Far North.

And so—farewell and good luck!

All I have seen of Scotland has attached me to it.

Journal of Miss Elvira Anna
Phipps (of London), 1840

BIBLIOGRAPHY

MY gratitude is larger than my memory and surer than my method, and the following are only a few of the sources from which I have derived information or helpful hints.

History of Scotland, by P. Hume Brown, M.A., LL.D.

The Making of Scotland, by Robert S. Rait, Historiographer-Royal for Scotland, Principal of the University of Glasgow.

Scotland: The Ancient Kingdom, by Donald A. Mackenzie.

The Medieval Castle in Scotland, by W. Mackay Mackenzie.

Literary and Historical Essays, by the Rev. Henry Gray Graham.

Historical Geography of Scotland, by W. R. Kermack, M.C., B.A., F.R.G.S.

Pennant's Tour.

Scotland in 1745 (anonymous).

A Journey to the Western Highlands of Scotland, by Samuel Johnson, LL.D.

Domestic Life in Scotland, 1488–1688, by John Warrack.

Traditions and Stories of Scottish Castles, by H. A. Millar, LL.D.

Witchcraft in the South-west of Scotland, by J. Maxwell Wood, M.B.

St Margaret, Queen of Scotland, by Lucy Menzies.

Edinburgh, by Gordon Home.

The Royal Mile (Edinburgh), by Robert T. Skinner.

Castle Memories (Edinburgh), by the Rev. J. N. Ogilvie, D.D.

Holyrood, by William Moir Bryce.

Recent Excavations and Researches at Holyrood, by W.T. Oldrieve.

The Call of the Pentlands, by Will Grant.

The Scott Country, by the Rev. W. S. Crockett.

Highways and Byways in the Border, by Andrew and John Lang.

Border Byways and Lothian Lore, by the Rev. T. Ratcliffe Barnett, Ph.D.

The History of Fife, by James Wilkie.

The Fringes of Fife, by John Geddie.

Stirlingshire, by W. Douglas Simpson.

Stirling Castle, by Eric Stair-Kerr.

Highways and Byways in Galloway and Carrick, by the Rev. Charles Hill Dick.

Mountain, Moor, and Loch (anonymous).

A Tour through the Highlands (1811), by T. Garnett, M.D.

Highlands, Highways, and Heroes, by D. C. Cuthbertson.

The Forty-Five, by Charles S. Terry, M.A., Litt.D.,Mus.D.,LL.D.

History of the Rebellion, by Robert Chambers, LL.D.

The Island of Mull, by John MacCormack.

Iona, Past and Present, by Alec. Ritchie.

Islesmen of Bride, by M. E. M. Donaldson.

Culloden Moor, by Peter Anderson.

The Isle of Arran, by the Rev. David Landsborough, D.D.

The East of Arran, by the Rev. A. Boyd Scott, D.D.

Glen Albyn (Abbey Press, Fort Augustus).

Where to Fish in Scotland, by P. Castle.

The Secret of the Spey, by Wendy Wood.

The Misty Isle of Skye, by the Rev. J. A. MacCulloch, D.D.

Pilgrimages in Moray, by H. B. Mackintosh, M.B.E., F.S.A.Scot.

Scottish Diaries and Memoirs, 1550–1746, by J. G. Fyfe, M.A.

Historic Scenes in Forfarshire, by William Marshall.

Our Highland Folklore Heritage, by A. Polson, F.S.A.Scot.

Stonehaven, by Provost Charles Burns.

Place-names of Scotland, by the Rev. J. B. Johnston.

Scotland for the Motorist, by J. Inglis Ker, F.R.G.S., F.S.A.Scot.

Motoring in Scotland, published by the *Glasgow Herald*.

Also the writings of Sir George Douglas, Bart., Sir Herbert Maxwell, Bart., George Eyre Todd, F.S.A.Scot., Neil Munro, LL.D., George Malcolm Thomson, Lewis Spence, J. B. Salmond, William Jeffrey, William Power, George Blake, C. M. Grieve, and innumerable newspaper and magazine articles published during the past five years.

My special thanks are due to Mr Chalmers Anderson for much practical assistance.